MICAH

Other Continental Commentaries from Augsburg

Genesis 1-11
Claus Westermann

Genesis 12–36
Claus Westermann

Genesis 37–50
Claus Westermann

Obadiah and Jonah
Hans Walter Wolff

Haggai
Hans Walter Wolff

Theology of the Psalms
Hans-Joachim Kraus

Psalms 1–59
Hans-Joachim Kraus

Psalms 60–150
Hans-Joachim Kraus

HANS WALTER
WOLFF

MICAH

A Commentary

Translated by
Gary Stansell

AUGSBURG
MINNEAPOLIS

MICAH
A Commentary

English translation copyright © 1990 Augsburg Fortress.

Translated from *Micha,* published by Neukirchener Verlag, Neukirchen-Vluyn, in 1982 in the Biblischer Kommentar series.

Copyright © Neukirchener Verlag des Erziehungsvereins GmbH, Neukirchen-Vluyn, 1982. English translation copyright © 1990 Augsburg Fortress, Publishers, Minneapolis.

Library of Congress Cataloging-in-Publication Data

Wolff, Hans Walter.
  [Micha. English]
  Micah : a commentary / Hans Walter Wolff ; translated by Gary Stansell.
    p.   cm.
  Translation of: Micha.
  Bibliography: p.
  Includes index.
  ISBN 0–8066–2449–3
  1. Bible. O.T. Micah—Commentaries. I. Title.
BS1615.3.W6413   1990
224′.93077—dc20   89–35669
                                                      CIP

Manufactured in the U.S.A.   AF 10–5302

94   93   92   91   90   1   2   3   4   5   6   7   8   9   10

To the
Society for Old Testament Study
in gratitude for the bestowal of
Honorary Membership

Contents

Translator's Preface

The English translation of the Book of Micah presented in this volume is a new one; based on the ancient texts, it seeks to reflect the exegetical decisions of the commentator. In the translation of the biblical text, words within brackets [ ] are considered by the commentator to be interpolations; words within parentheses ( ) expand or clarify what is implied but not expressly stated in the Hebrew text; words within single quotes ' ' represent a textual emendation discussed in the notes. For the spelling of proper nouns and place-names, the RSV is followed.

The translator acknowledges with affection and respect the advice, encouragement, and patience of the author, Prof. D. Dr. Hans Walter Wolff, D.D., D.D.hc, professor emeritus of Old Testament, University of Heidelberg, during the extended period of this project. For uncommon skill in editing and for a lively dedication to this undertaking, I am most grateful to Dr. Marshall D. Johnson of Augsburg Fortress. David J. Wartluft prepared the index of biblical references. Finally, I thankfully acknowledge the help of two colleagues at St. Olaf College: Prof. Norman Watt, Department of German, for occasional consultations on the technicalities of German syntax and grammar; Prof. Louis Janus, Department of Norweigian, for teaching my computer to write Greek and Hebrew.

GARY STANSELL
Department of Religion
St. Olaf College

Introduction

1. The Period

The book of Micah reflects the turbulence of several centuries, for only a small part of the prophetic sayings it presents to its readers are from Micah of Moresheth, who saw clouds of doom on the horizon as early as the neo-Assyrian era. The book also contains sayings from the neo-Babylonian period, a time when the storm broke and new prophetic voices accompanied the people through their experience of catastrophe. Finally, we recognize texts from a period in which an Israelite remnant in the Persian Empire was gathered together and painfully reconstituted— texts in which the prophetic voice in part also addressed itself to nations surrounding Israel. Hence, the words transmitted to us in the book of Micah are related to people from the most disparate phases of history, from the second half of the eighth century to around the first half of the fifth century. As to the details, many problems of dating the material remain unresolved.

It is certain, however, that Micah of Moresheth appeared in the second half of the eighth century. It is also certain that the book contains numerous sayings that stem not from Micah but from a much later period. These sayings frequently accounted for the fulfillment of the original prophecies of Micah and they provided further orientation for Israel's continuing path in the midst of the foreign nations. Finally, the book also makes audible the echo of the Israelite community in response to hearing the liturgical readings of the old and new words of prophecy.

A. We are unable to achieve certainty in assigning precise dates even to the original prophecies of Micah. Three texts can provide a step-by-step explication of the matter.

1. Outside of the book of Micah, Micah of Moresheth is mentioned only once, in Jer. 26:18. Within an account that dates from the beginning of Jehoiakim's reign in the year 608, Micah is mentioned as a prophet who appeared in the days of Hezekiah, king of Judah. Hezekiah reigned 29 years, from the third year of Hoshea, king of Northern Israel

1

(2 Kings 18:1f.), thus probably from 729 to 700 (cf. A. Jepsen and R. Hanhart, *Untersuchungen zur israelitisch-jüdischen Chronologie*, BZAW 88 [1964] 36ff. with A. Jepsen, "Zeittafel," supplement to W. Rudolph, KAT 13/3 [1975]). Jer. 26:18 cites the prophet's threat of Jerusalem's destruction that is transmitted in Mic. 3:12. Following this, in 26:19 it is reported that after Micah's harsh proclamation of disaster, Hezekiah did not condemn the prophet to death, as the Jerusalem authorities wanted to condemn Jeremiah in the days of Jehoiakim. Rather, it states that Hezekiah contritely repented. Scholars have been inclined to understand Hezekiah's reaction as an impetus toward his cultic reform which is mentioned in 2 Kings 18:4. However, this historical account makes no mention of such concerns on Micah's part; nor do Micah's prophecies— to the extent they have come down to us (on 1:7a, see below, p. 42, note 7a–a)—indicate any interest in cultic matters. Nor do his transmitted sayings address the king or even mention him, a fact that is especially remarkable in 3:9–12 (see below, p. 98). Micah's proclamation of Jerusalem's destruction as found in Jer. 26:18 and Mic. 3:12 is often placed in proximity to the seige upon the city made by the Assyrian Sennacherib in the year 701. However, in the motivation (3:9–11) for the disaster no connection with external political matters or military actions is to be recognized, as we find, for example, in Isaiah (30:1–5; 31:1–3). Instead of mentioning danger from the outside, defense against it, and a corresponding mistrust of Yahweh, it speaks only of injustice (v. 9) within the city. This injustice is exhibited expressly within the framework of an enormous building activity (v. 10) and an attendant religious security (v. 11). On account of this, Jerusalem will become a "heap of ruins" (see below, pp. 96ff.). Therefore, no evidence compels us to date Mic. 3 in the time shortly before Sennacherib's seige of Jerusalem. But which situation could better, or just as easily, fit Micah's proclamation?

2. The superscription of the book of Micah (1:1) takes us a step further. According to it, Micah was active as a prophet not only under Hezekiah, but also under his two predecessors, Jotham and Ahaz. According to the probable chronology, the period of Jotham's reign (as coregent with Uzziah, who was ill) is to be reckoned during the years 759–744; that of Ahaz, in 744–729. Given these dates, the possible period of Micah's activity is considerably expanded. To be sure, an uncertainty in the chronology must be taken into consideration. Although the beginning of Hezekiah's reign in the year 729 is made relatively certain by 2 Kings 18:1f., 9f.—according to it the beginning of the seige against Samaria (725) and the conquest of the city (722) also occurred during the reign of Hezekiah—nevertheless Sennacherib's campaign against Judah (701) is dated in 2 Kings 18:13 as the 14th year of Hezekiah's reign. Here we find—to be sure, only in this instance—a chronology according to which Hezekiah is said to have replaced his predecessor Ahaz not until 715, rather than as early as 729. Since according to 2 Kings 16:2 Ahaz reigned for 16 years, he would thus not have succeeded Jotham until 731. Consequently, the mention of Jotham in Mic. 1:1 would mean to say that Micah himself had already experienced the Assyrian assault upon the Philistine coastal plain in the year 734 (*TGI*[2] 56f.; *ANET* 283f.) and the loss of a considerable part of Northern Israel in the year 733. The superscription of the book therefore assumes

2

that, according to the chronology in 2 Kings 18:1f., 9f. as well as that presupposed by 2 Kings 18:13, Micah was active as early as the decade of the 30s in the eighth century. This makes it clear, however, that the prophet from Moresheth, along with his alert contemporaries, had to reckon with danger to Judah and Jerusalem from the Assyrian Empire under its determined Emperor Tiglath-Pileser III (745–727) and his successors no later than 734. The emperor's reactions to the Syro-Palestinian rebellions of 734/733, again in 721/20, and from 714/12 to 701 (see below, pp. 36f.), kept their fear continuously kindled. Such considerations provide us with a long span of time within which to date Micah's activity. From the viewpoint of foreign politics, therefore, 701 is by no means the only possible date of Micah's proclamation of disaster in 3:12.

3. On the other hand, a third text, 1:6–16, would suggest a different date for Micah's activity. The first thing to be noted is that the prophetic saying against Samaria in 1:6 must have preceded the conquest of the city, which was under seige for three years (725–722). Its very words announce the destruction of Samaria and all of her buildings. To be sure, there is also a brief, generally worded account of Shalmaneser V (727–722) which states that he destroyed the city; nevertheless, this presumably means only the city's fortifications. For his immediate successor, Sargon II (722–705), provides a more detailed report; according to it, the city, after it was conquered and its population deported, was immediately resettled by foreign peoples and even expanded in size. "I made Samaria larger than before," Sargon claims (*TGI*² 60; S. Herrmann, *A History of Israel in Old Testament Times* [1981²] 251; and see below, p. 53). Thus there is tension between Micah's threat to the city and the events of history. This makes Mic. 1:6f. intelligible only if its date is prior to 722.

To be sure, there have been attempts to date the immediately following saying in 1:8–16, like 3:(1–)12, at the time of Sennacherib's campaign against Judah and Jerusalem in 701. In view of the towns mentioned 1:10–15, scholars have called attention to Sennacherib's account of his third campaign (*TGI*² 67ff.), according to which he "beseiged and conquered 46 secure, unwalled Judean cities as well as countless small towns surrounding them" before he laid seige to the royal residence. It is claimed that Micah sketched the various stations of this campaign. But there are serious doubts to be registered against this view.

The words proclaimed against Judah and Jerusalem in 1:8–16 are inseparably connected as a rhetorical unit with the preceding saying against Samaria in vv. 6f. (see below, pp. 47ff.). In vv. 8ff. Micah has in mind the blow against the Southern Kingdom, which is the immediate continuation of the anticipated blow against Samaria. Only in this way is the threefold עד in 1:9 to be understood, as well as the "therefore" in 1:8 that makes an inseparable connection with the prophecy against Samaria. Moreover, several factors speak against the interpretation that the passage represents a sketch of the Assyrian campaign of 701: (1) in the prophets, metaphors of mourning (1:8) have the function of *proclaiming disaster;* they do not lament a past event. (2) Furthermore, after the campaign of Sargon II in 712, the fortified city of Gath no longer belonged to Judah but to Ashdod, which was occupied by Assyria; hence, 1:10a would be intelligible in its context only if its date precedes 712. (3)

3

Finally, the succession of place-names in vv. 10–15 does not present recognizable historical and geographical events; rather, in each case word-plays interpret the impending misfortune of individual towns (see below, p. 49). Accordingly, to date the passage at the time of Sennacherib's attack is unlikely; the connection of 1:8–16 with 1:6f., however, is unconditionally to be maintained.

In light of these considerations, 722 is the terminus ad quem for the entire text in 1:6–16 originally from Micah. We have to reckon with 734 as the terminus a quo, the year when the troops of Tiglath-Pileser III, in his first campaign against Palestine, stormed over Gaza in Philistia and on toward the south (*TGI*² 56), bringing terror to the inhabitants of Micah's homeland in the southwestern Shephelah. Soon thereafter, Damascus and Northern Israel were threatened from the north by Assyria. Shalmaneser V laid seige to Samaria from 725 to 722. Thus it is highly probable that Micah first appeared as prophet in the decade of 733–723 (see below, pp. 48f.). Whether 2:1–11 and 3:1–12 also belong in this decade cannot be absolutely demonstrated; however, it is not to be dismissed (see below, p. 8).

B. The texts contained in the book of Micah extend far beyond the final decades of the eighth century. In the first place, this is connected with the power and effectiveness of the man from Moresheth, as the quotation of Mic. 3:12 in Jer. 26:17–19 already indicates. In the days of Jehoiachim, the "elders of the land" have precise knowledge of his prophetic sayings. As once under Hezekiah, so even after a hundred years, the elders still seek to effect changes in the people's consciousness and judgment. This was 608. Thus it is not surprising when Micah's prophecy of Jerusalem's fall was recalled ten and then twenty years later, at the subjugation of Jerusalem by Nebuchadnezzar II.

There are new prophetic voices which take up Micah's prophecy and carry it further. "Now!"—this is how they make a connection with Micah's threats, especially with 3:12 (cf. 4:9, 11, 14). Among others, the sayings in 4:9–14 are the clearest reflection of the catastrophic events of the Babylonian era, particularly around 587. Micah 4:10 speaks precisely of the situation in which the treks to Babylon were organized in front of the gates of Jerusalem (2 Kings 25:7, 8–13, 28; Jer. 40:7, 13). Micah 4:11 relates to the situation during and immediately after the seige in which Nebuchádnezzar's troops, drawn from many nations, surrounded Jerusalem, and scoffers such as the Edomites voiced their scorn (cf. 2 Kings 25:1–4; Obad. 11–14). Micah 4:14[5:1] may allude to a particular event from the last phase of the siege in which king Zedekiah ("the judge of Israel"), after an attempt to flee, was deeply humiliated (cf. 2 Kings 25:4–7; see below, p. 137). The new prophecies pointed to the inevitability of judgment, but at the same time they inspired their audience to a new hope. Other sayings as well, e.g., 1:5, 13b, 5:9–12, 6:13, might derive from the difficulties brought on by the Babylonian years, although they do not make recognizable as clearly as 4:9–14 their connections with the events of the Babylonian epoch.

C. Toward the end of the exile and in the early postexilic period—thus during the time of Persian rule—the hope expressed in the book's prophetic sayings was given new and different connections. Prophecies of return from deportation (2:12f.; 4:6f., 8) were joined with new expectations for Jerusalem (see below pp. 118f.). Micah 4:1–4 already presupposes the reconstruction of the temple, since on the basis of its theme, word statistics, and redaction history, the text can belong neither to the preexilic nor even to the exilic period (see below, pp. 117f.). It may have been given its present form at the dedication of the temple in 515, or at least soon thereafter. The relationship of the nations to Jerusalem and to the remnant of Israel became greatly significant in the first century of the Persian era (cf. 1:2; 4:1–4, 5; 5:6–8, 14[7–9, 15]).

The latest connections to historical events among the postexilic texts are to be recognized in the literary additions to the book. Thus the prophecy about the return of the remaining exiles (5:2[3]; see below, p. 145) apparently intends to address the disappointment experienced by delay of the messianic promise (in 5:1, 3[2, 4]), and therefore it was presumably inserted into the text before Ezra (458). A similar hope—connected with the expectation that a fortified wall would be erected around Jerusalem—could have been given its present formulation in 7:11f. before the time of Nehemiah (445). Accordingly, it is likely that the latest postexilic passages in the book of Micah stem from the first half of the fifth century.

The historical background of all the prophecies contained in the book of Micah comprehends, therefore, a span of time of about 300 years.

2. The Man Micah

Even fewer biographical details about Micah have come down to us than about Amos, Hosea, or Isaiah. Only his name and the place of his origin and work are mentioned. Neither his father's name nor his profession is noted; neither his call nor his encounter with other persons is narrated.

Micah (with its variations) is one of the most frequently occurring and popular names, not merely within Israel. The Keil Inscriptions attest to the use of the name since the third millennium B.C.E.; and recently it was found in the materials discovered by the archeological expeditions at the royal city of Ebla in northern Syria (see below, p. 35). Today there are numerous bearers of this name who will carry it into the third millennium C.E.

The title of the book (1:1) contains the abbreviated form "Micah," the most frequent form of the name in the Old Testament. In Jer. 26:18, the only other instance in the Old Testament where our prophet is mentioned, the name occurs in the (older) consonantal text in its fuller form, Micahiah (see below, pp. 34f.). By naming their children Micahiah, parents wished to praise the incomparability of the God of Israel: "Who is like Yahweh?" The hymn that concludes the book in 7:18–20 offers the most appropriate commentary on the prophet's name: "Who is a God like you, who forgives sins . . .?"

The frequent mention of the name soon led to confusion. For example, the first three words spoken by Micah according to Mic. 1:2 ("Hear this, all you peoples!") have been erroneously added to the end of the prophecy of Micaiah ben Imlah in the Hebrew text of 1 Kings 22:28. This interpolation from the hand of a glossarist was not contained in the Hebrew text available to the translators of the Septuagint (see below, p. 41, note 1:2a). In Pseudo-Epiphanius (from the first or second century

5

C.E. [*Vitae prophetarum,* ed. Schermann (1907) 81, 5ff.]), Micah the prophet is confused with a person of the same name from the hill country of Ephraim spoken of in Judg. 17f. (according to Joachim Jeremias, *PJB* 29 [1933] 44f.). To avoid similar mistakes, the father's name is often added. The title of the book of Micah (1:1) and Jer. 26:18 give the name of his hometown: Micah, the Moreshite.

In 1:14a *Moresheth* is called Moresheth-Gath by Micah himself (see below, pp. 35f. and p. 62); the town is an offshoot settlement of Gath (see 1:10a). It is situated in the foothills of southwestern Judah, the Shephelah, as are other places Micah mentions in the same context (1:13–15). Among them we find the ancient fortress of Lachish (1:13a); as in 1:13a, Lachish is also mentioned alongside Moresheth (Muhrašti) already in the ancient Egyptian Amarna texts of the 14th century B.C.E.

The ancient town of Moresheth was quite probably located at modern Tell-ej-Judeideh, about 35 km southwest of Jerusalem (see below, pp. 35f.), in a favored elevated area 400 meters above sea level, with a view of the coastal plain. Militarily and politically, the region was of great significance. Thus Rehoboam had no less than five towns built into fortresses in the immediately neighboring area, among which Lachish was the best known (see below, pp. 36, 61f., 74). In this rolling terrain, access to the central Judean hill country and the way toward Jerusalem had to be made secure from the coastal highway and the Philistine plain. Although Moresheth is not named among Rehoboam's fortified cities in 2 Chron. 11:6–9, nevertheless the archeological evidence of jar handles imprinted with the royal stamp indicates that this town also maintained a thriving commercial connection with the capital city (see below, pp. 36, 62, 74). At the least, it was a part of the regular connections the neighboring fortresses had with Jerusalem.

Micah himself appeared not only in his hometown, where the prophetic sayings handed down to us in chapters 1 and 2 were most likely proclaimed (see below, pp. 54, 74), but also in *Jerusalem,* as is sufficiently indicated by 3:10, 12 (see below pp. 96f.). However, the presence in Jerusalem of a man from the provinces, who would have to make the trip of 35 km from Moresheth to the capital city, is everything but self-evident. That it was possible, and that Micah had the right, to speak publicly in Jerusalem can be accounted for if we inquire into Micah's civil office. After critical examination of the pertinent texts, I consider it possible that Micah functioned as a local elder (זָקֵן), or as a head of a clan (רֹאשׁ), in Moresheth, before and during the time when the office of charismatic prophet was bestowed upon him. He never calls himself a prophet, nor does the ancient Septuagint text of Jer. 26:18 name him thus. He was surely dominated by the specific authority of the prophet who acts as spokesman for Yahweh, beginning with the time he became certain of the doom that was approaching Samaria, Judah, and Jerusalem (1:6–9; see section 4 below, pp. 14f.). This is probably indicated in 2:3f. by the messenger speech against the authorities whom he indicted in 2:1–2 (cf. also 2:6f., 11); it becomes clearer by the way he presents himself in 3:8 in his direct confrontation with the prophets (3:5–7) and "heads" (3:1, 9–11) in Jerusalem. He knew himself to be an ambassador of a completely different sort than those professional prophets whom he opposed in 2:11 and 3:5, 11. Several individual motifs in the Micah tradition became more intelligible when we assume that he held the civil office of elder in and from Moresheth.

1. Among ten other persons named Micah in the OT, only he is identified by the name of his hometown and not by the addition of his father's name (as in 1 Kings 22:8; Hos. 1:1; Isa. 1:1, etc.) or his profession (as in Amos 1:1; Jer. 1:1; Ezek. 1:3). This is easily clarified by his appearance among the circle of "elders of the land" in Jerusalem; there he is simply known as the speaker from Moresheth.

2. The "elders of the land" or the "elders of Judah" assembled themselves in Jerusalem at the great festivals by particular invitation of the king (1 Kings 8:1f.; 2 Kings 23:1; cf. 1 Sam. 30:26); they probably could also come to Jerusalem on their own initiative, especially, as in the case of Micah, when they were impelled by a prophetic commission. If Micah was an elder or a clan chieftain, then it becomes easily understandable that he not only appeared in Jerusalem, but also that his prophecies were handed on by the "elders of the land" and even quoted by them a hundred years later (Jer. 26:17f.).

3. When Micah says concerning himself that he is filled with "justice" (מִשְׁפָּט), he is the representative of a task which (according to Mic. 3:1, 9, 11aα[1]) in the first instance is not performed by prophets (cf. 3:5–7, 11aβ), but by those whom he calls "heads" (רָאשִׁים). This title used by Micah corresponds less with the linguistic usage of the court (cf. below, p. 206 on 7:3) than with that of the ancient tribal orders within which he himself moves, probably as elder and clan chieftain (see below, pp. 97f.). In contrast to the Jerusalem "heads" themselves, he understands it to be his calling fearlessly and boldly to expose injustice (3:8; cf. 3:2–4, 9–11).

4. This he does in the interest of "his people." It is remarkable that he uses the word עַמִּי exclusively for that particular group of people entrusted to his care, presumably those especially from his hometown and its surrounding territory in the Shephelah (cf. 1:9, 10–15). In Amos, Hosea, or Isaiah, עַמִּי mostly occurs in the messenger speech and therefore means the people of Yahweh. When the term is used in a way similar to that found in Micah, then it is more of an exception and is found predominantly in woe cries such as Isa. 5:13; 10:2 (cf. 3:12), which presumably belong to the rhetorical forms of clan wisdom (see Wolff, *Joel and Amos,* 242–245).

In Micah's prophetic sayings, on the other hand, his personal sympathy is perceptible when he speaks of the "women of my people" or of "their children" (2:9) who have been driven from their houses; or of the men "of my people" who (carried away from their homeland?) as forced laborers in Jerusalem were mistreated in a cannibalistic manner (3:3, 10; cf. 3:5; see below pp. 82f., 100, 106f.; on עַמִּי in 1:9, see below, pp. 54, 59, 82).

Micah's active defense of those whom he calls "my people" is not the concern of a solitary, small landowner or even that of an (exceptionally) righteous estate owner who has regard for the distress of the little people; rather, it is best understood as that of an elder who is dedicated to "justice," in contrast to the authorities and the law courts. It is noticeable that Micah never calls people for whom he concerns himself the "poor" (אֶבְיוֹן), "oppressed" (דַּל), or "needy" (עָנִי) (as Amos and Isaiah usually do); it is the "husband" (גֶּבֶר) and "citizen" (אִישׁ) whose family and property he defends (2:2; see below, p. 78). His chief opponents in the Shephelah are therefore hardly the greedy estate owners (who are to be opposed according to Isa. 5:8), but rather the officials, officers, and soldiers from the garrisons in the region. As the "authorities" (2:1bβ), they have confiscated houses and land and have degraded free persons by turning them into working slaves. These members of the Judean troops act like enemy occupational forces (2:1f., 8–10; cf. especially 2:8aα and see below, pp. 74f., 78, 82ff.). Micah opposes them just as he opposes the "heads" in Jerusalem on behalf of his fellow countrymen; possessing the authority of an elder, he is responsible for justice (3:8).

It has often been noted that the book contains no record of Micah's call to be a prophet. From this we certainly cannot conclude that there was no such call. But 3:8 cannot be regarded as a substitute for it, for in this passage Micah makes absolutely no reference to Yahweh. This fact was so remarkable even to the ancient tradents that they felt it necessary to add the phrase "with the spirit of Yahweh" to v. 8 (see below, pp. 91f., note 3:8a). The original words of the prophet's self-presentation in 3:8 are almost like boasting speech that has parallels in expressions of self-assurance found in wisdom texts (cf. Sir. 24:1; Prov. 8:1ff., and H. W. Wolff, "Wie Verstand Micha von Moreschet sein prophetisches Amt?" VTSuppl 29 [1978] 413–415). Micah came before the authorities fearlessly and with an inner superiority. Within the simple social relationships of the provincial towns, the elder is at one and the same time a teacher of justice and of wisdom. His office comprehends different functions. Micah was especially dedicated to calling attention to injustice. He thus performed at the same time one of the main tasks of the classical prophets. In other respects, it remains for us to inquire of the texts whether the prophet Micah is better understood when he is considered to have originally performed the duties of an elder from Moresheth.

Concerning the *length* of Micah's activity as a prophet, we can only make conjectures. Given the small number of texts that have come down to us, it was more likely a limited period of time. In that the beginning of his public proclamation, according to 1:6, must in any case have preceded 722 (see below, pp. 53f.), it is therefore also unlikely that 1:8–16 or even 3:1–12 originated as late as 701 (the time of Sennacherib's military campaign; see below, pp. 53f., 97), that is, more than twenty years later. For Micah's public activity, this would suggest a briefer period of a few months or years in the decade between 733 and 722.

It is quite likely that the prophet himself wrote down (or dictated) the present selection of his prophecies in chaps. 1–3. This is indicated above all by the tiny redactional note in 3:1aα[1] ("but I said"; see below, p. 95). The note points back particularly to 2:11 and thus also to the sketch of the scene in 2:1–11. The written form of the first scene in 1:6, 7b–13a, 14–16 also contains the prophet's "I" in 1:8 (further cf. §5 below, p. 95). As an elder Micah was not only able to speak publicly; he mastered the art of writing as well. Thus it was presumably Micah himself who wrote down his proclamation in three scenes (see §3 and see below, pp. 12f.). Our commentary makes it probable that the following texts go back to Micah himself: 1:6 (conj.), 7b–13a, 14 (excluding the first word)–16; 2:1–

4 (conj.), 6–11; 3:1–4 (conj.), 5 (conj.)–8, 9–12. The following two sections proceed on the basis of this textual analysis.

3. The Language of Micah

A. *Style.* Each of Micah's sentences is clear and replete with colorful portrayals; not one line suffers from colorless conceptions or weak repetition. He carefully follows the order of events and, with a lively interest, notes their details and features. Past or future events are portrayed in a few brief strokes and in rapid succession. Even when Micah uses *parallelismus membrorum,* he moves quickly from fact to fact.

He sometimes emphasizes the climax of a speech by using *alliteration,* as for example at the end of the moving summons to lamentation over approaching disaster in 1:16: "Make large your *b*aldness like a *b*uzzard (vulture) . . .! (see below, p. 50); or at the original conclusion of the announcement of punishment in 2:4, with the quotation formulated as a two-stress bicolon: *šādōd neʾšaddūnū / śādēnū jeʾhullāḵ* ("We are fully ruined, our fields are divided"; see below, pp. 72f., 80). In 1:10–15 assonance alternates with alliteration, as do wordplays on sound with wordplays on meaning (see below, pp. 49, 59–64).

Micah's passionate accusations can also be expressed crudely and dramatically. For example, what the construction workers must suffer in Jerusalem he portrays with metaphors borrowed from the butcher shop. What the farmer in the Shephelah routinely does only to his cattle, the leaders in the capital city do to human beings: "remove the hide,"—"break the bones"—"devour their flesh" (3:2f., 10; see below, pp. 99f., 107f.). Such grimly agitated language corresponds to what lies on the other side, namely, the prophet's sympathy with his fellow countrymen who are entrusted to his care: the well-beloved sons who must go into exile (1:16); the women who are driven from their houses; and the small children, from whom life's necessities are taken (2:9f.). Micah's tenderest sympathy is not only reflected by the repeated emphasis that such things pertain to "his" fellow countrymen (עַמִּי in 2:8f., as in 3:3; cf. 1:9; 3:5 and see above, p. 7), but also by his choice of the unusual word תַּעֲנוּגִים (with suffix) in 1:16 and 2:9 (see below, pp. 64, 83).

To the daring *metaphors* in 3:2f. rooted in cattle raising (see above), we must add the imagery of the ox's yoke which, in the threat in 2:3b, is thought of as an instrument of torture: "You cannot remove your necks, nor can you walk upright" (see below, p. 79). He compares his cry of lament with the shudder and cry of the jackal and the whimpering of the ostrich; with the mourning custom of shaving the head, Micah calls to mind the bald-headed vulture. When the false prophets become deprived of their visions and of the word of God, they will no longer be able to find their way, as in the night, when the sun has gone down; it will seem as dismal as an eclipse of the sun in midday (3:6f., see below, pp. 103f.).

Possessing a clarity that is intensified by the use of imagery, Micah's language also reveals a lively quality. Its liveliness is heightened by the frequent use of *quotations.* We have already observed (see above) that the announcement of judgment (2:3f.) addressed to the authorities indicted in 2:1f. comes to a climax when, at the conclusion of the original prophetic saying, Micah puts into their mouth a lament over approaching

9

disaster: "We are completely ruined, our fields are divided" (2:4; on the text, see below, pp. 79f.). In the following verses, Micah first quotes three short sentences of protest from the authorities (2:6), then their counter-questions (v. 7a). As he struggles to make his audience understand, he further discusses (2:7b–9) their questions, which he has already quoted, emphasizing their guilt with a new quotation in v. 10a (see below, p. 83). Finally, with a concluding quotation, he comes to the theme of the kind of prophet his greedy audience would love: "I would preach to you of wine and beer!" (2:11aβ). Micah also illustrates the guilt of the leaders in Jerusalem by concluding his accusation with a quotation (3:11b) in which they call upon Yahweh with self-assurance, deflecting from themselves the prophet's announcement of disaster (see below, p. 108).

The prophet's use of quotations illustrates his enjoyment of and skill in personal encounter. This is confirmed by the fact that within the immediate context of these quotations, we almost always find the forms of *direct address* (second person plural; cf. 2:3b–4a, 8–10; 3:12aα). (On the frequent alternation between second and third person found else-where, see below, pp. 54, 75, 93). *Questions* also promote his contact with his audience. Corresponding to the questions which Micah formulates within his audience's quotations (2:7a; 3:11bβ) are those questions he himself poses: in 2:7b he puts counter-questions to the authorities; in 3:1b his rhetorical question to the "heads" in Jerusalem is intended to provoke them to agree that they are indeed responsible (see below, p. 98).

B. *Genre.* In the prophetic sayings which probably come from Micah, three genres are prominent: the judgment speech, the mourning cry, and the disputation speech.

1. The *judgment speeches* are found in 1:6f. (conj.); 2:1–4 (conj.); 3:1–4, 5 (conj.)–8, 9–12. They all exhibit a taunt form, usually of two parts, in which the accusation, as a rule, precedes (2:1f.; 3:1–3, 5, 9–11), and is often more detailed than, the announcement of disaster (2:3f. [conj.]; 3:4, 6–7, 12). The announcement of disaster, usually attached to the announcement by לָכֵן ("therefore," 2:3; 3:6, 12, except in 3:4, where אָז "then" is used), is the proof of guilt which provides the motivation for the announcement. Only in 1:6, 7b is the announcement followed by the accusation, where a כִּי-clause gives the motivation for divine punishment. The simple form of the two-part judgment speech accords with the manner and method of the elders who, sitting in the city gate of the villages, made their indictments, brought attention to legal infringe-ments, and explained their legal decisions.

This parallel is particularly deserving of our attention, because Micah usually introduces the punishment as the direct consequence of the guilt (a wisdom connection) to which he has pointed, without pre-senting the punishment as though it were brought on by the special direction of Yahweh (cf. 3:4, 6, 12). Only one saying (2:3a) has come down to us in which the announcement of disaster is a divine oracle that begins with the messenger formula ("thus Yahweh has spoken") and, at least in the first sentence, presents the "I" of Yahweh as the agent. That later generations thought that Micah departed in this regard from the norm of the prophecies contained in the tradition can be recognized in Jer. 26:18, where the formula "thus Yahweh has spoken" has been added to the quotation of Mic. 3:12 (see below, p. 110 and Wolff, "Amt," 410f.).

Within the Micah-texts that have been transmitted to us, the messenger formula at the beginning of 3:5 is quite probably secondary; in any case, it is not followed by words of Yahweh in the first person. Like 3:1 and 9, presumably the saying was originally introduced with a summons to hear: "Listen to this, you prophets!" (or with a woe-cry: "Woe to the prophets who . . ."); the following accusations, with their participial formulation, would fit with such expressions (see below, p. 94 and Wolff, "Amt," 409f.). On the other hand, the messenger formula preceding the Yahweh speech in 1:6 might have been erroneously omitted in the transmission process (see below, p. 47).

On various special characteristics in the arrangement and shaping of the prophetic judgment speeches in 3:1–12, see below, pp. 92f. Each has been introduced by a summons to hear in 3:1, 5 (conj.; see above), 9.

2. By contrast, the judgment speech in 2:1–4 exhibits an element that is central to the funerary lament. Sentences of accusation are introduced with the woe cry from the death lament (הוי; see below, p. 77). The woe cry belongs to the mourning ceremonies of the clan (see Wolff, *Joel and Amos* 243f.), and thus Micah as clan elder would be familiar with it.

Many other elements of the mourning ritual of the clan are found in 1:8–16. While the "Woe!" (הוי) laments the death of a person, in chapter 1 Micah summons himself (v. 8) and the inhabitants of several Judean towns (vv. 10–16) to lament over the destruction of the land and cities of Judah. This extensive *summons to lament impending destruction* connects the prophet's directives to perform mourning rites (weeping, rolling in the dust, lamentation, shaving the head bald in vv. 8, 10f., 16) with commands and reports about scenes of devastating war and capitulation (vv. 11–15). Beyond this, the prophet himself performs a symbolic action by going about "barefoot and naked" (cf. Isa. 20 and see below, p. 58) to signify the threat of imprisonment (cf. the proclamation of exile in 1:16bβ).

It is remarkable that in this summons to lament impending disaster, not one syllable speaks of the guilt of Judah or Jerusalem. The author of the Deuteronomistic interpolations in 1:5, 13b was aware of this omission and then filled it (see below, pp. 46f., 50, 65). Whereas the reports of disaster lead to various actions beside mourning rites, nevertheless at no point do they summon the people to pray, to repent, or to some act of worship. Micah is in no way connected with cultic functions. When Micah, following the brief proclamation of Yahweh's blow against Samaria (1:6, which receives its motivation only in v. 7b) and its continuation against Judah and Jerusalem (1:9, 12b), speaks of the consequences to the Judean villages in such an "a-religious" manner, this too becomes intelligible in light of his office as an elder from Judah.

3. The *disputation speech* probably belongs as well to the rhetorical forms of the elders at the city gate; the form occurs in 2:6–11. It begins with a quotation of Micah's opponents, who register their protest (v. 6) and then ask questions (v. 7a). In accordance with the style of the disputation (on הלוא in v. 7b, a typical element of the form, cf. 3:1b and 11:bβ; see below, pp. 73f.), a reply is then given, which, formulated as direct address (second person), immediately shifts from a general accusation (v. 8a) to concrete reproaches (vv. 8b–10). Micah's rejection of his oppo-

nents concludes with a sarcastic picture of the kind of accommodating prophet desired by the people (v. 11). Yahweh is mentioned only once; indeed, it is not Micah but the protesters who refer to him (v. 7a). The alternation between direct address (second person) and report (third person) reflects the course of the disputation speech: at first, in the style of a report (third person, v. 6a) Micah quotes his opponents (presumably before the assembly at the city gate); next, in the course of the indictment, he addresses them directly (second person, vv. 8–10); in conclusion, he again (in the third person, v. 11) refers to them as "this people over there" as he hands them over to the assembly for sentencing.

C. *Literary Compositions.* The disputation speech in 2:6–11 is to be seen in relation to 2:1–4 (conj.). The disputants are the authorities whom the prophet indicts in 2:1–2 and then threatens in 2:3–4 (conj.). Therefore the persons who are quoted in v. 6 need not be named a second time; their words in v. 6, commanding the prophet to be silent, are related to the prophetic judgment speech in vv. 1–4 which they have just heard. In addition, the "concerning this" in v. 6bα as well as "the reproach" in v. 6bβ point back to 2:1–4. The charges made in vv. 8–10 apparently are intended to provide detailed evidence for the accusations in v. 2.

Nevertheless, the connection between 2:1–4 and 2:6–11 is not that of a unified speech. Micah's quotations of his opponents' words in 2:6 indicate that between the judgment speech in 2:1–4 (conj.) and the disputation speech in 2:6–11, the authorities have voiced their objections, questions, and demand for the prophet's silence. Certainly, the references from vv. 6–11 back to vv. 1–4 are so numerous and close that we may assume that the basic text in 2:1–11 originates from the same time and place. The literary fixation of the address is therefore to be defined as a "sketch of a scene in which the prophet proclaims his sayings" (*Auftrittsskizze;* see below, p. 75).

On the basis of the first word in chap. 3 ("But I said"), we have already recognized the likelihood that Micah himself was responsible for putting his sayings into written form. Originally, this first word made a connection with the picture of the false prophet presented in 2:11 (see above, p. 8, and below, p. 94). In what follows in chap. 3, we must also reckon with a "sketch of a scene in which the prophet's speaks." For, on the one hand, the various sayings (vv. 1–4, 5–8, 9–12) are in every case clearly set off from each other by new introductory formulae; on the other hand, all three prophetic sayings are to be located in Jerusalem. In addition, whereas the circle of the addressees is arranged according to various offices, nevertheless, the circle is also addressed as a group (cf. 3:1a, 5a, 9a, 11a; see below, pp. 96f.). We probably cannot be as certain that each saying belongs to the same historical moment as we are in 2:1–11. Nevertheless, Micah himself probably intended to attest to his appearance in Jerusalem by providing three examples of sayings he proclaimed there, just as he had apparently given evidence in 2:1–11 of his disputation with the authorities in the Shephelah.

As far as we can tell, Micah had begun his literary work (see his "I" in 1:8) with the largest composition that is to be understood as a self-contained (uninterrupted) address, a transmitted whole, in 1:6 (conj.), 7b–13a, 14 (excluding the first word)–16. Placed at the very beginning of this composition is a fragmented judgment speech against Samaria (vv. 6f.; corrupt text in the first part of the passage), which is formulated as an oracle of Yahweh. Then, the composition contains a passage that is indissolubly connected with the judgment speech against Samaria (see below, pp. 47f.); here, with a very emphatic "self-summons" (first person) the prophet laments over the impending disaster (including a symbolic action in v. 8) which will come upon the cities of Judah and upon Jerusalem (v. 9). The reference to the incurable blow of Yahweh (v. 9) at the same time introduces the first strophe of the lament (vv. 10–12a), which speaks of six villages and of various kinds of misfortune over which the prophet laments. A second strophe commences with a reference to the doom which comes down from Yahweh against Jerusalem (v. 12b); here the prophet addresses his words to five additional cities of Judah (vv. 13a, 14 [minus the first word], 15). A sixth time words are formulated as direct address (v. 16), although the transmitted text does not contain a vocative. Since v. 16 is just as detailed as the prophet's "self-summons" in v. 8—v. 16 also includes an animal simile in the summons to mourning rites—this verse might be intended as a summary that is addressed to "(the daughter of) Judah" (see below, p. 64). Thus in this text we find a complete composition containing an extended lament over impending disaster to which has been prefixed an oracle of Yahweh against Samaria. We will have to take into account that Micah himself placed this extended summons to lament at the very beginning of his written traditions. He would have been impelled by the certainty that Yahweh was bringing unavoidable suffering upon Judah from the north.

According to all indications, Micah appended to this initial lament only two further sketches of scenes in which he delivers his prophetic sayings: (1) the cry of woe addressed to the (military?) authorities in his homeland, the Shephelah, followed by Yahweh's oracle of judgment and the disputation speech belonging to them (2:1–11); (2) the three examples of his activity in Jerusalem, which reach a climax in the unexpected proclamation of total annihilation of city and temple (3:1–12).

Along with the (rhetorical) structure of the extensive lament over impending disaster, one can see a remarkable ability at work in the literary composition of the three sketches of the prophet's sayings. It seems rather improbable that the author of this could be someone other than the elder from Moresheth. In this case, however, we can also assume that Micah has given written form merely to a selection of his prophetic sayings; he has, to be sure, chosen them with care.

D. *Later material.* In chaps. 4–7 we find hardly a text whose language is comparable to Micah's.

The sayings in chaps. 4–5 contain not one sentence of accusation or proclamation of judgment against Judah or Jerusalem. On the other hand, many of them presuppose that the judgment announced by Micah has already been fulfilled. Micah 4:1–8 and 5:6–14[7–15] primarily contain five unconditional promises for Jerusalem and (the remnant of) Jacob. The style of these promises is quite varied, and they have been supplemented by cultic or redactional additions (see below, pp. 114ff., 152f.). Somewhat more uniform in their structure are the three assurances of deliverance in 4:9–5:5[6] (after removal of the later additions), which lead the daughter of Zion beyond the disaster and distress which have befallen her in the meantime.

Only in three later texts in 6:2–7:7 do we find language that is somewhat more reminiscent of Micah's. In 6:2–8 the catchword מִשְׁפָּט ("justice" v. 8; cf. 3:1, 8, 9) occurs. Here it is the first of two other key themes in the climax of an artistically shaped didactic sermon which combines quite different genre elements (see below, pp. 167ff.). But in 6:8 Micah's theme of "justice" is not treated the same as in chap(s). (2–)3, where he points to injustice (3:8!) or speaks of justice as the motivation for judgment (3:1, 9!). The prophetic "teacher" in 6:2ff. is more concerned with Israel's return to Yahweh than with judgment (see below, pp. 182ff.).

The language of the original text in 6:9–16 (see below, pp. 188ff.) bears a stronger similarity to Micah's prophecies in chaps. 2–3 than all other texts in chaps. 4–7. A summons to hear (6:9b conj.) introduces a judgment speech comprising accusations (vv. 10–12a) and announcements of punishment (vv. 13–15 conj.). The text's structure as well as its theme are similar to that in the prophecies of the man from Moresheth, at least in its reference to Israel's guilt. Foreign to Micah are the question-style in the accusations and the exposition of Yahweh's judgment by means of a series of futility curses; particularly alien is the connection of both main parts by correspondence formulae (vv. 12a, 13) which are found only in the Jeremiah and Ezekiel tradition (see below, p. 188 and note 6:12a). Moreover, other linguistic details make a later date of composition more likely, although they belong entirely within the spirit of Micah's prophecy.

As a lament, 7:1–7 is distantly reminiscent of 1:8 and 2:1, while the substance of its accusations recalls Micah's exposure of injustice. However, not only is the rhetorical form of the woe-cry different; also the unjust officials are designated in a manner unlike that found in chaps. 2–3. Equally novel is the insertion of the warning (v. 5), and particularly the transition to hope at the conclusion, which is similar to the conclusion of the book of Hab. in 3:18 (see below, p. 203).

Thus the rhetorical and linguistic details of the three passages in 6:2–7:7 suggest not so much the authorship of Micah as that of a prophetic disciple who wants to continue Micah's work for a new era.

On 7:8–20, see below pp. 24f.

4. The Message of Micah

The heart and center of Micah's message can be stated briefly: Yahweh is bringing inexorable doom on Samaria, Jerusalem, and the cities of Judah. The guilt for this rests with the authorities and the leading citizens, such as judges, prophets, and priests.

That Micah's prophetic sayings have to do with *Samaria and Jerusalem* (in this order!) has already been stated in the title of the book. It is not impossible that the title goes back to a briefer form composed by an older editor of prophetic sayings, or by Micah himself, as a superscription for the three sketches of his prophetic sayings (see above, p. 8). It might have read: "Words of Micah the Moreshite, which he saw concerning Samaria and Jerusalem" (see below, p. 33). 1:6 and 1:9b, 12b;

3:12 provide confirmation that his sayings were addressed to both. For Micah, Samaria holds only initial significance. In the decade preceding 722, people generally knew how endangered was the capital city of the Northern Kingdom (see above, pp. 3f.). If destructive blows should strike Samaria—precisely this Micah proclaims (1:6) with certitude!—then Jerusalem would immediately be threatened, and along with it the *cities of Judah* (1:8f.). The man from Moresheth shows himself to be particularly concerned for his home region in the Shephelah. To the extent that we are able to identify the places, they are all situated not so far from Moresheth in the foothills of southwestern Judah (1:10–15; see below, pp. 35f., 59ff.). Village after village, city after city, will be exposed to the approaching doom, unknown settlements and also world-famous fortresses. Micah feels himself to be most deeply involved in the disaster that threatens; indeed, he precedes his fellow countrymen in mourning over the impending destruction, already going about "naked and barefoot," dressed like a dishonored prisoner (1:8; see below, pp. 58f.). At first it appears as though he were more concerned with the cities of his home region (also in 2:1–11; see below, pp. 74f.) than with Jerusalem. But then we find that he also works as prophet in the capital of Judah (3:1–12; see below, pp. 96f.).

What is the origin of the approaching disaster? While the destructive events are clearly sketched out, all of which point to military conquest, nevertheless "the conqueror" (1:15a) is not mentioned by name. (In the book of Micah, "Assyria" is only mentioned by a later voice in 5:5b [6b]; see below, pp. 147f.). The prophet Micah only now and then expressly points to *Yahweh* as the author of imminent catastrophe—much less than is to be expected in comparison with other prophets! Only in 1:12b and 2:3 does the tradition unambiguously contain the name of Yahweh; however, it is presupposed in 1:6 and it is probably to be restored to 1:9a by conjecture (see below, note 1:9a, p. 43); beyond these instances, cf. only 3:4 and 3:7b (on 3:5 see below, pp. 94f.). Of more significance to Micah than the historical background are the inexorable events themselves as they are to strike Samaria, Jerusalem, and Judah: Samaria will be demolished (1:6); Jerusalem will be completely destroyed, and even the temple mount will become a wilderness (3:12); the present authorities will become enslaved, losing their property (2:3f. conj.); the children of the people will be carried into exile (1:16); there are also hints of military occupation and flight (1:15). From those who think that they stand closest to Yahweh, he withdraws himself in total silence (3:4, 7, 12; on which see below, p. 108f.).

If we inquire about the *motivation* for the disaster, it is noticeable that in chap. 1—to the extent that it shows us the first appearance which the prophet wished to have put in writing—there is not one word about the guilt of Judah or Jerusalem (on the function of 1:5 and 1:13b as later additions, see below, pp. 46f., 51f.), to say nothing of a call to repentance. It is Yahweh's judgment as such which terrifies Micah and which he, in the first instance, is to proclaim to Judah. Consequently, at the later liturgical reading of the prophet's words, the theophany hymn in 1:3f., having been prefixed to the prophecies, announces Yahweh's epiphany for the purpose of judgment, and thus prepares the worshiping community to submit to Yahweh's judgment. Later in the book, when Micah

15

himself as an exception introduces a saying expressly as an oracle of Yahweh, it is an announcement of judgment (2:3).

However, in this last example, as in the other sayings in chaps. 2 and 3 (and in 1:7b as well as the later additions in 1:5, 13b), a detailed reference to the motivation for the approaching doom always precedes the announcement. This fits with the way Micah himself has characterized his life's work: "To declare to Jacob his rebellion and to Israel his transgression" (3:8b). To expose and to accuse of guilt—thus he describes the commission with which he "is filled." Is not precisely this, too, one of the essential tasks of the elders? To be sure. But beyond this Micah brings two further elements to his office as charismatic prophet: he places the guilty before a court of justice which is not administered in the gate of the village; rather, it is Yahweh who, comprehensively and conclusively, executes justice over Judah and Jerusalem. Moreover, the guilty (according to 3:8b) are not the individual members of his village; instead, Micah confronts "Jacob" and "Israel" with its wickedness and its sin, that is, the same entity for which he holds the heads and leaders of Jerusalem responsible, according to 3:1, 9.

If we ask more precisely *whom* in particular Micah accuses in his judgment speeches, then clearly it is not the people of Judah and Jerusalem as a whole; rather, it is exclusively the leaders in positions of responsibility: the authorities (2:1bβ; see below, p. 75), especially the heads, overseers, judges, priests, and prophets in Jerusalem (3:1, 5, 9, 11).

Why does he accuse them of guilt? Because they transgress against the people for whom Micah considers himself so responsible—a responsibility which they are supposed to carry out. What for Micah is the decisive criterion of his accusation? משפט, i.e., the orders and institutions of justice which guide and orient Israel (see below, pp. 105f., 109), and to which the heads and judges of Jerusalem should equally consider themselves obligated but which they abhor (cf. 3:1b, 9b with 3:8a). Accordingly, Micah can formulate his accusation against the leading circles in general terms: "They hate the good and love the evil" (3:2a), or "they twist all that is straight" (see below, pp. 98f., 106f.).

When Micah expresses himself in concrete terms, he appropriates catchwords for guilt from Israel's legal tradition: "covet," "rob," "oppress" (2:2; cf. Exod. 20:17a,b; Lev. 19:13, etc.; see below, pp. 7–8). But usually he provides the motivation for his words of judgment by precise descriptions of deeds and social interactions: to take away houses and fields (2:2); to treat men violently (2:2; 3:2f., 10); to strip away the cloak from innocent persons (2:8); to drive women and children from their homes (2:9); to take life's necessities as a pledge (2:10 conj.). In making such indictments, the prophet acts as lawyer in behalf of the defenseless. In this connection, his sentence of judgment sympathetically attends not only to the troubles of those who have been harmed (see above, §3, p. 9), but also to the psychological events connected with the guilt-incurring deeds: the violent actions committed against the landowners he traces back to the initial stage of covetousness, when plans were laid by night (2:1f.; see below, pp. 77f.). He exposes the economic motives both of the false prophets and of the unjust legal sentences handed down by the judges, when bribery decides between salvation and doom, between what is just and unjust (see below, pp. 101f., 106f.). Finally, he unmasks the

16

hypocritical sense of security of those who call upon Yahweh, while trampling his commandments with their feet (2:7f.; 3:4a, 11b; see below, pp. 81f., 108f.).

Nowhere in the texts that can be traced back to Micah (see above, p. 8) do we find a call to return, instruction in repentance, or a hope in salvation connected with, or following upon, the prophet's proclamation of "inexorable" (1:9; see below, p. 59) judgment. Moreover, in the recollection of his prophecy in Jer. 26:17–19, only his announcement of Jerusalem's destruction is cited, although this quotation is intended to motivate the king to return to Yahweh.

The message proclaimed by Micah, in the course of time, raised a series of questions which found their answers in the secondary passages in the book of Micah. We shall attempt to formulate the questions, and thus suggest in a preliminary way the various themes of the remainder of the book.

1:1—Where does Micah's message come from?

1:2—How are the nations to appropriate his message?

1:3–4—How can a later audience, listening to a reading of his words, be equipped for worship?

1:5 (7a, 13b)—What additional guilt has been evoked by Yahweh's blow against Samaria and Jerusalem?

Interpolations in 2:3–5—How is the announcement of disaster which Micah had addressed to the authorities during the Assyrian period transferred to the people of Judah and Jerusalem during the Babylonian period?

2:12, 13—What will become of the inhabitants of Judah who have been deported?

4:1–8—What will become of Jerusalem after its destruction?

4:9—5:5[6]—How will the "daughter of Zion" endure the time of collapse and then be led to a new hope?

5:6–14[7–15]—How will the remnant of Jacob and the foreign nations relate to one another in the future?

6:1—7:7—Which admonitions, judgment speeches, and laments were proclaimed by later prophetic voices as a supplement to Micah's message?

7:8–20—How did the later worshiping community respond to the message of Micah (and of his successors)?

Such a sequence of questions presupposes the results of a final redaction of the book of Micah as we now have it. The literary strata, having grown from Micah's written work into the present book, however, correspond only in part to the current sequence of chapters. Only with an analysis of these strata are we able to gain more precise knowledge of the themes contained in the book as a whole.

5. The Book of Micah

The structure of the book is complex. Initially, to be sure, we can distinguish with some clarity between four groups of texts in the final form of the book. It appears best to proceed from this final form.

In chaps. 1–3, the original material presented in the three "sketches" (see above, pp. 12f.) speaks only of guilt and judgment upon Samaria, Judah and Jerusalem. Reference is made to the salvation of Israel and of the foreign nations only in brief interpolations. By contrast, chaps. 4–5 exclusively proclaim future salvation for Jerusalem and Israel;

moreover, these sayings often include words about the future of the nations; not one passage mentions Israel's guilt in tones of accusation. But this is even clearer in the three latter passages in chaps. 6:1—7:7, which for their part only indirectly and quite marginally speak about the nations (see note 6:16c) or about future salvation (7:7). The fourth group of texts in 7:8–20 presents liturgical passages in which the worshiping community itself speaks (except in the interpolations in vv. 11–13).

Although the four groups of texts can be clearly distinguished according to their chief themes and also according to their addressees, merely the scattered interpolations indicate that the juxtaposition of the four main complexes is rather like intricate meshwork. For in most cases we find within the main complexes shorter or longer commentary (e.g., 1:13b; 5:2[3]; 7:11–12); liturgical pieces (e.g., 1:3f.; 4:5; 5:8[9]), or divergent prophecies (e.g., 2:12f.; 5:14[15]; 7:13). Alongside these cross-connections within the text-groups we find longitudinal connections, thin but clear threads between the text-groups that link one group to the other, such as the connection of 1:2 with 5:14[15]; of 3:8 with 6:8; or of 7:7 with 7:8ff.

This complicated meshwork, not so easily transparent, makes more difficult our understanding of the history of the book's formation. Frequently it allows only a relative chronology of limited pericopes. Only a few texts can be connected with an absolute chronology, such as the conquest of Samaria in 722 (1:6) or the destruction of Jerusalem in 587 (4:9–14[5:1]). Those texts related to the dedication of the temple in 515 (4:1ff.) and to Nehemiah in 445 (7:11) are themselves less certain.

Accordingly, it seems best initially to present the meshwork of the four large text-complexes so that the connections between passages in one text group and the threads that link the one group to a more distant group become clear; in this way it may be possible to achieve some clarity about the history of the book's redaction.

A. Micah 1–3. My analysis indicates that no less than six different interpolations have been inserted into the sketches of Micah's sayings; in my opinion, however, these interpolations can be traced back to no more than three distinguishable redactional processes.

1. The interpolations most often speak about *guilt:* in 1:5, 7a and 2:10b MT it is connected with the cultic realm; in 1:13b (+ the first word in v. 14) with the military sphere. Much about the style is reminiscent of the Deuteronomistic redaction of the book of Amos (see below, p. 46; on Hosea, cf. also Wolff, *Hosea* xxxii). Micah's accusations against social sins are expanded to include the guilt incurred in the cultic and military sphere. In 5:9–12[10–13], in an entirely different style, both military and cultic sins are proscribed by Yahweh himself as self-deification; the formulation, however, is not that of a prophetic accusation (see below, pp. 154, 161).

2. The same Deuteronomistic circles relate the *judgment* upon Jerusalem once proclaimed by Micah during the neo-Babylonian era (see notes 2:3a, 2:3c–c, 2:4a, 2:4f–f, 2:5a, and 3:4b). Now the circle of those who are threatened is enlarged, and the time-span between prophecy and fulfillment is expanded: not only the authorities but the entire people are the objects of divine punishment, while the expressions "on that day"

and "at that time" bridge the lengthened span of time. These supplements to the text made by the Deuteronomists fit the time around and after 587.

3. The liturgical prelude to the reading of Micah's prophecies in 1:3f. might also belong to the work of the Deuteronomistic tradents. These verses present a *theophany hymn* (similar to Amos 1:2) which, as a liturgical doxology of judgment, prepares the way for a ready hearing of the ancient prophecies at the time when the word of judgment was fulfilled (see below, pp. 51f.).

4. In addition to the liturgical transmission of the original Micah text (introduced in 1:3f. and given a new motivation in v. 5), there is also a *literary* transmission that stems from the Deuteronomistic school. It provides Micah's proclamation with the classic Deuteronomistic super-scription: "The word of Yahweh which came to Micah . . ." (1:1; see below, pp. 34f.; cf. also the interpolation in 3:8, according to which the "spirit of Yahweh" fills Micah, and see the discussion in note 3:8a).

5. In the *two prophecies of salvation* in 2:12, 13 we find language that is completely different from that of the Deuteronomistic tradents and commentators (nos. 1 to 4 above). These sayings already presuppose —unique in chaps. 1–3!—that Judah has experienced the dispersion of exile; they may have more in common with the prophetic proclamation of the early Persian era (cf. especially 4:6–7a and see below, p. 76).

6. A final, entirely different kind of supplement to Micah's proph-ecy is found in 1:2. There a *summons to the nations* calls all inhabitants of the earth (together with the following original words of Micah to Israel and with the theophany hymn that introduces them) to hear Yahweh, whom it presents as witness and plaintiff (see below, pp. 51, 54f.). This summons to hear addressed to all peoples is certainly the latest among the interpolations into the sketches of Micah's sayings. This reference to the peoples finds no parallel whatsoever within the first three chapters of the book, although they are certainly mentioned quite clearly and repeatedly in chaps. 4–5 (cf. as early as 4:1–3, 5, 11, 13; 5:6–8[7–9], 13[14] conj.); the most significant instance is in the concluding verse 5:14[15], which as a redactional ending is linked by its content to the introduction in 1:2 (see below, pp. 153f.).

If we compare the interpolations contained in chaps. 1–3 with the remaining sections of the book, we must note that the Deuteronomistic commentaries on the proclamation of guilt and judgment exhibit only insignificant connections of content with 6:1—7:7. However, the two salvation prophecies for the exiles in 2:12, 13 and the summons to the foreign nations (1:2) have clearly perceptible parallels in chaps. 4–5 (4:6–7a; 5:14[15])—and *only* there. Apparently, the sketches of Micah's say-ings (chaps. 1–3), including already the Deuteronomistic additions (see above nos. 1–4) and the later salvation prophecies in 2:12, 13, were combined with chaps. 4–5 by the redactor by means of 1:2.

B. Micah 4–5. Down to and including the years of the Babylonian catastrophe, Micah's prophecies of disaster remained a living tradition both in oral form, as is indicated by Jer. 26:17–19, and in written form, as is shown by the Deuteronomistic commentaries on the sketches of Micah's sayings. However, the original words of Micah were not only transmitted and commented upon; they were not merely introduced into liturgical ceremonies of lamentation, where they were read publicly (see below, p. 52). Rather, precisely at the time when Micah's threats were understood to be fulfilled in the disastrous events around 587, his prophecies also provoked *new prophetic voices* which accompanied Israel throughout this period of trouble and distress. We have already found evidence of the later exilic period in 2:12, 13. However, it is most likely that the new prophetic proclamation, which also has been brought into literary connection with Micah's prophecy (according to the evidence in the book as we now have it) commenced already at the time of Jerusalem's collapse, and then continued down to the first decades of the postexilic period. The analysis of chaps. 4–5 requires us to suppose that there were several phases. Each responds to the question: After the catastrophe of 587 and the years following, what would become of Jerusalem and of Israel in the midst of the nations of the world?

1. Micah 4:9—5:1, 3, 4a, 5b[5:2, 4, 5a, 6b] preserve the oldest passages. The reader can still sense the fiery breath of distressed people in these three sayings, which have been given a literary context in the middle of chaps. 4–5. In each instance, they begin with "Now!"; "And now!"; "Now!"; (4:9, 11, 14[5:1]). Apparently such expressions are intended to link these prophecies, which are addressed to the contemporary situation, to Micah's proclamation of disaster in 3:12, to which these new sayings presumably would in short order also be joined literarily (at first directly) (see below, p. 138). Each of the three sayings make perceptible the distress of its own time; then, in words of promise, they point the way to salvation (4:9–10; 4:11–13; 4:14—5:1, 3, 4a, 5b[5:1–5:2, 4, 5a, 6b]). What at first suggests the time around the year 587 is that the portrayals of the troubled situation fit no other phase in Judah's history so well (see below, pp. 137f.). Moreover, the language employed in the sayings is strongly reminiscent of Jeremiah; consequently, one should seek the author or authors within the circle of Jeremiah's disciples (see below, pp. 137f.). Here we find prophetic words of comfort in a new form (on the form and the extent of the three prophecies of deliverance, see below, p. 133f.).

Apparently two interpolations were added later to this group of sayings. The first one (5:2[3]) is easily distinguishable from its context. This saying presumably applies to those who had long waited in vain for a new ruler from Bethlehem. Referring back to the image of the woman giving birth (4:9), and looking forward to the return of the exiles, it offers them comfort (see below, p. 117; concerning the interpolation of the first word in 5:3b[4b], see below, pp. 135f.). Whereas these interpolations may have originated during the early Persian era, the second interpolation in 5:4b–5a[5b–6a] is probably to be dated much later (see below, pp. 137f., 147).

2. Micah 5:6–14[7–15]. To the early exilic promises of deliverance that begin with "Now!" (עתה[ו]), eschatological promises have been linked by the word "Then" (והיה) (5:6, 7, 9[7, 8, 10]; see below, p. 152). Employing a double simile, the first saying promises to the remnant of Jacob a future and a position of superiority among the nations, which will be accomplished by a divine miracle (5:6f.[7f.]). In the form of excommunication sayings, the second passage declares that Yahweh will purify the land of all the inferior works created by the military and religious sphere

(5:9–12[10–13]). While the first saying exhibits a thematic kinship to 4:13 (cf. also 4:7a), the second is related in content to the Deuteronomistic redaction in 1:5, 7a, 13b; 2:10b (MT). But the language in both passages is completely different from these verses; in the second saying, the nature of the promise is also different.

It becomes apparent how broad and rich is the circle of those who in exilic and postexilic Jerusalem seek out paths that lead to a new future. Here this is elucidated by two interpolations. In 5:8[9] we hear words of prayer that cry against the foreign nations, presumably out of disappointment over unfulfillment heretofore of the preceding words, which promise (in 5:7[8]) complete dominance over all oppressors. That the form is a cry of prayer suggests that the collecting of newer prophecies was taken up by the worshiping assembly. That such gatherings were above all services of lamentation within the exilic and postexilic communities is confirmed by the other interpolation in 5:14[15] (and 5:13[14]conj.; see below, p. 154). For in the style of an "oracle against foreign nations" Yahweh expresses his wrath and punishment (as an answer to the petition in 5:8[9]?) against "the nations who will not listen." The first person style ("I") of the Yahweh speech in 5:14[15] is appropriated from the excommunication sayings (mediated by 5:13[14]conj.?; see below, p. 159). At the same time, with 5:14[15], which points back to 1:2 (see below, pp. 159f.), the ring around the tradition now contained in chaps. 1–3 and in chaps. 4–5 is brought to closure by the redaction. But in our description of the chain of redaction, one link remains to be discussed.

3. Micah 4:1–8, as a collection of sayings, appears to be the latest passage in chaps. 4–5. It contains three eschatological sayings (4:1–4, 6–7a, 8), a liturgical statement of confession (4:5), and a redactional addition formulated in liturgical language (4:7b; see below, pp. 114f.). The individual parts are linked by their focus upon the question, What, in the end, will become of that Jerusalem which Yahweh "treated harshly"? (4:6b; cf. 3:12). The concise answers contained in the text available to the redactor may have induced him to place it immediately after Micah's harshest prophecy of Jerusalem's destruction (3:12), thus juxtaposing the images in each text as polar opposites; this pushed forward the older assurances of deliverance in 4:9—5:5[6] (see above, pp. 20f.). However, the redactor would immediately need these texts also, for in 4:8 he elaborates upon the older promise of the ruler who is to come forth from Bethlehem (from 5:1[2]) in order to proclaim the return of the Davidic kingship to the daughter of Zion (see below, pp. 115f.). He also appropriates an older word of promise in 4:6–7a which (like 2:12, 13) applied to the gathering together and return of the exiles. In content it is similar both to the promise that they will become a "mighty nation" (4:7aβ) and to the double promise for the remnant of Jacob in 5:6f.[7f.], which will become like a "lion in the midst of the nations." But to the promise contained in 4:6–7a the redactor gives a new intention with the addition of v. 7b: on Mount Zion Yahweh will prove himself to be king forever of the community that has returned home (see below, p. 124). The redactor places the greatest emphasis on the Jerusalem theme by putting the promise contained in 4:1–4 at the very beginning of the collection: the house and the word of Yahweh will become the highest goal of all peoples and the source of world peace. This radical hope, on the one hand,

harshly confronts the threat of annihilation in 3:12; on the other hand, it receives a dispassionate commentary in 4:5. Here, in a liturgical confession, the community declares that for the present all the nations still follow after their gods, whereas Israel alone, even now, embraces the God who in the end will become the peacemaker of all peoples. This passage (4:1–5) is hardly conceivable before the dedication of the temple in 515 (see below, p. 118). The same must be true of the final redaction of 4:1–8 and thus also of 4:1—5:14[15].

In summarizing the results, we note at first a far-reaching difference in the redaction history of chaps. 4–5 in comparison with that of chaps. 1–3. Nowhere in chaps. 4–5 do we find later interpretations from the Deuteronomists. The theme of "guilt—judgment" has been replaced by promises for Jerusalem, for the remnant of Jacob, and for the nations, after the time of the catastrophe brought on by the neo-Babylonians. Prophetic sayings which were initially proclaimed to members within the community are now arranged into three groups. Although the groups of sayings exhibit thematic connections, a detailed look at them reveals a fair amount of diversity in form: assurances of deliverance, excommunication sayings, unconditional promises, a confession, a petition, sayings against foreign nations. A plurality of authors is just as certain as is their contact within a school of redaction; the school at the same time is supported by, and does its work on behalf of, a worshiping community. It is responsible for the later redactional interpretations. The liturgical character of most of the interpolations (4:5, 7b; 5:8[9], 14[15]) supports our supposition that the collection of various exilic and postexilic prophecies were used as part of the liturgical readings in ceremonies of lamentation by the Jerusalem community (according to Zech. 7:3, 5; 8:19). Moreover, this "setting in life" of the collection, as well as the redaction which has linked chaps. 1–3 with chaps. 4–5 make it understandable that the sayings concerning foreign nations also decisively determine the framework (1:2; 5:14[15]; cf. also Wolff, *Obadiah and Jonah* 42ff.). Although the date of individual passages must often remain uncertain, nevertheless it is quite probable that the process of collection extended from the threat to and destruction of Jerusalem in the year 587 (4:9ff.), through the exilic period (4:6f.; 5:9ff.[10ff.]), down to the dedication of the second temple in the year 515 (4:1ff.).

C. **Micah 6:1—7:7.** A new summons to hear in 6:1 separates what follows from chaps. 4–5. In its almost clumsy prosaic form (6:1a), its connection with 5:14[15], and its appropriation of catchwords from 6:2b in 6:1b, v. 1 is distinguished from the summons to hear in Micah (3:1, 9) and from the call to the foreign nations in 1:2 (see below, pp. 166f.). The verse appears to be similar in function to 1:2 only in that it, too, takes words originally addressed to Israel (cf. 6:2b) and appeals to the nations to hear them, assuming that the connection of 6:1a with 5:14b[15b] is deliberate (see below, p. 169). Moreover, the following three texts (except in 6:2b) mention neither Israel nor Judah, neither Jerusalem nor Samaria, neither the daughter of Zion nor the remnant of Jacob. Are we to regard it as coincidence that the addressee of the instruction in 6:8 is "the person," and in 6:9 it is "the city"; that in 7:2 the pious person "upon the earth" and the honest one "among the people" are sought after? It is most likely that 6:1, as a connecting link from the redactor's hand, presupposes 1:2—5:14[15]; consequently, it would also have to be post-exilic. To be sure, this says nothing yet about the origin of the sayings in 6:2—7:7.

How far does the text-complex reach which has been connected to the preceding material by 6:1? Words of Yahweh (cf. 6:1a) in the strict sense are found only in 6:3–5, 9–16. But in the broader sense used by the redactor, which may in this regard be in accordance with the understanding found in 1:1 (see below, pp. 34f.), we probably have to consider 6:2—7:7 as "words of Yahweh." For not until 7:8 does it become perceptible that someone other than a prophet is the speaker, namely, the community. As the commentary will show in detail, 6:2—7:7 is composed of three, self-contained rhetorical units which in various ways treat Micah's theme of "justice" (cf. 3:1, 8, 9 with 6:8, 10–12; 7:2–6). All three texts probably were addressed originally to Israel (6:2!; "my people," 6:3, 5) and Jerusalem ("the city," 6:9).

1. Micah 6:2–8 presents an artistically shaped rhetorical piece, which appropriates the prophetic lawsuit speech (vv. 2–5) and then turns to problems connected with the cult (vv. 6–7), in order to teach "what is good" with stronger focus at the end (v. 8). The language recalls at significant points the pedagogical activity of the Deuteronomic-Deuteronomistic school. But various details make it probable that the present text has its origins in the postexilic era (see below, pp. 171f.).

The postexilic redactor presents a text for his own time in order to make a contemporary application of Micah's proclamation. For according to its content, this didactic sermon has no connection with the themes of chaps. 4–5. It does, however, relate to the main theme of Micah's sketches of his sayings in chaps. 1–3, although there is nothing more than a hint of accusation; of approaching disaster, there is no mention at all.

2. Micah 6:9–16, by contrast, contains sentences which bring indictment and announcement of disaster similar to those found in Micah's prophecies. The passage is also concerned with social conduct, which, to be sure, has to do with the sphere of deceptive commercial practices. More importantly, several characteristics of style and the content of v. 13a make it more likely that the passage has its origins after Micah's time (see below, pp. 189f.). Two briefer interpolations (v. 14aβ, bβ) and a longer, unquestionably Deuteronomistic addition (v. 16) indicate that the text found wider attention in the course of the sixth century. Two briefer interpolations exhibiting the language of wisdom (vv. 9aβ, 12b) could be even later.

But neither the basic text nor any of the interpolations exhibits a connection with the words of salvation prophecy in chaps. 4–5. However, its connection with Micah's prophecies and with the Deuteronomistic commentaries is closer in terms of theme but more distant in terms of language (see below, pp. 188f.).

3. Micah 7:1–7 contains one single lament over the total dominion of injustice in the land. Similar to Micah, here it is particularly the leading circles that are held responsible; unlike Micah, however, all other members of society are charged with offenses: "not one of them is just" (v. 2). The language is reminiscent of Trito-Isaiah (see below, p. 204). The speaker is to be thought of as a disheartened prophet (see note 7:1a); he does not prophesy disaster. The people's conduct already bears judgment

within itself. In the interpolation in 7:4b we find a prayer that reflects upon the day—proclaimed by the "watchers" or Yahweh, i.e., probably the earlier prophets—which has dawned with the universal chaos now present (see below, p. 207). But, in spite of everything, the voice of lament ends with a call to hope and trust (v. 7).

Again, the content of the lament in vv. 2–6 comes close to Micah's accusations, even if the circle of those who are guilty has now become boundless. But the completely isolated person uttering the lament does not expect a judgment that is yet to come. What does it mean that in watching he turns to God for deliverance (v. 7)? With such a statement of trust he remains far removed from the prophetic promises and the liturgical insertions in chaps. 4–5, especially in that he speaks without exception the language of the prayer of the individual. It is possible that this last lament, because of its prospect of hope, and in view of the songs of the community which follow beginning with 7:8, has been consciously placed at the conclusion of the three significant later passages in 6:2—7:7 by the postexilic redactor responsible for 6:1.

If we take an overview of these later passages, it can be established that they, to a greater or a lesser degree, clearly recall Micah's theme of justice in chaps. 1–3. However, it remains impossible to demonstrate that any of these texts originates during the preexilic period. Certain linguistic elements of the Deuteronomists in 6:3-5, 8, 16 (see below, pp. 170f., 197f.) are only indefinite reminiscences of the specific Deuteronomistic commentary in chaps. 1–3 (see above, pp. 18f.). But a different observation is all the more unambiguous: in no instance in these texts do we find a thematic connection with the new prophecies and with the liturgical insertions of the redaction in chaps. 4–5.

Accordingly, in the exilic and postexilic period, two different groups among the Jerusalem tradents of the prophets' words concerned themselves with Micah: on the one hand, there were circles of prophets proclaiming a new salvation who, in light of the fulfillment of Micah's sayings of doom, led Israel to a new future and in so doing concerned themselves with the destiny of the nations (chaps. 4–5); on the other hand, there were those circles of preachers who, at a later time, focused upon the guilt of social sins which Micah himself had censured (6:2—7:7). They were entirely dedicated to their own time and people, hardly taking notice of the foreign nations. That both groups had contact with each other is demonstrated by the book of Micah, for Micah was an authority to both groups, and both carried Micah's proclamation further, but in a manner that is indicative of each one's own unique characteristics.

D. Micah 7:8–20. The circles of salvation prophets stood in a closer connection with the liturgical ceremonies of lamentation. Thus in chaps. 4–5 we found liturgical insertions and elements of a liturgical nature (4:5, 7b; 5:8[9]) as well as sayings concerning foreign nations (4:11–13; 5:14[15]). These groups also edited the texts for the lamentation ceremonies in Jerusalem used on the anniversary of Jerusalem's fall and of the temple's destruction (Zech. 7:3, 5; 8:19). Also belonging to these texts are the Psalms used by the worshiping community to respond to the rereading of the old and the new prophecies. With the recognition that 7:11–12, 13 are explanatory glosses that exhibit the style of the interpolation in 7:4b, our exegetical analysis indicated that there are three different psalms (see below, pp. 216f.). 7:8–10, 14–20 is the only larger text-complex in which the community raises its voice (cf. previously the confession in 4:5, the prayer of supplication in 5:8, and the theophany hymn in 1:3f. that functions as an introit; see below, p. 52). After bracketing 7:11–13, there are also other grounds for concluding that the 7:8–20 is not a self-contained liturgy with responses uttered between a prophetic speaker and the community (see below, p. 215). The three psalms of the community are to be distinguished on the basis of style and function: a song of trust (vv. 8–10); a prayer (vv. 14–17); and a hymn (vv. 18–20). It is an open question whether the redaction intends that the three psalms be understood as a unit, or whether it considered the individual psalms to have a connection with the various strata of the book of Micah.

Micah 7:8–10 could have already been connected with the reading of chaps. 1–3. The song speaks more clearly than the others of confession of guilt and of acceptance of Yahweh's wrath. To this extent it best fits with Micah's proclamation. As a psalm of trust which expresses the hope of salvation, it certainly also echoes the first promise of deliverance in 4:9f.; and its motif of the rejection of the enemy's malicious joy *(Schadenfreude)*, associated with the oracles concerning foreign nations, sounds like an answer to the second promise of deliverance (4:11–13). Thus as a psalm of trust, 7:8–10 might have originated in direct response to chaps. 1–3 and 4:9–13 in the early exilic period, when Jerusalem still very much "sat in darkness" (v. 8b; nevertheless, cf. below, pp. 218f.).

The poverty-stricken community, returned from exile, speaks in 7:14–17; these verses ask for a new institution of Yahweh's office as shepherd, without clearly recalling texts such as 2:12, 13 and 4:6f. (cf. 5:2b[3b] and 3[4]; see below, pp. 86f., 123f.), which speak of the gathering and return of the flock scattered in exile. 7:14 refers more to the regaining of fertile pasture in the homeland (see below, pp. 225f.). Moreover, the intercessions for the nations (v. 16f.) do not in a more precise way correspond to the prophecies against the foreign nations in 4:13; 5:6–8[7–9], 14[15]. The general connection of the intercessions for Yahweh's people with the intercessions for the nations merely corresponds with the theme of future hostility or friendship that occurs frequently in the prophecies chaps. 4–5 (4:1–5, 11–13; 5:6–7[7–8]). Thus only in a general way can it be shown that the connections of 7:14–17 with chaps. 4–5 are closer than they are with chaps. 1–3.

Micah 7:18–20, a beloved hymn to the God who forgives sins, gives no indication of having a closer connection to any of the main strata in the book of Micah, yet it certainly echoes all of them. The reference to the multitude of sins that are to be removed (v. 19), and to the wrath that is not retained forever, is in the first instance suggestive of Micah's own proclamation in chaps. 1–3. But 6:2—7:6 also referred in various instances to the abundance of injustice. That no one can live without the forgiveness of sins receives its most pointed formulation in 7:2–6. The forgiveness of sins is, finally, also the presupposition of the proclamation of salvation that is attested in chaps. 4–5, although it remains unstated there.

Not one sentence in the three psalms makes it necessary to assume

25

that they were composed in order to make a precise and direct connection with the preceding chapters. Nevertheless, they were specifically attached to the book of Micah by redactors with liturgical interests. That only one of the psalms was ever sung after the reading of one part of the book is, finally, less probable than that all three passages were sung after the reading of the whole preceding book.

The interpolations in 7:4b and 7:11–13 belong to the latest glosses in the book. According to 7:11a they would have to be dated before Nehemiah, i.e., in the first half of the fifth century (see below, pp. 223f.). I see no basis for dating any interpolation in the book even later, unless it be the obscure saying in 5:4b–5a[5b–6a].

Conclusion: The redaction history of the book

The history of the book's redaction is, in our view, closely connected with the history of the proclamation of its prophetic sayings. At the beginning we find three sketches of scenes in which Micah proclaimed his sayings, penned by the prophet himself: (1) 1:6, 7b–13a, 14–16; (2) 2:1–4, 6–11; (3) 3:1–12 (on brief conjectures, see the textual notes accompanying the translation). The first Deuteronomistic commentaries on these texts are found in 1:5, 7a, 13b, as well as in the interpolations and changes in 2:3–5, 10b; 3:4, 5, 8; 1:1, and in the appropriation of the liturgical introit for the reading of the book in the setting of community worship in 1:3f. (theophany hymn).

From 587 down to the early postexilic period, there accumulated in chaps. 4–5 a collection of sayings from the prophets of salvation. It begins in the early exilic time with the promises of deliverance in 4:9—5:1, 3, 4a, 5b [5:2, 4, 5a, 6b]. Added to these in the late exilic time were sayings which promise the return of the exiles, found in 2:12, 13 as well as in 4:6–7a. These were followed by sayings which treat the relationship of the remnant Israel to the foreign nations (5:6–14[7–15] and other sayings which speak of the future of Jerusalem (4:1–8). At the same tim , previously known prophecies of salvation were reworked: to 4:6–7a was added v. 7b, and to 5:9–12[10–13] were added 5:8[9] and (v. 13[14] conj.) v. 14[15]. In addition, 5:1, 3[2, 5] was expanded by the addition of 5:2[3], on the one hand (see below, pp. 145f.), and by 4:8, on the other (see below, pp. 115f.). The conclusion of the collection of material in chaps. 4–5 is not conceivable before the dedication of the temple in the year 515 (see above, pp. 21f.). Connected with the final collection of chaps. 4–5 is the redactor's inclusion of chaps. 1–3 by means of the summons to hear addressed to all peoples in 1:2 (cf. 5:14[15]).

This postexilic redaction of chaps. 1–5 represents the results of a literary movement which, since early exilic times, grew in connection with the ceremonies of lamentation over the fall of Jerusalem (see below, pp. 38, 153f.). Here, on the one hand, appeared prophets who spoke about salvation and about foreign nations; on the other, the listening community of worshipers gave its response (4:5; 5:8).

In order to understand the history of redaction of the book of Micah, we have to reckon with an advanced school in Jerusalem which promoted traditions of salvation prophecy and universalism during the early Persian era. It handed on not only the prophecies of Micah which had been fulfilled in the meantime, including their Deuteronomistic commentary, but it was also productive in carrying on his work. In this connection, its own central theme was the future of the remnant of Israel, of Jerusalem, and of the nations. In addition, there must have been within this school of tradents a group which, by making loose connections with Micah's accusations, were oriented toward social criticism; thus they were interested in pressing, contemporary (early postexilic) abuses, as we find in the texts in 6:2—7:7. This group of texts was incorporated (after 5:14[15]; 6:1) by the school of redactors into the Micah traditions in 1:1—5:14[15], which were by that time available to them.

A final step of redactional activity by this school of tradents prepared the proclamation of Micah (chaps. 1–3), that of the new salvation prophets (chaps. 4–5), and also the later passages from the circles of the social critics (6:2—7:7), for liturgical use as readings within community worship, and added the three psalm texts (7:8–10, 14–17, 18–20) which functioned as the response of the worshiping community.

Several additions (presumably literary only), such as 5:4b–5a[5b–6a] and 7:4b, 11f., 13, remain difficult to incorporate into a redactional analysis; presumably, they are not to be dated prior to the fifth century.

6. Literature

For older literature on the Twelve Prophets, see Wolff, *Obadiah and Jonah* (1987) 23ff.

1. Commentaries on Micah: J. T. Beck, *Erklärung der Propheten Micha und Joel* (1898). J. Halévy, "Le Livre de Michée," *RSEHA* 12 (1904) 97–117; 193–216; 289–312; *RSEHA* 13 (1905) 1–22. B. A. Copass and E. L. Carlson, *A Study of the Prophet Micah* (1950). A. P. Hastupis, Tὸ βίβλιον τοῦ Μιχαίου (Athens 1969). L. C. Allen, *The Books of Joel, Obadiah, Jonah and Micah*, The New International Commentary on the OT 5 (1976). J. L. Mays, *Micah*, OTL (1976). A. S. van der Woude, *Micha* (1976).

2. General Studies on Micah: B. Duhm, "Anmerkungen zu den Zwölf Propheten. III. Micha," *ZAW* 31 (1911) 81–93; also reprinted as a booklet from *ZAW* (1911) 43–55. L. P. Smith, "The Book of Micah," *Interpretation* 6 (1952) 210–227. R. Meyer, "Michabuch," *RGG*³ 4 (1960) 929–931. A. E. Leslie, "Micah the Prophet," *IDB* 3 (1962) 369–372. J. M. Ward, "Micah the Prophet," *IDBSuppl* (1976) 592f. K. Koch, *The Prophets* 1, trans. Margaret Kohl (1982) 94–105 ("Micah of Moresheth").

3. The Text of Micah: J. T. Meek, "Some Emendations in the Old Testament: 1. Mic. 4:1 = Isa. 2:2," *JBL* 48 (1929) 162–163. J. T. Milik, "Fragments d'un midrash de Michée dans les manuscrits de Qumran," *RB* 59 (1952) 412–418. S. J. Schwantes, "A Note on Micah 5:1 (Hebrew 4:14)," *AUSS* 1 (1963) 107. Idem, "Critical Notes on Micah I 10–16," *VT* 14 (1964) 454–461. M. Moreschet, *"whr hbyt lbmwt y'r,"* *BetM* 12 (1966–67)/3.(31.) 123–126. D. K. Innes, "Some Notes on Micah, Chap. I," *EvQ* 39 (1967) 225–227. J. T. Willis, "On the Text of Micah 2:1aα–β, *Biblica* 48 (1967) 534–541. H. F. Fuhs, *Die äthiopische Übersetzung des Propheten Micha*, BBB 28 (1968). D. K. Innes, "Some Notes on Micah, Chapters II–V," 41 *EvQ* 41 (1969) 10–13, 109–112, 169–171, 216–220. M. Collin,

"Recherches sur l'histoire textuelle du prophète Michée," *VT* 21 (1971) 281–297. J. P. Oberholzer, "Micah 1:10–16 and the Septuagint," *HTS* 28 (1972) 74–85.

4. Literary and Redaction Criticism of Micah: B. Stade, "Bemerkungen über das Buch Micha," *ZAW* 1 (1881) 161–172. Idem, "Weitere Bemerkungen zu Micha 4 und 5," *ZAW* 3 (1883) 1–16. W. Nowack, "Bemerkungen über das Buch Micha," *ZAW* 4 (1884) 277–291. B. Stade, "Bemerkungen zu Nowack, über das Buch Micha," *ZAW* 4 (1884) 291–297. Idem, "Streiflichter auf die Entstehung der jetzigen Gestalt der alttestamentlichen Prophetenschriften," *ZAW* 23 (1903) 153–171 (163: Micha 1,2–4; 164–171: Micha 7,7–20 ein Psalm). G. Hylmö, *Kompositionen av Mikas Bok* (1919). K. Budde, "Verfasser und Stelle von Mi 4,1–4 (Jes 2,2–4)," *ZDMG* 81 (1927) 152–158. J. Lindblom, *Micha literarisch untersucht:* AAAbo.H VI:2 (1919). E. Cannawurf, "The Authenticity of Micah IV 1–4," *VT* 13 (1963) 26–33. B. Renaud, *Structure et Attaches Littéraires de Michée IV–V,* CRB 2 (1964). R. Tournay, "Quelques relectures bibliques antisamaritaines," *RB* 71 (1964) 504–536 (III. Michée, VI,9–16: 514–524). J. T. Willis, "Structure et Attaches Littéraires de Michée IV–V, by B. Renaud. 1964," *VT* 15 (1965) 400–403. Idem, "The Structure, Setting and Interrelationships of the Pericopes in the Book of Micah," *Dissertation Abstracts* 27 (1966–67) 1442. Idem, "The Structure of the Book of Micah," *SEÅ* 34 (1969) 5–42. Idem, "The Structure of Micah 3–5 and the Function of Micah 5,9–14 in the Book," *ZAW* 81 (1969) 191–214. A. S. van de Woude, "Micah in Dispute with the Pseudo-Prophets," *VT* 19 (1969) 244–260. J. T. Willis, "Fundamental Issues in Contemporary Micah Studies," *RestQ* 13 (1970) 77–90. Jörg Jeremias, "Die Deutung der Gerichtsworte Michas in der Exilszeit," *ZAW* 83 (1971) 330–354. I. Willi-Plein, *Vorformen der Schriftexegese innerhalb des Alten Testaments,* ZAWBeih 123 (1971) 70–114. A. S. van der Woude, "Deutero-Micha: ein Prophet aus Nord-Israel?" *NedThT* 25 (1971) 365–378. Th. Lescow, "Redaktionsgeschichtliche Analyse von Micha 1–5," *ZAW* 84 (1972) 46–85. Idem, "Redaktionsgeschichtliche Analyse von Micha 6–7," *ZAW* 84 (1972) 182–212. B. Renaud, *La formation du Livre de Michée. Tradition et Actualisation,* EtB (Paris) 1977. K. Jeppesen, "New Aspects of Micah Research," *JSOT* 8 (1978) 3–32. J. Vermeylen, *Du prophète Isaïe á l'apocalyptique* (1978) 570–601 ("Les relectures deutéronomistes des livres d'Amos et de Michée. B. Michée"). J. T. Willis, "Thoughts on a Redactional Analysis of the Book of Micah," *SoBl* 1 (1978) 87–109.

5. Style Analysis and Form Criticism of Micah: E. Sachsse, "Untersuchungen zur hebräischen Metrik. Jes 2,2–4; Mi 4,1–3," *ZAW* 43 (1925) 173–192. P. Watson, "Form Criticism and an Exegesis of Micah 6,1–8:" *RestQ* 7 (1963) 62–72. C. Hardmeier, *Texttheorie und biblische Exegese,* BEvTh 79 (1978). J. de Waard, "Vers une identification des participants dans le livre de Michée," in *Festschrift E. Jacob,* RHPhR 59 (1979) 509–516.

6. Tradition History of Micah: E. Nielsen, *Oral Tradition,* SBT 11 (1954) 79–93 (Micah 4–5). W. Beyerlin, *Die Kulttraditionen Israels in der Verkündigung des Propheten Micha,* FRLANT 72 (1959). W. Harrelson, "Nonroyal Motifs in the Royal Eschatology," in *Israel's Prophetic Heritage* (1962) 147–165. S. Herrmann, *Die prophetischen Heilserwartungen* *im Alten Testament,* BWANT 85 (1965) 144–154. B. Reicke, "Liturgical Traditions in Micah 7," *HThR* 60 (1967) 349–368.

7. The Man Micah: R. Meyer, "Micha," *RGG³* 4 (1960) 929. I. H. Eybers, "Micah, the Morashthite: the Man and his Message," *OTWSA* (1973) 9–24. H. W. Wolff, "Wie verstand Micha von Moreschet sein prophetisches Amt?" VTSuppl 29 (1978) 403–417. Idem, "Michas geistige Heimat," in *Mit Micha reden* (1978) 30–40; translated as "Micah the Moreshite—The Prophet and His Background" in *Israelite Wisdom: Theological and Literary Essays in Honor of Samuel Terrien,* ed. J. G. Gammie, W. Brueggemann, W. L. Humphreys, J. M. Ward (1978) 77–84; and also as "Micah's Cultural and Intellectual Background," in *Micah the Prophet,* trans. R. D. Gehrke (1981) 17–25. J. N. Carreira, "Micha—ein Ältester von Moreschet?" *TThZ* 90 (1981) 19–28.

8. The Time of Micah: N. Na'aman, "Sennacherib's 'Letter to God' on his Campaign to Judah," *BASOR* 214 (1974) 25–39. B. Z. Luria, "The Political Background for Micah: Ch. 1" (Hebrew; English summary), *BetM* 71 (1977) 403–412. N. Na'aman, "Sennacherib's Campaign to Judah and the Date of the *LMLK* Stamps," *VT* 29 (1979) 61–86.

9. The Theology and Message of Micah: W. Cannon, "The Disarmament Passage in Isaiah II and Micah IV," *Theol.* 24 (1930) 2–8. A. H. Edelkoort, "Prophet and Prophet," *OTS* 5 (1948) 179–189. E. Hammershaimb, "Einige Hauptgedanken in der Schrift des Propheten Micha," *ST* 15 (1961) 11–34; idem, *Some Aspects of Old Testament Prophecy* (1966) 29–50. A. S. Kapelrud, "Eschatology in the Book of Micah," *VT* 11 (1961) 392–405. F. C. Fensham, "Righteousness in the Book of Micah and Parallels from the Ancient Near East" (Afrikaans), *TGW* 7 (1967) 416–425. Idem, "The Divine Subject of the Verb in the Book of Micah," *OTWSA* (1973) 25–34. F. L. Hossfeld and I. Meyer, *Prophet gegen Prophet,* BiBe 9 (1973) 46–48. A. H. van Zyl, "Messianic Scope in the Book of Micah," *OTWSA* (1973) 62–72. J. L. Mays, "The Theological Purpose of the Book of Micah," *Beiträge zur alttestamentlichen Theologie. Festschrift Walter Zimmerli* (1977) 276–287.

10. Specific Problems of Interpretation: B. Stade, "Mich. 2,4," *ZAW* 6 (1986) 122–123. E. Nestle, "Miszellen. Micha 4,3," *ZAW* 29 (1909) 234. H. Donat, "Micha 2,6–9," *BZ* 9 (1911) 351–366. K. Fullerton, "Studies in Isaiah I: on Is 2,5 and Mi 4,5," *JBL* 35 (1916) 134–140. K. Budde, "Das Rätsel von Micha 1," *ZAW* 37 (1917–18) 77–108. Idem, "Micha 2 und 3," *ZAW* 38 (1919–20) 2–22. A. Bruno, *Micha und der Herrscher aus der Vorzeit* (1923). H. Gunkel, "Der Micha-Schluss: Zur Einführung in die literaturgeschichtliche Arbeit am Alten Testament," *ZS* 2 (1924) 145–178. R. C. Burkitt, "Micah 6 and 7: A Northern Prophecy," *JBL* 45 (1926) 159–161. W. C. Graham, "Some Suggestions towards the Interpretation of Micah 1,10–16," *AJSL* 47 (1930–31) 237–258. A. R. Osborn, "The Nature of True Religion Micah 6:1–8," *Bibl Rev* 17 (1932) 232–239. K. Elliger, "Die Heimat des Propheten Micha," *ZDPV* 57 (1934) 81–152, reprinted in *Kleine Schriften zum Alten Testament,* ThB 32 (1966) 9–71. J. H. Hertz, "Micah 6,8," *ET* 46 (1934–35) 188. Th. H. Gaster, "Notes on the Minor Prophets. 2. Micah 5,13; 6,10," *JThS* 38 (1937) 163–165. A. Jepsen, "Kleine Beiträge zum Zwölfprophetenbuch," *ZAW* 56 (1938) 85–100 (96–100). Z. Vilnai, "The Topography of Micah," *BJPES* 6 (1939) 127–131. H. M. Weil, "Le chapitre II de

Michée expliqué par le Premier Livre des Rois, chap. XX–XXII," *RHR*
121 (1940) 146–161. M. Zeidel, "Micha ch. VI (Its Parallels and a
Commentary), *Tarb.* 17 (1945) 12–20. B. Reicke, "Mik. 7 såsom 'mes-
siansk' text med sörskild hänsyn till Matt. 10,35f. och Luk. 12,53," *SEÅ*
12 (1947) 279–302. D. W. Thomas, "The Root *ṣn'* in Hebrew," *JJS* 1
(1949) 182–188. G. W. Anderson, "A Study of Micah 6,1–8," *SJTh* 4
(1951) 191–197. M. B. Crook, "The Promise in Micah 5," *JBL* 70 (1951)
313–320. Ph. Hyatt, "On the Meaning of Micah 6,8," *AThR* 34 (1952)
232–239. J. A. Fitzmyer, "*lᵉ* as a Preposition and a Particle in Mi 5,1
(5,2)," *CBQ* 18 (1956) 10–13. H. Wildberger, "Die Völkerwallfahrt zum
Zion," *VT* 7 (1957) 62–81. R. Köbert, "*môrad* (Mi 1,4) 'Tränke,'" *Biblica*
39 (1958) 82–83. A. Deissler, "Micha 6,1–8. Der Rechtsstreit Jahwes mit
Israel um das rechte Bundesverhältnis," *TThZ* 68 (1959) 229–234. A.
Ehrman, "A Note on יֵשׁ in Mic. 6,14," *JNES* 18 (1959) 156. H. J. Stoebe,
"'Und demütig sein vor deinem Gott,'" *WuD* 6 (1959) 180–194. C.
Westermann, "Micha 5,1–3," *Herr, tue meine Lippen auf* 5, ed. G.
Eichholz (²1961) 54–59. O. Eissfeldt, "Ein Psalm aus Nord-Israel. Micha
7,7–20," *ZDMG* 112 (1962) 259–268, reprinted in *Kleine Schriften* 4
(1968) 63–72. D. Squillaxi, "Il mistero di Betlem nel profeta Michea
(5,2–5)," *PalCl* 41 (1962) 763–766. E. R. Achtemeier, "How to Stay Alive
(Exercising Love in Terms of Mi 6,8)," *Theology in Life* 6 (1963) 275–
282. F. L. B. Gorgulho, "Notas sôbre Belem-Efratá em Miq 5,1–5," *RCT*
3 (1963) 20–38. H. Gottlieb, "Den taersende kuie Mi 4,11–13," *DTT* 26
(1963) 167–171. H. Donner, *Israel unter den Völkern,* VTSuppl 11 (1964)
92–105.176. J. Dus, "Weiteres zum nordisraelitischen Psalm, Micha
7,7–20," *ZDMG* 115 (1965) 14–22. A. Demsky, "The Houses of Achzib:
A Critical Note on Micah 1,14b (cf. 1 Chron. 4,21–23)," *IEJ* 16 (1966)
211–215. Th. Lescow, *Micha 6,6–8,* AzTh 1/25 (1966). B. Z. Luria, "Das
übriggebliebene Land und der Rest Israels," *BetM* 12 (1966–67) 18–28.
H. Cazelles, "Histoire et Géographie en Mi 4, 6–13," *Fourth World
Jewish Studies* I (1967) 87–89. G. Fohrer, "Micha 1," in *Das ferne und
nahe Wort. Festschrift Leonard Rost,* ZAWBeih 105 (1967) 65–80. O.
García de la Fuente, "Notas al texto de Miqueas," *Aug.* 7 (1967) 145–
154. Th. Lescow, "Das Geburtsmotiv in den messianischen Weissa-
gungen bei Jesaja und Micha," *ZAW* 79 (1967) 172–207. J. T. Willis,
"*Mimmᵉ kā lī yēṣē'* in Micah 5,1," *JQR* (1967–68) 317–322. K. J.
Cathcart, "Notes on Micah 5,4–5," *Biblica* 49 (1968) 511–514. J. T.
Willis, "Some Suggestions on the Interpretation of Micah I 2," *VT* 18
(1968) 372–379. Idem, "Micah IV 14—V 5 A Unit," *VT* 18 (1968) 529–
547. Idem, "*Micha 6, 6–8. Studien zu Sprache, Form und Auslegung,* by
Theodor Lescow," *VT* 18 (1968) 273–278. Idem, "A Note on ואמר in
Micah 3,1," *ZAW* 80 (1968) 50–54. A. S. van der Woude, "Micha 2,7a
und der Bund Jahwes mit Israel," *VT* 18 (1968) 388–391. J. T. Willis,
"The Authenticity and Meaning of Micah 5,9–14," *ZAW* 81 (1969) 353–
368. B. Chiesa, "'Altare solare' e culto jahwistico a Lachish," *BibOr* 12
(1970) 273–274. J. T. Willis, "Micah 2,6–8 and the 'People of God' in
Micah," *BZ* 14 (1970) 72–87. A. S. van der Woude, "Waarheid als
Leugen (Micha 2,6–11)," *VoxTh* (1970) 65–70. P. Bordreuil, "Michée
4,10–13 et ses parallèles ougaritiques," *Sem.* 21 (1971) 21–28. J. Coppens, "Le cadre littéraire de Michée V 1–5," in *Near Eastern Studies in
Honor of W. F. Albright* (1971) 57–62. L. Grollenberg, "Micha 7: Eine

Buss-Liturgie?" *Schrift* 17 (1971) 188–191. A. S. van der Woude, "Micha I 10–16," in *Festschrift A. Dupont-Sommer* (1971) 347–353. A. Ehrman, "A Note on Micah VI 14," *VT* 23 (1973) 103–105. B. J. van der Merwe, "Micah 1,12 and its possible Parallels in Pre-Exilic Prophetism," *OTWSA* (1973) 45–53. H. S. Pelser, "Some Remarks regarding the Contrast in Micah 5,1 and 2," *OTWSA* (1973) 35–44. J. P. van der Westhuizen, "The Term *'etnān* in Micah," *OTWSA* (1973) 54–61. A. S. van der Woude, "Micah IV 1–5: An Instance of the Pseudo-Prophets Quoting Isaiah," in *Symbolae biblicae et mesopotamicae F. M. Th. de Liagre-Böhl dedicatae* (1973) 396–402. P. J. van Zijl, "A Possible Explanation of Micah 5,13 in Light of Comparative Semitic Languages," *OTWSA* (1973) 73–76. V. Fritz, "Das Wort gegen Samaria Mi 1,2–7*," *ZAW* 86 (1974) 316–331. J. T. Willis, "A Reapplied Prophetic Hope Oracle," in *Studies in Prophecy,* VTSuppl 26 (1974) 64–76. J. Homerski, "'Panujacy' z Betlejem (interpretacja perykopy Mich 5,1–5)," *RTK* 22 (1976) 5–16. R. C. Lux, "An Exegetical Study of Micah 1, 8–16," diss., Notre Dame 1976 (Order No. 76-27.288), *Dissertation Abstracts* 37 (1976–77) 3717. J. Synowiec, "Jerozolima stolica uniwersalneso kró-lestwa Jahwe, Mi 4,1–4; Iz 2,2–4" (Polish; "Jerusalem, the Capital City of the Universal Kingdom of Yahweh, Mic. 4:1–4; Isa. 2:2–4"), *Króleshro Boze w Piśmie św.,* Lublin (1976) 17–33. S. Vergone, "Micah 4,14," (Hebrew; English summary), *BetM* 66 (1976) 392–401. O. Loretz, "Fehlanzeige von Ugaritismen in Micha 5,1–3," *UF* 9 (1977) 358–360. Idem, "Hebräisch *tjrwš* und *jrš* in Mi 6,15 und Hi 20,15," *UF* 9 (1977) 353–354. D. J. Bryant, "Micah 4,14–5,14: An Exegesis," *RestQ* 21 (1978) 210–230. R. P. Gordon, "Micah VII 19 and Akkadian *kabāsu,*" *VT* 28 (1978) 355. K. J. Cathcart, "Micah 5,4–5 and Semitic Incantations," *Biblica* 59 (1978) 38–48. D. Kellermann, "Überlieferungsprobleme alt-testamentlicher Ortsnamen," *VT* 28 (1978) 423–432. O. Loretz, "Die Psalmen: Beiträge der Ugarit-Texte zum Verständnis von Kolometrie und Textologie der Psalmen 2. Psalm 90–150," *AOAT* 207 (1979) 453–455 [on Mic. 5:4–5].

11. On Literature about the Book of Micah: G. Fohrer, "Neuere Literatur zur alttestamentlichen Prophetie: III.5.6 Micha," *ThR* 19 (1951) 316–317 (Literature from 1932 to 1939). Idem, "Neuere Literatur zur alttestamentlichen Prophetie: IIIf 7 Micha," *ThR* 20 (1952) 263 (Literature from 1940 to 1950). Idem, "Zehn Jahre Literatur zur alt-testamentlichen Prophetie. IX 7 Micha," *ThR* 28 (1962) 289–291. K. Jeppesen, "How the Book of Micah Lost Its Integrity: Outline of the History of the Criticism of the Book of Micah with Emphasis on the 19th Century," *StTh* 33 (1979) 101–131. Idem, "B. Renaud, *La Formation du Livre de Michée. Tradition et Actualisation* (1977)," *VT* 29 (1979) 251–256. G. Fohrer, "Neue Literatur zur alttestamentlichen Prophetie. 6. Micha," *ThR* 45 (1980) 212–216. J. Vermeylen, book review of B. Renaud, *La formation du livre de Michée* (1977), *Bibl* 61 (1980) 287–291.

12. Practical Theology: J. Heer, "Der Bethlehemspruch Micheas und die Geburt Jesu (Micha 5,1–3)," *BiKi* 25 (1970) 106–109. R. Zerfass, "'Es ist dir gesagt, Mensch, was du tun sollst'" (Mi 6,8), *BiKi* 25 (1970) 109–110. A. Maillot-A. Lelievre, *Actualité de Michée. Un grand petit prophète* (1976). H. W. Wolff, *Mit Micha reden. Prophetie einst und heute* (1978), English translation, *Micah the Prophet,* tr. R. D. Gehrke (1981).

The Title of the Book

Literature

Joachim Jeremias, "Moresheth-Gath, Die Heimat des Propheten Micha," *PJB* 29 (1933) 42–53. K. Elliger, "Die Heimat des Propheten Micha," *ZDPV* 57 (1934) 81–152. Idem, *Kleine Schriften zum Alten Testament,* ThB 32 (1966) 9–71. Z. Kallai מוֹרֶשֶׁת גַּת, *Encyclopaedia biblica* 4 (1962) 741–742. C. J. Labuschagne, *The Incomparability of Yahweh in the Old Testament,* POS 5 (1966). G. Johannes, "Unvergleichlichkeitsformulierungen im Alten Testament" (Dissertation, University of Mainz, 1968). P. Welten, *Die Königs-Stempel. Ein Beitrag zur Militärpolitik Judas unter Hiskia und Josia,* Abhandlungen des Deutschen Palästina-vereins 1 (1969). Z. Kallai, "The Kingdom of Rehoboam," *ErIs* 10 (1971) 245–254 and XVIIIf. P. K. D. Neumann, "Das Wort, das geschehen ist . . .," *VT* 23 (1973) 171–217. A. K. Jenkins, "Hezekiah's Fourteenth Year," *VT* 26 (1976) 284–298. G. Pettinato, "The Royal Archives of *tell mardikh-Ebla,*" *BA* 39 (1976) 44–52. G. M. Tucker, "Prophetic Superscriptions and the Growth of the Canon," in *Canon and Authority,* ed. G. W. Coats and B. O. Long (1977) 56–70. H. F. Fuhs, *Sehen und Schauen. Die Wurzel ḥzh im Alten Orient und im Alten Testament,* Forschung zur Bibel 32 (1978) 194–197. A. Archi, "The Epigraphic Evidence from Ebla and the Old Testament," *Biblica* 60 (1979) 556–566.

Text

1:1 The word of Yahweh[a] which came to Micah the[b] Moreshite[c] in the days of Jotham, Ahaz, and Hezekiah, the kings of Judah, which[d] he has seen[e] concerning Samaria and Jerusalem.

1a Gk (καὶ ἐγένετο λόγος κυρίου προς M.) corresponds to the beginning of the Jonah narrative.

1b Gk[B], etc. (τον του Μωρασθι) understands מרשתי as the name of the father, as do Coptic, Ethiopic, Arabic *(filium)* versions.

1c Targ (דממרשא) and Syr understand this to be the town Mareshah (1:15).

1d Gk (ὑπὲρ ὧν) connects the second relative clause to the kings of Judah; Vg *(quod)* correctly relates it to the דבר־יהוה *(verbum Domini),* for חזה does not occur in comparable texts without an accusative object (Isa. 1:1; 2:1; 13:1; Hab. 1:1; cf. Amos 1:1 and Wolff, *Joel and Amos* 116ff.), especially in those cases when על introduces object of the vision.

1e Targ (ראתנבי) translates with the words "he prophesies"; cf. Obad. 1 and Wolff, *Obadiah and Jonah* 31ff.; 44.

Form

The beginning verse has no syntactic or thematic connection with vv. 2ff. Rather, the superscription in v. 1 is placed before the following prophetic sayings in order to characterize them concisely and pointedly as "the word of Yahweh" (element *a*). The relative clauses add three explanations to the phrase "word of Yahweh." The first clause specifies the agent through whom (element *b*) and the time when (element *c*) the word came. The second clause states for whom (element *d*) these prophetic sayings are meant. All of these elements occur in the redaction of prophetic books; and each is found elsewhere at the beginning of collections of prophetic sayings: element *a* (דבר־יהוה) is the determinative, lead title in Hos. 1:1; Joel 1:1; Zeph. 1:1 (the phrase stands in a subordinate position in Jer. 1:2; Ezek. 1:3; Hag. 1:1; Zech. 1:1; Mal. 1:1); element *b* (אשר היה אל־ . . .) occurs in Hos. 1:1; Joel 1:1; Zeph. 1:1 (cf. Jer. 1:2a*a*; Ezek. 1:3a*a*); element *c* (. . . בימי) in Hos. 1:1; Amos 1:1; Zeph. 1:1; Jer. 1:2f. (a different expression is used in Ezek. 1:2; Hag. 1:1; and Zech. 1:1); element *d* (אשר . . . חזה על־) in Amos 1:1; Isa. 1:1 (cf. Isa. 2:1; without על־ in Isa. 13:1; Hab. 1:1). In Amos 1:1 and Isa. 1:1 the last element *(d)*, the reference to those addressed by the divine revelation, stands before the phrase specifying the time of the prophet's activity *(c)*. In Micah, element *d* appears to be a later addition. In the titles of prophetic books, we find a second relative clause, in addition to Mic. 1:1, only in Amos 1:1 and Jer. 1:1. Since it is highly probable that these latter two texts contain several stages of literary growth (see Wolff, *Joel and Amos* 116ff.), here in Micah we must also reckon with a secondary combination of two types of book titles. Moreover, that the two relative clauses stem from two different redactors is indicated by the fact that the second clause names Samaria and Jerusalem as the addressees, whereas the first clause mentions only kings of Judea and not kings of Israel (as do Amos 1:1 and Hos. 1:1).

Critics have usually considered the second relative clause (element *d*) as secondary (J. Wellhausen, J. M. P. Smith, J. Lindblom, I. Willi-Plein, Th. Lescow, W. Rudolph, J. L. Mays; cf. B. Renaud, 4–7), especially since elements *a, b,* and *d* do not otherwise occur together. The book superscriptions most closely related to Mic. 1:1, namely, Hos. 1:1 and Zeph. 1:1, contain no reference to the addressees of the word of God.

Too little consideration, however, has been given to the possibility that the second relative clause could have been part of an older form of the superscription. This older form of the superscription—occurring before elements *a* and *b*, which are otherwise not connected with *d*—would have read, in analogy to Amos 1:1, "Words of Micah, the Moreshite, which he saw concerning Samaria and Jerusalem" (דִּבְרֵי מִיכָה; B. Duhm; A. George; A. S. van der Woude 13; cf. also H. F. Fuhs 196f.). Or, in analogy to Isa. 1:1, the superscription would read: "Vision of Micah, the Moreshite, which he saw concerning Samaria and Jerusalem" (חֲזוֹן מִיכָה; cf. Obad. 1; Mic. 3:6; and Wolff, *Obadiah and Jonah* 44, and Jörg Jeremias, "Die Deutung der Gerichtsworte Michas in der Exilszeit," *ZAW* 83 [1971] 352f.).

Setting

Such an older form, in that it makes mention of Samaria and Jerusalem, provides an appropriate superscription to the preexilic collection of the original sayings of Micah in chaps. 1–3 (see above, introduction §5). This form of the superscription is to be compared with Isa. 1:1 and the earliest form of the superscription in Amos 1:1 (see Wolff, *Joel and Amos* 107f., 116ff.). It should not be surprising that in Judah, at the end of the eighth century, a similar style of redaction developed among those who collected the prophetic sayings of Amos, Isaiah, and Micah.

On the other hand, the adaptation and expansion of the superscription to its present form certainly did not take place before the exile. Setting forth this collection of prophetic sayings as "the word of Yahweh which came to Micah, the Moreshite, in the days of Jotham, Ahaz, and Hezekiah," is evidence of an advanced theological reflection. This is characteristic of Deuteronomistic redactors who edited and compiled preexilic prophetic sayings after the beginning of the catastrophe of exile (cf. the next closest examples in the superscriptions in Hos. 1:1 and Zeph. 1:1, and see Wolff, *Hosea* 4).

Thus merely an analysis of the book's superscription indicates that it contains two levels of literary activity, each separated from the other by a considerable amount of time. We will have to observe whether the person responsible for reworking the older superscription of Micah's sayings also worked as redactor elsewhere in the book, whether in the glosses on the ancient collection of sayings with chaps. 1–3, or in those chapters added later to complete the book as we now have it (chaps. 4–7).

As a help in dating the redactor's work on the superscription, the form of the name *Hezekiah* has received little attention. It is not (וְ)חִזְקִיָּה (2 Kings 16:20; 18:1—21:3; also Jer. 26:18f.), the form of the name indicating trust in the deity ("Yahweh is my strength"), common in the Deuteronomistic history. Rather, it is the slightly abbreviated form יְחִזְקִיָּהוּ, which expresses a petition for strength ("may Yahweh strengthen"; 1 Chron. 4:41; 2 Chron. 28:27; 33:3), found predominantly in the Chronicler's history. This form of the word, used as a petition, is already found in Isa. 1:1 and, shortened to יְחִזְקִיָה, also in Hos. 1:1, in addition to Mic. 1:1. Although this form of the name did not become common until the postexilic period, it should not be concluded that the redaction of the book was completed during the exile. The superscription type, דבר יהוה אשר היה אל־ occurs as late as the fourth century (Joel 1:1; see Wolff, *Joel and Amos* 20). Yet, in light of Hag. 1:1; Zech. 1:1; Mal. 1:1, the wording of Mic. 1:1 should not be attributed to an editor of the minor prophets as late as the third century (R. E. Wolff, *ZAW* 53 [1953] 115f.; idem, "The Book of Micah," *IB* 6:901). Nevertheless, the date of the final formulation of the superscription remains the broad span of time from the end of the sixth century to the fourth century.

Commentary

The editor intends for the entire book of Micah to be understood as an event of "Yahweh's word." In the classical prophecy of the eighth century, an individual prophetic saying is relatively seldom introduced as a "word of Yahweh" (Isa. 1:10; 28:13f.; Amos. 7:16). On the other hand, the formula for divine revelation ("the word of Yahweh came to . . .) quite frequently introduces a single prophetic saying in Jeremiah (1:4, 11, 13; a total of 21 times) and Ezekiel (3:16; 6:1; 18:5; a total of 41 times) (cf. further, P. K. D. Neumann, 174). But now in Micah, as in Hos. 1:1; Zeph. 1:1; Jer. 1:2f.; Ezek. 1:3; and Joel 1:1, large collections of various kinds of prophetic sayings have become a single event of the word of God. The "religion of the book" is in the making. The book of Micah is to be read as the word of God. Only in this way can it be genuinely understood.

The word of Yahweh has become indissolubly linked with the person Micah. The name is one of the most beloved in the OT and occurs in no less than six variations: מִיכָה, מִיכָיָה, מִיכָיְהוּ, מִיכָיָהוּ, מִיכָאֵל, מִיכָא. More-over, it occurs as a woman's name, מִיכַל (see KBL³ 545f. for the texts). The superscription in Micah has the form מִיכָה, which is the form that occurs most frequently in the OT (more than thirty times for seven persons). This abbreviated form was also read by Jer. 26:18 *Qere,* where-as the (older) consonantal text *(Ketib)* calls our prophet מִיכָיָה. Elsewhere in the OT the same person can be called by different names. Thus in Judg. 17:1, 4 the Ephraimite מִיכָיְהוּ is introduced; by contrast, he is referred to only by the abbreviated form מִיכָה beginning with Judg. 17:5 (until 18:31, a total of nineteen times). Similarly, Micah ben Imlah is called מִיכָיְהוּ in 2 Chron. 18:7f., 12ff. (as in 1 Kings 22:8ff.), but the abbreviated name מִיכָה is used when he is personally addressed in 2 Chron. 18:14. The frequent usage of the name easily led to confusion of one for the other. Thus Micaiahu ben Imlah early on was confused with Micah of Moresheth, as the secondary quotation of Mic. 1:2aα in 1 Kings 22:28b indicates. The addition of the word המרשתי therefore appeared indispensable in Mic. 1:1 as well as in Jer. 28:18. Whereas מִיכָא and מִיכַל are to be explained as abbreviated forms of מִיכָאֵל, the word מִיכָה is rather to be seen as the abbreviated form of מִיכָיְהוּ (M. Noth, *Personennamen* 107, 144). It is one of the oldest combinations of a personal name with "Yahweh" (Judges 17f.); the only other examples of such a combination from the pre-monarchic time are the names Joshua, Joash, Jotham, Jonathan, and Joel. In areas where Akkadian was spoken, the name-type "who is like . . ." *(mannu-kī)* was current (e.g., *mannu-kīma-Sin* = "who is like Sin"; *man-kī-bēli* = "who is like my lord"). In 1975 the excavations of Tell Mardikh in the ancient north Syrian royal city of Ebla, the name *Mi-Kà-Yà* together with the name *Mi-Kà-Il* was discovered (G. Pettinato). However, the ultima *-ya* is not a theophoric element which refers to a God named Yahweh, but is the diminutive name of endearment for *Mi-Kà-Il* (A. Archi). In view of such evidence, the name *Micah* (Michael) may be the oldest name that has survived more than 4000 years and remained undiminished in popularity down to the present time. Al-though such names in the form of a comparative question are rooted in polytheistic thinking, they became a part of a lively hymnic manner of speech (cf. Mic. 7:18!); these names do not belong to a particular polemic against foreign gods (cf. G. Johannes, 92, contra C. J. Lambuschagne, 71f.). Parents who named their child Micah (Micaiah) wished to praise Yahweh above all else.

The gentilic המרשתי denotes the town of Micah's origin, thus distinguishing him from all others in the OT who bear the same name. In addition to "Micah of Moresheth," the name of a prophet's hometown is given only for Elijah (1 Kings 17:1), Jonah (2 Kings 14:25), Amos (1:1), and Nahum (1:1). Since Jer. 26:18 also speaks of Micah "the Moreshite," it would seem probable that this epithet was given to him after his appearance in Jerusalem (cf. 3:9–12). The town of Moresheth may be identical with Moresheth-Gath (Mic. 1:14; see below, p. 62). Muḫrašti is already mentioned in the Amarna texts (*EAT* 335, 17); there, too, it occurs with Lachish (*EAT* 335, 16; cf. Mic. 1:13; on its identification with Moresheth, see J. A. Knudzton, *EAT* 1356). According to Joachim Jeremias the ancient town is to be located at *Tell ej-Judeideh*. It is situated in western Judah's hill country, about 35 km southwest of Jerusalem, 25 km northwest of Hebron, 15 km eastward from Gath (*'Arâq el-Menshîjeh),* a good 30 km west of Tekoa; about 400 m above sea level, on the border of the Shephelah, with a view of the coastal plain (Z. Kallai thinks Moresheth is to be identified with *Tell 'Ētūn,* southwest of Mareshah; for a different view, cf. P. Welten, 74f., 82, etc.). Thus Micah may have his roots among farmers who lived in a small town in an area bordering the coastal plain. But royal officials and soldiers from Jerusalem were present in the neighboring area, for no less than five of the fortified cities established by Rehoboam (2 Chron. 11:7–9; cf. 2 Chron. 19:5) lay in a circle less than 10 km from Moresheth: Azekah to the south; Socoh to the northeast; Adullum to the east; Mareshah to the south; Lachish to the southwest (cf. Mic. 1:13–15 and see below, pp. 61f.). These fortified cities were supposed to secure the entrance to Jerusalem from the coastal highway and the Philistine plain. Moreover, a large number of jar-handles (thirty-seven) bearing the royal stamp were found at *Tell ej-Judeideh* and an even larger number at Lachish (314), evidence for contact between these areas and the capital city (P. Welten, 82; also N. Na'aman, "Sennacherib's Campaign to Judah," *VT* 29 [1979] 61–86 [74]).

By Micah's time, travel had already achieved an increased military significance. For "in the days of the Judean kings Jotham, Ahaz, and Hezekiah," the new Assyrian kings had advanced deep into the Syro-Palestine area. The Northern Kingdom of Israel had already become tributary to Tiglath-Pileser III in 738/737 (*TGI*[2] 55; *ANET* 283), and had lost significant areas of its land in 733 (2 Kings 15:29); with the subjugation of Samaria in 725–722, Israel was finally overthrown (2 Kings 17:5ff.; *TGI*[2] 60; *ANET* 284f.). Moreover, the man from Moresheth could have been an eyewitness to the Assyrian advance into the Philistine coastal plain, concerning which there is evidence for the years 734 (*TGI*[2] 56f.; *ANET* 283f.; S. Herrmann, *A History of Israel in Old Testament Times* [1981[2]] 246ff.), 720 (*TGI*[2] 62), and 712/711 (*TGI*[2] 63f.; *ANET* 286), before Sennacherib in 701 advanced from the coastal plain through Micah's west-Judean homeland as far as Jerusalem (*TGI*[2] 67ff.; *ANET* 287ff.; 2 Kings 18:13ff.). In the meantime, there would have been lively traffic between the fortified towns in the neighborhood of Moresheth and the capital city of Jerusalem.

It is certain that Micah was active as a prophet during the time of Hezekiah (Jer. 26:18). Possibly even the prophecy against Samaria (1:6f.) belongs to this period, since, according to 2 Kings 18:10, Samaria fell in the sixth year of Hezekiah. It is uncertain, however, whether Micah appeared as early as the time of Ahaz, or even Jotham. The time of their reigns cannot be determined unequivocally, but they certainly began before 730, if not before 740. While the phrase which names the kings in the book's superscription probably belongs, at the earliest, to the end of the sixth century (see above, p. 34), it is possible that the author of the superscription follows a different chronology than that found in 2 Kings 18:10; perhaps it is the one in 2 Kings 18:13 and Isa. 36:1, according to which Hezekiah became king in 715, and thus not before the seige of Samaria (725), as 2 Kings 18:1, 9f. has it. In this way, the redactor responsible for this chronology, relying on Hos. 1:1 and Isa. 1:1, could have characterized Micah as a (younger) contemporary of Hosea and Isaiah (according to A. K. Jenkins, 2 Kings 18:13 originally had to do with the time of Ashdod's rebellion in 714–712 and therefore with the military threat of Sargon II). It is remarkable that, unlike Amos 1:1 and Hos. 1:1, there is no mention of a Northern Israelite king in Mic. 1:1, although Micah certainly proclaimed disaster also for Samaria; yet Micah was not active as a prophet in the Northern Kingdom.

The second relative clause in the superscription characterizes Micah's prophetic office. Here the word חזה no longer refers to a specific visionary experience (as in Num. 24:4, 16; cf. Wolff, *Joel and Amos* 124); rather, it denotes in general the reception of a revelation (cf. 3:6, and on חזון in Obad. 1, see Wolff, *Obadiah and Jonah* 44; further, see D. Vetter, *THAT* 1:535; A. Jepsen, *ThWAT* 2:822–835), especially since in 1:1 חזה modifies the phrase "word of Yahweh," imparting to it the meaning of a collection of prophetic sayings (cf. Is. 2:1; Amos 1:1).

The second relative clause accents the perception that the "word of God" has to do with "Samaria and Jerusalem." The redactor names Samaria first because in the transmitted corpus of Micah's prophecy, the capital of the Northern Kingdom is threatened before the capital of Judah (1:6f., 9; 3:12; see above, p. 33). At the same time, this corresponds to the order of historical events. That only the two capital cities are named fits with the later addition of the interpretative comment in 1:5b, whereas elsewhere in the summary statements in Micah (3:8; cf. 1:5a) as well as in other superscriptions, Israel (Amos 1:1) and Judah [and Jerusalem] (Isa. 1:1) are named.

Purpose and Thrust

The book's superscription, given the composition of its elements, emphasizes that the word of Yahweh should be understood both as mediated through history and addressed to the historical situation. Thus, the editor intends to indicate the book's place in history by including a chronology of the kings of Micah's time and by naming the book's addressees. The entire book is to be read as a concrete witness to the one "word of Yahweh." That every efficacious word of prophecy has its source in the "spirit of Yahweh" is emphasized by the Deuteronomistic redactor's gloss on 3:8 (see below, p. 96). He belongs to those circles that compared the ancient prophetic words with the historical events belonging to the fall of Jerusalem and to the exile. As a word that had in the meantime been fulfilled, Micah's ancient prophecy is now accepted as the valid word of God.

The reference to the person of Micah is understandably brief, probably out of respect for the original superscription handed on in the tradition. It is remarkable that Micah is not once given the title *prophet* (nor is the title found in Hos. 1:1; Isa. 1:1; Amos 1:1). Yet Micah himself certainly knows and speaks of other "prophets" (3:5, 6, 11). Nor is his father's name mentioned (cf., by contrast, Hos. 1:1; Isa. 1:1; Zeph. 1:1). Micah is distinguished from others bearing the same name only by the epithet "the Moreshite," which was necessary, at the latest, when he was active in Jerusalem (see above, pp. 35f., and Jer. 26:18). It is only his commission that is important. Since his word of judgment has in the meantime been fulfilled, it now deserves—especially in that it is an historical word—further attention from those whose are prepared to repent. The redactor is certain, in any event, that Micah's prophetic words contain binding knowledge for his own historical situation and are of exemplary significance for succeeding generations.

The Punishment of God

Literature

On Micah 1:2–16: K. Budde, "Das Rätsel von Micha 1," *ZAW* 37 (1917–1918) 77–108. W. Beyerlin, *Die Kulttraditionen Israels in der Verkündigung des Prophet Micha,* FRLANT 72 (1959) 12–15; 30–42. H. Donner, *Israel unter den Völkern,* VTSuppl 11 (1964) 92–105; 196. G. Fohrer, "Micha 1," in *Das nahe und ferne Wort. Festschrift L. Rost,* BZAW 105 (1967) 65–80. D. K. Innes, "Some Notes on Micah Chapter I," *EvQ* 39 (1967) 225–227. Jörg Jeremias, "Die Deutung der Gerichtsworte Michas in der Exilszeit," *ZAW* 83 (1971) 330–354. I. Willi-Plein, *Vorformen der Schriftexegese innerhalb des Alten Testaments,* BZAW 123 (1971) 70–75; 110–114. Th. Lescow, "Redaktionsgeschichtliche Analyse von Micha 1–5," *ZAW* 84 (1972) 46–85 (54–61; 82–84). Ch. Hardmeier, *Texttheorie und biblischer Exegese,* BEvTh 79 (1978).

On Micah 1:2–7: V. Fritz, "Das Wort gegen Samaria Mi 1,2–7*," *ZAW* 86 (1974) 316–331. H. F. Fuhs (see above, Literature on 1:1) 197–206.

On Micah 1:2–4: B. Stade, "Streiflichter auf die Entstehung der jetzigen Gestalt der alttestamentlichen Prophetenschriften," *ZAW* 23 (1903) 163–171 (163).

On Micah 1:2: J. T. Willis, "Some Suggestions on the Interpretation of Micah I 2," *VT* 18 (1968) 372–379.

On Micah 1:3–4: Jörg Jeremias, *Theophanie,* WMANT 10 (1977²). H. Schulz, *Das Buch Nahum,* BZAW 129 (1973).

On Micah 1:4: R. Köbert, "*Môrad* (Mi 1,4) 'Tränke,'" *Bibl* 39 (1958) 82–83. O. García de la Fuente, "Notas al texto de Miqueas," *Aug* 7 (1967) 145–154.

On Micah 1:6–7: A. Jepsen, "Kleine Beiträge zum Zwölfprophetenbuch," *ZAW* 56 (1938) 85–100 (96–99).

On Micah 1:7: J. P. van der Westhuizen, "The Term *'tnān* in Micah," *OTWSA* (1973) 54–61.

On Micah 1:8–16: K. Elliger, "Die Heimat des Propheten Micha," *ZDPV* 57 (1934) 81–152; idem, *Kleine Schriften,* ThB 32 (1966) 9–71. R. C. Lux, "An Exegetical Study of Micah I 8–16." Diss., Notre Dame (1976); *Diss. Abstracts International* 37 (1976–1977).

On Micah 1:10–16: W. C. Graham, "Some Suggestions towards the Interpretation of Micah I 10–16," *AJSL* 47 (1930–1931) 237–258. S. J. Schwantes, "Critical Notes on Micah I 10–16," *VT* 14 (1964) 454–461. P. Welten (see above, Literature on 1:1). A. S. van der Woude, "Micha I 10–16," *Festschrift A. Dupont-Sommer* (1971) 347–353. N. Na'aman, "Sennacherib's Campaign to Judah and the Date of the *LMLK* Stamps," *VT* 29 (1979) 61–86.

On **Micah 1:11**: D. Kellermann, "Überlieferungsprobleme alttestamentlicher Ortsnamen," *VT* 28 (1978) 423–432.

On **Micah 1:12**: B. J. van der Merwe, "Micah 1:12 and Its Possible
Parallels in Pre-Exilic Prophetism," *OTWSA* (1973) 45–53.

On **Micah 1:14**: A. Demsky, "The Houses of Achzib: A Critical Note on
Micah I 14b (cf. 1 Chron. 4:21–23)," *IEJ* 16 (1966) 211–215.

Text

1:2   Hear, O peoples, all of you![a]
           Listen,[b] O earth, and those who dwell in her![b]
        For[c] [the Lord][d] Yahweh will become a witness against you,
           the Lord from his holy temple.[e]

3   For behold:[a]
        [e]Yahweh comes forth from his place,
           he comes down '   '[b] upon the heights[c] of 'the'[d] earth.

4   Then the mountains will melt[a] under him,
           and the valleys will split,
        like wax in the fire,
           like water poured down[b] a steep place.[e]

5   [e]All of this is because of Jacob's rebellion,
           because of the error[a] of the house of Israel.[b]
        Who[c] is the rebellion of Jacob?
        Is it not Samaria?
        And who[c] are the high places[d] of Judah?
        Is it not Jerusalem?[e]

6 And I will make Samaria [into a ruin—the field][a] into a vineyard.
    I will hurl her stones into the valley,[b]
      her foundations I will lay bare.

7   [a]All her images will be destroyed,
          all her whore's images will be burned in the fire,
          all her idols I will demolish.[a]
  For with a whore's fee she gathered[b] (them),
    and they will again become a whore's fee.

8 Therefore I[a] will lament, I[a] will wail,
    I[a] will go[b] barefoot[c] and naked.
  I[a] will make lamentation like jackals
    and mourn like ostriches.

9 Indeed, inescapable is the blow of 'Yahweh,'[a]
    Surely, it comes as far as Judah.
  It reaches to the gate of my people,
    to Jerusalem.

10 In Gath do not 'boast'![a]
    Weep! 'Yes'[b] weep!
  In Beth-le-aphrah[c]
    'roll yourselves'[d] in the dust!

11 'Go away,'[a]
    O inhabitants of Shaphir,[b]
      naked, ashamed![c]
  The inhabitants of Zaanan[d]
    do not break forth.[e]
  [f](Raise) 'lamentation,'[f] O Beth-ezel,[g]
    one takes away from you[h] its[h] standing place.

12 'How'[a] good can be 'hoped'[b] for
    the inhabitants of Maroth.
  Indeed, disaster comes down from Yahweh himself
    to the gate[c] of Jerusalem.

13 'Harness'ᵃ the horses to the chariot,
     O inhabitants of Lachish!
          ᵉThis is the beginning of sin for the daughter of Zion,
          for in you the rebellions of Israel were found.
14   Therefore:ᵉ
     'Let one give'ᵃ parting giftsᵇ
     toᶜ Moresheth-gath.
     The buildings of Achzibᵈ are a deceit
     for the kings of Israel.
15 Again the conqueror 'comes'ᵃ to you,
     O inhabitants of Mareshah.
     Until the glory of Israel
     comes to Adullam.
16 Clip short (your hair), shave yourself baldᵃ
     for the children of your delight.
     Make yourself as bald as a vulture,
     for they go away from you into exile.

2a Gk (Ἀκούσατε, λαοί, λόγους) did not read מְלִים (thus K. Vollers, *ZAW* 4 [1884] 2; B. Renaud, 12); rather, Gk connected כלם to v. 2aβ (see note 1:2b: καὶ πάντες ὁι ἐν αὐτῇ). Concerning the grammatical incongruence, after the plural imperative, of the third person plural suffix ("all of them"), which is to be understood as a fixed possessive suffix, cf. Bauer-Leander §§61ki; 65y; Ges-K §135r. Job 17:10 speaks contra the view that this is an "asyndetic relative clause," as held by BrSynt §153c (cf. F. Horst, *Hiob,* BK 16/1, 243). MT is supported by 2 Chron 18:27 (1 Kings 22:28 MT, not Gk), where Mic. 1:2aβ has been inserted because Micah ben Imlah was mistakenly identified with Micah the Moreshite.
2b Gk (προσεχέτω ἡ γῆ καὶ πάντες ὁι ἐν αὐτῇ) entirely avoids the incongruence found in MT not only by connecting כלם (see note 1:2a) with v. 2aβ instead of with v. 2aα, but also by making the imperative feminine singular in MT (הקשיבי) grammatically congruent with ומלאָה (ארץ) by translating προσεχέτω.
2c The connection made by the copulative ויהי (jussive) approaches the function of a motivation clause; cf. Ges-K §158a and A. S. van der Woude 26.
2d 1QpMi places אדני after יהוה; MT has the usual sequence of the two words; B. Renaud (12) regards 1QpMi as the authentic reading because it is *lectio difficilior;* cf. J. T. Milik, *RB* 59 (1952) 413 and *DJD* I (1964) 77. Since אדני occurs in the parallel in v. 2bβ, the word in v. 2bα is certainly, as is frequent, an interpolation from *Qere;* cf. Wolff, *Joel and Amos,* note b on Amos 3:8); thus the word occurs in 1QpMi and MT at different places; Gk and 2 Mss do not yet have it, but Vg, Syr, and Targ already follow MT.
2e Verse 2 probably introduces the Micah tradition as a new eschatological-universal proclamation for postexilic times (see below, p. 51).
3a It appears arbitrary to read הִנֵּה instead of הנה יהוה for metrical reasons, as does BHS. For with כי הנה the author of the preceding summons to a lawsuit calls for attention to the following theophany account; the phrase as transmitted stands outside the rhythm of the following words in the verse, as in Amos 4:13.
3b 1QpMi and numerous Gkᴹˢˢ (cf. M. Collin, *VT* 21 [1971] 285, and J. Ziegler) presuppose only one of the two verbs; the poetic style also supports this (a three-stress bicolon, as occurs in the context). The verb וירד, which more seldom occurs in similar contexts, could be the original reading; the later addition of ודרך is easier to explain as a secondary harmonization with Amos 4:13 and Deut. 33:29; cf. Jörg Jeremias, *Theophanie,* WMANT 10 (1977²) 11, 22, and Th. Lescow, 54. V. Fritz 319 deletes וירד and vocalizes וְדֹרֵךְ according to Amos 4:13, but he is unable to explain how MT originated.
3c *Ketib* reads בָּמוֹתֵי (sing. בָּמָה); *Qere* has בָּמֳתֵי (*bomᵒtê;* sing. בֹּמָת; cf. KBL³; Ges-K §95o). The plene-form of *Ketib* is found elsewhere in Deut. 32:13 and Isa. 58:14.

41

In these texts as well as in the defective forms in Isa. 14:14; Job 9:8; Amos 4:13, *Qere* corresponds to the *Qere* found in Mic. 1:3. Thus the reading בָּמֳתֵי *(bom°tê)* occurs only in poetic texts and, as a rule, precedes accented syllables in the pause form (Jouon, *Gr* §97 Eb).

3d The reading הארץ in 1QpMi may be authentic. MT (ארץ) fits with the more frequently occurring form of the word in the phrase "high places of the earth"; cf. Deut. 32:13; Isa. 58:14; Amos 4:13.

3e–4e On the problem of the origin of these lines, see below, p. 52.

4a Instead of מסס *niph.* it appears that Gk (σαλευθήσεται, "totter") has read נָמוֹטּוּ (cf. Isa. 40:20; Pss. 46:5; 82:5) (or נָמוֹגוּ, Nahum 1:5?).

4b נגר *hoph.* participle.

5a *Ketib* and *Qere* read the plural; Vg *(in peccatis)* supports MT; however, Gk (καὶ διὰ ἁμαρτίαν) presupposes the singular (ובחטאת), as do Syr and Targ. In parallel to the singular פשע, the plural remains the more difficult reading and it therefore is probably the original reading. In v. 13b there occurs the opposite transition from singular חטאת to the plural of פשע. Not until 3:8b do both nouns occur in the singular. But 1:5a may belong to the same level of redaction as 1:13b; see below, p. 52. The transition from singular to plural can indicate heightening.

5b The proposal to read יְהוּדָה instead of בית ישראל *(BHS)* seeks to harmonize this with v. 5bβ; but it has no support in any text tradition.

5c 1QpMi reads מ(ו)ה ("what?") instead of מ(י)י. MT is, however, supported by Gk (τίς) and preserves the personification.

5d Gk (ἡ ἁμαρτία), Syr, Targ harmonize this with v. 5aβ; for the same purpose, Gk adds the word οἴκου (בית). MT is supported by σ' (τὰ ὑψηλά) and is to be retained as *lectio difficilior*. W. Rudolph's emendation בְּמוֹת ("even the death") is syntactically difficult, unclear in meaning, and without support in the text tradition.

5e–e A Deuteronomistic addition for the sake of clarification; see below, p. 52.

6a Merely the absence of the copula before למטעי כרם indicates that לעי השדה is the later addition of a catchphrase. It might derive from a comparison of the fate of Samaria with that of Jerusalem, as it is threatened in 3:12. It is more likely that the phrase is a misplaced fragment of the original prophecy against Samaria that presumably preceded the beginning of v. 6 (see below, p. 47). Moreover, the phrase fits poorly with the image of planting a vineyard. Gk translates the questionable addition with εἰς ὀπωροφυλάκιον ἀγροῦ ("to the hut of the vine-dresser in the field") and thus weakens the force of the threat after the manner of Isa. 1:8ab (cf. B. Renaud 14). Before the continuation of the verse, Gk has to insert *kai*.

6b גי occurs without an א only in this instance and in Josh. 8:11 (KBL³).

7a–a In v. 7aα² the word אתנן plural denotes inflammable cultic images placed in the sanctuary; in v. 7baβ, on the other hand, it means a prostitute's fee. To read אתנניה instead of אֲשֵׁרֶיהָ in v. 7aα² (J. Wellhausen; I. Willi-Plein, 71) is unfounded and unnecessary, in view of the history of the text. Rather, all three sentences in v. 7a are to be considered a later addition on the basis of the diction, style, and context; the diction is Hosean-Deuteronomistic (Jörg Jeremias, 336, note 28; cf. earlier E. Sellin). Verse 7aα¹ and 7aα² are formulated in the passive (whereas the verbs in v. 6 are in the first person, which is not continued until v. 7aβ); next to the threat of total destruction against the city (vv. 6, 7b), v. 7a makes a very specific threat against the cult. The contrary argument—that after the announcement of Yahweh's punishment there often follows a description of its consequences—does not apply here (as in Mic. 2:3; Hos. 13:8; Isa. 8:7f.; cf. Mic. 1:3f.; B. Renaud 45, contra Jörg Jeremias). For in these instances the object of the disaster then becomes the subject of the next sentence, as also in v. 7b; but in v. 7a, a new subject is introduced.

7b Syr, Vg *(congregata sunt)*, Targ (אתכנשו) presuppose קֻבָּצוּ because of the missing accusative object of the verb (thus already Ewald and Wellhausen); but the object of the verb is to be supplied according to the sense of v. 7b (see below, pp. 57f.).

8a The entire verse in Gk has the third person singular; thus it considers Samaria in the immediately preceding verses (vv. 6f.) to be the subject. In the same sense, Targ employs the third person plural; Syr has the imperative feminine singular; but Mur 88 supports MT.

8b The unusual plene form אילכה instead of אלכה can be regarded as a scribal error after אילילה; perhaps, however, this spelling means to emphasize the lengthened dirge-tone of the alliteration *(ēl—ēl)*.

8c Read שׁולל with *Qere* as in Job 12:17, 19; *DJD* 1 (1955) 78 also writes the defective form שׁלל. Also Gk translates שׁולל (actually, "undressed"), next to עָרום ("naked"), with the word ἀνυπόδετος, which it also uses to translate the more customary term for "barefoot" (יָחֵף) in 2 Sam. 15:30 and Isa. 20:2–4.

9a MT ("her wounds") may derive from an incorrect reading rooted in the many third feminine singular suffixes in vv. 6f. (cf. Gk in v. 8; see note 8a). The context favors the proposal to read מַכַּת יהוה (K. Elliger), for the predicates in v. 9a,b (אנושה—בָּאָה) require the singular ("wound"), and the following sentence in v. 9bβ (נגע) presupposes a masculine noun that would be provided by יהוה. The singular form is supported by Gk (ἡ πληγὴ αὐτῆς), Syr, Targ, Vg *(plaga eius)*. Nevertheless, יהוה is not attested in one of the ancient translations, although such a reading is supported by the content of v. 12b. This conjecture does reestablish a colon of three stresses, which one would expect from the context. Both the incorrect reading and the corrupt nature of the text must be ancient.

10a MT ("do not proclaim!") agrees neither with the ancient versions nor with the sense of the context. Gk (μὴ μεγαλύνεσθε = אַל־תַּגְדִּילוּ, "do not boast!") probably gives the original wording of MT, for the word תגדילו would explain not only the incorrect reading by MT (= Vg *nolite adnuntiare*), which was supported by reference to 2 Sam. 1:20, but also the incorrect reading by Syr (*l' thdwn* = אַל־תָּגִילוּ, "do not rejoice").

10b On the basis of the synonymous parallelism, אל ("not") should be understood as an incorrect reading of אַף (K. Elliger). Since Gk (Ακιμ), critics have repeatedly attempted to find a fitting place-name in v. 10aβ. The attempt is misguided, merely in the light of text-critical principles, which B. Renaud (20), regarding 1:10–16, summarizes somewhat as follows: (1) The textual basis should be MT; (2) each line (bicola with two stresses, bicola with three stresses, a colon with five stresses) names only one town; (3) a wordplay is made on the name of each town; (4) the content has the tone of a dirge.

10c In order to indicate to the modern reader how the wordplays in Hebrew might have sounded, see Wolff, *Micah the Prophet,* trans. R. Gehrke, 29–30; cf. also the similar attempt by L. P. Smith, "The Book of Micah," *Interpretation* 6 (1952) 210–227, especially 213. Concerning the word Beth-le-aphrah, K. Elliger raises doubts about the ל, since it is "entirely without analogy in the many instances where *byt* occurs with place-names in the OT." In θ' and Syr the letter ל is not translated. Was the ל perhaps intentionally added later to characterize from the outset an (otherwise unknown) Beth-aphra as "house for the dust"?

10d Following Gk (καταπάσασθε) most critics read with J. Wellhausen הִתְפַּלְּשׁוּ, which is without certainty supported by *Qere* and Mur 88. *Ketib* (הִתְפַּלָּשְׁתִּי) = "I have rolled myself") early on was corrected by *Qere* (הִתְפַּלָּשִׁי) with an imperative feminine singular ("roll yourself"); but the ב before Beth-le-aphrah supports Gk's reading (second person masculine plural imperative).

11a Since Duhm most critics correct and complete the beginning of the line with שׁוֹפָר הַעֲבִרוּ ("sound the shophar [alarm horn], you inhabitants of Shaphir"). Yet, more recent attempts at a solution, without resorting to conjectural emendations, are more commendable. A. S. van der Woude, in light of the similarity with Lev. 25:9, considers it unnecessary to insert the word שׁוֹפָר; by taking the superfluous ת from the last word in v. 10 (see note 10d), he reads תַּעֲבִיר. But the sense of the sentence surely becomes clearer if one stays even closer to MT: עִבְרִי can be an incorrect reading of עָבְרוּ; cf. also B. Renaud, 23f. The grammatical incongruence of the feminine singular יוֹשֶׁבֶת and the second masculine plural (לכם) is prepared for by the juxtaposition in v. 10a,b of the feminine name of the town with the plural denoting its inhabitants.

11b The place-name שָׁפִיר derives from the root שׁפר, "to be beautiful, pleasant" (KBL). Gk σ' (καλῶς) and Vg (*pulchra*) are familiar with the root, but fail to recognize the word as a proper noun.

11c By more radically altering the consonantal text עריה בשׁת is frequently connected with v. 11bα (see note 11e). MT connects the two words to v. 11a, perhaps intending the words to be an insult: *Shaphir* experiences in the deportation of its inhabitants "nakedness" and "shame"; perhaps בשׁת is a later interpolation since Gk had not yet translated it.

11d Arab curiously translates צאן with 'arāk or 'irak; it bases this on GkMss (cf. Ziegler 208), which have replaced the unknown Σεννααν with the word Σενναap = שִׁנְעָר, familiar from Gen. 10:10; 11:2; cf. D. Kellermann, 426f.

11e To remove עריה in v. 11aβ from its context with Shaphir and to connect it with the sentence about Zaanan (K. Elliger) remains an uncertain procedure that does not clarify the meaning of the verse (J. L. Mays).

11f–f Either one must think of this as a passionate lament, with an outburst of words (as in v. 11aβ), and understand מספד as a *status absolutus* מִסְפֵּד, that forms a noun clause with בית האצל ("[veritable] lament [is] Beth-ezel"? W. Rudolph); or, with S. J. Schwantes (457), one must complete the sentence by adding עָשָׂה in light of v. 8bα.

11g אֵצֶל used as a preposition indicates that something lies "by the side of, near to" something; the root אצל means "to take away." What would this have called to mind for the original audience?

11h The many attempts to harmonize the gender of the suffixes are still unsatisfactory. The transmitted text is not unintelligible if we take into account that the inhabitants of a city are often addressed in the second person masculine plural (cf. vv. 10a, 11a), while the city and its inhabitants as a whole appear in the singular. Grammatical incongruence is frequent, particularly in this passage (e.g., the third masculine singular suffix in עמדתו, where one would expect a feminine suffix, or, after the immediately preceding word, a plural). Gk also contains irregular changes between the second and third person in the singular and the plural.

12a MT ("for"? "indeed"?) is not intelligible in this context. Gk (τίς) reads מִי instead of כִּי; מִי can be understood here as an interjection ("how!"; cf. KBL³ 545, and Wolff, *Joel and Amos,* note on Amos 7:2b), but also as a question, "who?" if יושבת מרות is taken as a vocative in a rhetorical question and not as the subject of the sentence.

12b MT ("weak is"?) probably contains an incorrect reading; Gk (ἤρξατο) appears to have read הלל יָחֵל hiph. "to begin"?), while σ' (ἤλπισεν) read יִחֲלָה (יחל piel, "they can hope for"); thus the translators tried to make the sentence intelligible (thus already J. Wellhausen).

12c Gk (ἐπὶ πύλας), Targ (בתרעי), and Syr presuppose שְׁעָרֵי ("the gates"), which can be accounted for by dittography. MT is supported by v. 9b.

13a רתם is etymologically unclear, but Syr, Targ support the meaning "to hitch up," which the context suggests. The creative suggestions for attested verbs that would fit here (K. Elliger, 20: עֶרְכִי, "mobilize"; S. J. Schwantes, 458: אָסַרְתְּ, "harness"), in that they bear no resemblance to the transmitted consonants, remain more uncertain than any attempt to interpret the hapax legomenon. To vocalize it as an infinitive absolute, רָתֹם (W. Rudolph), avoids the grammatical incongruity and intensifies the sense of MT (imperative). In the remainder of the verse, it is strange that the horses are not mentioned before the chariot. Accordingly, H. Donner (95) reverses the word order (רֶכֶשׁ לַמֶּרְכָּבָה), but this destroys the alliteration לרכשׁ—לכישׁ (cf. B. Renaud, 25).

13e–14e Concerning the Deuteronomistic explanatory gloss, including the connecting particle, at the beginning of v. 14, see below, p. 52.

14a Although MT (second feminine singular imperfect *qal* of נתן) is supported by several Gk^Mss (δώσεις), it nevertheless remains unclear who is addressed. Gk^BQ etc. (δώσει), Vg *(dabit)* presuppose the third person, thus a form which would be understood to have an indefinite subject ("one") (Nowack reads יִתֵּן; Lindblom, יִתְּנוּ). W. Rudolph stays closer to the consonantal text (תִּתְּנוּ, "you will have to give"), which again leaves the question of the addressee unanswered (L. C. Allen).

14b On the meaning, cf. 1 Kings 9:16; for Ugaritic parallels, cf. Gordon, *UT:* 2Aqht 6.18, 28, *šlḥ* = to give (a gift). M. Buber translates "dowry."

14c עַל should be understood in the sense of אֶל or לְ (thus 1 Kings 9:16).

14d On Syh, cf. Ziegler, 103f.

15a Although Gk (ἀγάγω) supports MT (אָבִי) as a first person singular, yet MT surely must go back to יָבֹא and to an ancient scribal error that switched the letters (A. B. Ehrlich [1912]), since the first person singular would be an oracle of Yahweh, which the context excludes.

16a Who is addressed? K. Elliger (24) points out that Gk translates the penultimate word in v. 15 with θυγατρός, a word that corresponds to nothing in MT. Should we presume that the word בָּם in Gk's Hebrew text is the remnant of a textually corrupt and misplaced בַּת־צִיּוֹן, which originally stood at the beginning of v. 16? The phrase would reestablish the *qina* rhythm (3+2) in v. 16a and b. However, such a word of address to Jerusalem is not attested in any of Micah's unquestionably genuine sayings. It is more probable that v. 16 contained the phrase בַּת־יְהוּדָה. See below, p. 64.

Form

The first chapter of the book of Micah opens in a grandiose manner. It offers an increasingly breathtaking sequence of the most varied rhetorical forms. After the initial "summons to a judicial proceeding" against all peoples (v. 2), there follows a report, formulated in hymnic style, of God's manifestation and its devastating consequences (a theophany, vv. 3f.). Then comes an accusation against Israel (v. 5), which is closely connected with the foregoing verses (vv. 3f.). This is followed by an announcement of Samaria's destruction (vv. 6f.). The passage reaches its climax with Micah's own passionate self-summons to lament over the misfortune of Jerusalem and Judah (vv. 8f.), which turns into a barrage of summonses to lament in word and deed over the disaster (vv. 10–16).

Critical scholarship has not yet resolved the question whether Micah himself originally composed this chapter (thus K. Budde, J. T. Willis, B. Renaud); or whether it is the work of a redactor (thus Th. Lescow, J. L. Mays, B. Renaud). We must ask whether the seams connecting the individual units are of a literary or a rhetorical nature, and how best to account for the stylistic distinctions and tensions in the content.

[1:2] The scene opens with a "summons to hear" (v. 2a), a form that can exhibit a wide variety of connections with other forms (cf. Ch. Hardmeier, 311ff.). Here (according to v. 2b) we do not have a summons of witnesses to a judicial proceeding against Israel, as in Isa. 1:2; Deut. 31:28b (cf. Mic. 6:2) (thus erroneously Fohrer, 72f.). For in v. 2 it is not heaven and earth that are called upon as a cosmic forum, but all peoples and inhabitants of the earth. Indeed, they are called upon not as audience and witnesses, but as those involved and indicted, against whom Yahweh himself will be a witness. However, we should not interpret this as a word of judgment against foreign nations, as in Amos 1:3—2:3, the purpose of which would be simply to make the Israelite audience willing to listen, so that they are then all the more surprised when they themselves are accused and threatened (thus J. T. Willis and A. S. van der Woude, 22ff.). For the peoples do not stand parallel to Israel as the accused (as in Amos 1–2). They are convened to listen because Yahweh intends to witness against them (see below, p. 55). Parallels are to be found in those contexts where a summons to all nations is followed by a witness to Yahweh's exemplary action against individual, specific nations: Isa. 34:1ff. (Edom); 51:4f.; Jer. 31:10 (Israel), and especially Jer. 25:30f., where, in its present literary context, Yahweh's lawsuit with the nations is joined to an (immediately following) depiction of theophany; cf. J. L. Mays, 40. Since nothing in the diction would indicate that v. 2 is an original saying from Micah, it is most probable that the redactor has added this preface because he wants God's word of judgment against Israel to serve as an example for the nations; cf. further 5:14! The word ויהי connecting the bicola (v. 1a and v. 1b, each colon containing three stresses; see note 2c) also appears to be the literary work of the redactor rather than part of an original rhetorical unit (on אדני, see note 2d).

[1:3–4] The universalistic viewpoint of the editor of the Micah tradition, whom we perceive at work in v. 2, attached connecting particles (כי הנה) to the material provided to him by the tradition in vv. 3–4; these particles he prefixed to the balanced construction of the following three-stress bicolon. כי הנה introduces the citation of a hymn in Amos 4:13 just as it does here (cf. Wolff, *Joel and Amos* 216; 223). Thus the redactional seam consists of more than simply the כי (as B. Renaud, 31, supposes). Verses 3f. present a classic theophany account in hymnic style. The consistent two-part form is comprised of (1) a description of Yahweh's appearance which (2) causes a disturbance in nature. Jörg Jeremias has analyzed the comparable texts, from the Song of Deborah (Judg. 5:4f.) to texts from the postbiblical era. Rooted in Israel's victory celebrations, the genre was taken up by the prophets in their proclamations of judgment, especially in their oracles against foreign nations (cf. Jer. 25:30f.; Isa. 66:15f., but also Amos 1:2ff. [cf. Wolff, *Joel and Amos* 118f.] and Nahum 1:2a, 3b–8 [see also H. Schult, *Das Buch Nahum*, BZAW 129 (1973) 73–99, on the problem of the theophany hymns]). Thus the summons to the people to hear (v. 2), which prefaces vv. 3f., may also have been provoked by the theophany description (vv. 3f.). The repetition of v. 2b by v. 3a, sentences which do not constitute a parallelism, indicates, on the one hand, that vv. 3f. were available in literary form to the author of v. 2; and, on the other, that the redactional connection of the two pieces was made with some care. The wording of the theophany hymn exhibits remarkable connections with the following verses: cf. ירד in v. 3b with v. 12b; במות in v. 3b with v. 5bβ (and with 3:12b MT); אש in v. 4b with v. 7a. Whereas the two basic themes are common to all theophany accounts, each theme is capable of a variety of formulation.

[1:5] The theophany hymn is more closely connected with what follows in v. 5 than with what precedes in v. 2. Verse 5 provides the motivation for the announcement of Yahweh's theophany appearance to judge his people. The phrase "all of this" (כל־זאת) summarizes the motivation and is included within the rhythm of the three-stress bicolon (unlike the כי־ הנה in the transition from v. 2 to v. 3, or the ויהי between v. 2a and b). The rhythm of vv. 3f. is thus continued without interruption. The "high places" upon which Yahweh will tread (v. 3b) are now interpreted as the "high places of Judah," namely, Jerusalem (v. 5bβ; cf. also 3:12 MT, and see note 3:12c). The literary seam between v. 5 and vv. 3f. is obvious. The motivation for Yahweh's appearance is described as the guilt of Jacob and Judah. Verse 5a appears to contain vocabulary which stems from Micah himself. In 3:8 Micah states that his job is to proclaim the "rebellion of Jacob" and the "error of Israel." But in 3:8 the words "Jacob" and "Israel" refer exclusively to Judah and Jerusalem (cf. 3:1, 9). By contrast, in v. 5a Jacob is used to refer to the Northern Kingdom and its capital, Samaria; only "Israel" refers to Judah and Jerusalem. The commentator who included the theophany account thus appropriates Micah's language, on the one hand, to introduce the two chief addressees of chap. 1 and, on the other, to make a transition to Micah's own prophetic sayings. When v. 5b describes the guilt mentioned in v. 5a, its interrogative style is indicative of the commentator's urgent pedagogical intention, which above all is to bring his audience to a recognition of their guilt, and especially of their transgression in the cultic sphere (cultic "high places").

[1:6–7] With the beginning of v. 6, the first prophetic word of Micah confronts the reader. The formulation of v. 6 as a Yahweh speech distinguishes it from each of the previous verses. Yahweh, speaking in the first person, announces through his messenger that Samaria will be destroyed. This announcement of judgment, which is the main theme of this saying, has its particular motivation—even if only intimated—in v. 7b. This observation suffices to show that כל־זאת in v. 5a does not have a cataphoric (i.e., forward referring) function, and thus v. 5a and vv. 6f. are not to be incorrectly tied together. On the other hand, the transition (v. 5) from the theophany account (vv. 3f.) to Micah's judgment speech against Samaria (vv. 6f.) provides an explanation for the displacement of an original, rhetorical introduction to Micah's prophecy of doom in v. 6 (perhaps "thus has Yahweh spoken . . . into a ruin . . . the field"; see above, note 6a). Verse 7a could stem from the redactor whom we recognized in v. 5 (see note 7a–a). Like v. 5, v. 7a exhibits a special interest in the cult and also picks up another catchword from the theophany account ("fire," cf. v. 4b with v. 7aα²).

[1:8] The word "therefore" (על־זאת) joins a completely new type of prophetic saying to the previous verses. It is precisely at this point that an intense debate arises over the unity of chap. 1. Of decisive significance is the question whether על־זאת refers back to the preceding prophecy against Samaria (vv. 6f.) or to the following verses, i.e., whether it has an anaphoric or a cataphoric meaning. Gk clearly understood the phrase to refer back to the previous verses, since it takes Samaria to be the subject of the verbs in v. 8 (see note 8a). The same applies to the transmitted text in MT, wherein v. 9a ("her wounds") refers back to Samaria's impending doom.

A close connection between vv. 8ff. and vv. 6f. has been repeatedly disputed by recent scholarship. In the first place, chronological considerations were advanced: the prophecy of Samaria's destruction must have been proclaimed before 722, the date of Assyria's conquest of the city. On the other hand, vv. 8–16 were said to reflect Sennacherib's advance against Jerusalem in 701 (K. Elliger, among others). It was further argued that זאת in prophetic writings often points to subsequent verses (K. Elliger, *PJB* 29 [1933] 139 = ThB 32 (1966) 59, cites Hos. 5:1; Amos 8:4; Joel 1:2; Mic. 3:9; etc.; cf. also Gen. 42:39); in addition, על־זאת supposedly has a cataphoric meaning in Jer. 2:12 (W. Beyerlin, 12f.). Finally, it was questioned whether Micah prophesied the end of Samaria at all: how could one expect a prophet from Judah to mourn the punishment of the Northern Kingdom (W. Rudolph, 38)?

On the contrary, stronger arguments favor taking על־זאת as a connecting link between vv. 8ff. and vv. 6f. The threefold עד in v. 9 becomes fully understandable when "therefore" in v. 8 refers back to vv. 6f.; thus, it would be "the wound" against Samaria that continues on until it reaches "as far as" Judah and Jerusalem. Hence, the prophet's own lamentation is for both the Northern and the Southern Kingdoms of Israel. An even more compelling observation is that when על־זאת functions as a conjunction (preposition with a demonstrative pronoun; cf. BrSynt, §163) (similar to על־כֵּן), wherever it appears in the OT, it always has only an anaphoric meaning (cf. Amos 7:3, 6; 8:8; Jer. 4:28; Ps. 32:6; etc., a total of 19 times; see the precise investigation by B. Renaud, 39f.). Jeremiah 2:12 and 4:8 should also be considered here. על־זאת in 2:12 and 4:8 refers back to 2:11 and 4:7, respectively, and then clearly forms a transition to the following כי-clause in 2:13 and 4:8b. Thus, in the same way in Mic. 1:8 על־זאת first refers back to vv. 6f. and then clearly forms a transition to the following כי-clause. It is significant that על־זאת never stands at the beginning of a literary or rhetorical unit; it always summarizes preceding verses and draws consequences from them (B. Renaud, 40). Thus, it functions differently from the single demonstrative pronoun זאת, upon which K. Elliger bases his interpretation. על־זאת is used especially to signal a turning point within a train of thought, if at the same time there is a transition to a different rhetorical form. Thus in Neh. 13:14 על־זאת makes a transition from a report to a petition; similarly, in Mic. 1:8 the phrase indicates a change from a prophetic announcement of judgment in vv. 6f. to Micah's self-summons to lament. Finally, it should be noted that על־זאת in v. 8 is an inseparable part of the verse's prosody (the same is true of כל־זאת in 1:5a). Only with this connecting phrase is the colon of three stresses complete.

If it is then unlikely that על־זאת has a cataphoric meaning, the question of the passage's date must now be addressed. First, let us consider the question from a form-critical perspective, which means our answer will be only approximate. Has the destruction which is lamented in vv. 8–16 already taken place, or does it lie in the future?

[1:8–16] These verses present a very artistically shaped series of calls to lamentation which are connected with instructions pertaining to an enemy's hostilities. The passage opens with the prophet's self-summons to mourn. The motivation given for his mourning (v. 9) at the same time commences two strophes which contain summonses addressed to small towns in Judah. Just as the first strophe, announcing disaster for Judah and Jerusalem, is introduced by a כ-clause with perfect verbs, the second strophe is introduced in the same way in v. 12b. The two strophes (original wording found in vv. 10a,b, 11a,ba,β, 12a and in vv. 13a, 14a,b, 15a,b, 16) each name six Judean towns (the name of the last town in the second strophe has become lost in the transmitted text; see note 16a). The first two prosodic units of the first strophe (v. 10a,b) summon to rites of mourning, as do the last two prosodic units in the second strophe (v. 16a,b). The remaining verses of both strophes contain summonses and reports concerning military actions. The *qina* meter (3+2 stresses in each colon) predominates in the individual verses, to the extent that textual corruption permits such a judgment (e.g., vv. 9bβ, 12b, 13a, 14b, 16b). The genre of the passage is a "summons to lament disaster" (cf. C. Hardmeier, 355ff.). Metaphors belonging to the dirge, such as occur in Amos 5:2, are not found here. Thus, according to its genre, the passage is not to be understood as a "political dirge" (K. Elliger). In addition to the rites of mourning mentioned in the passage, there are also declarative statements about, and summonses to, a catastrophic war. The destruction of the land and its cities is threatened (cf. Amos 5:16f.; Isa. 22:4ff.; 23; Jer. 9:16–21). Not one syllable suggests that the lamentation is connected with a religious ceremony; nothing is heard concerning a summons to prayer or repentance (unlike Joel 1:13–20; 2:12–17). In a thoroughly secular manner, the prophet sees himself and his people confronted by an unavoidable catastrophe. Does this correspond to the prophet's secular office of elder (see above, introduction §3)?

But now we must address the question whether Micah speaks of a past or a future destruction. Scholars have been attracted to K. Elliger's reference to events of 701 and his hypothesis that this passage is a song that describes these events. We offer four reasons that speak against Elliger's interpretation. (1) In OT prophetic texts which are form critically parallel to Mic. 1:8–16, the funerary metaphors in the dirges and laments over destruction always function as a proclamation of impending doom (Amos 5:2, 16f.; Isa. 3:25—4:1; 32:11–14; Jer. 9:16–21). (2) The fortress of Gath (v. 10a) no longer belonged to Judah after Sargon II's military campaign of 712/711 (2 Chron. 11:8), but to Ashdod, occupied by Assyria (*TGI*[2] 65f.; *ANET* 286). Thus K. Elliger (15f.) is obliged to alter arbitrarily the clearly attested reading "Gath" in v. 10a. Had Micah been interested in the sequence of towns connected with the destructive events of 701, he would not have omitted Azekah, the first of the fortresses to fall (N. Na'aman, 68, 84). (3) Micah is not guided by historical and geographical events, but by the names of the towns as such, and by the interpretation of their misfortune by using wordplays: plays on sound (vv. 10a, 14b) and on meaning (vv. 10b, 12b) can be combined (vv. 11a, 12b). Micah presupposes that *nomen est omen*. (4) Given our observations on the rhetorical connection of vv. 8–16 with vv. 6f. by means of על זאת (v. 8), it is impossible to date vv. 8–16 later than 722 (see above, pp. 47f.).

These conclusions show that the perfect verbs in vv. 9a,b, 11b, 12b and v. 16bβ speak of the future, and that the summonses to mourn in vv. 10a,b, 11bβ, 16a,ba, as well as the reports of military hostilities (vv. 11a, 13a, 14a,b, 15a,b) can only have the function of actualizing a future catastrophe. Just as the impending disaster caused the prophet to lament (v. 8), he now reveals to each town in his homeland the threatening confusion it faces; his words are like a vehement "Kapuzinade" ("tirade," J. Wellhausen) in which short sentences fall like hail, reminiscent of Abraham of Santa Clara.

[1:13b] Only two sentences within vv. 10–16 are later literary additions. Verse 13b fits neither the style nor the mood of its context: it contains neither a wordplay nor a cry of distress. Instead, in a wordy prose style, v. 13b speaks of the sin and guilt of the daughter of Zion. It is apparently an interpolated commentary on the previous prophecy concerning Lachish (v. 13a; cf. היא in v. 13bα). The catchwords for sin and guilt as well as the reflective and explanatory style (nominal clause, passive verb) recall v. 5. Moreover, "daughter of Zion" occurs in the book of Micah only in secondary material (4:8, 10, 13). The לכן (v. 14aα), which is quite extraneous to the context, also connects v. 13b with what follows.

[1:16] This verse is different from all preceding sentences in that it contains no place-name. (See note 16a for various conjectures.) The mention of deportation (v. 16bβ), when combined with the conjectured reading "daughter of Zion," has led to the supposition that the concluding verse, together with v. 13b, were added to the passage at the time of the exile (cf. G. Fohrer, 76; J. L. Mays, 60). But the argument is weak: "daughter of Zion" is not in the text; a completely different addressee could have begun v. 16. And should we assume that Micah himself was incapable of fearing deportation? (Against such an assumption, cf. vv. 11 a,bβ,γ, 14a.) Above all, the imperative verbs well befit the structure of the summons to mourn, and the alliteration corresponds with the poetic character of the entire passage. Moreover, the animal simile is a part of the mourning ritual only in v. 16 and in the introductory self-summons of the prophet in v. 8. And the summons to an unnamed audience in v. 16 is just as long as the summons in v. 8; both are twice as long as all other verses concerning or addressed to Judean towns. Thus, we have in v. 16 an artistic rounding off of an extensive lament over disaster begun in v. 8 (cf. B. Renaud, 57f.). The occurrence of the infrequent word for "pleasure, delight" (תענוגים) within a quite similar context in a genuine Mican prophecy (2:9) lends support to the assumption that v. 16 is authentic.

These primarily form-critical observations lead to the conclusion that 1:2–16 is a redactional unit, but not an original rhetorical unit. Only vv. 6, 7b, 8–13a, 14–16 constitute an original rhetorical unit. Clearly distinguishable rhetorical forms occur in these verses; however, the transitions from the announcement of judgment in the style of a messenger speech (vv. 6, 7b) to the self-summons to mourn (vv. 8f.), and then to the summons to lament disaster addressed to the Judean towns (vv. 10–13a, 14–16), are stylistically and thematically so closely woven together that a later redactional arrangement of these verses is unlikely.

However, v. 13b (including the first word in v. 14) and, with less clarity, v. 7a, give indication of being later additions to the text. They appear to be related to v. 5, whose interpolation must have replaced the beginning of v. 6. On the other hand, this same interpolation, together with the hymnic theophany report in vv. 3f., provided a new introduction to the ancient Micah traditions. From this second stratum (vv. 3, 5, 7a, 13b) a third stratum can be distinguished by means of a redactional seam (at the beginning of v. 3a). This third stratum (v. 2), the latest introduction added to the passage, opens up a universalistic horizon.

Setting

Where do these three strata have their place of origin? As we consider the various possible answers, we will evaluate at the same time our hypotheses, formulated thus far, concerning the form and relationship of the strata within the text. Many interpreters still think of v. 2 as a prophecy of Micah, which enables them to praise the inclusive range of his prophecy. This requires them to see "the whole of chap. 1 aimed at surprising the reader" (W. Rudolph, 39), for nowhere in the following verses does Yahweh speak a word of judgment against the nations. Does Micah intend to play a casual trick on his audience by deceptively presenting himself as a salvation prophet before Israel? One might suggest that already in the Song of Deborah a summons to hear addressed to kings and princes (Judg. 5:3) immediately precedes a song praising God's theophany (vv. 4f.). But even this comparison indicates the difference between unbroken poetic speech and a literary preface which requires a short transitional phrase ("for behold," v. 3; see above, pp. 45f.). Moreover, the language, style, and content of the "summons to a legal proceeding" addressed to a universal audience ("people," "earth") in v. 2 is clearly distinguishable from Micah's manner of speech. When Micah summons his audience to hear him (3:1, 9; but also cf. 6:1, 2, 9), the imperative verb has no parallel in the second half of the line. Nor do the words "people" (עמים) and "earth" (ארץ) occur in the chapters which unquestionably contain Micah's sayings (chaps. 1–3); however, these words do occur in the sayings in chaps. 4–5, which are to be dated after Micah's time. Indeed, here the "nations" become the essential theme (גוים, 4:2, 3, 7; 5:7, 14; and equally as frequent, עמים, 4:1, 3, 5, 13; 5:6, 7, as in the opening summons in v. 2), and Yahweh appears as "Lord of the whole earth" (כָּל־הָאָרֶץ, 4:13). At the end of this collection of sayings in 5:14, the word "to hear" from the opening summons is used once more, but now for the purpose of characterizing those who come under divine punishment as "people who do not hear." This series of observations necessitates the conclusion that 1:2 is to be ascribed to the editor of the sayings in chaps. 4–5, who thus made this addition to the ancient Micah tradition in chaps. 1–3. At this point, all we can say about him is that he must have been a theologian with a universalistic orientation who, not until the postexilic, Persian era, took up and supplemented the ancient prophecy of Micah with words that provided a new aspect. Support for this conclusion is also found in the close connection between 1:2 and Isa. 34:1f., a text which, according to H. Wildberger's thorough examination, belongs at the earliest to the end of the sixth century (*Jesaja 28–39*, BK 10/3, 1341). Moreover, Isa. 26:21aα, dated by Wildberger in the fifth century (BK 10/2, 910f.), picks up Mic. 1:3a, with the connecting phrase כי הנה, a phrase which derives from the author of v. 2. More detailed arguments must await our investigation of chaps. 4–5.

[1:3–5] A considerable amount of time separates the composition of v. 2 from Micah and his prophecy. This is already suggested by the observation that the traditions available to the universalistic redactor present a not inconsiderable reworking of Micah's sayings. This editing was accomplished by that renowned Deuteronomistic school which wrote a comprehensive historical work and which endeavored to preserve and to understand the preexilic prophetic writings. In that we considered vv. 3f. to be indissolubly connected with v. 5, and thus a form-critical unit (see above, p. 46), we would also attribute the theophany hymn to the author of v. 5. Verses 3f. can hardly stem from the author of vv. 6f.: in vv. 3f. Yahweh is presented in the third person and effects a tumult in nature, whereas in vv. 6f. Yahweh speaks in the first person and effects historical events. Verses 3f. can easily be accounted for as the work of Judaic redactors who in a similar fashion also introduced the book of Amos with a theophany hymn (on Amos 1:2, cf. Wolff, *Joel and Amos,* 121f.; on the "introductory function" of the theophany hymn, cf. also H. Schulz [1973] 83 and Nahum 1:2–8). The hymnic inauguration of a collection of prophetic sayings is best understood as an introduction to a liturgical reading. One might imagine that in the years after the catastrophe of 587, the remnant of the Jerusalem community, as they would worship in a ceremony of lament, gained a new understanding of the original prophetic words. With the help of the early prophecies of disaster they came to recognize the destruction as God's righteous judgment. It would have been precisely with such hymnic passages that the congregation, as it looked back upon the past, affirmed "the validity of the catastrophe of the exile as proof of divine punishment and power to judge" (F. Horst, "Die Doxologien im Amosbuch," *ZAW* 47 [1929] 45–54; reprinted in *Gesammelte Studien,* ThB 12 [1961] 155–166; on the parallels to this interpretation in Amos, see Wolff, "Das Ende des Heiligtums in Bethel," *Festschrift K. Galling* [1970] 287–298; reprinted in Wolff, *Gesammelte Studien,* ThB 22 [1973²] 442–453, and *Joel and Amos* 111f.; on the important community festivals of lament in Jerusalem after 587, cf. Wolff, *Obadiah and Jonah* 19f., 42, and idem, "Obadja—Ein Kultprophet als Interpret," *EvTh* 37 [1977] 273–284). Before the community could expect a new word from God, it had to hear anew the earlier prophecies and acknowledge them in repentance. For an introit, the liturgist would appropriate, by means of a theophany hymn, the theme and tenor of the ancient victory songs and make the hymn applicable in his own day to the conquered people of Israel.

Verse 5 indicates that vv. 3f. are meant to be understood entirely within the spirit of the Deuteronomist. As it had with Amos (1:9–12; 2:4f.; see Wolff, *Joel and Amos* 139f., 151f.), so the Deuteronomistic school is here dedicated to uncovering Israel's guilt, whereas Micah himself in vv. 6–16 is concerned entirely with the impending doom from Yahweh. The exilic interpreter in v. 5a makes use of one of Micah's sayings in 3:8b in order to express his own denunciation of cultic sins. The "high places" (v. 5bβ) are for his tradition not only grounds for the destruction of the Northern Kingdom (2 Kings 17:9; cf. 23:15, 19f.) but also for Judah and Jerusalem (2 Kings 23:8, 13). The didactic questions (v. 5b) present another correspondence with the Deuteronomistic commentary in Amos (2:10–12; 5:25f.). Perhaps v. 7a (see above, p. 47), and most likely v. 13b, derive from the Deuteronomists (see above, p. 50). These "early exilic disciples of the prophets" (Jörg Jeremias [1971] 351) proclaim the old message of Micah in a new way in order to bring a judged people to a recognition of Yahweh's justice and thus to repentance.

A. Jepsen (*ZAW* 56 [1938] 96) suggested that vv. 6f. have their origin in Hosea's prophecy. But this interpretation is eliminated by the insight that v. 7a derives from Deuteronomistic circles who were especially interested in making use of Hosea's preaching (Wolff, *Hosea*, xxxif.). It is further made untenable, along with the suggestions that vv. 6f. are to be dated in a much later period (Th. Lescow, 83; V. Fritz, 330), in that v. 8 unconditionally presupposes that the prophecy against Samaria (v. 6) is a genuine saying of Micah (see above, pp. 47ff.). The beginning of v. 6 gives the impression of being fragmentary. The corruption in the text may have arisen when vv. 3–5 were placed before v. 6, if—according to our supposition—the written tradition of Micah's sayings was already available to the Deuteronomistic commentator. That a first literary tradition came from Micah himself is suggested both by 3:1a ("and I said") and by the prophet's first person speech in 1:8. This makes it all the more necessary for the first person Yahweh speech in v. 6 to have had an introduction that was replaced by v. 5 and perhaps taken up in part into 1:1 (see above, p. 47; also note 6a, and below, p. 57). The tradents responsible for handing on the written prophecies of Micah in the eighth century may have had a connection with circles of elders in Judah who, according to Jer. 26:17–19, cited the tradition in public (cf. B. Renaud, 386; Wolff, VTSuppl 29 [1978] 403–417 [408f.]).

Thus we have to distinguish three literary strata in 1:2–16: (1) a primary level which derives from Micah himself and was transmitted in the eighth century (vv. 6, 7b–13a, 14–16); (2) the exilic commentary of the Deuteronomistic school (vv. 3–5, 7a, 13b); (3) the universalistically oriented interpretation from the Persian era (v. 2).

[1:8–16] The problem of dating this first, lengthy passage must now be discussed. The announcement of judgment against Samaria and the summons to lament addressed to the towns of Judah were seen to have formed an inseparable rhetorical unit, as the word "therefore" in v. 8a originally referred back to vv. 6f.; and the "blow" against Judah (v. 9) is expected to fall, not because of other new reasons, but precisely because the blow against Samaria must makes its way further toward the Southern Kingdom (see above, pp. 47f.).

The terminus ad quem must therefore be 722, for v. 6 announces the complete destruction of Samaria and its buildings. However, after almost three years of seige, the city was indeed conquered and its inhabitants deported, but Sargon II himself reports in addition: "The town I rebuilt better than it was before and settled therein people from countries which I myself had conquered" (*ANET* [1950] 284); cf. also 2 Kings 17:24. The terminus a quo would have to be 734, when Tiglath-Pileser made his first campaign into Palestine. At that time his troops had already stormed into the Philistine city of Gaza and gone farther toward the south (*ANET* [1950] 282; *TGI*² 56). This surely must have brought profound terror to the towns of Micah's own region—towns which overlooked the coastal plain from the Shephelah. Soon Jerusalem also was to be oppressed from the north by attacks from the Syro-Ephraimite coalition (Isa. 7:1ff.). The Northern Kingdom of Israel was attacked by Assyrian armies, which amputated extensive regions in the north, east, and west (2 Kings 15:29; *ANET* 283f.; *TGI*² 58f.); her southern border lay only 15 km from Jerusalem. Hence, Micah will have appeared as prophet between 733 and 723, more probably in the second rather than the first half of the decade at the time of the acute seige on Samaria in 724–723. For he of course saw the "blow" coming from the north (cf. vv. 6 and 9; on this see 2 Kings 17:5f. and H. Donner, 102–105; P. Welten, 157ff.).

It is a matter of dispute where Micah proclaimed this prophecy. Scholars have often thought of Jerusalem, in parallel to chap. 3 (K. Elliger, et al.), which is of course mentioned in vv. 6 and 12; but Jerusalem is never directly addressed in the passage. By contrast, of the eleven Judean towns mentioned (in vv. 10–15), at least six are directly addressed (to the extent that the corrupt text allows, their names are: Gath, Beth-le-aphra, Shaphir, Beth-ezel, Lachish, Mareshah). Furthermore, in connection with Moresheth-gath an unnamed entity is directly addressed in the second person feminine form in v. 14a; the second person feminine form is also addressed in v. 16a and b, although the transmitted text leaves the addressee unnamed. In v. 14a (לכן is secondary, see above, p. 50) as well as in the first prosodic unit in v. 16, one accent is lacking for the *qina* meter. Should one not expect at least in this summary conclusion that יהודה would be the addressee (v. 9bα)? In that the passage names many of the Judean towns which are addressed, perhaps we should rather assume that there was a large gathering at one of these places. A. S. van der Woude (19ff.) suggests that it was at Lachish. But Moresheth-gath, Micah's hometown, ought not be excluded from consideration, especially if the addressee in v. 14a were Judah, which perhaps has dropped out of v. 16; or if, as J. L. Mays (60) thinks, Moresheth-gath itself were the addressee in v. 14a. Since all the locatable towns named in the text lie in a circle of barely 15 km around Moresheth, it would not be entirely unlikely that some kind of a district meeting, for unknown reasons, was called by Micah, one of the "elders of Judah" (see above, introduction §2). In any case, this is still more likely than Jerusalem. To think here of a worship service of lament by no means recommends itself, since there is no mention of any prayer or call to prayer, nor is there any kind of act of repentance. Furthermore, Yahweh is mentioned in this passage only with extreme restraint. But this is completely different in the reworking of the text during the exile.

Commentary

[1:2] But preceding the verses of an exilic redaction is an even younger passage in v. 2, which initially calls for the attention of all the nations. The solemn two-part summons to listen lends a kind of official significance to what follows (cf. Hos. 5:1 and Wolff, *Hosea* 97; on this see C. Hardmeier, 311f.). In parallel to "all peoples," the "earth and its inhabitants" are summoned to hear; this does not mean the entire earthly creation (as in Pss. 24:1; 50:12; Jer. 8:16, etc.), but human beings who are capable of listening (as in Isa. 23:1). The second half of the verse almost sounds like a motivation clause which has been added to the summons in

v. 1a (see note 2c). Occasionally it is regarded as a secondary addition (J. Lindblom; E. Sellin; J. Lippl). The transitional ויהי, however, is probably indicative only of the literary character of the universalistic redaction in v. 2 (see above, pp. 45f.). Nevertheless the ויהי, together with the contents of v. 2b, is indispensable in view of the function of this opening verse and its continuation in chaps. 4–5. What the peoples are supposed to hear serves not to increase their knowledge but to determine their lives. Yahweh comes as "witness against" them, as witness for the prosecution, therefore as accuser. This meaning for עד with ב is unambiguous, according to Deut. 31:26; Jer. 42:5; Zeph. 3:8 (Gk) and Mal. 3:5 (further citations in J. T. Willis, 337f.; it does not mean "witness in your midst," as B. Duhm, 44; G. Fohrer, 69; D. K. Innes, 225, et al. suggest). Yahweh appears "from his holy palace"; the phrase היכל קדשו can refer to the temple in Zion (Ps. 68:30; Isa. 6:1), but here it most probably means the heavenly sanctuary (cf. Ps. 11:4; Hab. 2:20), since v. 2 already presupposes v. 3 (see above, p. 46), according to which Yahweh "comes forth from his place and treads upon the high places of the earth." The accuser of the peoples appears as "Lord." Thus Yahweh already in v. 2 is attested as "Lord of the whole earth," as later in 4:13. The world's fate is determined by its listening to him (cf. 5:14). This summons to a legal proceeding, however, does not merely foreshadow the later prophecies concerning the nations in chaps. 4–5. Rather, this summons probably has been placed here because the nations are indirectly to discern Yahweh's indictment of them from the example of Yahweh's dealings with Israel as presented in chaps. 1–3. Whatever happens to Israel affects the whole world. The entire human universe is placed under the same indictment first brought against Israel.

[1:3] The following theophany account derives from a tradition in which the deity comes against the nations with whom Israel fights (Judg. 5:4ff.; Ps. 18:8ff.; Isa. 26:20f.; Jer. 25:30 [Isa. 63:19—64:2]). Similar theophany motifs are well known among the peoples in Israel's environment: the god Assur splits the mountains; Adad shakes the earth; Martu causes fire to rain; and Ishtar causes herself to rain as fire upon the land (documentation in Jörg Jeremias [1977] 88ff.). Thus the preceding summons to the nations to hear is appropriately placed. We noted (above, p. 51) that the Micah tradition available to the universalistic redactor already contained the theophany account as the opening passage. The redactor responsible for vv. 3ff., however, thinks of the theophany (as the one in Amos 1:2) directed against Israel (cf. v. 5 and see above, pp. 46f.). A comparison of the individual statements with other theophany accounts indicates that the poet, on the one hand, utilizes substance and form that is strongly shaped by the tradition; on the other hand, insofar as it is discernible, he does not take up the very wording of a written text, but newly formulates oral tradition come down to him from some distance. In so doing, he fits the theophany somewhat into the present context (as in Amos 1:2; cf. Wolff, *Joel and Amos* 118f.).

    The participial formulation in the first clause (v. 3a), followed by perfect consecutive verbs (vv. 3b, 4aα) and an imperfect verb (v. 4aβ) indicates that these events are imminent, as also in Isa. 19:1; 26:21 (Ges-K §116p). Not one word describes Yahweh's appearance; immediately his deeds (v. 3) and then their effects (v. 4) are praised. His "coming forth" in the theophany tradition means his "marching out" to battle (Judg. 5:4; Zech. 14:3; Ps. 68:8; Isa. 26:21). He leaves "his place," which in v. 2b was already interpreted as "his holy palace." Yahweh is imagined to be in heaven, for from there he "comes down" upon the heights of the earth (on ירד see Isa. 63:19; Ps. 18:10; cf. also Jer. 25:30). The mythical picture, attested in Ugarit and Deut. 33:29bβ, in which the deity as victorious warrior sets his foot upon the conquered monster "earth," is no longer recognizable here (otherwise: A. S. van der Woude, 30; cf. M. K. Wakeman, "The Biblical Earth Monster in the Cosmogonic Combat Myth," *JBL* 88 [1969] 313–320 [319f.]). Rather, the choice of the word במות, in the light of Hos. 10:8 (Wolff, *Hosea* 176), similarly Amos 4:13 (idem, *Joel and Amos* 224), appears to prepare for v. 5bβ (on ירד, cf. 1:12).

[1:4] Within the hymn, the "heights" upon which Yahweh treads are then characterized simply as "mountains" (v. 4a) in the report on the effects of Yahweh's actions. The mountains represent permanence, height, power from primeval times (Ps. 90:2; 95:4; Zech. 4:7); the "lowlands," valleys, on the other hand, are the fruitful, inhabitable areas preferred by people (Judg. 1:19, 34; Hos. 2:17; Ps. 65:14). Yahweh will totally destroy both. It is on this that the accent lies. Therefore, after Yahweh's appearance (a bicola with three stresses, v. 3), the effect is described by two bicola with three stresses: v. 4a presents it directly; v. 4b with a comparison. The similes in v. 4bα and bβ elucidate v. 4aα and aβ, respectively. If the mountains melt like wax in fire (Ps. 97:5), they no longer exist (concerning "fire," cf. v. 7a); the verse more likely refers to an earthquake than to a volcanic eruption (cf. Judg. 5:4f.; Ps. 97:4f.). When the plains of the valley are split into steep ravines (cf. Hab. 3:9b; Zech. 14:4), they become exactly opposite of what humans find inhabitable, like a turbulent flood dispersed and atomized (cf. מגרים in v. 4bβ with והגרתי in v. 6b) upon rocky slopes. In like manner is Yahweh's action on earth when he goes forth against his enemies.

[1:5] Not until v. 5 are we told against whom Yahweh advances. In the spirit of Micah, the Deuteronomistic preacher (see above, pp. 46f.) intends to explain why "all this"—namely, Yahweh's coming forth for judgment (vv. 3f.)—has happened; he does this by making use of Micah's own words in Mic. 3:8b. The real cause of the catastrophes, now belonging to the past, of 722 for Samaria and 587 for Jerusalem, he attributes to their guilt. The word פשע places the accent upon intentional criminal rebellion against the law itself (1 Kings 12:19; Jer. 2:29); חטאת emphasizes the objective error of one who loses the way and is confused (Judg. 20:16; Prov. 19:2). Here both verbs equally characterize the guilt of the transgression. Who is responsible, whether far or near, for these catastrophes? With such a question, the historically conscious interpreter of the prophetic word provokes the audience to think along with him, as they prepare themselves to follow the reading of the ancient prophecy. The answer is: both of the capital cities. Thus the Deuteronomistic school had come to discern parallels in history (2 Kings 17:1ff., 19ff.); thus it had perceived in eighth-century prophecy's chief accusations against the officials and leaders a connection with the capital cities (Amos 3:9–11; Mic. 3:9–11). Thus among the prophets contemporaneous with the Deuteronomistic school, at the time of the transition to the exilic period, the capital in the north and that in the south come to be thought of as two sisters, beladen with guilt (Jer. 3:6ff.; Ezek. 23:1ff.). And thus did the Deuteronomistic preacher conclude from the immediately following prophecy from Micah, which sees Samaria and Jerusalem brought to disaster by one and the same blow from Yahweh (v. 6 and v. 9; on the "high places of Judah," see above, p. 52).

[1:6] Micah's first prophetic saying could not have begun with a perfect consecutive verb with Yahweh speaking in the first person (B. Duhm; A. Jepsen). At the least, the present wording will have been preceded by the messenger formula, perhaps followed by הִנֵּה + participle or a clause in the imperfect. This clause could have contained the fragments (לְעִי and הַשָּׂדֶה) which are in the wrong place in the transmitted text (cf. 2:3; 3:5, 12; also 1:3f. and see above, p. 47). Nevertheless, hardly any essential content of the verse will have been lost, especially since the motivation for Yahweh's actions does not follow until v. 7b. The prophetic utterance has to do with Samaria. The hill of Samaria, with a height of 450 meters, was purchased by Omri around 880 (1 Kings 16:24) and made into a fortress; he and his successor Ahab enlarged the city, making it their royal residence (cf. A. Alt, "Der Stadtstaat Samaria," *Kleine Schriften* 3:262f.). Prior to this, this hill had remained unpopulated; perhaps its elevation above the surrounding basin-shaped valley made it suitable for vineyards. In any case, Micah's prophecy announces that, in place of the prospering capital city, vineyards will be planted and the city returned to its previously unsettled condition. Its splendid buildings will be demolished down to their foundations, and the squared stones of the city-walls will be thrown straight down the steep slopes into the valley; the word נגר *hiph.*, which otherwise denotes the pouring out of liquids (Ps. 75:9; 2 Sam. 14:14; cf. Mic. 1:4bβ), suggests here Yahweh's superior power with which he destroys the walls of the palace and fortress in Samaria. The "laying bare" of the foundation stones is at the same time an act of violation (Lev. 18:6–19; Hos. 2:12 [10]; Ezek. 16:37). A comparison of the linguistic usage in v. 6a with Ps. 79:1 and in v. 6b with Ps. 137:7, confirms the supposition that Yahweh's action here comes not in the form of an earthquake (thus J. Lindblom; E. Sellin; W. Beyerlin, et al.) but a military conquest. (On the historical events around 722, see 2 Kings 17:24 and p. 53 above.)

[1:7] The twofold occurrence of the word "whore's fee" in v. 7b fits with the act of violation by means of "laying bare" in v. 6. This makes v. 7a appear to be a secondary addition (see note 7a–a); its vocabulary suggests that here the Deuteronomistic redactor has made use of concepts drawn from Hosea (cf. Jörg Jeremias [1971] 336). Just as the Deuteronomistic lector in v. 5bβ is mindful of Jerusalem's cultic high places, so here he thinks of the idols in the form of cultic images. Micah's word "whore's fee" may have suggested this to him; however, by putting it in the plural (unique in the OT) he gives to the word the meaning of "whore images" (on the figurines of female deities in the cultic high places, cf. 2 Kings

23:13; on the archeology of female and male images of the gods, cf. K. Galling and P. Welten, *BRL²* 99–119).

Micah's view, by contrast, is directed to the magnificent buildings of the royal city of Samaria. It is not to be ruled out that he, too, borrows something from Hosea (J. Lindblom, 137f.) when he speaks of "whore's fee" (Hos. 9:1; cf. 2:14[12] and Deut. 23:19). However, like Hosea himself, he hardly has in mind idols overlaid with gold or silver derived from melted coins from religious brothels—idols which would have been captured by invading soldiers and used in like manner. Possibly the commentator of v. 7a may have understood it in this way (cf. L. C. Allen, 274; A. S. van der Woude, 35; B. Renaud, 15). Rather, similar to Hos. 8:8–10 (cf. 12:2 [1] and on the text see Wolff, *Hosea* 132f. and 143), Micah probably had in mind that Samaria gave commercial goods and tribute to the great power Assyria, and therefore "gathered" "whore's wages," which made possible the splendid buildings for the royal residence. The "whore's wages" as such must now be given up. For this interpretation, the decisive questions center on determining the object in v. 7bα and the subject in v. 7bβ. Since only Samaria in v. 6 can be considered the subject of v. 7bα (looking beyond v. 7a), the most likely object of the verb is the palace buildings, with their walls and foundations (v. 6), which Samaria "has brought together" and "must again give up."

[1:8] This destruction of Samaria is, to begin with, what drives Micah to intense mourning (on עַל־זֹאת, see above, pp. 47f.). The prophet, himself the first to see the impending catastrophe, must be the first to suffer under its approach. סָפַד is the chief term for the mourning ritual and refers especially to the cry of woe (Amos 5:16f.), perhaps also to the simultaneous smiting of the breast (Isa. 32:12); יִלֵּל *hiph.* means "to wail" and is usually accompanied by tears (cf. v. 10a). But Micah summons himself not only to lamentation and wailing; he performs a symbolic act by going "barefoot and naked" (Ch. Hardmeier, 358), which as such strengthens and completes the announcement of disaster. Usually, these symbolic actions are understood merely as a part of the mourning ritual. At the most, this could apply to going barefoot (2 Sam. 15:30; cf. Ezek. 24:17, 23); however, a person in mourning does not go naked, but wears sackcloth as a mourning loincloth (Gen. 37:34; 1 Kings 21:27; Joel 1:8, and see Wolff, *Joel and Amos* 29f.) and covers his head (exactly as in the case of David's going about barefoot, 2 Sam. 15:30). The sackcloth was worn not merely to mourn the death of a person, but to lament the destruction of city and land (Isa. 15:3; Jer. 48:37; Lam. 2:10). Elsewhere the OT states only once that someone goes about "barefoot and naked"; indeed, it is said of Isaiah (20:2–4). This is without question a symbolic action which means to represent the threat of being taken prisoner (cf. also Amos 2:16). This corresponds precisely with Micah in v. 8, for at the end of Micah's summons to lament stands a prophecy about deportation (v. 16bβ). Thus, a prophetic symbolic action has been combined with the lamentation. Indeed, the mourning rite can be considered a part of the symbolic action. When Micah compares his own lamentation with the howling of the jackals and the moaning of the ostrich, it is not fortuitous that he considers himself in community with those who must dwell in the wilderness because of Samaria's desolation.

[1:9] But why is the Judean prophet so deeply affected by the destruction of Samaria? Certainly, for Micah the Northern Kingdom of Israel is just as much a part of the old Israel as for the Judean prophet Amos who, at the first of this ministry, interceded with Yahweh also on behalf of the Northern Kingdom (Amos 7:2, 5). But v. 9 indicates that Micah goes a step further.

Micah recognizes that the same blow which strikes Samaria will also reach Judah and Jerusalem. מכה is used elsewhere not only for the "blow" which smites an individual, and for the corresponding "injury" (Prov. 20:30; 1 Kings 20:35), but also means "defeat" and "devastation" that a city or state experiences from a military "blow" (1 Kings 20:21; Jer. 19:8; 50:13). אנוש(ה) means that a wound is "incurable" (Jer. 15:8), a day "disastrous" (Jer. 17:16), and a blow "inescapable" (such as an arrow, Job 34:6 MT). Micah mentions neither Assyria nor any other human power as the agent of this "blow"; however, he is extraordinarily reluctant to use the name of God. If the name *Yahweh* originally stood in this verse (see note 9a), then in addition to v. 12b, it is the only other instance. It is the consequences of Yahweh's intervention that predominate in these verses.

Micah begins vv. 9a and 9b with a deitic כי, an agitated, oathlike "indeed." Verse 9a,b provides the motivation, on the one hand, for his own expression of lamentation and, on the other, for the following cries to the Judean towns. Why does he name Judah before Jerusalem? Is it because the state belongs before the capital city (as in v. 5b and Isa. 1:1)? Or because the conqueror will first cross the state border and then arrive at the capital, even though the enemy comes from the north instead of from the coastal highway? Or because Micah is speaking before Judeans in the land of Judah rather than in the capital city (correspondingly reversed in Isa. 3:1, 8)? The last is probably correct, because Micah refers to Jerusalem only as the "gate of my people." Here it should be observed first of all that without exception, Micah names his oppressed fellow countrymen "my people" (2:8f.; 3:3, 5), for whom he regards himself responsible as one of their elders (Wolff, VTSuppl 29 [1978] 411f.). These are the Judean small landholders (Th. Lescow, 50). But to what extent is Jerusalem the "gate" of his people? Does Micah think of the capital city as the center of legal administration and government for the entire land (W. Rudolph; J. L. Mays)? In this regard, Micah does not expect much from Jerusalem for his people (see chap. 3!). Or are we to imagine that when the enemy captures the gate of a city, the entire city has fallen? This would mean that when Jerusalem, "the gate of my people," has been taken, then all of Judah, down to the last small landholder, has been taken by the enemy. A. Alt thought of it in this way: When the enemy comes from Samaria, then Jerusalem is the "gate" through which it must pass before it can inundate the land of Judah (*Kleine Schriften* 3:373). The subsequent verses, in my opinion, point in the direction of this interpretation.

[1:10] The city of *Gath*, until 712/711 a Judean fortress (2 Chron. 11:8; see above, p. 49), is the first summoned to leave aside its boasting and to participate in weeping and lamentation. The location of the town is still a matter of debate (cf. L. C. Allen, 279, note 73; M. Weippert, *BRL²* [1977] 85f.; *IDBSuppl* [1976] 353). However, P. Welten's detailed argument

(68–81), which suggests that ancient Gath was situated at *Tell šēh aḥmed el-'arēny = 'Arâq el-Menshîyeh,* finds additional support from the proximity of Gath to Moresheth-gath *(Tell ej-Judeideh;* it lies barely 15 km east of *'Arâq el-Menshîyeh).* That Gath belonged to Judah at that time is supported by the discoveries of royal stamps (P. Welten, 79). Even this first summons addressed to Gath, as in those which follow, contains a wordplay in the form of alliteration *(gat-tag dīlu).*

To this play on the sound of words, the following summons adds a play on the words' meaning: Beth-le-aphra ("house of dust") is to roll itself in the *'āfār* ("dust"). The prophet commands the performance of an act of mourning that is otherwise attested as a part of a lamentation over disaster (cf. Jer. 6:26; 25:34: Ezek. 27:30). Beth-le-aphra has not yet been located; K. Elliger (125ff.=47ff.) supposes that it is to be identified with *eṭ-Ṭaiyibeh* on the way from *Beit-Jibrîn* to Hebron.

[1:11] Likewise, the location of the following four towns in vv. 11–12a remains entirely uncertain (on particular suggestions, cf. L. H. Grollenberg, *Bildatlas zur Bibel,* index; R. Vuilleumier [1971]; and L. C. Allen [1976], in each case, ad loc.). Owing to the corrupt text, what Micah says about these towns is difficult to understand. If we remain with the transmitted text, the prophecy concerning Shaphir is a summons (as in v. 10a and 10b) to its inhabitants. However, the summons is not an urgent call to mourning but to flight, not as escape from the enemy, but—if indeed the words "naked!" "ashamed!" originally belong in the text (see note 11c)—flight into captivity. Similarly, in v. 8 the prophet himself prepares to go about "naked and barefoot" (on the anticipation of deportation, cf. especially v. 16b). The play on words here is a play on meaning: what is graceful (שפיר = "beautiful," "fair" [*BDB*]) will be disgraced.

Military catastrophe is also the context for understanding the colon which speaks of *Zaanan.* If the town צאנן (this spelling occurs nowhere else in the OT) is identical with צְנָן in Josh. 15:37 (thus most recently D. Kellermann, 426f.), then according to the context (v. 33), the town was situated in the Shephelah. For the first time, the prophet makes a declarative statement instead of a summons. The sound of the name Zaanan suggests to him the verb יָצְאָה. When used in a military context, this verb can have two meanings: frequently it means "to march off" to war (thus also 1:3, see above, p. 55); but it can also mean "to escape" (thus 1 Sam. 14:41). The anticipation of deportation in the context (see above) makes this latter sense more likely: "Zaanan will not escape."

Beth-ezel also does not occur elsewhere in the OT. For some reason Micah includes this town in the extensive lamentation (see note 11f–f). Its inhabitants are to mourn because their עֶמְדָּה has been taken from them. Does this word mean their "standing place" (KBL), their shelter? Is he thinking of the destruction of the city? Or does the word refer to their "endurance" (Ges-B), their steadfastness, their place of residence? The previous intimations of exile suggest the last meaning. Here there is no alliteration. I am able to find only in יקח ("one takes") a reminiscence of the basic meaning of the root II אצל ("to remove") from the word *Beth-ezel;* thus, there is a play on the meaning of the town's name.

[1:12] The play on the meaning of words is clearer in verse 12, the only place in the OT where the town *Maroth* is mentioned. In this case, there is no similarity of meaning in the town's name and the following explanatory clause, as is probable with Beth-ezel. Rather, as is likely the case with the word *Shaphir,* the verse contains an intended contrast: "good" (טוב) and "bitter" (מר) are well-known opposites (Isa. 5:20; Job 21:25). The name *Maroth* already seals the fate of all hope for good. With this sixth town the first strophe comes to an end, having begun with a כי-clause concerning Judah and Jerusalem (vv. 9–12a).

An emphatic כי and a statement about the gate of Jerusalem (see above, p. 49) make a new beginning in v. 12b. If the singular "the gate" (MT) preserves the original text (see note 12c), then this represents the same meaning found in v. 9 (see above, p. 59): Jerusalem is the gate of entry into Judah for the enemy from the north, inasmuch as the land is, in a narrower sense, Micah's home. The transmitted text now states that Yahweh himself is the cause of all disaster; doom comes down from him. The similarity of the statements in v. 9 and v. 12b may well be an additional support for the conjecture "Yahweh's blow" in v. 9a (see note 9a). The pun in v. 12b contains a play on the sound as well as on the meaning of the words: in addition to the alliteration of ירד with ירושלם and of רע with שער, there occurs a contrast in meaning (as in v. 11a and v. 12a) between רע ("disaster") and שלם ("salvation"), which is suggested by the word *Jerusalem.*

[1:13] The statement about Yahweh's judgment on the capital, however, is once again only the prelude to a return to Judah's fate. With *Lachish* in v. 13a, mentioned for the first time, the text speaks of a town (after Gath in v. 10a) which is frequently named in the OT and which is also identifiable with a fair degree of certainty. *Tell ed-Duweir* is generally considered to be the ancient location. It is situated halfway between Jerusalem and Gaza, about 10 km southwest of Moresheth *(Tell ej-Judeideh)* and a good 40 km southwest of Jerusalem, in the hill country of the Shephelah (cf. H. Weippert, *BRL*² 196–198; *IDBSuppl* 526). Recently S. Mittmann has cast doubt on this (according to D. Kellermann, *VT* 28 [1978] 428; he suggests *Tell Eitun*). *Tell ed-Duweir* was one of the most significant fortresses of Judah near the Philistine plain, as is indicated by a double wall that encircled the city in the ninth and eighth centuries (cf. M. and Y. Aharoni, "The Stratification of Judahite Sites in the 8th and 7th Centuries B.C.E.," *BASOR* 224 [1976] 73–90). Having already been mentioned in the Amarna texts (together with Moresheth, see above, p. 36), it will have belonged to the cities where chariots and horses were stationed, built by Solomon, according to 1 Kings 9:19; 10:26. In 2 Chron. 11:9 Lachish is listed as one of Rehoboam's fortified cities. In his campaign of 701, Sennacherib captured Lachish and immediately made it his headquarters (2 Kings 18:14, 17; 19:8). His victory over the city was so important to him that he had it pictured in a relief in Nineveh (cf. *AOB* 138; 140f.; a much better reproduction in *ANEP* 371–374). The city's ability to resist attack is attested even later in Jer. 34:7. This ample documentation of the military significance of Lachish makes it understandable that Lachish would be called upon to harness its steeds to the chariots.

The colon offers the most artistic alliterations, first with *rk* (המרכבה לרכש) and then even fuller *la.kš* (לרכש־לביש). Horses were harnessed to a chariot by placing around the neck of one or two pair of horses a yoke which was fastened by a strap at the throat. The wagon shaft was connected to the middle of the yoke (cf. W. Weippert, "Pferde und Streitwagen," *BRL*² 250–255 (especially 253) and the illustration, p. 70). What is the meaning of Micah's command to harness the chariots? The context excludes the possibility that it is for the purpose of battle. The prophet likely thought of the enemy's order for deportation (cf. v. 11a and v. 16b), which would have included taking the chariots as spoils of war. Sargon II's report of his conquest of Samaria attests to this: "I led away as booty 27,280 people, including their chariots. . . . 200 wagons I added to my royal corps" (*TGI*² 60).

At this climax to the prophet's summons, the Deuteronomistic liturgist again adds his own commentary. In a didactic style he calls attention with a demonstrative היא (thus in the third person; "that, there") in v. 13bα to Lachish's military potential, but then in v. 13bβ— uncertain in its prose style—he returns to direct address (as in v. 13a) to Lachish (בך). He characterizes the fortified city and its weaponry as the "apex" of rebellion of the daughter Zion, indeed, as the chief sin. If ראשית is understood not in a qualifying but in a temporal sense, then we would have to consider this as a reference to the historical beginnings of the completion of the fortifications under Solomon and Rehoboam (see above). But the substantive interpretation probably is to be preferred over the temporal. Here the Deuteronomistic commentator expresses a view that corresponds to Mic. 5:9–12 [10–13], where military self-security and cultic idolatry are mentioned together (as in v. 13b, along with vv. 5b and 7a). With this focused accusation, the Deuteronomist recalls a theme expressed in Hosea (10:13ff.; 14:4) and Isaiah (2:7; 31:1ff.) that also found an echo in the Deuteronomistic royal law (Deut. 17:16). Trust in "many horses" has replaced trust in Yahweh.

[1:14] "Therefore" Jerusalem and the cities of Judah will be destroyed, as Micah further describes in what follows; this is what the commentator wishes to say by adding the לכן at the beginning of v. 14a. In the original text Micah now turns to his own hometown (concerning its location, see above, pp. 35f.). That the town is now called *Moresheth-gath* is generally explained by its origin as an offshoot settlement from Gath (*BHHW* 2:1238). An unnamed entity is requested to present to the town "parting gifts." The expression apparently belongs to the sphere of marriage customs. According to 1 Kings 9:16 (cf. Exod. 18:2) this would refer to the dowry which the bride's father presents to her as she departs from her own family and enters unfamiliar surroundings. In our passage the accent lies upon the act of departure into that which is alien. With the name of the town the Hebrew ear would perceive a play on the meaning of the word ארש *(piel,* "to be betrothed," "to make the bride one's own forever"; cf. Wolff, *Hosea* 52) in the word *Moresheth,* either as the *pual* participle מְאֹרָשָׂה (thus Deut. 22:23, 25, 27) or even the form מְאֹרֶשֶׂת (Rudolph, 48), "betrothed," "bride." Hence, this summons as well makes an indirect reference to a deportation into exile.

Achzib is situated only slightly more than 5 km east of Moresheth, if the town, as is probable, is to be identified with *Tell el-Beida* (K. Elliger, *BHHW* 1:21f.). Joshua 15:44 also places Achzib in the Shephelah (vv. 33ff.). The nominal clause offers a perfect play on the sound of the word, except for a variation of one vowel. אכזב means "what is deceptive," especially the "deceitful brook," or dry wadi, where one expects to find water, but is disappointed (Jer. 15:18; Job 6:15–20). In what sense, though, are "the houses of Achzib a disappointment for the kings of Israel"? A. Demsky has made it plausible that the Achzib mentioned in v. 14 is identical with כְּזִיב in Gen. 38:5 and כֹּזֵבָה in 1 Chron. 4:22, where the name occurs with Mareshah (4:21), as it does here (v. 15a). Now, 1 Chron. 4:21–23 lists the professional guilds of linen workers and potters, who were in the service of the king of Judah. This list could have been originally compiled in the second half of the eighth century in the archives of the royal court in Jerusalem; it is undoubtedly preexilic (cf. also K. Galling, ATD 12 [1954] 25). It would be more precise to characterize the "houses" of Achzib as "workshops" (cf. Jer. 18:2 בֵּית הַיּוֹצֵר for the potter's workshop). Achzib was therefore one of the towns where earthen pots were made, which bore on their handle the inscription למלך (cf. P. Welten); numerous examples have been found in Lachish and Moresheth, among other places. These workshops would have to shut down their operations because of the impending catastrophe; and thus the "kings of Israel" would be deceived, i.e., disappointed. It is not surprising that Micah calls the rulers in Jerusalem "kings of Israel," as he also speaks of the inhabitants of Jerusalem as "Israel" in 3:1, 8, 9.

[1:15] *Maresha* (v. 15a) lies approximately 7 km southwest of Achzib and 5 km south of Moresheth; it is to be identified with *Tell Sandaḥannah* (K. Elliger 100ff. = 25ff.; *BHHW* 2:1147f.; *IDBSuppl* 566f.). According to 2 Chron. 11:7 the town belongs to the system of fortifications; according to Josh. 15:35, it is a part of the settlements in the Shephelah (vv. 33ff.). Micah hears in the name Mareshah the root ירש, which can mean not only a peaceable "taking possession of," but also a brutal "ousting from one's property," "supplanting," "conquering." Hence, the verse also announces that a foreign "conqueror" and "power of occupation" is coming (as in Jer. 8:10). This is the only mention in chap. 1 of the actions of a human enemy. Does the word עֹד presupposes an earlier military oppression which now begins "anew"?

Adullam is also known as a fortified city (2 Chron. 11:17) in the Shephelah (Jos. 15:33, 35). The attempt has been made to identify Adullam with *Khirbet esh-Sheikh Madhkur* (R. Bach, *BHHW,* 1:28f.). The wordplay appears to be only a play on meaning. In the history of David's rise to power, Adullam signifies the low point in his life; in utter affliction, David fled to a cave (1 Sam. 22:1) in the rocky refuge of Adullam (2 Sam. 23:13). When Micah speaks of the "glory of Israel coming to Adullam," then the phrase כבוד ישראל must refer to the contemporary "king of Israel," who, in correspondence to v. 14b, must be the Davidic king in Jerusalem. The prophet announces that he, as his forefather, will flee to the cave of Adullam in extreme affliction and necessity. Similarly, in David's dirge in 2 Sam. 1:19, Saul and Jonathan are called "the honor" (הַצְּבִי) of Israel.

In retrospect, it is remarkable that the towns named in the second strophe (vv. 13–15) are significantly better known, both to the OT and to archaeologists, than those in the first strophe (vv. 10b–12a). Moreover, they represent in several instances a particular connection to the history of Jerusalem and its kings (vv. 13, 14b, 15b). We found that all identifiable towns form a circle of a two-to-three-hour walk from Moresheth, in the Shephelah. Is it possible that the unknown places first addressed by the prophet were quite small settlements in the immediate neighborhood of Moresheth?

[1:16] Micah concludes this passage with a final summons to mourning by commanding that his addressees perform the rite of shaving the head bald. גזז frequently denotes the shearing of sheep (Gen. 31:19; 38:12f.; Isa. 53:7, etc.); קרח is always used for the cutting of human hair to make one completely or partially bald. In Jer. 7:29 the same command is issued, in the second person feminine singular as here, and connected with the inhabitants of the cities of Judah and the streets of Jerusalem (v. 34). According to Jer. 16:6, cutting the hair is an act that accompanies the singing of a dirge; more often, it accompanies the lamentation over the destruction of a city or country (Isa. 3:24; 15:2; Jer. 47:5; 48:37; Ezek. 7:18; 27:31; cf. Job 1:20). With this act, the person who mourns removes his natural adornment. No less than three imperatives call for the cutting of the hair. The third imperative represents a heightening, in that it requires an especially extensive removal of hair, in contrast to a smaller tonsure, which was also customary (on the different forms of baldness as a sign of mourning [shaving of a bald edge around the head; of the forelocks; of the entire head], cf. Wolff, *Joel and Amos* 329). Micah had compared his own voice of lamentation with that of the jackal and the ostrich (v. 8b). Now his audience, of whom he demands shaved heads, is likened to the vulture, whose totally naked head and neck appear so striking (cf. *Brockhaus Enzyklopädie* 7 [1969] 38 [illustration]; J. Feliks, *BHHW* 1:533f.).

Now the reason for all of this lamentation becomes more clearly expressed than in the preceding verses: the children will be sent into exile. Whose children are these? The summarizing character of v. 16 suggests that they are the inhabitants of all the towns of Judah, even if Judah (or בַּת־יְהוּדָה) was not the original addressee (cf. Lam. 1:15; 2:2, 5 and see above, pp. 45f., 54). They are called בני תענוגים the dearly beloved children, the joy and delight of the mother Judah. The root ענג suggests pleasure, comfort, and longing; תענוג is used elsewhere for luxury (Prov. 19:10), delight (Eccles. 2:8), charm (Song of Sol. 7:7[6]). In 2:9 Micah speaks of pleasant houses of contentment and security. Verse 16 says that the "children of delight" will be taken off into exile. This states harshly (perfect verb!) what Micah himself had already intimated with the words "barefoot and naked" (v. 8), and what he made known more or less clearly by the commands to Shaphir (v. 11a), Lachish (v. 13a), and Moresheth (v. 14a); in principle, however, every clause in the passage presupposed this. The land will be divested of its inhabitants (on גלה, cf. Zobel, *ThWAT* 1:1020; also v. 6b, אגלה).

Purpose and Thrust

In this passage we have seen Micah's first passionate summons to his people. What is particularly characteristic of the text is best seen by way of comparison. Isaiah had also prophesied threatening disaster for all of Judah (8:7f.). He had clearly made reference to Assyria and to Judah as a whole. Previously he had declared that the people's guilt was the cause of Yahweh's punishment (8:5). Isaiah had also announced the fall of Samaria (Isa. 28:1–4, as had Amos [3:11] and Hosea [14:1] before him).

What is different in Micah?

1. He does not mention Assyria; only once does he prophesy that a "conqueror" will come (v. 15a). Micah is completely dominated by the dreadful disaster he perceives about to descend upon the cities of Judah. He presents a brief messenger speech from Yahweh (first person) concerning Samaria (v. 6), but then immediately speaks of his own involvement (first person) by means of a self-summons (v. 8). As appears self-evident, Micah, in the midst of his very concrete summons and proclamation, only incidently names Yahweh as the author of the dreadful blow which also reaches to Judah and Jerusalem (perhaps in v. 9a, see note 9a; then in v. 12b). His main theme is the land's grave distress.

2. In Micah the prophecy concerning Samaria is not separated from that concerning Judah. The word spoken against Samaria contains no particular addressee. Its sole function is to proclaim unambiguously the blow, which will reach as far as Judah and Jerusalem (cf. the עַל־זֹאת, and see above, pp. 47f.). Therefore, the announcement of Samaria's destruction evokes the prophet's mourning and symbolic action (see above, p. 58), with which he immediately calls on the cities of Judah to respond to the impending destruction with lamentation and preparedness. Samaria, the prophet, Jerusalem, and Judah have been attacked as one.

3. Whereas Isaiah names Judah to refer only to the land as a whole, it is characteristic of Micah that he addresses eleven different towns individually. As far as we know, they all are located in his homeland in the narrow sense, the Shephelah. Unimportant and otherwise-unnamed towns are mentioned along with world-renowned fortresses. With his own particular art in using wordplays, Micah connects the impending destruction so indissolubly with each individual place-name that no member of his audience could forget it. This is apparently his main intention: to proclaim the inescapable approaching catastrophe in such a manner that his audience cannot fail to perceive it. He does this most unambiguously when he speaks of their departure into exile.

4. It is remarkable that in this chapter, Micah, in contrast to Isaiah, utters not one syllable about Judah's guilt. He will have much to say about it in the prophetic sayings of the next two chapters. In chap. 1, however, in connection with Samaria, he alludes only once—with the phrase "whore's wages," perhaps borrowing an expression from Hosea's prophecy that he may have found compelling—to the city's guilt of unfaithfulness and greed. No word of accusation is spoken to Judah and Jerusalem. For a complete understanding of Micah, this possibility should be kept in mind, namely, that in this first passage he speaks exclusively of an approaching judgment. For him this must have been what was essential and necessary.

5. The time came when tradents and interpreters supplemented Micah's saying with words of accusation. Thus, we observed that the Deuteronomists added vv. 5, 7a, and 13b. It is probable that after the judgment which had broken in upon Jerusalem in 587, they preached

about idol worship and military self-security as the cause of the catastrophe. Perhaps it was members of the same circles who sang also of Yahweh's lordship over the powers of nature in the words of the theophany hymn (vv. 3f.) and thus, in a time of judgment on Israel, bowed in prayer before Yahweh's punishment (see above, pp. 51f.).

6. Finally, we found that a preface (v. 2) has been added to the Micah traditions that had been redacted by the Deuteronomists. The preface presents a universal summons to all nations to prepare themselves for Yahweh's indictment. Here for the first time we recognize the intention to take Micah's judgment speech to Israel as a preliminary model for God's lawsuit with the world.

Thus in Micah 1:2–16 we are presented with a multiphased history of prophetic proclamation. The reader gains a remarkable impression of how, in the light of an historical catastrophe, the most different and opposing circles are shaped into a community of people overcome by the judgment of God: Samaria and Judah, the prophet and his people, animals and human beings, small towns and the capital city, important fortresses and little settlements, Israel and all nations, the earth and its inhabitants. In the face of divine catastrophe they are able to recognize their common fate and they find themselves called upon to accept it.

This is most certainly not all that Micah and those who transmitted his message have to say, but here in the first chapter we have a prophetic witness which is not to be overlooked.

Micah 2:1-13

Woe to the Oppressors!

Literature

On 2:1–13: K. Budde, "Micha 2 und 3," *ZAW* 38 (1919/1920) 2–22. H. M. Weil, "Le chapitre II de Michée expliqué par le Premier Livre de Rois, chapitres XX–XXII," *RHR* 121 (1940) 146–161. H. Donner, "Die soziale Botschaft der Propheten im Lichte der Gesellschaftsordnung in Israel," *OrAnt* 2 (1963) 229–245; reprinted in P. A. H. Neumann (ed.), *Das Prophetenverständnis in der deutschsprachigen Forschung seit Heinrich Ewald,* WdF 307 (1979) 493–514. D. K. Innes, "Some Notes on Micah, Chapter II," *EvQ* 41 (1969) 10–13.

On 2:1–5: B. Stade, "Mich. 2,4," *ZAW* 6 (1886) 122–123. A. Alt, "Micha 2:1–5. ΓΗΣ ΑΝΑΔΑΣΜΟΣ in Juda," *Festschrift S. Mowinckel* (1955) 13–23; reprinted in idem, *Kleine Schriften* 3:373–381. F. Horst, "Das Eigentum nach dem Alten Testament," (1949) ThB 12 (1961) 203–221. J. T. Willis, "On the Text of Micah 2:1aα–β," *Biblica* 48 (1967) 534–541. Jörg Jeremias, "Die Deutung der Gerichtsworte Michas in der Exilszeit," *ZAW* 83 (1971) 330–354. W. Janzen, *Mourning Cry and Woe Oracle,* BZAW 125 (1972) 62–64. H. J. Krause, "*hôj* als prophetische Leichenklage über das eigene Volk," *ZAW* 85 (1973) 15–46 (28–31). J. Ebach, "Sozialethische Erwägungen zum alttestamentlichen Bodenrecht," *Biblische Notizen* 1 (1976) 31–46. G. W. Ramsey, "Speech-Forms in Hebrew Law and Prophetic Oracles," *JBL* 96 (1977) 45–58. Ch. Hardmeier, *Texttheorie und biblische Exegese,* BEvTh 79 (1978).

On 2:6–11: H. Donat, "Micha 2,6–9," *BZ* 9 (1911) 351–366. A. Wolf, "*l' z't hmnḥh* (Mich 2,6–11)," *BetM* 11 (1966) 14–41. A. S. van der Woude, "Micha 2,7a und der Bund Jahwes mit Israel," *VT* 18 (1968) 388–391. Idem, "Micah and the Pseudo-Prophets," *VT* 19 (1969) 244–260. A. Ehrman, "A Note on Micah II 7," *VT* 20 (1970) 86f. J. T. Willis, "Micah 2,6–8 and the 'People of God,'" *BZ* 14 (1970) 72–87. A. S. van der Woude, "Waarheid als leugen (Mi 2,6–11)," *VoxTh* 40 (1970) 65–70. F. Stolz, "Der Streit um die Wirklichkeit in der Südreichsprophetie des 8. Jh.," *WuD* 12 (1973) 9–30 (18f.).

On 2:12–13: J. M. P. Smith, "Mi 2, 12," *AJSL* 37 (1920/1921) 238f. Ch. Toll, "Die Wurzel *PRṢ* im Hebräischen," *OrSuec* 21 (1972) 73–86.

Text

2:1 Woe[a] to those who plan injustice and 'crimes'[b]
    on their beds.
  At dawn they accomplish it.
    [c]For it is in the power of their hand.[c]
  2 They covet fields and seize (them),[a]

houses, and take[b] (them).
They oppress[b] a man and his house,
[c]a person and his inheritance.
3 Therefore thus has Yahweh spoken,
    Behold, I am planning disaster [against this clan],[a]
from which you [b]cannot remove your necks,[b]
    nor can you again walk upright.
        [c][For it is an evil time].[c]
4   [On that day][a]
then one will recite a proverb among you,
    then he will wail with lamentation [it has happened][b] 'and'[c] say,
"We are completely ruined,
    [f][the land of my people 'will be measured,'[d]
    O how he takes from me (the land) as retribution[e]][f]
our fields 'are apportioned.'[g]"
5   [Therefore[a] no one will be there for you[a] who
        casts the measuring cord in a land allotment
        within the assembly of Yahweh].[a]

6 "Stop preaching!" they preach.
    "One should not preach about these things!"[a]
    "The reproach[b] does not 'apply'[c] (to us)."
7 "Is (then) the house of Jacob 'accursed'?"[a]
    "Is Yahweh impatient?"
        "Or are such deeds his?"
Is it not so that my[b] words mean well
    for him who[c] lives uprightly?
8 But 'against'[a] my people
    you 'come forth'[b] as enemies.
From 'lovers of peace'[c] you strip away the cloak,[d]
    from unsuspecting wanderers who dislike[e] strife.
9 The women[a] of my people you drive away
    from their[b] pleasant homes.
From their[b] children you take
    the 'bed-chamber'[c] forever:
10 "Up and away with you!
    For here (you have) rest no longer."[a]
On account of a 'trifle'[b]
    [c]'you take a grievous pledge'.[c]
11 If[a] a person would go about[b] with windy[c] words
    uttering deceit and lying;
"I will preach to you about wine and beer!"
    —he would then be a preacher for this people.
12   Bring home, I will surely bring home[a] all of you[b] Jacob.
        Assemble, I will surely assemble the remnant of Israel.
    I will bring them together like sheep in a 'fold',[c]
        like a herd inside of the 'pen'[d]
            [g]['and'[d] there will be a tumult[e] of[f] people].[g]
13   He who makes a breach[a] goes before[b] them; they break
        forth,[a,c]
        they pass through the gate and leave by it.
    Their king marches before them,
        Yahweh at their head.

1a Gk (ἐγένετο) incorrectly read יְהִי instead of הוֹי.
1b According to J. M. P. Smith, O. Procksch, A. Weiser, R. Vuilleumeir, A. S. van

der Woude, et al., two reasons account for why ופעלי רע is a later prose addition: (1) a second participle following תשבי would anticipate the execution of nocturnal plans which are to be carried out in the daytime (v. 1b!); (2) the phrase adds too many stresses to the *Qina* prosody (3+2) which occurs regularly in the following verses. However, Gk, Syr, Targ, Vg, support MT. There is hardly any support for the attempt to retain MT's reading by translating פעל with "to devise" (Th. Lescow, 50) or "to plot," "to contrive" (B. Renaud, 61ff.; cf. also J. T. Willis [1967]). MT ("those who plan injustice and do evil") should probably have only the vocalization corrected to read וּפֹעֲלֵי; then the word would not stand as a participle parallel to חשבי; rather, as a noun, it would be a second object of חשבי and function as a parallel to און (thus J. Halévy, *RSEHA* 12 [1904] 110). Against deleting the phrase *metrum causi* is the consideration whether five full stresses still remain (conjectures *metrum causi* are highly uncertain because we know as little about the rules of Hebrew prosody as about the syllable counts of the original oral articulation; when in doubt MT ought to be preferred).

1c Gk (διότι οὐκ ἦραν πρὸς τὸν θεὸν τὰς χεῖρας αὐτῶν) and Vg *(quoniam contra deum est manus eorum)* no longer correctly understood the Hebrew expression, although a' (οτι ισχυεν η χειρ αυτων) did; similarly, σ' and θ'. See below, p. 77.

2a Gk adds ὀρφανούς ("orphans") as an object of the verb.

2b Gk (κατεδυνάστευον καὶ διήρπαζον) nonsensically reverses the order of ונשאו ועשקו.

2c While ו preceding איש is missing in many Mss and versions (see BHS), it nevertheless fits the style of the context (cf. v. 2aβ); its omission, where it occurs in the Mss and versions, is to be accounted for by haplography.

3a על־המשפחה הזאת separates חשב from its object (רעה) (in contrast to v. 1a) and does not fit the direct address style of the following verses (K. Marti; J. M. P. Smith). Moreover, the phrase will not have been originally placed "immediately after the divine oracle formula" [v. 3aα I. Willi-Plein, 74). This rhetorical style is less appropriate to Micah, who names his addressees more precisely, than it is to the redactors, who, as the context also suggests, are from the Deuteronomistic school. These Deuteronomistic editors have used this same phrase in other, ancient prophetic sayings in order to give them a different, more general addressee to fit a later time; e.g., Amos 3:1b (see Wolff, *Joel and Amos* 174f.) and Jer. 8:3 (see Jörg Jeremias, 335f.).

3b-b J. M. P. Smith, followed recently by I. Willi-Plein and B. Renaud, has proposed that מצוארתיכם be read instead of צוארתיכם משם. Smith understands משם to be a secondary combination of שם (which he sees as dittography from תמישו [!]) with the preposition (מ(ן which, he postulates, was originally prefixed to the following word. Smith thinks that by removing משם from the text, two difficulties are eliminated: (1) שם elsewhere has only a locative meaning; (2) it is preferable for תמישו to have "yoke" instead of "neck" as its object. However, it must be stated that: (1) שם does not always have a locative meaning; as Ps. 132:17 and Hos. 13:8 indicate, the word can modify events (KBL: "temporal"). (2) The act of "removal" (מוש *hiph.*) can certainly have "neck" as its object, as is indicated by several other examples where the act of placing under the yoke has "neck" as its object (Jer. 27:8, 11, 12; Neh. 3:5). Moreover, for Micah's train of thought in what follows, it makes more sense to say that the neck is not free than that the yoke cannot be removed (cf. already K. Budde, 4).

3c-c The redactor interprets the disaster aimed at a particular group of people as an entire epoch of doom; cf. Amos 5:13b.

4a This familiar connecting formula (Hos. 2:18, 20, 23; Amos 8:9; 9:11; Isa. 7:18, 20, 21, 23) is more likely from the hand of the redactor seen in v. 3aβ,bβ than from Micah.

4b נהיה has been understood as an alternate form (as attested in Qumran) of נהי (lamentation) (cf. J. Carmignac, *VT* 5 [1955] 351); however, placed next to נהי, it is more probably incorrect dittography (B. Stade), which was then understood by the redactor as a confirmation of the loss of the land that had taken place in the meantime (היה *niph.* third person singular perfect): "it has happened" = "it has thus taken place"; cf. 1 Kings 12:24; Joel 2:2. B. Renaud (75) supposes this to be intentional dittography.

4c This interpolation caused either וַ (some MT^Mss, Syr, cf. *BHS*) or ל (Gk reads λέγων, presupposing לֵאמֹר, cf. 3:11) to be omitted.

4d Gk (κατεμετρήθη) presupposes יָמַר (מדד *niph.*) and adds ἐν σχοινίῳ ("with the measuring line") to elucidate the word in accordance with v. 5aβ. MT (מוּר *hiph.* "he changes") has a subject (or object?) missing; cf. Jer. 2:11; Lev. 27:33; ד is often misread as ר.

4e שוב inf. *pil.* "to bring back," "to pay back"; or is לשובב in apposition to לי ("to me, the rebel")? Cf. exilic texts, Jer. 3:14, 22; 31:22; 49:4; Isa. 57:17 and B. Renaud, 76. The interpretation remains uncertain.

4f–f The abrupt transition from the first person plural of the context to the first person singular indicates an interpolation (cf. Jörg Jeremias, 333ff.). It appears to be a commentary on the original bicola with two stresses שדינו—שדינו יחלק, which transfers the lamentation of the oppressors to the entire nation. In v. 4ba the object of ימיש is to be found in the שדינו of the original text.

4g Gk (διεμερίσθησαν) read *pual* יְחֻלָּק.

5a A second לכן after v. 3 is unexpected; however, it should not be deleted (thus B. Duhm) by itself. Rather, it is the introduction to the redactor's interpolation. Cf. the לכן in 1:14 which is part of the later interpretation added in 1:13b; further, cf. 5:2. Moreover, all of v. 5 may be recognized as secondary by the singular address לך, which corresponds to the first person singular of the secondary addition in v. 4aβ,ba. The לך should not be arbitrarily changed to לָכֶם (thus A. B. Ehrlich). MT is supported by Gk (σοι) and Vg *(tibi)*. The entire sentence, which is prose, departs from Micah's strict poetic style (Th. Lescow, 50; cf. already K. Marti and J. M. P. Smith).

6a After נטף *hiph.* the subject of the speech is introduced by ל; the same is true of v. 11 (the second ל) (KBL 613; otherwise, Rudolph).

6b כְּלִמּוֹת fits the singular verb better (Jer. 23:40). However, after the singular verb the plural noun in the transmitted text is also possible; cf. Ges-K §145o (Deut. 32:35; 1 Kings 11:3; Isa. 8:8).

6c MT (סוג *niph.* "to turn oneself away") is difficult to understand, given the context ("the calamity does not turn aside"?). Worth considering is Buhl's (Ges-Buhl) suggestion to read יַשִּׂיג, from נשג *hiph.* ("to reach, hit the mark").

7a The passive participle of אמר in MT is quite unusual and is not intelligible (but cf. B. Renaud, 91f.: "Can that be said?"). Since G. Richter, (*Erläuterungen zu dunklen Stellen in den Kleinen Propheten* [Gütersloh, 1914]) and Klostermann, critics have assumed that the word is a misreading of an original הֶאָרוּר (see BHS), a word which has a clear meaning in this context. A. Ehrmann thinks that here, in accordance with Job 3:3, אמר can also have the same meaning as ארור.

7b Gk (οἱ λόγοι αὐτοῦ) presupposes דבריו, which makes it fit with v. 7a ("Yahweh's spirit" and "his deeds"); but this suggests that Gk's reading is more likely secondary. MT, which is supported by Syr and Targ, presupposes that v. 7b ("my words") is a transition from the quoted words of the opponents (vv. 6–7a) to prophetic speech which follows (cf. vv. 8f.).

7c (יושר) הַ introduces an independent relative clause and functions here as a substitute for אֲשֶׁר; cf. BrSynt §150a; Ges-K §138i,k.

8a MT ("and yesterday") is supported only by σ' (Jerome has *ante unam diem*); accordingly, "my people" would be the subject. But according to the following context, עמי is the object of the verb and the injured party, whereas the subject is addressed in the second person plural. Hence the original beginning of the sentence might have been something like וְאַתֶּם עַל־עַמִּי (J. Wellhausen).

8b MT (קום *pil.,* "has stepped forth") takes עמי to be the subject, which accords with the misreading at the beginning of the sentence (see note 8a); but if אַתֶּם were the original subject, then תְּקוּמוּ should probably be read in parallel to the verb in v. 8bβ.

8c The beginning of v. 8aβ is also quite corrupt and difficult to reconstruct with certainty. MT ("opposite a cloak"?) requires conjectural emendation to make it fit the context. Parallel to the beginning of v. 8b, helpful suggestions have been offered: שְׁלֵמִים or מֵעַל־שָׂלֵם (KBL³ 527, plural; or L. C. Allen = BHK, singular); v. 8b supports the plural.

8d MT is usually translated as "splendor" (KBL³); it is often presumed that at the end of the word a ה is missing because of haplography. However, אדר perhaps also denotes an ordinary "cloak" (L. C. Allen). In the context in MT, the preceding שַׂלְמָה serves to help secure this meaning. L. C. Allen finds in the ה of the word שלמה (MT) the original article for אדר(ת) which would have become incorrectly attached to שָׂלֵם due to misunderstanding of the word.

8e שׁוּבֵי should be taken as a *qal* passive participle in a construct chain, which in this instance substitutes for the preposition מִן; cf. Joüon, *Gr* §121n.

9a Gk (ἡγούμενοι λαοῦ μου, "the leaders of my people") apparently read נְשִׂיאֵי; Gk also completely misunderstood v. 9b. Here is one of the many instances of how difficult to read, and how corrupt the transmitted Micah text was for translator and scribe; and how necessary it still is to reconstruct the text in many of the passages. Mur 88, Syr, Vg support MT. On Gk in 2:9, cf. B. Renaud, 95f.

9b The grammatically correct suffixes would be in the third feminine plural, which are presupposed in Gk, Syr, Vg, and Targ; but Micah should not be expected to exhibit precise grammatical congruence; see note 1:11h.

9c MT ("my majesty") gives the verse a theological interpretation, probably in light of Ps. 8:3, 6 (children are also crowned by God with majesty); in the context of Micah's words, the suggestion to read הֶדֶר is considerably more intelligible (J. Halévy, *RSEHA* 12 [1904] 115; *BHS:* הֲדָרוּ). Preceding this it speaks of the mothers' houses; afterwards, it speaks of rest. (Perhaps the suffix was added to the word by a misreading of the text.)

10a Verse 10a should be interpreted as words spoken by those whom Micah accuses, and thus it corresponds to the quotations in vv. 6–7a.

10b MT ("unclean") should be taken as a *qal* infinitive *(ṭom'ā)* used as a noun; however, since this would be entirely without parallel, perhaps the word should be vocalized as the usual noun טֻמְאָה (a frequent reading since H. J. Elhorst [1891]). Gk (ἕνεκεν ἀκαθαρσίας) presupposes MT but connects the phrase to the first half of the verse. The word belongs to the language of the priest: of 37 occurrences, 20 of them are found in Leviticus and Numbers, and 8 in Ezekiel; cf. F. Maas, *THAT* 1:664–667. Since the time of A. B. Ehrlich (1912) and K. Budde (12), critics prefer to read מְעַט מְאוּמָה, which fits the context quite well. The reading in MT may be explained by reference to the Deuteronomistic redaction of the text (see below, p. 76). For the Deuteronomists the word טמאה means cultic uncleanness.

10c–c A. B. Ehrlich supposes that the ancient vocalization probably read תַּחְבְּלוּ חֲבֹל, deriving the words from II חבל, which has to do with the giving of a pledge for security. In this case, the consonantal text is entirely retained, except that the ו is attached to תקבל. MT is best explained, following Jörg Jeremias (339f.), as due to Deuteronomistic redaction. It is typical for the Deuteronomists to use a singular address form (cf. v. 5, where the second person singular refers back to "my people" in v. 4aβ), which it achieves by transposing the ו from תחבלו to the following חבל and making it a copula. By vocalizing the word as a *pual,* תְּחֻבָּל, deriving from III חבל ("to be ruined," "to be destroyed"), the Deuteronomist now says, "On account of an uncleanness you will be destroyed, and the destruction is painful." This changes Micah's accusation into an announcement of disaster. Gk (διεφθάρητε φθορᾷ, "you will perish in the destruction") understands the sentence in the same way, but it already read the verb form as a plural. The change from *pual* to *piel* of III חבל must be due to a post-Deuteronomistic vocalization—

apparently based on a correct understanding of the context (vv. 8f).—which accuses the addressees of being "destroyers": "You bring destruction, and that destruction is painful." Thus we see a history of interpretation of v. 10b that developed in three phases, without a significant change in the consonantal text.

11a Mur 88 has לא instead of לו; cf. לָא in 2 Sam. 18:12! Gk (οὐδενὸς) and Vg (including לו and an אָנֹכִי, has *utniam non essem*) also read a negation. לא is probably a secondary misreading of לו rather than vice versa; thus also B. Renaud, contra M. Collin, *VT* 21 (1971) 284.

11b The original wish-particle לו is immediately followed by a participle preceding a finite verb in other passages as well (cf. Joüon, *Gr* §121j; 2 Sam. 18:12; 2 Kings 3:14; Ps. 81:14); this makes it unnecessary to vocalize the word as a perfect (J. Wellhausen, J. L. Mays).

11c Here רוח follows הלך as *accus. adverbialis*, as in Isa. 33:15 (הֹלֵךְ צְדָקוֹת); Mic. 2:3 (תלכו רומה); cf. Ges-K §118m,q; Meyer³ §106,2f.). Luther struggles with the positive meaning of רוח in Vg *(vir habens spiritum)* and at first translated it in his lectures with *ventosus = vanus, qui moveretur ad ventum;* then in 1532/1534: "were ich ein loser schwetzer" (if I were an irresponsible babbler); finally, in 1539 (retaining only the "I" from the Vg; see note 11a): "wenn ich ein irregeist wäre" (if I were a misleading spirit); WA 13,271, lines 34ff.; *DB* 4, 249, line 7 (G. Krause, *Studien zu Luthers Auslegung der Kleinen Propheten,* BHTh 33 [1962] 105.

12a אסף can be used for the "taking in" of a wife (2 Sam. 11:27), a refugee (Isa. 20:4), or a stray animal (Deut. 22:2) into one's own house.

12b Gk (σὺν πᾶσιν) read כֻּלוֹ or כֻּלָם and harmonized the word with the third person style of the context. Vg, Syr, Targ support MT.

12c MT ("Bozrah," according to Gen. 36:33; Amos 1:12, is an Edomite city; according to Jer. 48:24, a Moabite city) is not supported by any ancient translations; Gk (ἐν θλίψει) and Syr presuppose בְּצָרָה. The remainder of the verse, and also σ', θ' (εν οχυρωματι), Vg *(in ovili),* Targ (בגו חטרא) suggest the reading בַּצָּרָה (W. Nowack).

12d MT presents a quite unusual form: דבר ("word"?) with both an article and a suffix! Gk (κοίτης), σ', θ' (ερημου), Vg *(caularum),* Targ (דירא) suggest the reading הַדֹּבֶר ("the pasture"; cf. Isa. 5:17); the final letter ו (suffix) should be joined to the next word as a copula.

12e MT (הום *hiph.* third plural feminine, "to cause a tumult") is often vocalized תְּהֵמֶינָה (המה *hiph.,* "to make an uproar"; cf. Isa. 17:12) to make it intelligible. The plural form may be due to the collectives צאן and עדר; cf. Ges-K §145b,c. However, see note 12g–g!

12f מן indicates the agent, as in Gen. 9:11; 19:36; 32:13; cf. BrSynt §111b.

12g–g Probably a gloss, with the ו serving as an explicative; next to the parallel cola, the phrase appears to be superfluous. Perhaps the final two words were intended merely as a commentary upon "fold" and "pen" following Ezek. 36:38 (cf. Ezek. 34:31), which speaks of "flocks of men" (צֹאן אָדָם); then the verb form would have been derived from תִּהְיֶינָה (thus Ezek. 36:38aβ): "the waste cities will be filled with flocks of men" (RSV).

13a C. Toll (80), with considerable grounds, translates: "A powerful one . . . they are strengthened." However, in this context the emphasis on "breaking out" is decisive, for it makes possible the departure and return.

13b Gk (διὰ τῆς διακοπῆς), owing to haplography of ה, read עַל הַפֶּרֶץ ("through the breach"); Mur 88, α' (ἀνέβη), Vg *(ascendet)* lend certainty to MT.

13c B. Renaud (106) supposes that פֶּרֶץ should be read instead of פרצו (diplography of ו); Syr and Targ translate a singular form. But after the word לפניהם, the plural is more likely.

Form

The second chapter of the book of Micah is distinguished from the previous as well as from the following material by a change to new rhetorical forms, different addresses, and new themes. Chapter 2 exhibits three different sections: vv. 1–5 contain a prophetic accusation with an announcement of judgment; vv. 6–11 present Micah's disputation speech with his audience; vv. 12f., a later addition, contain two proclamations of salvation. But also within the first two rhetorical units several additions are discernible.

[2:1–5] The first saying (vv. 1–4) is a rather trim, two-part prophetic *judgment speech*. A "woe cry" commences the indictment of a number of powerful persons who have committed transgressions against others. The somewhat longer sentences in v. 1 characterize the accused parties in a personal way. Then in v. 2 the style changes; strictly parallel statements about their sinful actions exhibit the rhythm of the dirge (3+2 stresses). The first part of the unit (vv. 1–2) provides the motivation for the second part, introduced by "therefore," which has the form of a messenger speech (v. 3a). The second part presents an announcement of doom, addressed directly to the accused (second person plural in vv. 3ba, 4aa). According to what is perhaps the original text, this part contains mostly three-stress bicola. A climax is reached with the quotation of a cry of distress, formulated in brief bicola with two stresses (2+2) that are made more pointed by alliteration. Concerning the later additions to the text, see note 3a, c–c; 4a, b, f–f; 5a. The accusations and announcements of judgment are verbally connected with one another: against those who "plan evil" (v. 1a) Yahweh himself "plans evil" (v. 3a); those who rob the "fields" of others (v. 2a) will have their own fields taken from them (v. 4bβ); the "woe cry" of the prophet (v. 1a) finds its correspondence at the end of the passage in the "lament of woe" spoken by those whom the prophet accuses (v. 4aa, bβ). Given these parallels, there is no need to question the rhetorical unity of the woe cry and the messenger speech. The word הוי, which belongs originally to the death lament (1 Kings 13:30; Jer. 22:18; cf. Wolff, *Joel and Amos* 242, and see below, p. 77), and נהי, which is specifically used to lament a disaster (here in v. 4a, also in Jer. 9:18; Ezek. 32:17ff.; cf. Ch. Hardmeier 333ff.), indicate, as in 1:8–16, that Micah has an intimate knowledge of mourning rituals in the clan.

[2:6–11] A prophetic disputation follows the judgment speech against the rulers. It divides into two main parts and a brief conclusion. At the outset, the prophet quotes his opponents (vv. 6–7a); then he answers them (vv. 7b–10), closing with a sarcastic picture of the kind of prophet they would like to have (v. 11). The zeal of those who debate with Micah is indicated immediately by the short sentences that confront the prophet at the beginning of the passage. He first cites three negatively formulated sentences spoken by his opponents (אַל, לֹא, לֹא, each placed at the beginning of a sentence), with which they reject his prophecy and its content (v. 6). These are followed by three equally short rhetorical questions (v. 7a) which expect a no to Micah's prophecy of judgment. According to MT, v. 7b is already a part of Micah's response (see note 7b). Introduced by the word הֲלוֹא, it begins with a counter-question regarding the basic content of prophetic proclamation that expects an affirmative answer (v. 7b). That Micah refers to himself with the first person singular suffix attached in the word דברי—meaning his own words rejected by his opponents—is clear from the style of the prophetic disputation, as the same suffix attached to word עמי would indicate (vv. 8, 9). Cf. the corresponding reply of Amos when he is sent away from Bethel (Amos 7:13f.); further, note the frequency with which הלוא begins a reply within a disputation (Amos 5:20; 9:7a, b; Micah 3:1b, 11b; Zech. 7:7; Mal. 1:2b; cf. Wolff, *Obadiah and Jonah* 49f.). Although until now Micah quoted his opponents only in the third person before a larger audience (v. 6a), after his opening counter-question (v. 7b), he begins to address his opponents directly in vv. 8–10. With this main section of the disputation speech, the prophet expands the motivation for the accusation in vv. 1f., thus supplementing the motivation for the announcement of judgment (vv. 3f.), which for its part is apparently not taken up again in the original text (but cf. note 10c–c). The disputation is rounded off by the conclusion in v. 11. Verse 11 picks up the word נטף *hiph.,* used for prophetic speech three times in the questions at the beginning of the passage, and uses it twice in a bitterly sarcastic tone. Verse 11 again departs from the direct address style.

[2:12–13] The two sayings in v. 12 and v. 13, which are proclamations of salvation, present a completely new theme in the book of Micah. Cola with four stresses predominate, but in both sayings the length of the colon is shortened toward the end. While v. 12 presents a Yahweh speech, v. 13 is prophetic speech. In v. 12 at first Jacob is addressed in the second person singular, but then the remnant of Israel is spoken about in the third person. In v. 13, on the other hand, the object of Yahweh's saving action is spoken about only in the third person. In v. 12 the verb forms are only in the imperfect; in v. 13, instead of the imperfect, perfect and imperfect consecutive verbs are used. Distinctions between verb forms are sufficient to indicate that these two sayings did not originate from the same source: next to the promise (v. 12) stands a prophetic saying that establishes what has already taken place (v. 13). Yet, before we inquire into the origin and the relationship of these two verses to each other, we must discuss the setting of the preceding passages in chap. 2.

Setting

[2:1–11] Whom did Micah indict in vv. 1–2, and where did he utter these words? In contrast to chap. 3 (vv. 10, 12), Jerusalem is not mentioned once in chap. 2. It is probable that Micah proclaimed these words in his hometown, Moresheth, or in the surrounding region, a conclusion similar to the results of our investigation of 1:10–16 (see above, p. 54). At *Tell ej-Judeideh,* assuming that this is Micah's home (see above, pp. 35f.), a particularly large number of jar handles bearing the royal stamp have been found in widely scattered locations (see above, p. 36 and P. Welten, *Die Königs-Stempel* [1969] 81f., 170–172). If not precisely here, then surely in the immediately surrounding fortresses of Azekah, Soho, Adullam, and Mareshah (see above, pp. 36, 61ff.), we may assume that members of the royal court, officials, military commanders, and soldiers —groups who were part of a permanent occupation—would have taken charge of farms and comfortable homes. If Micah belonged to the "elders of the land" (see above, §2 of the Introduction), we would already have grounds for assuming that Micah took the side of the oppressed of his people, i.e., the people of his own region (cf. עַמִּי in vv. 8 and 9). If the oppressed people in 3:3, 10 refers to men from the Shephelah who were forced to labor in Jerusalem, then it becomes intelligible why Micah especially takes the side of the women and children in his homeland (vv. 9f.). The *addressees* of this text, therefore, are the personnel belonging to the military occupation and royal administration in the fortified cities in Moresheth's environment.

Accordingly, Micah's opponents in the disputation speech in vv. 6–11 are not to be found among circles of false prophets, but within the ranks of military and civil officials, insofar as they felt themselves addressed by his own prophetic judgment speech in vv. 1–4. They command him to be silent according to v. 6; they are "this people there," who wish for themselves a prophet who would preach about wine and beer (v. 11); they are indicted, in direct address (vv. 8–10), for hostility against the people of the land. Those persons before whom Micah holds his debate (third person plural in v. 6a!) may be the elders at the gate and thus the representatives of his suffering people. If the "powerful" people (cf. v. 1bβ) seek to silence not only Micah but a number of others (v. 6a), then included with the prophet are probably his associates from among the circle of elders as well as his disciples.

Although in the basic texts in 2:1–4 and 2:6–11 we have the same addressees and the same theme, nevertheless 2:1–11 is not a self-contained rhetorical unit. Between the judgment speech in 2:1–4 and the disputation in 2:6–11, the objections of the opponents were voiced, which Micah then (partially?) cites in 2:6–7a. Nevertheless, because the quotations in vv. 6–7a and the accusations in vv. 8–10 carefully refer back to vv. 1–4, we may assume that both passages in 2:1–11 originate from the same time and place. The present literary deposit of the basic text therefore may be properly regarded as the sketch of a scene *(Auftrittsskizze)* involving the prophet's dispute with his opponents (cf. Wolff, *Hosea*, p. xxx).

A later interpretation within vv. 3–5 and v. 10 can be distinguished from the basic text; it is made recognizable by the arrangement of the sentences in the translation and is discussed in the notes. This later interpretation expands almost exclusively the announcements of judgment, and it does so in three particular ways. (1) It expands the company of those who are involved; whereas Micah addressed a limited group of rulers, now it is the entire nation: "the fields of my people 'will be measured'" (v. 4aβ); in v. 3aβ, correspondingly, the phrase "against this family" has been inserted. The word מִשְׁפָּחָה is used by the redactors to refer to the entire community of Israel (as in Amos 3:1b), inasmuch as they stem from a shared history of salvation (cf. Jer. 8:3; 33:24). (2) The new interpretation makes clear that there is a temporal distance between Micah's prophecy and its fulfillment, which the redactors see fulfilled in their own age: "on that day" (v. 4aα); an entire epoch is affected: "for this is an evil time" (v. 3bβ); the beginning of a momentous time of mourning is confirmed: "it has happened" (v. 4aα). (3) The connections of the great judgment with salvation history are reflected: "how (the land) is taken from me as retribution" (or: "from me, a rebel"; see note 4e) (v. 4b); in the assembly of Yahweh a great division of the land by lot will no longer take place (v. 5); here it is probable that important catchwords from the

original Micah text are picked up by the redactors ("portion of land"—
חלק—in v. 4aβ taken from שדינו יחלק in v. 4bβ; "remove"—מוש *hiph.*—in
v. 4bα taken from 3bα). But on the whole, the later additions now speak
not of the rulers and their landed property, as did Micah, but of the
nation and its land in the "assembly of Yahweh" (קהל יהוה is not found
once in the rest of the prophetic corpus). Micah's quotation of the rulers'
words about driving out women and children (v. 10a) is understood by
the redactors as a prophecy announcing the exile; they add a new motivation for the exile by the word "uncleanness" (see note 10b, c–c). Thus
in the Babylonian era the Deuteronomistic school of tradents also actual-
ized this prophecy of Micah in order better to understand the catastrophe
of 587 (cf. Jörg Jeremias, *ZAW* 83 [1971] 330–354).

[**2:12–13**] These prophecies of salvation, which were appended to our
passage, stem from a still later period and a different circle of editors than
those who inserted a new interpretation into vv. 1–4 and vv. 6–11. To be
sure, two reasons have been offered for dating vv. 12–13 at the time of
Micah: (1) they are words of the false prophets who seek to contradict
Micah, and (2) they are Micah's own prophecy from his later period,
around 701. Scholars from time to time, from Ibn Ezra in the Middle
Ages down to A. S. van der Woude, have seen these verses in connection
with the false prophets. However, in the text there is no appropriate introduction, as in 3:11 or even in 2:6, nor do we find a clear contradiction
of Micah's prophecy, as in 2:6–7a. To interpret vv. 12–13 in terms of
Micah's late period (around 701) is possible only by very carefully
weighing the connections with other prophecies from Micah, such as the
connection of "gate" in v. 13 with gate of Jerusalem in 1:9, 12 (thus L. C.
Allen, 301). The decisive question here is whether the language of both
passages indicates a relationship closer to Micah and his contemporaries,
or instead to the prophecy of the exilic or postexilic time. Since the work
of B. Stade (*ZAW* 1 [1881]) this latter alternative has been repeatedly
accepted. Reminiscences of Deutero-Isaiah's prophecy and of the (secondary?) material in Jeremiah and Ezekiel are on the whole quite conclusive; thus, it is most likely that such hopes of salvation from the early
Persian period were added to the book of Micah by a late redaction. I
mention here only the most striking connections: the image of Yahweh in
v. 12 as a shepherd who gathers his sheep should be compared with Isa.
40:11; Jer. 23:3; 31:7, 10; Ezek. 34:13ff.; Yahweh in v. 13 as the king who
goes before his people should be compared with Isa. 43:15; 52:7, 12.

How v. 13 relates to v. 12 remains a difficult question. While v. 12
promises that Yahweh the shepherd will gather the scattered remnant of
Israel, v. 13 affirms that Yahweh the king will break out of a fortified city
and lead his people forth. The two verses complement each other in a
manner similar to Isa. 40:11 and Isa. 52:11f. Perhaps v. 13 was necessary
because "fold" and "pen" in v. 12 could be understood as places of
imprisonment, especially because of the incorrect reading of "Bozrah"
(see note 12c). However, that both prophetic sayings stand juxtaposed
could also reflect a simple anthological style of redaction from the early
postexilic period (B. Renaud, 114).

In any case, a prophecy giving assurance of salvation, current among the remnant of Israel in the early Persian period after the great judgment upon Israel, has been added to supplement Micah's proclamation. Both verses are distinguished from the supplements to chap. 3 found in chap. 4 in that they make absolutely no mention of Jerusalem and Zion. Perhaps these redactors operated on the premise that Micah's prophecy, particularly in chaps. 1–2, was compiled in his Judean home in the Shephelah.

Commentary

[2:1] The prophet introduces a new saying with the cry of "woe" (cf. Wolff, *Joel and Amos* 242ff.). The "emotional-affective content" of the interjection הוֹי derives from the dirge, or death lament (1 Kings 13:30; Jer. 22:18; 34:5; cf. Ch. Hardmeier, *Texttheorie* 174ff.; 233ff.; 302ff.). For whom such a lament is expressed, or whoever is accused by means of the cry of woe, is proleptically drawn into the domain of the sepulchre. What follows the cry of woe describes how its addressees run headlong into disaster (cf. Prov. 5:5; 11:19). With his cry of woe, Micah anticipates the threat of disaster which, according to vv. 3f., he is commissioned to proclaim. Those who must bear this judgment are identified by their deeds, not by name or office. This makes it easier for later generations to recognize themselves in the prophet's pronouncements. The route to death begins with "planning." Those who in their thoughts calculate how to bring disaster upon others through "injustice" (on אָוֶן, see R. Knierim, *THAT* 1:81–84) submit themselves to the power of destruction. They do "what Yahweh hates" (Prov. 6:18). By conceiving of harm, they are led to plan concrete "deeds" (see note 1b); instead of spurning "evil" (Ps. 36:5b [4b]), they commit crime. These plans are conceived "in their beds." The plural form with -ōt refers to individual beds (unlike the ending -īm, which more likely denotes the whole; see D. Michel, *Grundlegung einer hebräischen Syntax* [1977] 37, 63). Micah focuses more sharply than Isaiah (in the closely related saying in Isa. 5:8–10) on particular individuals, their evil spiritual origins, and the birth-place of their exploitative undertakings. As they lie on their beds, their plans flourish. That their evil thoughts prevent them from sleeping is an image of transgressors found in wisdom material (Ps. 36:5a[4a]). They do not dream; they calculate. These greedy people are not sluggards; on the contrary, they are restless. As in Amos, where they tensely await the end of the sabbath, so in Micah, they wait for "morning light," when they can "accomplish it," namely, the evil they have been conceiving. Their success is guaranteed because "it is within the power of their hand." This fixed expression occurs in four other instances in the Old Testament: Gen. 31:29; Deut. 28:32; Prov. 3:27; Neh. 5:5. In v. 1 אֵל does not mean "God," as Gk and Vg incorrectly thought; rather it means "power," "might" (IV אֵל); cf. W. Rudolph, *Esra-Nehemia*, HAT 1/20, 128; otherwise, F. M. Cross, *ThWAT* 1:279. The words of this verse characterize Micah's audience not only according to their deeds, but also according to their potential as men of authority. It is therefore clear that Micah does not speak in an unfocused manner to the people; rather, he makes an accusation against a particular elite. Their power is the basis (כִּי, v. 1bβ!) for the laying of their plans; it also provides the possibility for the execution of these plans.

Power corrupts when it does not follow wisdom's admonition: "Do not withhold good from those to whom it is due, when it is in your power to do it" (Prov. 3:27).

[2:2] The brief, percusive sentences that follow in v. 2 at first indicate how quickly the covetousness of the powerful elite leads to robbery and oppression. These sentences give concrete expression to what v. 1b calls "injustice and crimes." By means of ancient Israel's fundamental laws, Micah exposes the transgressions of the powerful. With the word "covet" he places their nightly provocations within the purview of divine law. "Do not covet!"—that is the only commandment which appears twice in the Decalogue (Exod. 20:17a,b; cf. further Exod. 34:24; Josh. 7:21; also Prov. 12:12a). Covetousness is the impulse that drives Micah's opponents to commit the resultant criminal acts. The words for "robbing" and "oppressing" occur together also in the catalogue of prohibitions in Lev. 19:13 (further, cf. Ps. 62:11 [10]; Ezek. 18:18; 22:29). It is forbidden to use force against property (robbery) as well as against persons (oppression) (on Amos 3:10, cf. Wolff, *Joel and Amos* 193f.). Those indicted by the prophet "rob *fields* and take *houses*." This might refer to officials and soldiers from royal troops who lived in the fortified cities during times of military quiet (see above, pp. 74f.); it may also include certain greedy landed property owners in the Shephelah, of whom Isaiah also spoke (5:8ff.). Whereas the word "houses," which occurs together with "fields" in v. 2a, certainly refers to buildings (cf. also v. 9a), the singular *"house"* in v. 2b must surely also mean the family. In his commentary in v. 9 (see above, p. 73) Micah expressly refers to women and children as well. Proverbial wisdom has also issued warnings against violent oppression of other persons (Prov. 14:31; 22:16; 28:3). However, there and also in Amos (Amos 4:1; 5:11ff.; cf. Isa. 3:14f.), those in need of protection are called poor and needy. Remarkably, Micah never speaks of those who have been harmfully treated as "poor" and "needy." He has in mind the *"man"* capable of military service (גבר), the *"citizen"* who possesses full legal rights and obligations (איש), whose rights and freedoms have been violated. To this status especially belongs landed property as "hereditary possession" (נחלה). Even in the ancient Egyptian instructions from Merikare we read (line 47): "Do not drive out a man from the land of his fathers" (*ANET* 415; cf. *Ergänzungsheft*, ATD 1 [1975] 71). According to Israelite laws governing land tenure, Yahweh, the owner of the land (Lev. 25:23; Num. 36:2,7), invests his people with land as a pledge of their liberation. The property inherited from the fathers is therefore unsalable; nor can it be exchanged for a different piece of property (1 Kings 21:3). Micah 2:1–3 might be a commentary on the episode about Naboth's vineyard in 1 Kings 21 (W. Brueggemann, *The Land* [1977] 97). Micah sees that the destruction of the ancient Israelite rural society by a few powerful persons and their unjust actions is in full swing (cf. Donner, *OrAnt* 2 [1963] 229–245; H. J. Boecker, *Recht und Gesetz im Alten Testament* [1976] 77–81).

[2:3] A concise "Therefore thus has Yahweh spoken" abruptly changes the scene. The word "therefore" (v. 3a), referring back to the preceding verses, makes the cry of woe with its indictment of wrong-doing (vv. 1–2) into the motivation for the punishment immediately to be proclaimed by the prophet. Since Yahweh has already commissioned the prophet to speak in his behalf, the proclamation of doom is presented in the form of a messenger speech. The messenger speech exhibits both of its typical elements: the messenger formula (v. 3aα) and Yahweh's first person messenger speech itself (v. 3aβ) (cf. Wolff, *Joel and Amos* 135ff.). The extent and nature of the punishment are determined precisely by the extent and nature of the guilt (see above, p. 73). The word הנני followed by a participle sounds the alarm to give utmost attention to Yahweh's action; in 118 out of 125 instances this call for attention is spoken by Yahweh (P. Humbert; cf. Wolff, *Joel and Amos* 58, 142). Yahweh's already-existent plan opposes the plan of the powerful. Their evil action (פעלי רע, v. 1) is met by the doom (רעה, v. 3) sent by Yahweh. A synthetic manner of thinking is represented in the word (רע(ה: it means "evil" in the sense of active wickedness, and "disaster" in the sense of suffering brought on by wicked actions—two sides of the same coin. The common element is doing *harm:* those who do harm will experience harm (see Wolff, *Obadiah and Jonah* 153, 165). Hence, they experience the "fruit of their devices" (Jer. 6:19; cf. 11:17 and Ps. 28:3f.).

If the first sentence of the messenger speech attests to Yahweh's own intervention (v. 3aβ), then what follows elucidates the consequences, first for the powerful elite personally (v. 3b), then as regards their property (v. 4). The violence they use against person and property they themselves will experience. In v. 3b the messenger speech shifts to the style of direct address (second person) to those under indictment. Behind the brief phrase ("you cannot remove your necks nor walk about upright") clearly stands the image of the yoke. This is not a reference to a general politico-military subjugation (Isa. 10:27; Jer. 27:8; 28:14; 30:8; Ezek. 24:27; Deut. 28:48); rather, it strongly emphasizes the personal effect upon the powerful individual who, without offering resistance, will be overpowered by an alien force. (Of note is the simple, grammatical observation that here we find the only instance of the plural of "neck" formed by the ending *-ōt,* which refers to the many individual "necks"; by contrast, there are ten instances in which the plural has the ending *-īm,* according to D. Michel, *Grundlegung* 37, 42, 62f.) Whoever enslaves a person will himself become a slave; the oppressor will be placed under the yoke. Perhaps Micah actually saw the troops stationed in the fortified cities departing for the prisons of Assyria.

Micah's eight-century prophecy against the powerful circles living in his region was heard and applied in a new way by later interpreters who lived during the Babylonian era. They picked up the word רעה and used it a second time with emphasis: "This is an evil (רעה) time!" not only for a few people in power, but for all (for "this clan," v. 3a) (see above, p. 75).

[2:4] With the connecting formula "on that day," the redactor also applies to his own time this lament from Micah's prophecy—a lament first placed by Micah only in the mouth of his powerful contemporaries (see note 4a). Micah proclaims to them that "one" (ישא, with an indefinite subject, according to Ges-K §144d) will recite a proverb concerning them. משל has a broad scale of meanings, from didactic proverb to taunt song to lament over disaster. The word is more precisely defined in what follows, as is often the case (Hab. 2:6; cf. Isa. 14:4). Here it stands parallel with נהי, the lament over disaster (cf. Amos 5:16; Jer. 9:9, 17–19; 31:15; Ezek. 32:17ff.). In contrast to the dirge, with its 3+2 rhythm (see v. 2), the lament over disaster (נהי) apparently prefers the two-stress bicola (2+2) (Jer. 9:18 and probably also Ezek. 32:17ff.; on Ezek., see W. Zimmerli, *Ezekiel* 2 [Hermeneia], 170). The ancient, original text in Micah probably read (see notes 4f–f, g):

šādōd nᵉšaddŭnu—šādēnū jᵉhullāḳ.

The alliteration of the *s* and *d* consonants as well as the assonance of the predominantly dark *a* and *u* sounds should be noted. The content is unambiguous. שדד (on נדנו, first plural *niph.* perfect, cf. Bauer-Leander, 439, §58p′) describes not merely a general destruction but a specific plundering and devastation of the land (Amos 3:10; Hos. 7:13; 9:6; 10:2; Obad. 5; Joel 1:15) and the destruction of fortifications (Hos. 10:14). The fields taken by the powerful (v. 2) will be divided up anew, like the land of Amaziah the priest after his deportation, according to Amos (7:17).

The later interpretation of this verse inserts a bicolon with three stresses into the original two-stress bicolon. This later expansion presents a lament over the entire nation and its loss of land during the Babylonian exile.

[2:5] This verse (see note 5a) supplements the interpolation in v. 4 in a verbose prose style with terminology drawn from traditions rooted in the sacral land allotment. The introductory "therefore" may have been intended to connect with a previous word of indictment (cf. v. 3 and 1:14). Among the later additions to vv. 1–4, the word "therefore" could possibly provide a link to the (uncertain) self-lament over apostasy in v. 4bβ (see note 4e). According to its content, v. 5 supplements the previous prophecy of disaster: whoever has been dispossessed of his land can no longer expect his lost property to be returned in a future sacral distribution of the land. The verse laboriously incorporates vocabulary drawn from traditions of the first allotment of the land in Joshua 14f. and 18–20; cf. esp. Josh. 17:14; 18:8, 10; Num. 26:52–56. The wording of the phrase "casting the measuring line in the allotment of land" appears to be particularly artificial; it has been proposed that either חבל or גורל be deleted (A. Alt, 337). However, v. 5 defies all attempts to emend by conjecture; indeed, because of the complicated difficulties it poses, the verse is hardly to be attributed to Micah. We ought to regard it as the redactor's attempt to make Micah's announcement of judgment understandable for the generation of the exile with the help of the ancient tradition of land allotment.

[2:6] With v. 6 a disputation speech commences in which Micah responds to the provocative objections from the audience to whom he addressed his words in 2:1–4 (see above, pp. 73f.). He introduces their words without any closer description of their person: יטיפון, "they preach." Who are "they"? Scholars have often thought this refers to the false prophets who opposed Micah. However, all evidence suggests that "they" refers to the authorities, indicted in vv. 1–2 and threatened with disaster in vv. 3–4, who oppress the small landholders. For (1) only when this is the case would any description of these persons in v. 6 be superfluous; (2) the additional accusation in vv. 8–10 elucidates only the accusation in v. 2; and (3) the strict demand for silence in v. 6 is most likely to be expected from those in a position of "authority" (v. 1bβ).

But why does Micah characterize their manner of speech with the word נטף *hiph.,* a word which they themselves used to describe Micah's prophetic speech? This usage is made intelligible by the fact that נטף *hiph.* introduces a derisive overtone when used for prophetic speech. The word נטף, most often occurring in *qal,* means "to drip," "to trickle," "to flow" (Judg. 5:4; Joel 4:18; Amos 9:13). In the prophetic writings of the eighth century, the only other occurrence of נטף *hiph.* is in Amos 7:16; indeed, there the usage is the same as in v. 6: prophetic speech is forbidden. In this setting such a contemptible overtone is understandable. Here the word refers to a passionate, zealous manner of speech in which spittle sprays forth; colloquially, we would say "slobbering" or even "babbling." If we translate the word with "to preach," then a pejorative tone of over-zealous volubility is to be perceived. Later in Ezekiel the word has lost its disparaging meaning (cf. Ezek. 21:2–7). (Gk still understands the word to mean "to drip, trickle," when it [incorrectly] thinks of crying tears: μὴ κλαίετε δάκρυσι, μηδὲ δακρυέτωσαν). Therefore when Micah says, "they babble nonsense," he responds to them with the same derisive word his audience used to forbid his prophesying.

Coordinate with the general prohibition to speak (v. 6a), introduced by אַל, stands a categorical prohibition, introduced by לֹא, forbidding Micah to speak on a specific theme. The word לאלה refers to the content of his prophecy (see note 6a; cf. the corresponding meaning of ל in Isa. 29:16; Jer. 28:8, 9). That a demonstrative pronoun can refer back to the substance of the prophet's speech is again confirmed by the close connection of the disputation speech with the judgment speech within the same scene.

The next four brief sentences quoted by Micah are hurled in the prophet's face by his opponents in an attempt to justify their demand that he keep silent. First, it is apodictically stated that his words (as accusation) do "not apply" to the audience; or perhaps that his words (as announcement of disaster) "will not be fulfilled" (see note 6c). Micah's prophecy is summarily degraded and dismissed as "insult."

[2:7] In v. 7a the content of Micah's prophecy is placed in question three more times. The first question (assuming the conjecture in note 7a is correct), utilizing the word "curse" from the cultic sphere, responds to the cry of woe (v. 1), familiar to Micah from the dirges sung within the clans. But Israel knows itself especially as the "house of Jacob" which has been placed under an incontestable blessing (e.g., Gen. 49; cf. Exod. 19:3ff.; Isa. 8:17). The second question refers to the common confession that Yahweh is patient and long-suffering (Exod. 34:6; Pss. 86:15; 103:8; 145:8; Neh. 9:17; Joel 2:13, and see Wolff, *Jonah and Obadiah* 167). According to his audience, Micah presupposes on the contrary that "Yahweh's breath has become short" (קצר רוח), i.e., Yahweh has been provoked to wrath and impatience (on this terminology, see Wolff, *Anthropology of the OT* 37). And also in the third question the authorities oppose Micah with the ancient traditions of salvation and the hymnbook, when they compare Micah's proclamation of Yahweh's impending actions with the tradition of Yahweh's saving deeds (Pss. 77:12 [11]; 78:7).

Micah opposes such unflinching certainty of salvation in v. 7b (see note 7b and above, pp. 73f.). In response to the quotation of six brief sentences of protest, Micah first of all poses a counter-question, formulated as a long, markedly serene sentence that takes up the controversial topic of salvation theology. He challenges his audience to consider whether the intention of his words is not goodness and blessing as well. The question, however, is, for whom? Micah takes the side of the person who "lives uprightly." This refers of course to those who are ill-treated by the authorities who embrace a salvation theology. The authorities hold discussions about God, while God is concerned with the disaster they cause the farmers, who justly wish to preserve their own freedom and the land entrusted to them.

[2:8] Thus in v. 8 Micah proceeds to a renewal of his accusation, now formulated in direct address, and provides more precise evidence for what was said in a brief and lively manner in v. 2. The direct address in the second person plural, made uncertain in v. 8aα by the corrupt text (see notes 8a,b) is not open to question in vv. 8aβ, 9a,b. And thus this sudden change from v. 7b to v. 8aα, marked by a forceful "But you," is made textually indisputable. In the previous judgment speech the announcement of disaster (vv. 3f.) was formulated in direct address; now also the renewed indictments. The first is of fundamental significance. It indicates that (1) the prophet's attacks against the authorities are mainly in the interest of his people; and that (2) those he accuses are found to be enemies of his people.

Concerning (1): The suffix in עמי refers not to Yahweh but to the *prophet,* who speaks in the first person. For in a disputation speech (vv. 6–11) the prophet speaks, not Yahweh; the prophet compares his own words ("my words" in v. 7b) with the words of his opponents (vv. 6, 7a). Moreover, Micah seldom has Yahweh speak in the first person (1:6; 2:3, on 3:5 see below, pp. 94, 110). Also in 3:3, the prophet clearly refers to his people with the word עמי, for in v. 4 Yahweh is spoken of in the third person. Moreover, in Mic. עם does not refer to the nation of Judah, but to the more limited circle of his fellow countrymen in his home region of the Shephelah (cf. עמי for "the people of Bethlehem" [Ruth 4:9] or for the "people gathered round an individual" [1 Kings 19:21; 2 Kings 4:41; Gen. 32:8, and KBL 711]). As an elder of the clan, Micah considers himself responsible for them.

Concerning (2): "As an enemy" they arise against his people. This simile is particularly intelligible if those accused by these words belong to the royal Judean troops occupying the fortified cities around Moresheth. Their attacks are like those of a foreign, indeed, hostile military power. In Israel, a sense of community is demonstrated neither by nationality nor by mouthing the creed (v. 7a), but by attitudes and actions of love and kindness. "Not all who are descended from Israel belong to Israel; and not all [who] are children of Abraham . . . are [therefore] the children of God" (Rom. 9:6–8). The Judean militia—insofar as Micah speaks to them—conduct themselves, however, as enemies in the land.

After this general reproach, Micah corroborates his charge of hostility and also his indictment in v. 2 by setting forth specific instances of his opponents' conduct.

Instance 1 (v. 8aβ,b): Those who walk about peaceably are robbed of their clothes. In a verse containing several textual uncertainties (see notes c, d, e) the verb תפשׁטון is not to be contested. It means "to undress," "to unclothe"; in 3:3 it recurs in a deft metaphor for "to skin" ("they strip away their flesh"). The transmitted text in v. 8 further indicates that the objects of the verb are pieces of clothing belonging, in fact, to citizens who, going on their way peacefully (cf. Judg. 9:25), have nothing to do with "war." (Here is another word that suggests that Micah disputes with military personnel.) This part of the accusation probably gives evidence of personal assault connected with robbery (v. 2); perhaps the prophet refers to attacks from plundering troops (cf. Exod. 22:5f.).

[2:9] Instance 2 (v. 9a): Women are driven from their homes. No compelling reason suggests that they are widows; nor does v. 9b speak of orphans; (cf. Exod. 22:21). Generally, the word אשׁה, unlike אלמנה, refers to a married woman (1 Sam. 30:5 and 1 Kings 7:14 are exceptions). These could be wives of the men taken to Jerusalem who are required to do forced labor there (cf. 3:2f., 10). Micah again emphasizes that these are "women of *my people*"; as an elder, he is particularly concerned about their well-being. They are *"driven out."* The word גרשׁ is a further allusion to actions of a foreign conqueror (Num. 22:6, 11; Exod. 23:28ff.; Pss. 80:9; 78:55). This is the way the Judean occupational forces treat their own people. These people in power chase the women *"from their pleasant dwellings."* (On תענג see above, p. 64 on 1:16). When Micah speaks of "comfortable homes," his tender sympathies are evident. He denounces not only such public injustices, but also the heartlessness of Judean against Judean, of the powerful against the powerless. Jesus warns against "those who devour the widows' houses" (Mark 12:40).

Instance 3 (v. 9b): Even the children fall prey to their covetousness. עללים more likely refers to small children (II עול "to nurse") than to more grownup children (בחורים Jer. 6:11; 9:20; Lam. 4:4). What is taken from them? MT contains the word הדר. Does this recall Ps. 8 (see note 9c), or does it refer to the valuable land of one's inheritance (cf. Jer. 3:19)? In connection with small children, it more likely means "bedchamber" (חֶדֶר). Moreover, this reading is suggested both by the reference back to "their" mothers and their houses (v. 9a), and by the mention of "rest" in the immediately following verse (v. 10a). What is textually certain, at least according to MT, is that something of importance is "taken away *forever.*" Here as well, the prophet's sympathy is evident.

[2:10a] Micah emphasizes the brutality of those whom he accuses by quoting in v. 10a their own words that demand expulsion. The sentence should probably be understood as words directly addressed to the women and children by those who would dispossess them. The alternative—that the prophet speaks to the dispossessors who are to be driven from the land—should not even be considered, because v. 10b itself is also part of the accusation, and because there is no recognizable transition to an announcement of judgment. Moreover, the grammar of the demonstrative particle זאת, as well as the content, "the rest," is to be connected with words of the authorities and their reference to houses and bedrooms in v. 9. But Micah has them speak of מנוחה, a word which denotes the "rest" connected with Yahweh's salvation; "rest," together with "property" (נחלה, cf. v. 2) constitute the guarantee of Yahweh's gifts of salvation (see Deut. 12:9; 1 Kings 8:56; Ps. 95:11). Whoever pretends to be certain of his own salvation (v. 7a) destroys Yahweh's saving gifts among his people.

[2:10b] Instance 4 (v. 10b): They exceed the legal bounds of holding mortgaged property (see note 10c–c). It is probable that the original text stated that even for a *trifle* they placed great financial burdens on the people (see note 10b: מְעַט מְאוּמָה; cf. Amos 2:6bβ: for the debt of a pair of sandals a person was sold into slavery). The transmitted text clearly indicates that those who were thus mistreated experienced aggravation and pain (נמרץ). Thus Micah provides four examples (vv. 8–10) of how those in power (v. 8a) are hostile to his people and break the law (v. 2).

The transmitters and editors of the text in the Babylonian era (see above, p. 75) understood the command from those who would dispossess the women and children (v. 10a) as the prophet's banishment of the people into exile and, accordingly, also interpreted v. 10b as a prophecy of disaster. The word "trifle" was misread as the word "unclean" and probably understood with reference to the idol worship denounced in Jer. 19:13; Ezek. 22:15; 24:13; 36:25, 29; 39:24. The understanding that the text speaks of idol worship led to the reading "painful destruction" (see note 10c–c) as a reference to expulsion from the land.

[2:11] Having shown by concrete example the distress of his fellow countrymen and the guilt of the authorities, Micah then concludes with a bitterly humorous picture that contrasts with the prophetic office to which he knows himself to be called. Instead of prophesying about real transgressions and themes of substance, these other prophets, whom Micah's opponents find so desirable, go about doing and saying nothing. Here רוח means "windy," in the sense of unstable, empty; windy words are empty words (Job 6:26; 16:3). Windy prophets are prophets who say nothing (Jer. 5:13; Isa. 41:29; cf. Hos. 9:7). They camouflage and twist the facts with lies. These prophets like to take up the favorite theme of the offices and soldiers: alcoholic drinks for every taste. שכר ("beer") forms a wordplay on שקר ("lies"). (On the different kinds of beer in OT times, cf. D. Kellermann, *BRL*² 48f. On the critique of alcohol consumption, cf. in the prophets, Amos 4:1; 6:4–6; Isa. 5:11f., 22; 28:7f.; 56:12; in proverbial wisdom, Prov. 20:1; 21:17; 23:20f., 29ff.; 31:4–7). For Micah's opponents, beer and wine, as gifts of the land, may also count as the pledge of salvation and security; cf. Lev. 26:5; Deut. 28:4, 11; Amos 9:13; Joel 2:24; 4:18. נטף *hiph.* is grammatically construed with a double ל, with the first ל designating the addressee and the second the subject matter of the speech (cf. v. 6aα). That the addressee appears in the singular form (לך) does not necessarily suggest that this is a private oracle; rather, it could also correspond to the phrase "this people" in v. 11b. Once again it becomes clear that Micah's opponents in this dialogue are not the false prophets themselves, but an audience which finds this kind of prophet desirable.

Now in v. 11 Micah uses the contemptible word נטף *hiph.*—a word that the authorities had first applied to Micah's prophecy and which he threw back at them (v. 6a)—for the "babbling" of the false prophets.

[2:12] Here a new voice is heard. Long cola, serene in nature, each containing four stresses, impress upon the audience powerful words of comfort. In v. 12aα a promise is uttered in the form of a divine first person speech, emphatically stated by means of absolute infinitives. Such a manner of giving assurance is hardly to be found in Ezekiel, Jeremiah, and Deutero-Isaiah, nor even in the similar prophecy in Mic. 4:6. Here אסף has a comforting tone (see note 12a). Its antonym is in this case עזב "to forsake" (Isa. 10:14). In words which promise a gathering together of God's scattered people, one senses a tone which expresses God's affectionate (re)assembling of his people. Only with קבץ *piel* does the author use a word which, occurring frequently in the promises of the sixth century, denotes the bringing together and reuniting of Israelites scattered among the nations (cf. Isa. 40:11; 43:5; Jer. 23:3; 31:10; Ezek. 34:13; Zeph. 3:19). None will be left out ("Jacob, all of you!"). Jacob, who is culpable, surely remains the bearer of the promise. In this context, the "remnant of Israel" means the diaspora among the nations, as in Jer. 23:3; likewise, the "remnant of Jacob" in Mic. 5:6f.

So that faith might be awakened, v. 12aβ, with a different vocabulary, presents a third promise to unite Israel. Again, we have a Yahweh speech presented in the first person, without directly mentioning his name or his office as shepherd. Israel, however, is portrayed as a flock, again an allusion to the exilic tradition of promise (cf. Isa. 40:11; Jer. 23:3; 31:10; Ezek. 34:12). The goal of bringing Israel together remains obscure. The imagery of the "fold" and of the "pen" (see notes 12c, d) suggests not Jerusalem, but rather a foreign city (thus MT: Bozrah), perhaps Babel (Isa. 48:20; 52:11f.), whence all the exiles are to return to their own country. But there is no mention of this yet in v. 12 (see below on v. 13). V. 12 emphasizes only the promise of a grand bringing together of all who have been dispersed. The later interpolation in v. 12bβ, no longer clearly intelligible, indicates that this will be a huge assembly of people (see notes 12e, g–g).

[2:13] In different words and with a different style (see above, p. 74), v. 13 contains something more of the unanswered question about the destination of those in the diaspora who are to be reassembled. It is as though v. 13 comments upon Yahweh's first person speech (v. 12) (Yahweh is presented in the third person). The subject of the commentary appears to be the "fold" and the "pen." Nor can this commentary refer to Jerusalem, for upon departing from the city, one goes down, not up (עלה), from Jerusalem. Moreover, the salvation which is hoped for would not be a departure from, but a return to, Jerusalem (1 Kings 12:27f.; Isa. 40:9f.; 52:7–12; Jer. 31:6; Ps. 122:4). In light of Deutero-Isaiah, the commentator could have had in mind the exodus from Babylon to Jerusalem. It is a novum for Yahweh to be called "One who makes a breach"; the word is a singular participle. The verb פרץ has Yahweh as its subject in other texts, where it is used for breaking through the wall of a fortified city (Ps. 80:13 [12]; 89:41 [40], or for breaking through the enemy's lines (with the

simile of a bursting dam in 2 Sam. 5:20; cf. 1 Chron. 15:13; 2 Sam. 6:8).
The following mention of a (city) gate suggests the image of breaking out
of a fortified city; the thought is not of a city besieged by the enemy, but of
a captive city (Isa. 48:20; 49:9). Yahweh is the one who breaks forth,
bursting first through the barricades. The multitude follows him, passing
(עבר) through the gate, finally making an exodus (יצא) into freedom. On
the catchword (יצא) for the exodus from Babylon that is used here, cf.
again Deutero-Isaiah (48:20; 49:9; 52:11, 12; 55:12). We also find an
allusion to Deutero-Isaiah's message when v. 13 calls Yahweh *king*
(41:21; 43:15; 44:6; 52:7), as well as in the twofold emphasis (v. 12aα,bβ)
that Yahweh "goes before them" (Isa. 52:12; cf. 45:1f.). The concluding
phrase "Yahweh at their head" picks up again the twofold occurrence of
לפניהם. Thus the main theme of the passage is clear. It is Yahweh who,
going before his people, prepares a way for their escape from prison and
their exodus into freedom (cf. Exod. 13:21f.; Ps. 68:8[7]). It remains only
for Israel to follow.

The background of the exilic situation is what connects vv. 12 and
13. Both verses presuppose Micah's message of judgment as it has been
handed down in chaps. 1 and 2. 1:16 is a direct threat of exile (presupposed indirectly in most of 1:10–15; see above, p. 76); the exile is
presupposed in 2:3–5, 10, at least in its edited and reworked form.

Purpose and Thrust

Micah is the most eloquent in these two passages (2:1–4; 6–11) when he
speaks of wrongdoing. Standing at the center is his accusation that the
weighty commandments against covetousness, stealing, and oppression
(v. 2) have been broken. But it is primarily the officials, officers, and
soldiers in the fortified cities near Moresheth who have injured the small
landowners of the Shephelah and their inherited property (see above, pp.
44f.). Compared to a similar woe-saying in Isaiah (5:8), what is distinct in
Micah's accusation is that, on the one hand, he describes the personal
history of those who have been engaged in violence (v. 1a); on the other,
he evokes sympathy for the oppressed, providing even the details of their
misery (vv. 8–10).

Micah exposes the roots of their transgression in the thoughts,
desires, and plans that consume these individuals as they lie sleeplessly in
their beds. Thus in v. 1 Micah makes clear how their inner thoughts are
caught up in "covetousness" (v. 2; cf. Exod. 20:17). Greed becomes
dangerous when it is linked with power, i.e., with the potential for its
realization (v. 1bβ). Power augments temptation and even gives birth to
it. "Everyone to whom much has been given, of him much will be
required" (Luke 12:48); also required is great resistance against entice-
ments. Just as Micah discloses the inner path to oppression of persons
and property, so he offers directions for sensitizing the conscience. He
does not find the primary harmfulness and danger in the economic
orders, but in the secret plans which grow out of uncontrolled avarice and
desire. Covetousness is idolatry (Col. 3:5). Rejecting the conscience leads
to the shipwreck of faith (1 Tim. 1:19).

Micah, however, inquires not only into the personal antecedents
of their acts of violence, but into the concrete results for the injured

parties as well. He gives sympathetic expression to the bitter distress resulting from the assault, expropriation, expulsion, and foreclosure that his peaceloving fellow countrymen must endure. Security (v. 8b) and comfort (v. 9a) disappear; instead of rest (v. 10a), there is pain (v. 10b). Thus Micah illustrates the end result of their guilt.

At the same time, Micah is relatively brief in his portrayal of the *punishment* which threatens this misuse of power (vv. 3–4). Nevertheless, he not only makes a connection—as in the traditional formulation of the *jus talionis*—between the extent and type of transgression and its correspondingly apportioned punishment (robbed fields will again be robbed, see p. 73). He also mentions the historical antecedents of the punishment in the plans of God (v. 3a), as well as the personal effects of this punishment: he describes the suffering of those under the yoke of punishment (v. 3b) and he gives voice to their lament over the loss of their land (v. 4). Again, Micah is sensitive to the personal fate of people who leave the paths of an upright life, whose dancing is turned into lamentation. Yet, the punishment of the responsible authorities entails at the same time the overthrow of the economic orders. Just as divine plans advance against human plans, so Yahweh's power works inexorably against human power. Micah's message is stated clearly by Paul: "Whatever a man sows, that he will also reap. For he who sows to his own flesh will from the flesh reap corruption" (RSV, Gal. 6:7f.; cf. Matt. 7:2; 2 Cor. 5:10).

The early exilic interpretations that were added to the prophet's words apply Micah's insights to an entire generation (see above, pp. 75f.). Today, whoever would understand the truth of Micah's proclamation must not only study his perception of the hidden roots of guilt and punishment; he must also carefully consider the responsibilities of power and its consequences in light of the standards of the modern world.

Whenever such reflections lead to personal actions, there will be no lack of *dispute,* to which Micah himself was exposed (vv. 6–11). He was not the only prophet to whom silence was suggested (cf. Amos 7:16; Isa. 30:10; Jer. 26:9). At the least, he was expected to limit the topics he preached about (v. 6aα); at all events, he was told concerning the politics of power and economics: "Do not speak of these matters." Micah reacted, becoming even more precise, by naming entirely concrete examples (see above, pp. 82ff.). In doing so, he takes up the objections and questions of his opponents (vv. 6–7a). Micah's proclamation of the revealed word is accomplished not only in monologue, but in dialogue as well, as we indeed see from his unavoidable disputation, his argumentative defense of his message, and his resistance to the objections voiced by his opponents. The content of the disputation is about the whole truth of salvation. Micah fights against a pious-appearing, selfish half-truth that in reality is but a partial truth about the security of salvation. To be sure, this half-truth appropriates God's saving gift of the land, while it disdains the gift in relation to the small landholders. God's salvation history with Israel teaches it that the freedom of the powerful is limited by the freedom of the weak. Humankind never stops learning from the recognition that love for God is impossible without love for the weaker brother or sister. For the sake of his love, there must be struggles and disputes

87

whose goal is to recognize those particular instances which can be changed.

Verses 12 and 13 presuppose that in the meantime, a catastrophic judgment has occurred. What remains? A remnant of Israel, scattered among the nations, under foreign domination, separated from each other, without land, captives under subjection. This remnant community applies to itself the twofold *promise* that Deutero-Isaiah especially addressed to those in exile: the scattered nation will be brought together again by the good shepherd; he will go before them and lead them to freedom. This promise is offered with no conditions attached. It applies to those Israelites who survived. For Jesus' sake, those "who are not of this fold" (John 10:16) may also hear this voice and follow him who "goes before them" (cf. John 10:4 with Mic. 2:13aα,bα,β). Could any follower of Jesus forget—after the experience of judgment—what Micah did on behalf of his fellow countrymen, when he disputed with the authorities and proclaimed their guilt and punishment?

No Answer from God

Literature

J. Halévy, "Le Livre de Michée (Chapitre III: III, 1–12; IV, 8–10)," *RSEHA* 12 (1904) 193–216. K. Budde, "Micha 2 und 3," *ZAW* 38 (1919/1920) 2–22. A. H. Edelkoort, "Prophet and Prophet (Micah 2,6–11; 3,5–8)," *OTS* 5 (1948) 179–189. G. Quell, *Wahre und Falsche Propheten* (1952) 115–126. J. A. Soggin, "Der prophetische Gedanke über den heiligen Krieg als Gericht gegen Israel," *VT* 10 (1960) 79–83. M. Moreshet, *"whr hbyt lbmwt y'r,"* *BetM* 12 (1966/1967) 4 (31) 123–126. F. C. Fensham, "Righteousness in the Book of Micah and Parallels from the Ancient Near East" (Afrikaans), *TGW* 7 (1967) 416–425. J. T. Willis, "A Note on ואמר in Micah 3,1," *ZAW* 80 (1968) 50–54. D. K. Innes, "Some Notes on Micah, Chapters III and IV," *EvQ* 41 (1969) 109–112. J. L. Crenshaw, *Prophetic Conflict,* BZAW 124 (1971). Jörg Jeremias, "Die Vollmacht des Propheten im Alten Testament," *EvTh* 31 (1971) 305–322. Idem, "Die Deutung der Gerichtsworte Michas in der Exilszeit," *ZAW* 83 (1971) 330–354. F. L. Hossfeld; I. Meyer, *Prophet gegen Prophet,* Biblische Beiträge 9 (1973) 46–48. F. Stolz, "Der Streit um die Wirklichkeit in der Südreichsprophetie des 8. Jh." *WuD* 12 (1973) 9–30 (18f.). G. Münderlein, *Kriterien wahrer und falscher Prophetie,* EHS.T 33 (1974) 23–32. U. Müller, "Keramik," *BRL*[2] (1977) 168–185. H. F. Fuhs, *Sehen und Schauen. Die Wurzel ḥzh im Alten Orient und im Alten Testament,* Forschung zur Bibel 32 (1978) 194–197.

Text

3:1 But I said:[a]
Listen here,[b] you heads of Jacob,[c]
   you leaders[d] of the house of Israel!
Is it not your responsibility
   to be concerned for justice?
2 Who hate the good
   and love[a] the evil,[b]
who strip off their skin from them[c]
   and the flesh from their[c] bones,
3   '[a] they devour the flesh of my people
   [and strip off their hide from them][b]
and break their bones,
they chop them up 'like flesh'[c] into the pot,

like meat[d] for the cauldron.
4 Then[a] when they cry out to Yahweh,
    he will not answer them.
He will hide his face from them [at that time][b]
    because[c] their deeds are evil.[d]

5 Thus Yahweh has spoken[a] concerning the prophets,
    who lead my[b] people astray:
[c]When they have something to bite with their teeth,
    they[d] call out salvation;[c]
but when someone does not give what they desire,[e]
    then they declare war against him.
6 Therefore
it will be night for you, without[a] vision,
    darkness[b] will come upon you, without[a] divination.
The sun will go down upon the prophets,
    the day will be darkened above them.
7 Then the seers[a] will be ashamed
    and the diviners dejected.
[b]They will all cover their beard.[b]
    For there is no answer from God.[c]
8 By comparison I, I am filled
    with authority [with the power of Yahweh],[a] justice and cour-
           age,
to proclaim to Jacob his rebelliousness
    and to Israel his error.

9 Listen to this,
    you heads[a] of the house of Jacob,
        you leaders[b] in the house of Israel,
who detest justice
    and twist all that is straight,
10 'who build'[a] Zion with blood,
    and Jerusalem with injustice.
11 Her heads give judgment for a bribe,
    her priests give instruction[a] for pay,
        her prophets divine for money.
And yet they rely on Yahweh and say,
    "Is not Yahweh in our midst?
        Disaster will not come upon us!"
12 Therefore because of you
    Zion will be plowed into an open field,
        Jerusalem will become a heap of ruins,[a]
            and the temple mount[b] will be given over to the 'beasts'[c] of
            the forest.

1a Gk (καὶ ἐρεῖ) presupposes וְאָמַר ("and he will say"); Syr, וַיֹּאמֶר; Vg (*et dixi*) and Targ (ואמרית) support the first person form in MT.
1b Gk adds "this" (ταῦτα) following v. 9a (זֹאת).
1c Gk (οἶκον Ιακωβ) and Syr harmonize v. 1aα with v. 2aβ ("house of Israel") and with v. 9aα ("house of Jacob").
1d Gk (οἱ κατάλοιποι = "the remaining ones," also in v. 9a) goes back to an unknown textual antecedent; perhaps Gk heard in the word קצין a reminiscence of קֵץ, קָצֶה, קָצֶה ("end").
2a Gk translates ζητοῦντες ("to seek").
2b *Qere*'s reading (רָע), standing parallel to טוֹב, is to be preferred to *Kethib* (רָעָה); cf. 2:1; Isa. 5:20; Amos 5:14; the meaning is the same.

2c Since at this point in the text there is no antecedent for the third person plural suffixes, one might consider transposing v. 2b after v. 3a; then the collective עַמִּי (v. 3aα) would serve as the antecedent; cf. I. Willi-Plein, 80f. However, in the present redacted version of the text, which connects this passage with 2:1–11 by means of ואמר in 3:1aα (see below, p. 95), the suffixes are to be construed with the oppressed people spoken of in 2:2, 8f., whom Micah calls "my people" there as well as here (v. 3:3a).

3a Gk (ὃν τρόπον) reads כַּאֲשֶׁר; cf. v. 3bα and v. 4bβ. However, even ואשר appears grammatically and rhythmically superfluous. Could it stem from dittography of שאר with metathesis of א and שׁ (cf. B. Renaud 122)?

3b The sentence repeats and elucidates v. 2bα (see below, p. 99); it adds a third colon to the bicola otherwise found in the prosodic units in vv. 2b–4. On משׁ *hiph.* and its meaning, see above, pp. 82f. on 2:8aβ, and Th. Lescow 47f.

3c Gk (ὡς σάρκας), Targ (שארהון) have read בְּשָׁאֵר, which is probably the original reading, in light of the following parallel וכבשׂר (J. Wellhausen). The misreading could be traced to a jump of the eye back to וַאֲשֶׁר in v. 3aα.

3d Literally: "like flesh."

4a On the conditional undertone of אז, cf. Ps. 56:10[9].

4b The expression not only overloads the verse's rhythm but it also clashes with אז in v. 4aα, which speaks of an impending consequence; it also extends the length of time between the threat and its fulfillment; see above, p. 75 on 2:4aα[1] and Jörg Jeremias, "Deutung" 347.

4c Here כאשר has the function of providing the motivation, as in Num. 27:14; 1 Sam. 28:18; 2 Kings 17:26.

4d Gk (ἐπ᾽ αὐτούς) presupposes an additional עֲלֵיהֶם ("with them"), probably due to dittography of עלל(ל)יהם(מ).

5a Here perhaps the messenger formula is from the redactor's hand; see below, p. 94.

5b The first person suffix refers to the prophet, not to Yahweh, as *BHS* suggests. Micah never presents the expression "my people" as spoken by Yahweh (cf. 1:9; 2:8f.; 3:3); elsewhere in the first person speech form, the "I" is also the prophet speaking (1:8; 2:7b; 3:1aα, 8); Yahweh speaks in the first person less often (1:6; 2:3).

5c–c Gk (Syr, Vg) takes both participles in v. 5aβ and v. 5bα, and also the following finite verb, and makes them parallel: "who mislead my people, who bite with their teeth and who preach peace." On the other hand, even Targ has more appropriately understood v. 5bα as parallel to v. 5bβ,γ, and interpreted the participle in v. 5bα as a conditional protasis to the following perfect verb.

5d Gk inserts ἐπ᾽ αὐτὸν ("to him"), corresponding to עליו in v. 5bγ, which has its antecedent in "my people" in v. 5aβ.

5e On the translation, see below, pp. 102f.

6a Gk (ἐξ ὁράσεως . . . ἐκ μαντείας) understands מן as referring to the origin (cf. BrSynt §111h) of the revelation; the context (vv. 6b, 7), on the other hand, requires that the preposition be understood as privative ("without") or substitutive ("instead of") (Ges-K §119v,w; BrSynt §111f).

6b Gk (καὶ σκοτία), Vg *(et tenebrae)* vocalize the word, in parallel to לילה (v. 6aα), as the noun וְחָשְׁכָה; MT, supported by Syr, vocalizes the word as the more usual verb form ("it will become dark"), instead of as a noun, which the synonymous parallelism would make more likely.

7a Gk (οἱ ὁρῶντες τὰ ἐνύπνια) paraphrases ("those who see dreams"); similarly Vg *(qui vident visiones),* "those who see visions."

7b–b Gk (καὶ καταλαλήσουσι κατ᾽ αὐτῶν πάντες αὐτοί) interprets with the words "and they all shall ridicule them."

7c Gk (οὐκ ἔσται ὁ εἰσακούων αὐτῶν) probably had a text with some words missing, perhaps אין ענה להם ("no one answers them"); thus B. Renaud 131.

8a את־רוח יהוה proves to be a later commentary on the verse (already J. Wellhausen): (1) it interrupts the three-stress colon ("authority—justice—courage,"); (2) it overloads the prosody of the unit; (3) grammatically, it adds a superfluous אַתֶּם (without a copula!) to a colon that, with its three stresses, otherwise contains no אַתֶּם. Cf. also σ´ and J. Ziegler.

9a Gk, which had translated רָאשֵׁי in v. 1 with αἱ ἀρχαί, has οἱ ἡγούμενοι here.

9b See note 3:1d above.

10a With Gk (οἱ οἰκοδομοῦντες), Targ (בָּנִן), Syr (bānîn), Vg (qui aedificatis), and the preceding verse, the plural בֹּנֵי or בֹּנִים (cf. Hab 2:12) is to be expected.

11a Gk (ἀπεκρίνοντο) either presupposes יַעֲנוּ (cf. Gk, Mic. 6:3, 5), or freely interprets MT in light of the priests' main function of teaching ("they answered"); cf. Hab. 2:11–13.

12a In contrast to the quotation of this prophetic saying in Jer. 26:18 (עִיִּים), here an Aramaicized plural has been transmitted (cf. Bauer-Leander §63t,u). Is the alliteration with צִיּוֹן intentional (W. Rudolph)? On Gk, see note 1:6a above.

12b Targ (בֵּית מַקְדְּשָׁא), Vg (mons templi) render an appropriate translation of הַבַּיִת. With this prosaic, terse expression ("mount of the house") perhaps Micah intends to deconsecrate the temple.

12c In MT ("into wooded heights") one would expect to find the *status constructus* בָּמוֹתֵי (cf. 1:3). Gk (ἄλσος), σ´ (ὕψος), θ´ (βουνόν) presuppose the singular בָּמַת and refer to a sacred grove, as indeed the "heights" can point to Canaanite cultic places. However, in view of the previous two clauses, it is unlikely that Micah thinks Jerusalem will be turned into a pagan high place. The unusual plural form, the connection with יַעַר (see below, pp. 108f.), the preposition לְ, and the preceding words of threat, make A. B. Ehrlich's conjecture (לְבֶהֱמוֹת) quite probable; cf. 5:7 and M. Moreshet, *BetM* 12 (1966/1967) 123–126.

Form

Chapter 3 is clearly marked off as a unit: its prophecies of doom are entirely different from the hope expressed by the promises in 2:12f. and 4:1ff. But 3:1–12 is also to be distinguished from the scene sketched out in 2:1–11; this is already apparent in that in 3:1–12 Micah speaks to his audience not only concerning their deeds and words, but particularly concerning their office (cf. 2:1f., 8 with 3:1, 5, 9). This new way of introducing the addressee in terms of an office, occurring in chap. 3 for the first time in the book, is also an immediate indication that the chapter comprises three different rhetorical units of almost the same length: vv. 1–4; 5–8; 9–12. Each of these three sayings presents a self-contained unit, with the two basic elements of an accusation and a concluding announcement of disaster connected either by "then" (v. 4) or by "therefore" (vv. 6f., 12). To this extent, we have three examples of the classic *judgment speech* in chap. 3. The particular features of each unit are seen in additional form elements. Thus in the first saying (vv. 1–4), a rhetorical question preceding the accusation at first reminds the authorities addressed here of their official responsibilities (v. 1b). This provides the basis for the accusation. The second prophetic saying (vv. 5–8) reaches a climax in a very unusual personal statement from Micah, expressing with finality a contrast between him and the prophets he accuses (v. 8). Verse 8 presents Micah in complete antithesis to the prophets and elucidates both his accusation that they are weak and dependent (v. 5b), as well as his threatening declaration that their prophetic revelations will come to an end (vv. 6f.). A special form-critical element in the third saying is found in the climax of the accusation, where Micah uses a quotation (v. 11b) to document the religious self-consciousness of the officials. Against this backdrop, the announcement of disaster in v. 12 is especially gruesome.

Nevertheless, besides the individual characteristics of each of these sayings, we should also take note of a congruity that derives from their possessing the same basic structure. Most noticeable of all is that in the first and third sayings, the same addressees—the "heads (of the house) of Jacob" and the "leaders of the house of Israel"—in almost the same formulation, are summoned to hear (vv. 1a, 9a). In the course of the accusation in the third saying, after the "heads" and "priests" are named the "prophets" (v. 11b) are also mentioned, to whom the independent middle saying was addressed in vv. 5–8. In the second as well as the third saying, an accusation against covetousness is made (vv. 5b, 11a). Yet the second passage, concerning the prophets, is also connected with the first, concerning the political officials; indeed, the connection is made in the announcement of disaster: both prophets and officials will be subjected to divine rejection and silence (vv. 4, 6f.). This judgment will be fulfilled when the Jerusalem temple, the guarantee of God's salvation, is given over to destruction (vv. 11b–12). Thus these sayings not only dovetail together; they also exhibit form-critical similarities. Such a close connection of each passage with the other raises the question whether vv. 1–4, 5–8, 9–12 derive from the same scene and whether—similar to the judgment speech and the disputation speech in 2:1–11—the composition of chap. 3 should be understood as the sketch of a scene *(Auftrittsskizze)* in which Micah appears to speak to a gathering of people.

If we assume that 3:1–12 presents us with a particular scene, as we also found in 1:10–16 and 2:1–11 (see above, pp. 54, 75), this would account for the frequent transition from the prophet's direct address in the second person plural of those he accuses and threatens, to the form of a pronouncement of accusation and judgment in the third person plural. Thus the prophet, looking first at various groups whom he accuses, then turns his glance to a larger audience. With the summons to hear and the naming of the addressees' official responsibilities, the first saying begins in the style of direct address (v. 1). But then the accusation (v. 3), like the announcement of legal consequences (v. 4), changes to the third person. Next, after the prophets are initially accused in the third person (v. 5), come words of threat initially formulated in the second person style (v. 6a), followed by an announcement of the consequences in the third person (vv. 6b–7). The transition from the accusation in the third person (v. 5) to the announcement of judgment in the second person (v. 6a) is also found in Micah in 2:1f. and 3, 3:9–11, and v. 12 (cf. 2:6f. and vv. 8f.), transitions which do not indicate a change in the group that is addressed. Thus it appears misleading when A. S. van der Woude (99; 112) suggests that, on the basis of the direct address style (second person) in v. 6a, Micah speaks in 3:5–8 to the leaders (3:1, 9) concerning the prophets. To be sure, the transition from direct address style in v. 6a again to the third person in vv. 6b–7 can be explained by the prophet's turning to speak to the political authorities. In the third saying we find initially only the summons to hear formulated in the second person style (v. 9a), whereas the entire accusation is in the third person (vv. 9b–11). However, Micah utters the threat of judgment at the conclusion again in direct address to the officials ("because of you," v. 12). On the whole, therefore, direct address is predominant in the introductory summons to hear (vv. 1, 9a); this is balanced by the concluding announcement of judgment presented in the second person (vv. 6a, 12) and the third person (vv. 4, 6b–7). The accusation, on the other hand, is made throughout chap. 3 in the third person (vv. 3, 5, 9b–11). The transition from the initial direct address to the accusation is made smoothly and imperceptively by the participial style found in v. 2 and vv. 9b–10.

Participles also commence the accusation in v. 5. In the transmitted text, it is remarkable that the participles follow upon the messenger formula, "Thus Yahweh has spoken (concerning the prophets who . . .)." Occurring elsewhere in Micah only in 2:3, this formula in v. 5 does not introduce a first person Yahweh speech (as in Mic. 2:3, and in many other instances); for the participial phrase, המתעים את־עמי, standing in apposition to the messenger formula, expands it. The suffix ("*my* people") refers therefore to the prophet; moreover, God is spoken about in the third person in v. 7. The participles in v. 5aβ, ba could possibly fit better with an introductory woe cry (הוֹי הנביאים; cf. 2:1 and Th. Robinson 137; G. Quell 116). In this chapter it is even more likely that a summons to hear originally opened this passage, since of course in v. 2 and vv. 9b–10 the accusation addressed to the officials also begins at the outset in participial style. Thus it may be assumed that שִׁמְעוּ־נָא הנביאים was the original beginning of the passage (H. F. Fuhs, 207). In either case, the redaction of the text produced a two-stress bicolon, the same prosody which follows immediately in v. 5ba. Thus the messenger speech formula in v. 5 probably stems from the hand of the redactor (cf. J. L. Mays 81f.). This also explains the present prose style in v. 5a, which would be unusual in the original context.

The prophetic sayings in chap. 3 are poetic in form and almost exclusively in synonymous parallelism. Lines with three stresses predominate, with three-stress bicola (3+3) occurring in the first two sayings. In the first saying, this applies to v. 1a (without the redactional ואמר; on this see below, pp. 95f.) and to vv. 2b–4 (see notes 3a, 3b, and 4b); only in v. 1b and 2a do we find two pointed, shorter prosodic units (v. 2a, two-stress bicola). The second passage also contains strict bicola of two stresses at the beginning (v. 5ba) and in v. 7aα; otherwise, there are unambiguous three-stress bicola (vv. 5bβ, 6a,b, 7b, 8a; see note 8a). Verse 8b marks the conclusion of the second passage with a three-stress followed by a two-stress colon (3+2). The third passage presents itself as the climax of the scene *(Auftritt)* by changing to prosodic units with tricola. Even the summons to hear in v. 9a should be read as a three-stress tricolon. After two sentences containing a divergent prosody (five stresses: v. 9b, 2+3; v. 10a,b, 3+2), there follow in v. 11a,b, and in v. 12aβ-b three powerfully surging tricola of three stresses each (3+3+3). The synonymous parallelism of each of the tricola indicates that these verses do not contain bicola of three stresses (3+3), as is often incorrectly supposed. The announcement of disaster in the final prosodic unit (v. 12) is effectively set off from the accusation in the preceding prosodic units by the connecting phrase "therefore because of you"; as an anacrusis (like the לכן in v. 6aα), the phrase stands outside the prosody of the three-stress tricolon and, by virtue of its position at the beginning of the verse—

allowing the prophet to catch his breath—suggests a tense *retardando* before the prophecy of doom against Jerusalem.

Especially in light of this climax, it is surprising how little editing has been done to this chapter, which contains such offensive material particularly in the third passage. The apparent interpolations within v. 3 (see notes 3a, b) have merely stylistic significance. Only two interpolations have any theological significance: "in that time" (v. 4; see note 4b), a phrase which bridges the time-span between Micah's proclamation and the destruction of Jerusalem; and "with the power of Yahweh" (v. 8; see note 8a), which makes clear the source of Micah's authority.

Remaining problems are found in the prose introduction in v. 5a and the first word of the chapter in v. 1, which also stands outside the prosody of the chapter.

Setting

The word ואמר in v. 1 belongs unquestionably not to the oral proclamation but to the redaction of this first saying. The word provides significant information concerning the setting of the chapter's literary transmission. The first person reading "and I said" is text critically quite certain (see note 1a) and points to Micah himself as its author. As the tradent of his own sayings and sketches of scenes in which he speaks, Micah stands within a community of contemporary prophets otherwise unknown to us. This is confirmed by a glance at Amos (7:1–8; 8:1–2; 9:1–4; cf. also 5:1 and Wolff, *Joel and Amos* 107), Hosea (3:1; Wolff, *Hosea* xxix), and Isaiah (6:1ff. and Wildberger, *Jesaja 1–12,* BK 10/1, 239ff.). But in Micah, it should not be assumed that this is a fragment of an autobiographical narrative (see E. Sellin, A. Weiser; cf. Th. Lescow, 47–50). Quite probably the simple statement "and I said" is merely an indication that the following collection of sayings, like the previous ones, goes back to Micah himself (cf. also J. L. Mays, 24). This is already suggested by the first person style in 1:8 ("therefore I will lament . . ."); by 2:7 ("my words mean well . . ."); by the repeated phrase "my people" (1:9; 2:8f.; 3:3, 5); and finally 3:8 ("But I, I am filled . . ."). Even though ואמר—belonging to the first person style that runs through these passages like a red thread—has been given its present position in 3:1 by the redactor's hand, the word suggests that the oldest collection of Micah's sayings goes back to his own dictation or writing.

To what is the word ואמר connected? It is highly improbable, as A. S. van der Woude (94) has proposed, that here Micah begins his response to the false prophets, whose words are said to be found in 2:12f., and that in chap. 3 Micah provides new reasons to oppose their hopes for salvation. There is certainly no instance in 3:1–12 where a connection is made to 2:12f. On the contrary, chap. 3 has new addressees and a new theme. Moreover, in 2:12f. there is evidence that it is a later addition (see above, p. 76). Thus, it seems likely that ואמר is meant to connect with 2:11, making 3:1–12 the conclusion to the previous sketch *(Auftritts-skizze)* of the prophet's public oration. Such a connection is understandable in light of the content. Compared with the prophets "who slobber about wine and beer" (2:11aβ), Micah offers a new, contrasting picture from his own preaching in 3:1–12. Accordingly, the copula takes on an adversative meaning: "*But* I said" (cf. J. L. Mays, 23f., 77f.). Since ואמר makes a connection that is merely redactional in nature, nothing prevents our supposing that it provides a transition from the theme of covetousness of the soldiers and officials in the Shephelah (2:1–11) to the theme of injustice of the authorities in Jerusalem presented in this new scene-sketch. The contrast with the kind of prophets desired by "this people here" is made especially pointed in 3:8.

This initial word in 3:1a makes it clear that some time has elapsed between Micah's oral proclamation and the formation of his sayings into literary tradition. Perhaps this can help clarify the stylistic unevenness in V. 5a noted above (see p. 94). The difficulty, on the one hand, is that the messenger formula (v. 5a) begins a saying which is not a messenger speech: instead of the expected first person speech of Yahweh, we find "God" referred to only once in the third person ("from whom there is no answer"). On the other hand, the saying itself begins with the participial style that usually follows not the messenger formula but a "woe cry" (as in 2:1) or a summons to "hear" (as in 3:1, 9; see above, p. 94). We must investigate whether such a stylistic problem is to be explained by some special intention of Micah himself, as tradent (see below, p. 101), or whether it is in fact better to suppose that the verse was later re-worked by a redactor.

We have recognized such a later hand in 1:5, 13b, and in the interpolations within 2:3–5, 10. Given the observation that the messenger formula prefaces Mic. 3:12 when it is cited in Jer. 26:18, an expression not used by Micah himself in 3:12, then one would of course expect that similar circles of redactors most likely added the formula to 3:5 as it occurs in the present text. It might be the same Deuteronomistic interpreters who also added the expression "in that time" to Micah's threat in 3:4 (similarly 2:4a). This threat, originally referring to an impending (אז) act of Yahweh, is connected by this interpolation to a more distant future event, which in the meantime took place with the catastrophe of 587 (cf. Jörg Jeremias, 335, 347).

Finally, the explanatory phrase את־רוח יהוה inserted into 3:8 is also to be attributed to these same Deuteronomistic circles of the early sixth century. The prophets of the eighth and seventh centuries were remarkably strict in their avoidance of speaking about the "spirit of Yahweh" or the "power of Yahweh" in reference to their prophetic office. Micah himself uses the phrase "spirit of Yahweh" only in the quotation of his opponents (2:7a; cf. also Mic. 2:11a; Hos. 9:7 and Wolff, *Hosea* 157). Not until Ezekiel does the phrase appear with reference to the specific experience of the prophetic call (11:5, 24; 37:1; cf. further W. Zimmerli, *Ezekiel* 2, 657). Within the Deuteronomistic history, the phrase "spirit of Yahweh" occurs sixteen times from Judg. 3:10 to 2 Kings 2:17. The readers of Micah's proclamation of disaster at the time of the destruction of Judah and Jerusalem around 587 are to learn that the authority of this prophet derived alone from the "power of Yahweh," something Micah himself did not find it necessary to say.

The ancient prophecies in this chapter were sayings proclaimed in Jerusalem itself. This is sufficiently clear from vv. 10 and 12. Since 3:1 has the same addressee as 3:9, and since the prophets in vv. 5–7 are not to be separated from the political leaders (cf. vv. 6–7 with v. 4 and v. 5b with v. 11a), all the sayings in this chapter were no doubt proclaimed first in Jerusalem. We may suppose that the locality was the outer court of the temple; there, according to Jeremiah 26 (v. 2), on a similar occasion when Jeremiah threatened city and temple with disaster (v. 6), the legal authorities of the royal court gathered with priests and prophets, and also with the "elders of the land" (vv. 8–17). If Micah had been a member of the elders of Judah, it is certainly intelligible that precisely in this place he would have stood to proclaim his message about one hundred years earlier. The audience whom he faced and addressed as he indicted the political leaders and the prophets, speaking about them in the third person, may in particular have been circles of elders from the land who had gathered in the forecourt of the temple (cf. Wolff, "Micah's Cultural and Intellectual Background," in *Micah the Prophet,* trans. R. Gehrke [Philadelphia: Fortress Press, 1981] 17–25; idem, "Wie verstand Micha von Moresheth sein prophetisches Amt," SVT 29 [1978] 408ff.).

The date of this scene cannot be precisely determined. The Assyrian crisis, when the notion of security was propagated, as illustrated in v. 11b, need not be pushed forward to the time around 701, when Sennacherib besieged Jerusalem. If Micah already saw the seige of Samaria as a threat also to Jerusalem (on 1:6–9, 12b, see above, pp. 53f.), and if he already at that time referred to the Judaic authorities as "Israel" (cf. 1:14f. with 3:1, 8, 9), then we cannot with certainty exclude (thus Rudolph, 70) the sayings in chap. 3 from the decade between the Syro-Ephraimite war (733) and the conquest of Samaria (722).

Commentary

[3:1] It is conceivable that in the forecourt of the Jerusalem temple, Micah addressed and summoned to attention a congregation of the capital city's officials, and that among them there may also have been elders and citizens from the provincial areas. Whom did Micah address in this first saying? In v. 1, and also in v. 9, it is the "heads (of the house) of Jacob" and "leaders of the house of Israel," phrases parallel here, but not in any other OT texts. Although the word ראשׁים (plural) by itself occurs frequently (but usually in the singular), and קצין by itself is found in at least ten instances, their parallel placement as addressees is something peculiar to Micah. In only one other instance do these designations of an office stand side by side (Judg. 11:11). Do these words denote two offices, or are they two words for the same office? In Judg. 11:6 the elders of Gilead at first ask Jephthah to be their קצין, which in that context means "military leader" (cf. also Josh. 10:24). After a victorious battle he also becomes ראשׁ, "head of all inhabitants of Gilead" (Judg. 11:8, 9, 11); i.e., he becomes the chief custodian of the law. Then the name Jephthah also occurs in the list of the "minor judges" (12:7). This function of a "head" as civil judge appears to be predominately denoted by the word ראשׁ and also by קצין in Micah's time. This is evident in our passage from vv. 1b, 9b, and 11a in chap. 3. Micah's contemporary Isaiah also speaks of the "leaders of Sodom" (קציני) in Jerusalem (Isa. 1:10) and apparently refers to men responsible for justice not only for persons who have no legal standing (widows, orphans) (v. 17), but also for those who suffer various needs, such as the poor and sick (cf. Isa. 3:6f.). Accordingly, the responsibility for overseeing community welfare services belongs to the

office of leader. According to Prov. 6:7 and 25:15 the קָצִין is leader and
overseer of the community's work; he is responsible for keeping order.
The "head" (רֹאשׁ) and his duties derive from ancient functions within the
tribe and the clan (cf. J. R. Bartlett, "The Use of the Word רֹאשׁ as Title in
the Old Testament," *VT* 19 [1969] 1–10). In the era of the kings,
according to 2 Chron. 19:8, "heads of important families," together with
priests and Levites, were appointed as a judicial committee to render
judgment against capital crimes and apparently also to give counsel to
local judiciaries, particularly those in fortified cities (cf. 2 Chron. 19:5, 10
and G. Macholz, "Zur Geschichte der Justizorganisation in Juda," *ZAW*
84 [1972] 314–340). This explains why the prophet Micah, especially if
he was one of the elders in Judah, also addressed the "heads" and "overseers" in Jerusalem in the interests of his countrymen in the Shephelah
(v. 3: "my people"). Even if both these designations of office were originally rooted in different functions—as indicated by the Jephthah story,
as well as by the occurrences of קָצִין in Isaiah and in Proverbs—nevertheless Micah addresses them both in relation to the responsibility for
justice that each has (cf. v. 1a,b, and also vv. 9a,b and 11a). Micah's
choice of words for these offices goes back to premonarchic conceptions
(he never speaks of the king and his officials [שָׂרִים], unlike Hosea, in
related matters; cf. Hos. 5:1). Accordingly, he assigns to them responsibility for "Jacob" and "Israel," which unquestionably means Judah and
Jerusalem (cf. vv. 10, 12)—as previously in 1:14f. he used the ancient
name of the tribal confederacy "Israel" to mean the state of Judah. Micah
is closely connected with the conceptions of tribal life in ancient Israel.

Micah speaks immediately to the officials concerning their responsibilities. His conviction about their responsibilities is expressed by a
rhetorical question that allows them no choice but to agree with him
(Ges-K §150e). Their job is to see that justice (מִשְׁפָּט) is done. In 2 Chron.
19:8 the judicial council in Jerusalem is responsible for the מִשְׁפַּט יהוה.
Here, too, Micah uses reserve in mentioning Yahweh by name; instead,
he presents Yahweh's name on the lips of his own opponents (2:7; 3:11).
מִשְׁפָּט means ancient Israel's administration of justice in all areas of life
and the corresponding legal decisions which protect persons with no legal
standing (Isa. 1:17); these decisions, like life-giving waters (Amos 5:24)
and light (Hos. 6:5), bring blessings for all. The word דַּעַת denotes the
necessary, obligatory relationship of the Jerusalem authorities to justice.
The word means not only a knowledge of justice, but a charitable
devotion of the whole person to the practice of justice; it means the
utilization of justice for the benefit of people who are threatened by
wrong. The authorities whom Micah addresses cannot dispute the fact
that when justice is understood in this way, they are indeed responsible.
Thus they have been caught fast by the prophet's rhetorical question.

[3:2a] The accusation follows immediately upon this reference to the
authorities' obligations. Micah at first characterizes the heads and leaders
in a fundamental way (v. 2a), and then he proceeds, with a series of
metaphors, to offer his critique in detail (vv. 2b–3). He presupposes the
simple definition of מִשְׁפָּט: it teaches the distinction between good and
evil. Whoever concerns himself with the practice of justice will love the
good and hate the evil (thus precisely Amos 5:15a; cf. also Isa. 1:16f.). In

Micah's judgment, the Jerusalem authorities have completely corrupted this basic principle: they are plainly characterized (with participles) as persons who hate the good and love the evil. Isaiah (5:20, 23) elucidates the findings of the court in the legal process: they call evil good, and good they call evil. This same characterization of justice and the just judge found in Amos, Isaiah, and Micah has no model in the legal texts of the Pentateuch; but the antithesis of "good and evil" and also of "love and hate" is certainly found scattered in wisdom texts (Prov. 1:22; 9:8; 12:1; 13:24; 14:22; 28:5, 6; Pss. 34:15 [14]; 37:27). Thus Micah begins his accusation by stating that those who ought to be aware of their obligations to administer justice, owing to their basic orientation, not only pervert justice in individual cases; in their evil inclinations and in their zealousness, they also live in direct contradiction to their responsibilities. V. 2a presents this in a cutting, two-stress bicolon (2+2).

[3:2b–3] Six statements follow, each with three stresses (three bicola with three stresses, if 3aα² is secondary; see note 3b). While the participial style of v. 2a is initially continued (v. 2b), v. 3 changes to declarative statements in the perfect. The language used expresses extreme agitation, with metaphors borrowed from the bloody work of the butcher. The passionate rhetorical style is evident from the repetitions; next to the mention of skin and bones, the prophet speaks four times of "flesh," either stripped from the bones (v. 2bβ) or chopped up for the kettle (v. 3b; see note 3c) and eaten (v. 3a). But the sentences do not place each event in this logical order. In an agitated style, the eating of flesh is mentioned before it has been chopped for the kettle (cf. v. 3a with 3b). The prophet is not concerned with a narrative coherence but with grim, individual actions, each of which as metaphor provides evidence for the accusation that these officials "love evil." No other prophet speaks in such a coarse manner. To be sure, Amos speaks once about "trampling the head of the poor" (2:7), and Isaiah refers to "grinding the face of the poor" (3:15). But the description of such a series of barbarous deeds, in which people are treated like slaughtered cattle, was left to the prophet from among the farmers in Moresheth.

In v. 2b the colon begins with an indictment of "robbery" (גזל); the word already occurred in 2:2, where its accusative objects are "field" and "houses." Here "the skin" is robbed, i.e., stripped away, torn off ("from them"; the interpolation in v. 3aα² offers a necessary commentary on גזל, with its object "flesh," by taking the word פשט hiph. from 2:8bβ, where it means "to strip away"). The word גזל therefore provides the transition from the concrete accusation to a metaphorical use of language. According to Isa. 61:8, Yahweh "loves משפט" but "hates robbery." When v. 2b speaks of tearing away the skin, it probably does not present a metaphor for the "robe," which according to 2:8 is "stripped away." On the whole, the metaphors more probably make a general reference to bloody deeds such as those connected with the building of Jerusalem (cf. v. 10). The people themselves, Micah intends to say, are exploited to the point of destruction: their bones are broken, their flesh chopped into pieces and devoured, and even their skin is stripped away. Especially during oppressive times, when for example a city endured an extensive siege, or when there was devastating famine, Israel encountered the beginnings of canni-

eat flesh of other person

balism (2 Kings 6:26–30; Lam. 4:10). However, what is now happening in Jerusalem is an unheard-of economic cannibalism practiced by the heads and leaders. The accusation that they "devour the flesh of my people" denounces both the brutal actions and covetousness of the leading circles (cf. Pss. 14:4; 27:2; Prov. 30:14). They take their pleasure in life at the expense of those whom they oppress. The motivation for Micah's intervention can be recognized in the reference to his fellow countrymen (עמי), for whose defense he feels himself responsible. Nor does this passage speak of the poor people, as we find in Isa. 3:15 or Amos 2:7 (and elsewhere in these two prophets). Micah speaks in behalf of his small landholders, who suffer under violent measures at home, and perhaps also under the burden of obligatory labor in Jerusalem. In Micah we find combined a heartfelt sympathy and a sense of justice.

Why does v. 3b speak especially of "chopping" meat for the kettle? The basic meaning of פרש is "to spread out," but it can also be used for violent separation of what belongs together, e.g., for the scattering abroad of animals in a herd (Ezek. 34:12); or for the disintegration of military forces whose remaining troops are scattered to the winds (Ezek. 17:21). Thus, here it means "to break up," "to cut up." It may be the application of an allegorical interpretation when commentators understand this to be Micah's concern for the dividing up of families, as it is expressed in 2:2b, 9a,b. For Micah's metaphors do not derive from free plays on words; rather, they always have a connection with concrete facts. Two words for "cooking pot" stand side by side. סיר is the customary word for pot; cf. Exod. 16:3, "fleshpots of Egypt"; Jer. 1:13, "a boiling pot, facing away from the north." קלחת was perhaps a larger pot, such as those used in the temple (1 Sam. 2:14). Archaeologists have found a wide variety of similar ceramic ware, mostly with two handles, dating from the Iron Age (cf. U. Müller, 178f.; 183). Pieces of cut-up meat cooked in pots were removed with a fork (1 Sam. 2:14). In each of these sentences the crudeness and hedonism of Micah's opponents are combined to provide evidence for the prophet's central charge: hate of good and love of evil.

[3:4] With v. 4 the finite verbs in the perfect (three times in v. 3) change to the imperfect (also three times in v. 4aα,β,bα); v. 4bβ returns again to the perfect. The clauses in the imperfect are introduced by אז; they describe actions which have not yet taken place, but which logically follow. The subject of the first clause (v. 4aα) is still the third person of those indicted by the prophet in v. 3; but in the second and third clauses, Yahweh is the subject (v. 4aβ, ba). Apparently, emphasis is to be placed on the second and third clauses; thus the first sentence appears to be a protasis, and the introductory אז in this context takes on a temporal-conditional undertone ("whenever"). The situation proclaimed by the prophet is that those who flay the skin from human beings will utter a great cry of distress to Yahweh. The reason for their cry is not yet given. The prophet focuses on the actual distress which results when Yahweh does not respond to their outcry. What Micah says is nothing different from the experience found expressed in wisdom thinking: "He who closes his ear to the cry of the poor, will himself cry out and not be heard" (Prov. 21:13). But the threat is intensified in v. 4ba. Not only will there be an interruption of verbal communication; what is more, Yahweh will hide his countenance from them. Whenever Yahweh conceals his פנים, he removes his presence, his "turning toward" (פנה) someone; he withholds his salvation and help (Ps. 80:4[3], 8[7]), his protection and peace (Num. 6:24–26). Hence, the prophet completely calls into question the very existence of those whom he accuses. The two clauses that speak of Yahweh's refusal to answer prayer and to offer his presence sound like an answer of rejection in response to the cry of Psalm 27:7–9, "Be gracious to me and answer me! . . . hide not thy face from me." The dreadful alternative of God-forsakenness rears its head.

The final clause (v. 4bβ), which returns to the perfect tense used in the accusation (v. 3), concludes the passage by again emphasizing the basis for Yahweh's refusal to answer and to offer his presence. The misery that will come upon the heads and leaders corresponds precisely to the distress they themselves brought upon Micah's people; it corresponds (כאשר) to the malice of their deeds, to their love for evil. They did not answer the cry of suffering people, nor were they present to help them. The word רע in v. 2a is picked up again in the word הרעו in v. 4b.

[3:5] The new prophetic saying in vv. 5–8 makes a thematic connection with the proclamation of God's silence in v. 4. For the question about God's answer is the question about how prophecy functions (cf. vv. 6f.). The "heads" and "leaders" could call upon the Jerusalem prophets to help them oppose Micah. Micah declares to them that this ray of hope will be swallowed up by darkness.

If not Micah, then surely it was a later redactor of this prophecy who particularly deemed this saying about the prophets important enough to introduce it with the words "Thus Yahweh has spoken"; i.e., the prophecy is the express word of Yahweh against the deceptive oracles of the Jerusalem prophets. These prophets, together with priests and judges (v. 11a), may well have had a legitimate function, as is apparently presupposed in Isa. 28:7; Hos. 4:4f.; Jer. 2:8, 26; 6:13; 26:16. They were particularly responsible for uttering the intercessory prayers of those who brought their griefs to them; for questions seeking the oracles of Yahweh; and for offering appropriate counsel to individuals and to politicians as well (cf. Jörg Jeremias, "Vollmacht," 308, with further bibliography).

Micah does not deny that his prophetic opponents, in accordance with the duties of their office, have until now sought and also received answers from God in nocturnal visions (vv. 6f.). He does question, however, whether their prophetic pronouncements correspond with the revelation received from Yahweh. It is precisely because of this discrepancy between reception of the divine word and its proclamation that Micah accuses them of an intentional misleading of his people. They are guilty of תעה, which in the *qal* form means "to wander about," "to lose one's way" (Gen. 21:14; Exod. 23:4), and can also mean "to stagger" (of drunkards, such as priests and prophets according to Isa. 28:7). Accordingly, the *hiph.* participle of תעה in v. 5 characterizes the Jerusalem prophets as persons who "lead into error,". "mislead" the people; or who induce a spirit of confusion that causes the people to stagger about aimlessly (Isa. 19:13f.). These are the prophets who according to 2:11 are well-received by "that people"; prophets who "drivel about wine and beer." Isaiah also refers to the Jerusalem leaders simply as "those who mislead" (3:12, 9:15); and Jeremiah in particular, like Micah, calls the prophets misleaders (23:13) since they do not lead the people from their evil ways to repentance (23:32). When the writer of Lamentations looked back on the causes for the destruction of Jerusalem in 587, he said, "Your prophets have seen for you false and deceptive visions; they have not exposed your iniquity to lead you to repentance. They had deceptive visions for you, false and misleading" (2:14). Micah saw and prophesied concerning the prophets' very deceptions long before this. They mislead "my people," Micah says, not without a note of sympathy. Here again, he means those people who are exposed to the covetousness and violence of the authorities (2:8f.; 3:3) and who now have also been given up to the prophets' repulsive and hostile words (v. 5bγ).

Micah demonstrates the spuriousness of these misleading prophets by showing how they relate to their audience. The prophets' words correspond not to Yahweh's instructions, but to the ability of the hearers at any given time to fulfill their personal wishes. These fall into two categories, as the two parallel sentences in v. 5b indicate. The conditions under which the prophets give favorable or unfavorable information are mentioned in the first sentence by a protasis formulated in participial style; and in the second by an אשר-clause (Ges-K §116w). שלום, complete salvation, i.e., peace, prosperity, happiness, success, health, is promised to those who give the prophets something to bite with their teeth. Again, Micah expresses himself in crude language (cf. 3:2b–3). Elsewhere, the verb נשך is used only for the bite of a snake (Amos 5:19; 9:3; Prov. 23:32; Num. 21:8f.). Does the word suggest the lethal character of the prophets' bite? The verse does not of course refer to their usual livelihood which, for the ancient seers, consisted of donations of food and provisions (1 Sam. 9:7f.; 1 Kings 14:2f.; 2 Kings 4:8f.; 8:8f.). For the prophets employed in the temple, such provisions were regulated in a manner concerning which we possess little information (cf. Amos 7:12; Luke 10:7; in 2 Kings 5:15f., Elisha refused to accept any presents). Rather, this has to do with special payments that possess the nature of a bribe; cf. v. 11aβ. Private gain becomes a criterion for what is prophesied. What comes out of the mouth of these prophets depends upon what has been put into it.

A malicious response is received by whoever "does not give them what they desire." Since Gk (οὐκ ἐδόθη εἰς τὸ στόμα αὐτῶν) and Vg (si qius non dederit in ore eorum) down to the most recent commentators (R. Vuilleumier, L. C. Allen, J. L. Mays, B. Renaud), a very close parallel in content has been perceived between v. 5bβ and the preceding sentence in v. 5bα, and thus the usual translation, "who does not put anything into their mouth." In my opinion, A. S. van der Woude (109f.) was the first to recognize that this cannot be the original meaning of these words. For "to place in the mouth" would have to read שים בפה (Exod. 4:15; Num. 22:38; Deut. 31:19, etc.) or נתן בפה (Deut. 18:18; Jer. 1:9; 5:14; etc.). The frequently occurring phrase על־מה (נתן) always means (to give) "according to the word/command/wish"; cf. Gen. 45:21; also Gen. 41:40 and 43:7; Num. 3:51; 2 Kings 23:35; etc., cf. Ges-B, 635). Here פה denotes not the organ but—as frequently—its function (cf. H. W. Wolff, *Anthropology of the Old Testament* 28, 77f.), that is, "speech," "command," "wish." Thus it becomes clear that, according to the original meaning of the word, these prophets not only accept bribes, but they also utter particular wishes or even make demands. Again, Micah thinks not only of poor people who can pay nothing, but also of honest and thoughtful persons who refuse to meet such expectations. These are particular individuals, as is indicated by the third person singular יתן, as well as by the third singular suffix of עליו. Against such persons these prophets "declare war." Used by Micah in a sarcastic manner, this expression is reminiscent of the cultic preparations for holy war (Josh. 3:5; 1 Sam. 13:8–12). It does not refer to war in general (Jer. 6:4; Joel 4:9 [3:9]), but to personal hostility. Incidentally, it becomes clear that false prophets themselves can also preach doom. They are false prophets because their preaching of salvation or doom is determined not by the will of Yahweh but by their own interests. "Money talked louder than words" (J. L. Mays, 83). "Here we find two remarkable images of the prophet: arrogant and self-satisfied, with their mouths full, they intone an oracle of salvation for the benefit of their host; or, rejected, going about as beggars, they give vent in their presumptuous agitation to passionate threats. These are superlative expressions of mocking directed to God's servants, upon whom other persons have developed a slavelike dependence, without perceiving their shamelessness" (G. Quell, 119). Micah is enraged by such a desecration of the prophet's charismatic office.

[3:6] But before Micah himself takes a personal stand against this deception, he utters a word of judgment against these prophets; introducing his prophecy with "therefore" (v. 6), he at first addresses them directly (second person plural). It is remarkable that in contrast to his other pronouncements of judgment, here Micah is more verbose; usually, it is the accusation that is more extended.

Verse 6 is concerned with the existence or nonexistence of prophets and thus at the same time with Micah's own existence (v. 8). The לכן that introduces the announcement of judgment makes a connection between the threatening punishment and the prophets' present behavior. Whoever speaks falsely in behalf of Yahweh will have the word taken from him. The authority granted the prophet through his call was the presupposition for his professional status. The misuse of authority leads to its destruction. "Night" and "darkness" will no longer be brightened by any kind of prophetic revelation. The words חזון and קסם probably refer to two different modes of receiving revelation: here חזון still has the ancient meaning of visionary experience; beside it קסם recalls the practice of divination (Ezek. 21:26). Both are represented as legitimate means of prophetic knowledge. Thus in v. 7a the "seers" (חזים) and the "diviner" (קסמים; cf. also v. 11aβ), almost synonymous in meaning, are mentioned as two kinds of "prophets" (נביאים) (H. F. Fuhs, 208). It should be noted that Micah does not deny to them their previous gift of prophecy (cf. on the other hand the strict criticism of divination in Deut. 18:10, 14; in addition, Num. 23:23; 1 Sam. 15:23; 28:8; 2 Kings 17:17). He gives them credit entirely for their charismatic insight into the will of God; to this extent they are as much a prophet as he is. Micah is not at all concerned about the methods they use to attain knowledge of God. But he has sharply focused on the misuse of the authority of their office: they subordinated their divine knowledge to their interests in monetary gain. Because of their greed, they have stifled any discernible revelation, or abbreviated it, or superimposed upon it their own ideas and desires. Therefore their knowledge of God will be darkened, the source of their prophetic insight sealed up.

In no less than eight clauses Micah prophesies the end of their existence as prophets. The first two sentences (v. 6a) tell the prophets plainly that they will be deprived of their source of revelation. The proclamation that there will be "night" ("without vision") and "darkness" ("without oracle") not only emphasizes the loss of every means that orients the prophets, but is especially indicative of the disaster that is about to befall their very lives (cf. Amos 5:18; Isa. 8:22). In v. 6b Micah addresses his words to a larger audience; here in two further clauses he speaks of the sun setting upon the prophets and of the darkening (of the sun) by day (cf. Amos 8:9b). Light from these prophets can no longer be expected to enlighten the path of Israel. The prophets themselves are handed over to darkness, without revelation.

[3:7] Without metaphor v. 7a spells out the consequences of the prophets' loss of vocation. Once their inability to be guided by revelation manifests itself, they will find that shame replaces position and influence. Previously, they could with power and strength speak of peace or war, salvation or doom; now they must stand about, timid and dejected. The meaning of חפר can perhaps best be expressed in Dutch: "Zij zullen dan . . . met de mond vol tanden staan en geen woord . . . meer kunnen uitbrengen" ["They will have their teeth in their mouth (i.e., be stupified) and not be able to say a word."] (A. S. van der Woude, 114). V. 7b emphasizes their shame: "They shall cover their moustache." This gesture, known from Ezek. 24:17,22, is a sign of mourning; but it also belongs to the conduct of the leper, who was required to cry out, "Unclean, unclean!" (Lev. 13:45). For Micah, this gesture may also mean that the prophets will simply have nothing more to say.

Micah gives the motivation for their actions in a penultimate concluding כי-clause: "There is no answer from God." In the other sayings contained in the Micah tradition, the prophet in no other instance uses the word אלהים. It may be that he takes up a fixed term used in prophetic circles; cf. דעת אלהים in Hosea (4:1; 6:6, and see Wolff, *Hosea* 67). This climax to Micah's announcement of disaster for the prophets corresponds in content to the doom spoken against the politicians in v. 4. Verses 6f. are clearly an explanatory comment on v. 4: the heads and leaders no longer find an answer (to their inquiry) from God because the prophets no longer have a word of God revealed to them. It is precisely in times of crisis that there is need for such revelation (e.g., 1 Kings 22:5ff.; 2 Kings 19:2ff.). But Micah must declare that especially at such times there will be no word from God, and as a result the prophets will become silent.

[3:8] On the other hand, Micah sets himself in contrast to the misleading prophets in a most unusual sentence that expresses "defiant boasting" (G. von Rad, *Old Testament Theology* 2:203). In verbal combat the word ואולם introduces the development of a sharp antithesis within one's own speech (cf. Num. 14:21; Job 2:5; 5:8; 13:3). "I, I am filled"—this is not an allusion to a prophetic call account, nor is it merely a report of a brief commissioning (thus J. L. Mays, 84f.; W. Rudolph, 73; A. S. van der

Woude, 116). For מלא is never used in the accounts of a prophet's call. Whenever the word occurs in comparable texts, it refers rather only to a being filled up (with words), as in Jer. 6:11; 15:17b; Job 32:18. The word מלא points to the impossibility of holding in or suppressing words that fill a person to overflowing (here cf. v. 8b). Micah contrasts his own "fullness" with the "emptiness" of those prophets who no longer receive an "answer from God."

Micah's "strength" stands in contrast to their weak dependence on those who provide them with money. כֹח means physical and psychic strength to stand up against opposition and discouragement (cf. Isa. 40:29, 31; כֹח refers primarily to the strength of God himself: Isa. 40:26). The interpolation את־רוח יהוה is an explicit allusion to this (see note 8a above, pp. 91f.). In the second place, Micah names משפט, the "justice" that fills up to the brim the empty shell of his humanity. It has been suggested that together with the subjective gifts of "strength" (כֹח) and "courage" (בגורה), the third object of the verb, משפט, is also to be understood here as something subjective, namely, the prophet's consciousness of justice or his reasoning faculty. But our distinction between subjective and objective hardly applies to Israelite thinking. If indeed we take "strength" and "courage" as objective gifts a person is endowed with, then משפט is all the more that which fills Micah as an "object." It is certainly the same orientation-giving sense of justice with which the heads and leaders should be concerned (v. 1b), the basic principles that teach a person how to distinguish between good and evil (v. 2a), between right and wrong (v. 9b). If Micah is filled with "justice," he thereby stands in competition with the politicians whom he indicts. If Micah himself, as an "elder of Judah," is a custodian of justice, then this competition becomes more easily understandable (cf. Wolff, "Amt" 407). When we think in particular of Micah's prophetic proclamation (v. 8b!), we perceive in the word משפט, in addition to the meaning of "ordinances for justice," even more the sense of "legal decision" (Exod. 21:1, 31), "verdict" (G. Liedke, *THAT* 2: 1006: "judicial sentence"). Furthermore, to pronounce the legal sentence now deserved by the Jerusalem leaders requires a third gift, גבורה, the bravery needed by a warrior, a גבּור. The prophet, acting as plaintiff, needs the fortitude that is entirely lacking in the false prophets, namely, civil courage. גבורה also refers to a manner of superiority that is inseparably bound up with wisdom (Job 12:13; Prov. 8:24; Isa. 11:2). It must be possessed by those who would speak unpopular things.

But this is Micah's task: "to proclaim" what no one likes to hear. נגד *hiph.* means literally "to stand opposite to (נֶגֶד) something" so that it can be seen; "to confront"; "to charge or reproach." He is obligated to confront Jacob with his פשע, i.e., his rebellion and apostasy (cf. 1 Kings 12:19), his attitude of opposition to justice; and his חטאת, his failure to achieve the goal assigned to him (Judg. 20:16). He must charge with injustice "Jacob" and "Israel," i.e., all of the ancient people of God who live on in the Judah and Jerusalem of his time. Micah must address them as the people of God, to whom Yahweh once made known his will (cf. W. Beyerlin, 16). Micah claims for himself the same sphere of responsibility he assigns to the heads and leaders he addresses in 3:1, 9.

It is important to note that according to the personal statement in

v. 8, Micah sees his chief task in exposing the guilt of his audience. This corresponds to the fact that in chaps. 2–3 more space is devoted to the prophet's accusations than to his announcements of disaster, which clearly predominated in 1:1–16. He does not say that his charges of guilt should lead to repentance (thus Lam. 2:14!; cf. Ezek. 20:7f.). On the contrary, in this context his words of indictment clearly introduce the announcement of punishment (v. 12), which is also the consequence of the accusation (v. 4 and vv. 6f.). For Micah's understanding of his prophetic office, it is striking that he immediately responds by comparing himself ("by contrast, I") in strength and courage not only with the prophets as his colleagues (vv. 5–7); he also clearly stands as a rival to the leaders, heads, and judges (vv. 1, 9, 11a). For Micah is empowered to conserve and promote the very thing they neglect: justice.

[3:9] After a new "summons to hear," which is parallel to v. 1a, Micah does not again charge the leaders and heads with responsibility for justice, as at the beginning of the scene in v. 1b. Rather, he immediately characterizes them according to their entirely reprehensible relationship to משפט. They "detest" justice. תעב piel describes a sense of aversion. Just as others are repelled by filth and refuse, they find the practice of justice highly disagreeable. Amos 5:10 offers a concrete example: "They detest him who speaks the truth." The practice of justice hinders their reckless treatment of the neighbor; it stands in the way of their avarice and pleasure-seeking. Therefore, they are not only unconcerned with justice (v. 1b); they even "pervert" it. עקש piel describes an action that twists what is straight. But "straight" (ישרה) in the vocabulary of wisdom is the word for what is right, what is just. The wisdom teachers use this word frequently when they speak about the perversion of justice: Prov. 8:8f.; 10:9; 28:18; Job 33:27. Concerning such experts in distortion, Isaiah says that they make darkness out of light and light out of darkness, bitter out of sweet and sweet out of bitter (5:20). Micah presumably thinks of their preference for "perverted ways" (Prov. 10:9; cf. Amos 2:7). Those who ought to defend justice have become tyrants of injustice. Micah issues a fundamental rebuke against their rejection of justice, which he verifies by referring to three particular kinds of behavior: (1) they mistreat other people (v. 10); (2) they accept bribes (v. 11a); (3) they affect a pious self-security before God (v. 11b).

[3:10] Concerning (1): Micah alludes to the vigorous building program in Jerusalem, which was enlarged to an extraordinary degree under Hezekiah. Mushrooming alongside human dwellings were fortifications and public buildings, storage for grain, new wine and oil, and stalls for cattle (2 Chron. 32:27f.). The difficult construction of the Siloam tunnel, which brought water from the well of Gihon into the center of the city, was a technical feat. The tunnel was dug out of the rock for a length of 512 meters; it was .45–3.0 meters high and 58–65 cm wide (cf. H. J. Stoebe, BHHW 3: 1795f.). The tunnel of Siloam was merely the outstanding example of undertakings that required large colonies of laborers, men who no doubt were recruited from the countryside of Judah, including Micah's home territory. Micah tells us that the impressive enlargement of the capital city could only be accomplished by blood and wickedness. The plural דמים means spilled blood (Gen. 4:10; Exod. 22:1; Ps. 5:7). עולה is a word for malice that also occurs elsewhere in connection with murder: 2 Sam. 3:34; 7:10; Hab. 2:12. Micah's words probably refer not only to construction accidents with fatal consequences, but also, in light of his charge concerning injustice, to the extreme mistreatment of laborers, or even to their death sentence. What Jeremiah accused King Jehoiakim of a hundred years later (Jer. 22:13–17) will presumably have already taken place at the time of Micah under those in positions of responsibility; cf. also the stoning of Naboth in Jezreel (1 Kings 21). Perhaps the קצינים addressed by Micah had the function of overseeing (Prov. 6:7) construction procedures and, accordingly, were responsible for the laborer's welfare (Isa. 3:6–7). Negligence of these matters was as much to be censured as the neglect of the "heads," who were especially obligated to attend to matters of bloodguilt that came before the judiciary (cf. 2 Chron. 19:10 and G. Ch. Macholz, 328f.; see above, pp. 97f.).

[3:11a] Concerning (2): With v. 11a Micah begins the second accusation: the "heads" in their capacity as judges are guided not by justice but by money. They do not make their decisions and pass their judgments according to the standards of the traditional orders of justice in Israel but according to the size of the bribe slipped into their pockets. שחד denotes a gift given secretly ("in the bosom," Prov. 17:23; 21:14) to the judge by the person involved in a legal case; the bribe is proof of his ability to pervert justice (Prov. 17:8). Just as proverbial wisdom struggles against the craze for personal profit accumulated in official dealings, so the Old Testament legal material indicates that this theme remained relevant at all times (Exod. 23:8; Deut. 16:19; 10:17; in the ancient dodecalogue of curses in Deut. 27:25, bribery is mentioned even in connection with shedding innocent blood; cf. Mic. 3:10a). How flagrant the corruption was in Jerusalem during Micah's time is confirmed by Isaiah (1:23; 5:23). According to him, it is especially the poor, the widows, and the orphans who suffer under corruptible judges. This must have been a principal source of oppression in those days.

The priests, too, were caught up in accepting bribes. But here it is not so much the idea that the priests, as part of the council of judges in Jerusalem, worked together with the family heads in passing legal judgments (2 Chron. 19:8); indeed, they are not addressed by Micah concerning their practical legal decisions (as are the judges), but concerning their teaching (ירה *hiph.*). As stewards of the Torah, their duty is to keep alive the traditional ordinances and their validity (Deut. 33:10; Hos. 4:6; Deut. 17:8–11; cf. G. von Rad, *Old Testament Theology* 1:245ff.). Thus, within the council of judges their function is not only to teach and counsel, but also to watch over the conditions for admission to the sanctuary; one of these conditions is to reject a bribe against the innocent (Ps. 15:5). Nevertheless, even the priests' teaching is governed by money.

If a poor person in deepest distress goes to a prophet to receive personal counsel (1 Sam. 9:6), he finds that these, too, are already captivated by silver (see above, pp. 102f. on 3:5). The danger of bribery for the prophets is indicated in Num. 22:18; 1 Kings 13:7ff.; 2 Kings 5:15f.;

Neh. 6:12f. Micah is indignant over how widespread has become the practice of bribery, reaching even to persons who bear spiritual responsibilities.

[3:11b] Concerning (3): In v. 11b it becomes clear that the corruptible authorities profess an unshakable trust in God; here the accusation reaches its climax, at the same time expressing the self-irony of those whom the prophet indicts. The quotations should be understood not only as statements made by the prophets, who are named last within the group, but especially as expressions of certainty from all the officials mentioned in v. 11a; this is indicated by the prosody of v. 11, which has two three-stress tricola (corresponding to the three-stress tricola in v. 12; see above, p. 94). "To lean upon Yahweh" is synonymous with "to believe" and "to trust" (cf. Isa. 10:20; 31:1; 50:10). As in the Songs of Zion, those whom Micah quotes know "Yahweh to be in their midst" (Pss. 46; 48; 76). Therefore they can only reject the prophet's threat of "disaster" (רעה; 3:4, 6f.; cf. 2:3; cf. Amos 9:10b). They consider themselves immune and untouchable, and indeed, can no longer sense the contradiction between their dedication to profit and their verbal loyalty to Yahweh. They are oblivious to the hypocrisy of their faith, since they no longer consider Yahweh as the Lord of their life or the helper of those who suffer.

[3:12] It must have been like an exploding bomb when Micah hurled against these pietistic, self-satisfied opponents his final word of judgment, formulated in direct address: "Therefore because of you!" What the prophet must now say about Jerusalem applies to a city which the leading circles ruthlessly made to serve their own purposes by enlarging and fortifying it for their own pleasure and security. What, however, will become of their own concerns when the law of God is no longer permitted to have a voice among them?

"Zion will be plowed into an open field." This does not mean, for example, that Zion will be plowed up into "arable land"; for here שדה denotes open country (where, for example, wild animals are hunted, Gen. 27:3). Zion's beautiful, paved courts will be turned into an uninhabitable land. By using the passive voice (תחרש) Micah is able to speak of Yahweh with great restraint; nor does he introduce the announcement of disaster (v. 12) as a divine oracle, as do the elders later on in Jer. 26:18. Indeed, Micah has just cited the misuse of Yahweh's name (v. 11b).

"Jerusalem will become a field of ruins." It is improbable that Micah places Jerusalem next to Zion in order to refer to another part of the city. J. Simons (*Jerusalem in the Old Testament* [1952], 235f.), thinks that, preceding the reference to the temple mount, Zion denotes the ancient Jebusite city on the southeastern hill, while Jerusalem refers to the mass of living quarters situated on the southwestern hill of the city. This distinction is unlikely after v. 10, where Zion and Jerusalem are used synonymously. The buildings made with blood (v. 10) will thus become rubble. A gruesome end comes upon Jerusalem's building program, reflecting the words of the proverb, "Unless Yahweh builds a house, those who build it labor in vain" (Ps. 127:1).

That the sentences in v. 12 move to a climax in the third sentence is unmistakable: "The mountain of the house [upon which the accused ground their security] will be given over to the 'wild animals' of the forest." Here, too, Micah avoids using the name of Yahweh. For him, Yahweh has long ago ceased to dwell in this house. Moreover, human beings will no longer be found here. יער denotes the wilderness, the thicket with its scrub which—as for all cities under a curse—is given over to wild animals, jackals, hyenas, lions, bears, owls, and ostriches (cf. Jer. 13:19–22; Jer. 50:39; Zeph. 2:13–15). In this way, Samaria's misfortune also reaches to Jerusalem, as Micah saw it coming in 1:6–9, when he already howled like a jackal and mourned like an ostrich (1:8).

The enormous impact this unique judgment speech must have had upon Jerusalem is shown by the fact that the people still talked about it more than a hundred years later (Jer. 26:18f.). Never had any prophet dared to speak in this way in or concerning Jerusalem—not even Isaiah preached so severely, comprehensively, and destructively (1:21–26; 5:14; 22:1–14). It is now hardly possible to clarify the relationship of Hezekiah's reform (reported in 2 Kings 18:4–5) to his own repentance (according to Jer. 26:19) and to Micah's prophetic activity. However, the lament in Ps. 79:1 sees Micah's prophecy fulfilled in Israel's history: "They have laid Jerusalem in ruins."

Purpose and Thrust

משפט is the key word in Micah's three prophecies concerning Jerusalem. The Jerusalem heads and leaders (vv. 1, 9) as well as the prophets (v. 8) are to be measured by "justice." It is justice that provides the criterion for the prophet's accusations. In each instance, announcements of disaster are preceded by accusations (3:2–3, 5, 9b–11) which, on the whole, are more comprehensive than the announcements. Moreover, Micah himself characterizes his chief office as that of plaintiff (v. 8), which he serves on behalf of justice, by his strong and courageous work. M icah thus shows himself to be one of the great champions of justice. He expends his energy for the sake of "his people" (3:5), who are exploited physically (vv. 2f.) and cheated of their rights (vv. 9b–11a). The courage of the man from Moresheth may be seen in his attack against political and religious authorities in the capital city. He charges them with brutality and pleasure-seeking, even with cannibalism, as well as with perversion of justice: they accept bribes because of their avarice (vv. 5, 9b, 11a). The prophets have degraded themselves by becoming "cunning researchers of the market" (G. Quell, 122). They lull themselves to sleep—no doubt with the other officials—by means of a slogan expressing religious self-security: "Yahweh is in our midst"; however, their deeds contradict this sanctimonious statement. They are guided neither by Yahweh nor by justice; rather, they are absorbed with their own well-being, with the "morality" of making a buck. Micah's accusations should be a warning to the church not to allow its prophetic office to degenerate; instead, this office must remain vigilant and courageous in speaking out against injustice, not only in the world but, above all, among its own ecclesiastical leaders.

Micah joins to each accusation of injustice an announcement of the consequences, introduced by "then" in v. 4 and by the compelling and conclusive "therefore" in vv. 6 and 12. In each instance the content of the verdict corresponds to the content of the crime. Whoever refuses to hear the cries of mistreated people will experience the silence of God. Beginning with v. 4, the general theme of the chapter's proclamation of judgment becomes God's movement toward hiddenness. The prophets, who are professional intermediaries for those seeking answers from God, will become completely disoriented in their visions of the night: "No answer from God" stands over their future life and work (vv. 6f.). The prophetic message is decisive for the legitimacy of the office; the office does not decide the legitimacy of the message (see above, pp. 103f.). All judicial, priestly, and prophetic officials together must learn that a Jerusalem built with blood and injustice can only become a pile of rubble; that a misused sanctuary can only become a wilderness (v. 12). Yahweh has bound his presence not to a locality but to the word. In the word of justice, and in the proclamation of Micah, his witness, Yahweh's presence is to be found; in the midst of all God's hiddenness and in view of the destruction of his city, he remains efficaciously present in the midst of divine judgment.

Here we ought to take note how reticent Micah himself is in speaking of Yahweh. It is remarkable that Yahweh's name is mentioned neither at the beginning of Micah's prophetic sayings (on the messenger formula in v. 5a, see above p. 96) nor in the transitions to the threats of judgment (vv. 4, 6f., 12). Later, in one particular instance, this gave rise to the need for additions to the text (thus in Jer. 26:18, the messenger formula is inserted when Mic. 3:12 is quoted). In comparison with his contemporaries Amos, Hosea, and Isaiah, it is an astounding phenomenon that Micah does not present God as speaking in the first person in any of these sayings concerning Jerusalem, not even in the climax of the threat of destruction to Jerusalem; instead of a particular reference to Yahweh's authority, in v. 12 we find a passive construction ("Zion will be plowed up"). It speaks merely of the "mount of the house," not of the "mount of the house of Yahweh." In light of the call accounts contained in the other classical prophets, what is most obviously missing in Micah is a reference to Yahweh's commission; nor is "justice" even referred to as the "justice of Yahweh" in the bold sentence in v. 8 when the prophet introduces himself.

How are we to understand Micah's strange silence when it comes to using the name of Yahweh? Is it advisable for him to be reticent because his opponents frequently use the name of Yahweh? Micah says concerning them: "They will cry out to Yahweh . . ." (v. 4); "They rely on Yahweh and say, 'Is not Yahweh in our midst?'" (v. 11b). Or does his reticence stem from wisdom thinking (cf. H. W. Wolff, "Amt," 413ff.)? In either case, Micah's unusually infrequent mention of the name of Yahweh emphasizes his demand that his opponents recognize that they misuse God's name, revelation, and protection for their own glory or profit. The judgment he is commissioned to proclaim points up the outrageous discrepancy between their faith and their conduct. In this regard, Micah strikingly anticipates and interprets the words of Jesus: "Not everyone who says to me 'Lord, Lord,' shall enter the kingdom of heaven, but he who does the will of my father who is in heaven" (Matt. 7:21).

The New Jerusalem

Literature

B. Stade, "Bemerkungen über das Buch Micha," *ZAW* 1 (1881) 161–172. E. Nestle, "Miszellen. Micha 4,3," *ZAW* 29 (1909) 234. K. Fullerton, "Studies in Isaiah: On Is 2,5 and Mi 4,5," *JBL* 35 (1916) 134–140. E. Sachsse, "Untersuchungen zur hebräischen Metrik. Jes 2,2–4; Mi 4,1–3," *ZAW* 43 (1925) 173–192. K. Budde, "Verfasser und Stelle von Mi 4,1–4 (Jes 2,2–4)," *ZDMG* 81 (1927) 152–158. J. T. Meek, "Some Emendations in the Old Testament: 1. Mi 4:1 = Isa 2:2," *JBL* 48 (1929) 162–163. W. Cannon, "The Disarmament Passage in Isaiah II and Micah IV," *Theology* 24 (1930) 2–8. G. von Rad, "Die Stadt auf dem Berge," *EvTh* 8 (1948/1949) 439–447 = ThB 8 (⁴1971) 214–224; Eng. trans. in *The Problem of the Hexateuch and other essays,* trans. E. W. Trueman Dicken (1966) 232–242. E. Nielsen, *Oral Tradition,* SBT 11 (1954) 79–93. H. Wildberger, "Die Völkerwallfahrt zum Zion," *VT* 7 (1957) 62–81. A. S. Kapelrud, "Eschatology in the Book of Micah," *VT* 11 (1961) 392–405. C. Westermann, "Micha 5,1–3," in *Herr, tue meine Lippen auf* 5, ed. G. Eichholz (²1961) 54–59. E. Cannawurf, "The Authenticity of Micah IV 1–4," *VT* 13 (1963) 26–33. B. Renaud, *Structure et attaches littéraires de Michée IV–V* (1964). H. Cazelles, "Histoire et Géographie en Mi 4,6–13," in *Fourth World Congress Jewish Studies* 1 (1967) 87–89. H. M. Lutz, *Jahwe, Jerusalem und die Völker,* WMANT 27 (1968). E. Lipiński, "באחרית תימים dans les textes préexiliques," *VT* 20 (1970) 445–450. O. H. Steck, *Friedensvorstellungen im alten Jerusalem,“* ThSt Zürich 111 (1972) 69–71. A. S. van der Woude, "Micah IV 1–5. An Instance of the Pseudo-Prophets Quoting Isaiah," in *Symbolae biblicae et mesopotamicae F. M. Th. de Liagre-Böhl dedicatae* (1973) 396–402. J. S. Kselman, "A Note on Isaiah II 2, *VT* 25 (1975) 225–227. W. H. Schmidt, "Epiphanias. Jesaja 2,1–5," *GPM* 30 (1975) 66–74. B. Renaud, *La Formation du Livre de Michée* (1977) 150–195. B. S. Childs, *Introduction to the Old Testament as Scripture* (1979) 428–439. H. Wildberger, *Jesaja 1–12,* BK 10/1 (²1980) 75–90. H. Cazelles, "Qui aurait visé, à l'origine, Isaïe II 2–5," *VT* 30 (1980) 409–420.

Text

4:1 But one day,[a] when the times change,[b]
      then the mount of Yahweh's house[c] will[d]
    stand firm[e] as the peak of the mountains;
      it[f] will be lifted up above the hills.
    The[g] peoples[h] will stream[i] to[j] it,

111

2   and many nations[a] will come [and say],[b]
"Come, let us go up to the mount of Yahweh,
  to the house of the God of Jacob,
that he may teach[c] us the basis[d] of his ways,
  that we may walk in his paths"[e].[f]
For out of Zion instruction will go forth,
  Yahweh's word from Jerusalem.

3 He will judge between the [many][a] peoples,
    adjudicate for the multitude of nations [far away].[b]
Then they will beat their swords[c] into plowshares
  and their spears into pruning hooks.
Nation will not take[d] up sword against nation,
  neither will they[e] learn war any longer.

4 They will sit, each under his own grapevine
    and under his own fig tree—and none will disturb him.
    For the mouth of Yahweh Sebaoth has spoken.

5 Though all peoples walk (still in their way),[a]
    each in the name of its god,
we ourselves will walk
      in the name of Yahweh, our God
      forever and ever.

6 On that day, utterance of Yahweh,
  then I will assemble[a] the lame[b]
    and will gather the scattered
      and those[c] whom I harshly[d] treated.[e]

7 And I will[a] make the lame into (new) descendants[b]
    and those far away[c] I will make into a mighty nation.

Yahweh will be king[d] over them
  on Mount[e] Zion
    from now on and for evermore.

8 And you, O tower of the flock,
    fortified hill of the daughter of Zion,
to you will come[a] and enter
    the former sovereignty,
      the kingship of the daughter of Jerusalem.[b]

1a והיה at the beginning of a unit emphasizes the futurity of what follows; it also indicates a contrast with what precedes it literarily (3:12!); cf. Hos. 2:1 following 1:2–9.

1b The ancient translations recognize that the Hebrew expression characterizes the final end of all previous days (Gk: ἐπ ἐσχάτων τῶν ἡμερῶν; Targ: בסוף יומיא) and thus their turning point (Vg: *in novissimo dierum*). See below, p. 114.

1c Gk of Mic. (τὸ ὄρος τοῦ κυρίου) does not presuppose בית; however, בית is presupposed in Gk of Isa. 2:2 in an expanded phrase (τὸ ὄρος τοῦ κυρίου καὶ ὁ οἶκος τοῦ θεοῦ); this expansion is intelligible in view Isa. 2:3aα² = Mic. 4:2aα². Gk of Mic. abbreviates the Gk of Isa. in Mic. in v. 1aα (B. Renaud [1977] 151); MT (בית) is supported by Vg *(mons domus Domini)* and Targ (טור בית מקדשא); the unusual expression הר בית־יהוה is found also in 2 Chron. 33:15.

1d יהיה strengthens the durative-future aspect of the following participles (. . . נכון ונשא); cf. 1 Kings 2:45 and Joüon, *Gr* §§121e; 154m. Gk translates ἐμφανές (also in Isa. 2:2); however, this does not suggest that Gk has a different literary source (Th. H. Robinson, HAT 1/14³, 141, thinks Gk translates יראה; J. T. Meek proposes יחזה). Gk merely intended to avoid repeating καὶ ἔσται (B. Renaud [1977] 152).

1e In Isa. 2:2, נכון is placed before יהיה. In Mic. the word-order conforms not only to the rules of syntax (verbal adjective or participle stands after an auxiliary verb), but also to the *parallelismus membrorum* (נבון//ונשא).

1f הוא is omitted in Isa. 2:2, but the prosody of this line, a three-stress bicolon, requires it.

1g Isa. inserts כל־ and thus with this word emphasizes a universalistic view; cf. כל־העמים contained in the literary addition v. 5a, and see note 3a.

1h Isa. reads in v. 2b הגוים and in the parallel in v. 3a, עמים; the Isaiah text therefore reverses the order of the nouns found in Micah. The same reversal of עמים־גוים (Mic. 4:3a) is found in Isa. 2:4a; in each case the translations follow MT. J. Vermeylen, *Biblica* 61 (1980) 290, supposes that Mic. 4:1–3 has been brought into harmony with Mic. 4:11–13.

1i Gk (σπεύσουσι) reads וּמָהֲרוּ; in Isa. 2:2 Gk translates with ἥξουσιν. Vg *(fluent),* a' (ποταμωθήσονται) support MT.

1j Gk^{WQtxt,etc.} (Gk^{V,etc.} ἐπ αυτον) and Vg *(ad eum)* apparently understand עליו in the sense of אליו (found in Isa. 2:2b).

2a See note h on v. 1.

2b ואמרו should be read as an unstressed, initial beat (anacrusis); it stands outside the rhythm of the three-stress bicolon, but it is also attested by Isa. 2:3 and by all the versions.

2c Isa. 2:3 contains the defective form וירנו; Gk. of Mic. 4:2aβ (δείξουσιν) reads וירנו which misconstrues the subject to be "mount" and "house" (instead of Yahweh). Gk Isa. of 2:3 (ἀναγγελεῖ) confirms the singular verb in MT.

2d The singular in Gk (τὴν ὁδὸν αὐτοῦ) approaches the partitive understanding of מן with the plural (מדרכיו = "something of his ways," which is more closely defined in v. 3). See below, p. 121 on understanding MT.

2e The expected vocalization of ארח plural with suffix would be אָרְחֹתָיו; cf. KBL³, 84a,b on ארח ("way") and אֹרְחָה ("caravan").

2f The quotation of the saying of the nations ends here, since v. 2b is already more closely connected with v. 3a; see below, p. 121.

3a רבים is not found in Syr nor in Isa. 2:4aα; there, as in Mic. 4:1b–2aα, an adjective occurs only in the second member of the line (רבים instead of עצמים in Micah); thus in both cases a heightening is achieved by the style. On the basis of the verse's rhythm, one might suppose that רבים in Mic. 4:3aα was added later to emphasize a universalistic viewpoint, similar to the כל־ in Isa. 2:2b (see above, note g on v. 1).

3b עד רחוק, not found in Isa. 2:4, overloads the rhythm of the three-stress bicolon; the gloss underscores the universalism.

3c In Isa. 2:4bα¹ the word has the shorter suffix attached: חרבותם; Micah harmonizes the form with the longer suffix in the parallel חניתתיהם.

3d Gk (ἀντάρη) reads the singular ישּׂה, as in MT Isa. 2:4bβ, and interrupts the— grammatically correct—series of verbs in the third person plural.

3e The נ-*paragogicum* is not found in Isa. 2:4bγ.

5a Gk interprets by adding: τὴν ὁδὸν αὐτοῦ.

6a On the meaning of the word, see above, p. 86.

6b For this infrequent term (elsewhere only Gen. 32:32; Zeph. 3:19), Gk (συντετριμμένην) translates with "downtrodden"; Vg *(claudicantem)* with "hobbled"; Targ (מטלטליא) with "banished."

6c In translating the relative particle with οὓς, Gk correctly sees in the singular objects of the verbs אסף asap and קבץ qabas *piel*—objects naturally expected to be plurals—a collective sense, i.e., the flock (2:12) of the exilic community (4:7).

6d Gk (ἀπωσάμην) has in mind those who have been banished; Vg *(quam adflixeram),* the ill-treated.

6e The last member of the line (a two-stress tricolon) needs nothing to complete it, as B. Duhm and E. Sellin suppose. Although Targ (להון) presupposes an additional לָהֶם, which would clarify the object of the verb, it departs from the style (third person feminine singular as object) that is continued in v. 7.

7a The perfect consecutive has the same cohortative sense as the two previous synonyms, אספה—אקבצה; cf. Joüon, *Gr* §119j.

7b On the meaning of שארית, which is usually translated "remnant," see below, p. 124.

7c The singular form can be understood as a *niphal* participle of הלא. In light of the cry "stand back," "go away" (הלאה; Gen. 19:9; Num. 17:2; cf. Amos 5:27), its sense could be "that which is far off" (KBL³, 235); the feminine singular is congruent with the preceding forms in v. 6 (הצלעה and הנדחה). Gk (τὴν ἀπωσμένην; cf. note 6d) understands the word in a similar way. Since J. Wellhausen the word is often read as וְהַנַּחֲלָה ("the weak"; cf. Ezek. 34:4, 21); Vg *(quae laboraverat)* instead may have presupposed וְהַנִּלְאָה ("the exhausted"; cf. W. Rudolph and B. Renaud [1977] 182). MT is to be preferred on the basis of *lectio difficilior*.

7d The proposal to read וּמָלַכְתִּי instead of ומלך יהוה (*BHS*) arbitrarily brings this verse into congruence with the first person speech of God in vv. 6–7a.

7e Syr presupposes an additional וּבִירוּשָׁלַם, as in Isa. 24:23.

8a The first vowel in תֵּאתֶה is a contraction of the first two vowels in תֶאֱתֶה (as לֵאמֹר; cf. Joüon, *Gr* §73g).

8b Gk (ἐκ βαβυλῶνος) inserts the word "Babylon" for the place of their departure, in accordance with v. 10.

Form

Micah 4:1–8 contains three different complexes of sayings: vv. 1–5; 6–7; and 8. The boundaries are marked by the introductory formula in v. 6a, by the concluding formulas in v. 5b and v. 7b, and also by the change of theme. The sayings are linked together by the question concerning Jerusalem's future. However, according to their style, origin, and content the sayings are quite different. The first two (vv. 1–5; vv. 6–7) can by no means be taken by themselves as self-contained units. Let us begin by examining the three complexes according to their stylistic unity and rhetorical forms.

[4:1–5] In vv. 1–5, v. 5 initially can be clearly distinguished from vv. 1–4 as a later addition, for in vv. 1–4 a conclusion is reached with v. 4b ("for the mouth of Yahweh Sebaoth has spoken"). What follows in v. 5 is a shift from a promise (vv. 1–4) to a confessional statement; here the people of Yahweh (first person plural) go a different way from that of "all peoples." Thus the promise of the nations' pilgrimage to Zion, which is expected to lead to great peace in the future, is placed in sober antithesis to the present situation. In this way v. 5 critically comments on a pre-existing tradition of promise.

But even the promise itself (vv. 1–4) appears to contain levels of redactional activity, especially in comparison with Isa. 2:2–4, a passage that almost precisely corresponds to vv. 1–3. In Isa. 2:2–4, there is nothing similar to Mic. 4:4. The content of v. 4 goes a step further than vv. 1–3; it joins to the announcement of peace among nations a promise about the life of individuals. This promise appears to be a redactional addition. The concluding sentence itself in Mic. 4:4b, which is not found in Isa. 2:4, also seems to be a secondary addition, especially since no actual Yahweh speech precedes it. The core of the passage, in which Isa. 2:2–4 and Mic. 4:1–3 are in accord, instead presents an unconditional promise for the nations that speaks about Yahweh only in the third person, and only in the middle section (v. 2–3a) of the passage. Indeed, the main point here in vv. 2–3a is the word of Yahweh, whereas what precedes (v. 1) gives the detailed presuppositions for, and what follows (v. 3b) announces the consequences of, his word. Verse 4a portrays a further consequence. The variations in the parallel passage in Isaiah are indicative of oral tradition, which became fixed in writing in different phases. This explains the twice-occurring interchange of עמים and גוים (see note 1h), the different position of נכון (see note 1e) and the two interpolations in v. 3a (see notes 3a, b) that give it a universalistic emphasis.

The structure of this promise in the book of Micah permits a division into four strophes. The first strophe (vv. 1–2aα¹), three bicola of three stresses each, presents a vision of the towering grandeur of Jerusalem's temple mount, and of the nations' streaming to it. The second strophe (vv. 2aα²–b), a three-stress bicolon, reports the audition of words summoning the nations; further, it expresses the expectation that they will hear the voice of Yahweh, emphasized by a two-stress bicolon. Again, a three-stress bicolon presents the fulfillment of this expectation. The third strophe gives a promise of what Yahweh's voice will speak (v. 3a), formulated as a three-stress bicolon; it also tells of the peace-bringing consequences (v. 3b), expressed by two further three-stress bicola (on the overloaded meter, see notes 3a, b). Three-stress bicola thus clearly predominate; they are interrupted by a two-stress bicolon only at the climax, in the middle of the second strophe. The fourth strophe (v. 4), which has not been included in Isa. 2, is different from the preceding verses also in its prosody, for it contains three cola with four stresses each. The later addition in v. 5 combines a three-stress bicolon with a two-stress tricolon, the latter giving emphasis to this confessional statement.

[4:6–7] Whereas the grand promise of peace among nations speaks of Yahweh only in the third person, the core of the second complex is an oracle of Yahweh. In vv. 6–7a, after the introductory formula, each sentence is dominated by the "I" of Yahweh, which is the subject. This "messenger speech" is an unconditional promise for a defeated and scattered people in exile. Here a two-stress tricolon is combined with a three-stress bicolon, similar to that found in v. 5. In v. 7b a prose sentence follows. Apparently, v. 7b is intended to connect with vv. 6–7a, since the עלהם would otherwise have no antecedent. Yahweh's kingship extends to the lame and the dispersed who, according to the promise, will become a powerful nation. Nevertheless, whereas the suffering people in vv. 6–7a are always spoken about in the singular (to be understood in a collective sense), in v. 7b the third person plural is used. That v. 7b is a later addition can also be recognized by the stylistic change: now Yahweh is spoken of in the third person instead of the first person style of the messenger speech in vv. 6–7a. The thematic focus of the secondary addition is on Yahweh's kingship "on Mount Zion." Nothing is said about Mount Zion in the Yahweh speech in vv. 6–7a. The redaction that is recognizable in v. 7b takes the transmitted promise, and, by placing it into the context of chap. 4, gives it a special meaning.

[4:8] In v. 8, the third complex, unlike the first and second, no stylistic or thematic break can be recognized. A uniform style of address (second person) distinguishes v. 8 from the preceding complexes; what connects v. 8 to the previous context is its unconditional promise to Jerusalem-

Zion. Can it be said that v. 8 is joined to vv. 6f. (B. Renaud [1977] 149ff.)? Certainly, the image of the flock, which has been considered to be a connecting element, is not carried out in vv. 6f., as in 2:12, and the promise of the return of the Davidic monarchy in v. 8 stands rather in a certain tension with the redactional addition concerning Yahweh's kingship in v. 7b. But v. 8 itself must also be taken as redactional. It connects, however, not with the preceding but with the following context, namely, with 5:1[2], 3[4], the highpoint of the transmission complex 4:9—5:5[6] (see below pp. 134f.).

Numerous parallels in vocabulary require the supposition that, within the context of the question concerning the new Jerusalem, v. 8 is a redactional imitation of 5:1[2], 3[4] and was placed at the end of the Jerusalem-promises in 4:1–8 and before the older tradition complex 4:9—5:5[6] (cf. B. Renaud [1977] 280f.). To be noted are the following parallels between 5:1[2], 3[4] and v. 8: (1) the introduction of direct address with the word ואתה; (2) the similarity of "come forth from you" (ממך יצא) and "to you shall come" (עדיך תאתה ובאה); (3) the announcement of a "ruler" (מושל) and one "who rules" (הממשלה); (4) the ruler's origin "from of old, from ancient days" (מקדם ממי עולם) becomes the "former" (הראשנה) [dominion]; (5) the ruler is presented as a shepherd (5:3[4]), cf. עדר in 4:8. These numerous correspondences cannot be accidental. The difficulty is how to explain the levels of redaction that produced the present text.

If the original core of the transmission-unit 4:9—5:5[6] is older than the sayings in 4:1–8 (see below, pp. 137f.), then 4:8 stands in the same redactional relationship to the unit (4:9—5:5[6]), and thus especially to 5:1[2], as v. 7b does to vv. 6–7a. The process of redaction then reaches beyond the boundaries of 4:1–8. Micah 4:8 takes the older promise addressed to Bethlehem (5:1) and connects it to Zion-Jerusalem. Here for the first time in the book of Micah we become acquainted with the beginning of a consciously conceived prophetic literature. It takes the smaller rhetorical units and, guided by certain key questions, gives the units a written form that exhibits the redactor's interpretation.

Setting

The key questions here are provided by the literary setting of this collection of sayings. The ancient Micah tradition reached a climax with 3:12, which threatened the complete destruction of Jerusalem and the Zion temple. Jer. 26:17ff. provides evidence of how the memory of this prophecy remained alive from generation to generation. After the catastrophe of 587, Micah's prophecies were read and interpreted in the exilic ceremonies of lamentation for the purpose of awakening a sense of humility before God. This is indicated by the literary additions in 1:5, 13b, 2:3–5, 10 (see above, pp. 75f.). With hope rekindled in the exilic community after the preaching of Ezekiel and his disciples, and also of Deutero-Isaiah, and, finally, with the first arrival in Jerusalem of those returning from exile, the certainty began to grow that Micah's proclamation of destruction was not the last word from God. Thus joined to Mic. 3:12 were a collection of prophetic voices that initially were intended to provide answers to the question: What, then, will happen in the future to the destroyed city of God? As a collection of sayings that appears to have been shaped later into a self-contained unit in chaps. 4–5, it has a different literary character than the glosses from the Babylonian period that were inserted into Micah's prophetic sayings. For this reason, therefore, the collection presumably belongs to the Persian era, probably not until after the exilic period and the restoration of the temple.

In light of these provisional literary findings, in the succeeding literary analysis we must now ask in detail: What is the original setting in life of these collected sayings and fragments of sayings? What are the possibilities of a more precise dating of the material? How are the redactional connections to be understood?

[4:1–5] The first passage, a declaration about the worldwide importance of the "mount of the house of Yahweh," immediately stands in antithesis to the fearsome judgment prophesied in 3:12. This orally transmitted saying (see above, pp. 114f.) is characterized as a divine oracle by the secondary addition of v. 4b (although the passage itself does not contain a first person Yahweh speech; cf. vv. 1a, 2b, 3a). And as such it was proclaimed within the worship service, as is indicated by the conclusion in v. 5, which connects the passage with the present by means of this confessional statement from the worshiping community. That the parallel text in Isa. 2:2–4 also has a liturgical setting is confirmed by a similar concluding statement in v. 5: "Come, O House of Jacob! Let us walk in Yahweh's light!" Can more be said about origin of the divine oracle's core section?

Critical scholarship has shown the improbability of three attempts at dating the passage. (1) H. Ewald (*Die Propheten des Alten Bundes,* 1867) thought that Isaiah and Micah derived the oracle from a common source; similarly, most recently, R. Vuilleumier. Moreover, A. S. Kapelrud supposed that the passage is a cultic oracle rooted in the ancient New Year festival of the celebration of Yahweh's enthronement. (2) C. W. E. Nägelsbach (*Der Prophet Jesaja,* 1877) thought Micah was the author, whose text he found better preserved and transmitted in a more complete form. But since the passage's content sharply contrasts with Micah's message, (3) A. S. van der Woude thought that here also (as already in 2:12f.; see above, p. 76, for opposing arguments) are words of Micah's opponents, the false prophets; that in the first person plural in v. 5b they themselves speak, while the remainder of the text is an old prophecy of Isaiah's which they quote in opposition to Micah. In assigning vv. 1–3 to Isaiah, A. S. van der Woude is in agreement with H. Wildberger. However, the dating of the passage in preexilic times has become more and more unlikely. The decision rests on the question whether, in comparison with traditional older material, the text also contains words and phrases that are demonstrably specific to postexilic times and that present difficulties for dating them in preexilic times (B. Renaud [1977] 175). This is the case to a great extent. It is not individual examples but their sum which is conclusive. (1) "The mount of the house of Yahweh" (v. 1aα) is found elsewhere only in 2 Chron. 33:15. (2) That the peoples "stream together" (I נהר v. 1b) is said elsewhere only in Jer. 51:44. (3) "Many peoples and mighty nations" (v. 3a), formulated with these very words, occurs elsewhere only in Zech. 8:22, where the nations make their way to Jerusalem to seek Yahweh. (4) "To lift up the sword" and "to learn war"

(v. 3bβ) occur elsewhere in this phraseology only in 1 Chron. 5:18. (5) The expression באחרית הימים (v. 1aα), used to designate a completely new kind of event, occurs nowhere else as an introductory formula; as an eschatological term it is not found until postexilic times (Hos. 3:5 [secondary addition]; Ezek. 38:16 [secondary addition]; Dan. 10:14 and 2:28 [Aramaic]; cf. Deut. 4:30; 31:29; in addition, Gen. 49:1; Num. 24:14; Jer. 23:20; 30:24; 48:47; see below, p. 119). These word-statistics point clearly to the time of the Persian Empire.

The scholars who support a preexilic date for the origin of this saying have argued that the themes of the nations' pilgrimage, of the unique significance of Zion, and also of lasting peace, are already to be found in Isaiah and in the Songs of Zion in the Psalter (cf. especially H. Wildberger, *Jesaja,* BK 10/1, ad loc.). Aside from the difficulties of convincingly dating the appropriate texts in Isaiah and the Psalms, it must furthermore be asked whether we can locate a time in the history of Israel's proclamation when the three themes now joined together in our text were combined into one prophetic message. These three themes are (1) the focus on Zion as the goal of the pilgrimage and the place where divine instruction issues forth; (2) the universal scope of the nations' journey to Zion; (3) the effecting of a lasting peace throughout the whole world. It should especially be noted that in the combination of traditions under discussion, the texts in Mic. 4:1–4 and Isa. 2:2–4 have absolutely nothing particular to say about Israel. We do not find anything approaching similarity to the strong universal accent given with the simultaneous combination of these three themes until Trito-Isaiah and Zechariah. A comparison of Isa. 56:3–7, 66:18–23; Zech. 8:20–22, 23, on the one hand, with Isaiah's proclamation concerning Zion in 14:28–32 and 28:14–18, on the other, shows without doubt that this prophetic promise in Micah stands much closer to the postexilic texts.

The literary setting, word-statistics, and themes point to the same date. If we note that our passage repeatedly speaks of the "house of Yahweh" (v. 1a) or of the "house of the God of Jacob" (v. 2a), the resulting terminus a quo is the completion of the postexilic temple in spring of 515 B.C.E. (Ezra 5:15; cf. S. Herrmann, *History of Israel* [²1981] 305f.).

That Mic. 4:1–4 was used liturgically at the dedication of the temple, as Th. Lescow (*ZAW* 84 [1972] 76) supposes, is certainly possible, especially since the passage fits not only with the joyful character of the festival, but also with the support for rebuilding the temple given by the Persians (Ezra 5:6—6:12). Moreover, the motifs of the grandeur of the mount of God, and of the peoples' pilgrimage contained in hymns sung at temple dedications, have had their counterparts for centuries in the Mesopotamian area (cf. F. Stolz, *Strukturen und Figuren im Kult von Jerusalem,* BZAW 118 [1970] 78f.; see below, p. 120).

The commentary in v. 5, made on the occasion of a later liturgical reading of vv. 1–4 (see above, p. 117), shows that a sobering distance had been clearly placed, for that present moment, between the way of the Jewish community and way of the nations. Verse 5 exhibits the same tendency known from the period between Haggai (2:10–14), Malachi (2:10–12), and Ezra (Ezra 10; Nehemiah 8).

[4:6–7a] Verses 6–7a, however, presuppose that there are still weakness and dispersion, the afflictions of exile; yet the passage expresses hope for Yahweh's work of gathering and empowering the exiles (cf. p. 86 above on 2:12). Thus the redactor combines quite heterogeneous sayings; lacking any systemactic principles to guide his editing, his work appears rather to be anthological. Verses 6–7a, too, represent preexisting material that was available to him. The purpose for which he uses it is made clear with his own supplementary comment (see above, p. 115) in v. 7b: the gathering, strengthening, and returning home of the exiles is the precondition for Yahweh's accession to his final royal dominion "upon Mount Zion" (a similar reference is missing in 2:12f., see above, pp. 86f.). In this way, the redactor also relates this passage to his guiding question: What will happen to Zion in the future, after Yahweh had previously "treated his people harshly"? (v. 6b)—a reference to the fulfillment of judgment in 3:12.

[4:8] To the answer given in v. 7b, which announced Yahweh's royal dominion, v. 8 appends a saying expressing the expectation that in Jerusalem Davidic rule will be restored. As indicated by the comparison with 5:1[2], 3[4] in our form-critical analysis (see above, pp. 115f.), this third saying in the initial complex (vv. 1–8) of chaps. 4–5 is a bridgepost that suggests to the redactor now to include an older block of tradition available to him. This block of tradition (4:1ff.), presumably attached previously to 3:12, provides in its present larger context the reason for the redactor's hope (4:9—5:5; see below, pp. 137f.).

Commentary

[4:1] The phrase והיה באחרית הימים in v. 1 is by no means a familiar introductory formula. Rather, the expression באחרית הימים comes, as a rule, at the end of a sentence (e.g., Gen. 49:1; Num. 24:14; Jer. 23:20; etc.). The phrase primarily denotes "the posterior" of time, as "that which is behind you"; as such, it cannot yet be discerned. Thus, it is the time which follows, i.e., the future (cf. E. Jenni, *THAT* 1:110–118; H. Seebass, *ThWAT* 1:224–228; E. Lipiński). The phrase refers more clearly to the hiddenness of the future than the formula הנה ימים באים, which is more familiar as an introduction of prophetic sayings (1 Sam. 2:31; Jer. 7:32; 31:31, etc.; see H. W. Wolff, *Joel and Amos* 206). The most frequent use of the phrase is found in the later interpretations added to prophecies from the exilic and postexilic periods; there, it is usually connected with the idea of a turning point in time (Hos. 3:5; Jer. 23:20; 48:47; 49:39; cf. also Deut. 4:30; Jer. 30:24; Ezek. 38:16). The conception that time has a purpose, or even an end, appears to be remote; however, the notion of a comprehensive change within time in the future is clearly indicated. In light of this, we are to understand the beginning of our passage as referring to the expectation of a *change of times* (see note 1b). It raises this question: In the time that follows, what new thing will come?

Indeed, three exceptional events are announced: that the temple mount of Zion will tower over all the mountains; that the multitude of nations will stream to it to be instructed; that as a result, the implements necessary for waging war will be destroyed.

The first strophe speaks of a vision about the future grandeur of the temple mount (v. 1a) and the corresponding commotion among the nations (v. 1b–2aα[1]). Here the phrase הר בית־יהוה, found elsewhere only in 2 Chron. 33:15, means Mount Zion (cf. v. 7b). Previous to this in 3:12, it was called הר הבית; this has a chilling ring to it, as if Yahweh had already departed from his sanctuary (see above, pp. 108, 110). Now, however, there begins a new emphasis on *Yahweh's* dwelling-place, as seen also in v. 2a, which again speaks of the "mount of Yahweh" and of the "house of the God of Jacob." All that is yet to be heard in the following verse will be accomplished by the presence of God. To be sure, what is said concerning the mount of Yahweh's temple, in fact, means Yahweh himself. Ps. 48:2f.[1f.] says it even clearer: "Great is Yahweh . . .; his holy mountain, beautiful in elevation, is the joy of all the earth. . . ." Here the unshakable stability (נכון) and especially the towering grandeur of God's mountain is emphasized, for it stands as the "peak of the mountains" (ב-*essentiae*) and "will be lifted up above the hills" (comparative מן). The geological change turns Zion into the center of the world. This presents an indirect polemic against other divine mountains, known to us from Ugarit to Mesopotamia (cf. G. Wanke, *Die Zionstheologie der Korachiten,* BZAW 97 (1966) 64ff.; 109ff.; Sh. Talmon, *ThWAT* 2:481ff.; further bibliography in B. Renaud [1977] 170f.). F. Stolz (*Strukturen und Figuren im Kult von Jerusalem,* BZAW 118 [1970] 78ff.) cites these words from a hymn of Gudeah concerning the building of the temple, sung at its dedication ceremony:

O House, great tower of the land of Sumer, grown up together with heaven and earth, Eninu, a great brick structure given to Enlil by good fortune, beautiful mountain, standing there to the amazement of all people, which rises above all lands: The house is a great mountain, reaches to heaven, is like the sun-god, fills the inner parts of heaven, which . . . in the land of the enemy killed many, has given to people a secure place to live, has guided the land of Sumer.

Zion's grandeur is Yahweh's grandeur. The height of the temple mount, making it visible as the center of the earth, attracts the nations.

[4:2] After the vision of the towering temple mount of Yahweh, the third, three-stress bicolon of the first strophe presents the prospect of a great pilgrimage of peoples: They "stream" to Zion as they once "streamed" toward Babylon to the god Bel (Jer. 51:44), whom Yahweh punished, taking away its booty. Hence the "mountain of the house" is not given up to "the 'beasts' in the forest" forever (3:12). It is difficult to perceive here any difference between עמים ("the peoples of the Canaanite environment") and גוים (the wider "world of the nations"), as Th. Lescow (66) maintains (cf. A. R. Hulst, *THAT* 2:318f.). The synonymous use of both terms emphasizes that the peoples come "in great number" (רבים). עמים רבים approaches an inclusive sense (cf. "the masses" in Exod. 23:2) which means "all"; in Isa. 2:2b/3a כל־הגוים is parallel with עמים רבים, and in Mic. 4:5a the statements concerning the peoples are recapitulated with the phrase כל־העמים (cf. Joachim Jeremias, *TDNT* 6:537).

For what purpose do the nations stream to Zion? To bring Israel's sons and daughters home from exile, as Isa. 49:22 and Isaiah 60 indicate? Do they wish to offer their treasures as worshipful tribute to the newly dedicated temple (Hag. 2:6ff.; Isa. 60; Ps. 72:10f.)? Or do they wish to confess Yahweh as the only God (Isa. 45:14f.; Psalm 87)? Toward the end of the exile, the nations' pilgrimage to Zion was thought to have various goals. Here in the second strophe, in the audition following the vision, the nations themselves express a different goal. In the first three-stress bicolon, we hear the peoples summon one another; and in the following two-stress bicolon the goal is stated; in the concluding three-stress bicolon, its realization is expressed. The peoples are not signaled to approach Zion, as for example in Isa. 49:22; rather, they encourage each other in astonishment over the grandeur of Zion, where they freely gather themselves together (thus also in Zech. 8:20–22). עלה is a term for the pilgrimage to Jerusalem, as in Jer. 31:6; Ps. 122:4; Zech. 14:17; etc. What is emphasized is that they will make a pilgrimage to the "mount of *Yahweh*" and to "the house of the *God of Jacob*." The phrase "God of Jacob" occurs nowhere else in the prophetic writings, although it occurs frequently in the Psalms (in the Songs of Zion, Pss. 46:8[7], 12[11]; 76:7[6]; 84:9[8], and in other cultic songs such as Pss. 20:2[1]; 75:10[9]; 81:2[1], 5[4]; 94:7; further, 114:7; 146:5; also Exod. 3:6, 15f.; 4:5; 2 Sam. 23:1). Here we are in the realm of cultic traditions.

The intention of the pilgrimage is expressed briefly and precisely, and is emphasized by a two-stress bicolon. Not merely any kind of service is to be performed for Yahweh on the way to Jerusalem and there in the sanctuary (Ps. 102:23[22]); it is not that people should and would serve God. Rather, they are to wait upon the action of God. Nevertheless, the verse does not picture the gift of boundless fertility, which can issue forth from the temple (as in Joel 4:18 [3:18]; Ezek. 47:1–12; Zech. 14:8). What is solely awaited is the instruction of Yahweh's word. Here ירה *hiph.* does not have the specific meaning of priestly instruction and decision (as in 3:11); rather, it denotes Yahweh's own word that points the way, his תורה, which is no longer to be distinguished from the דבר־יהוה, his prophetic word (v. 2b; cf. Jer. 18:18; Amos 3:1; Ezek. 33:30, etc.). This instruction has as its object the "ways" and "paths" of Yahweh (as in Ps. 25:4; cf. Ps. 18:22[21]; Hos. 14:10[9]). The preposition מן in the word מדרכיו is not to be understood in the partitive sense, as though Yahweh instructs the peoples in only "one part of his ways." Rather, מן refers to the "point of departure" and the "origin" of Yahweh's teaching (BrSynt §111e, h; cf. note 2d). Yahweh's instructions have their foundation in the ways that he himself goes with people, and in the corresponding directions toward these paths. The goal of Yahweh's teaching is to direct the steps of the nations. Yahweh's instruction does not provide knowledge in general; rather, it leads to a concrete "walking in his paths." Therefore his instruction is called "way," and his word is called "path" (cf. v. 2a and b). The nations themselves hope for a way out of their international confusion. The quotation of the words of the nations in which they encourage each other may well conclude at the end of v. 2a. For in v. 2b the first person plural style is not continued; instead, the initial כי introduces the motivation for the hope of the nations (cf. note 2f). The movement of the nations toward Zion and to Yahweh's instruction corresponds to an opposite movement that goes out from Zion. Indeed, the promised "exodus" of the word of God from Jerusalem provides the primary basis and reason for the nations' coming to Zion. In Deutero-Isaiah it is the Servant of

Yahweh who carries forth the Torah to the nations (Isa. 42:4; cf. 49:6; 51:4). The chiastic formulation of v. 2b provides a concise ending to the second strophe.

[4:3] The third strophe (v. 3) describes what results from the encounter when, moving in opposite directions, the nations make their way toward Zion, and the word of Yahweh moves out into the world of the nations. Three three-stress bicola promise: (1) Yahweh's reconciling arbitration (v. 3a); (2) the disarmament of the nations (v. 3bα); and (3) the end of all military activities (v. 3bβ). The subject of שפט and הוכיח is Yahweh, whose "word" was declared in v. 2b. Now the "word" is more closely defined as שפט בין, i.e., as an "arbitration between (warring) nations"; and as יכח hiph., i.e., as an impartial establishment of what is just (cf. H. W. Wolff, *Hosea* 76; idem, *Joel and Amos* 246). עצום primarily refers to a multitude of people and often stands parallel to רב, but it can also allude to power (see below, p. 124 on 4:7). Thus the accent lies on Yahweh's establishment of justice by his word among the great nations, as well as on the institution of a comprehensive peace to which it leads (cf. also the secondary additions to the verse, according to notes 3a and b). Yahweh, the judge who establishes peace solely by his justice, leads the world to a resolution of its conflict and thereby makes weapons unnecessary. His words create insight, so that the nations themselves will recast their weapons into farming implements, whereas, according to Ps. 46:10[9], Yahweh himself destroys all instruments of war (cf. also Ps. 76:3f., 9–13 [2f., 8–12]). Here it is stated that the people in the pagan world, guided by the word of Yahweh, will themselves make these changes. They will renounce the use of weapons against each other, and they will abolish, now and for the future as well, the knowledge of how to wage war. The way is paved for a genuine turning point in time, when Yahweh's justice will issue from Zion and establish entirely new goals for the dealings of the nations.

[4:4] In v. 4 a further hope for the future of individuals (unknown in Isaiah 2) is joined to the expectation of a new community in v. 3. Peace and righteousness will affect each person. Instead of fleeing into the narrow confines of a fortified city, as in times of war, with the coming of the new age, each person will sit peacefully in the open "each under his own grapevine and his own fig tree." One can sit pleasantly "under" the grapevine as well as under the fig tree because the grape tendrils were allowed to climb up into the fig tree. "Since fig trees were frequently planted in the vineyard, it being suitable there (not so the olive tree), occasionally the grapevines were allowed to creep up into the fig tree. There they developed without any particular cultivation, increasing the amount of shade with their large leaves" (thus according to a report from G. Dalman, *AuS*, 4:315). Grapes and figs are the most precious fruits of the land. To be able to sit underneath them means, first, security from danger of war. Thus in the postexilic age, the days of Solomon were thought of as the golden age of peace (according to 1 Kings 5:5; cf. also 2 Kings 18:31). Furthermore, this phrase also means to live in joy (cf. 1 Kings 4:20 with 5:5 and 1 Macc. 14:11f.) and in neighborly friendship (Zech. 3:10). Every disturbance, all cares and anxieties, are expressly excluded: "none shall disturb him"; "no one shall terrorize him." In contrast to vv. 1–3, v. 4a appears to speak about circumstances in Israel, as the above-mentioned parallels especially indicate. The sentence "no one disturbs" is above all a guarantee of the defense against external enemies who might threaten any aspect of secure life in Israel (cf. Ezek. 34:28; 39:26; Lev. 26:6). The entire passage, from v. 1 up to and including the secondary addition in v. 4a, is brought to a conclusion in v. 4b, which indicates that the words are from an authorized prophet; the prophet is the "mouth of Yahweh" who has spoken (cf. Hos. 6:5; Isa. 30:2). This concluding formula (without צבאות) is found in Isaiah also in postexilic passages (1:20; 40:5; 58:14).

[4:5] A confessional statement, made by the Jerusalem community in difficult times, is joined to the divine oracle that concerns the world of the nations. Although the faithful in Jerusalem know Yahweh's word applies to "many" (v. 2a), "a multitude of nations" (v. 3a), "all peoples" (v. 5a), they soberly recognize that in the present situation the nations do not seek after the God of Jacob. "They lead their life" (ילכו picks up לכו from v. 2aα and ונלכה from v. 2aβ) each "in the name" of its god, i.e., in the mission, by the authority, and with trust in their gods. The כי indicates that this fact is acknowledged for the present; on the concessive meaning of כי ("although," "even if"), cf. Isa. 54:10; Prov. 6:35 and KBL³, 449 no. 12). In v. 5b the Israelite community (with prefixed "but we"), in contrast to the nations, are the people who even now walk in the name of the God Yahweh, i.e., in response to his instruction, walk in his way (cf. v. 2). With a solemn liturgical conclusion לעולם ועד, cf. Pss. 45:18 [17]; 145:21; also 119:44, etc.), they explain that they have forever entered upon the way made accessible to them, the path to the ultimate goal which one day all nations will take (v. 2).

[4:6–7a] With the phrase "on that day" the redactor adds a second promise, whose fulfillment will be simultaneous with the new era announced in v. 1; the fulfillment of the promise is given in v. 7b. The divine oracle formula נאם יהוה (elsewhere in Micah only in 5:9) is connected with vv. 6–7a, an oracle which (in contrast to vv. 1–4) has the "I" of Yahweh as its subject. This first person singular is employed in the three dominant verb forms we first met in 2:12 (see above, p. 86 on קבץ, אסף and שים); here (vv. 6–7a), however, the simile of the flock is not carried out. Nor are the persons mentioned in these verses addressed directly (as in 2:12aα); instead, they are spoken about (third person) by means of participles. Do the feminine singular forms refer to the "congregation" (עֵדָה; cf. Jer. 30:20 in the context of vv. 18–21)? Or do they merely emphasize the tenderness of the promise? (But see below on Ezekiel 34!) Initially (v. 6a) and then once more (v. 7a), the congregation to whom the promise applies is characterized as "those who limp," "the lame." צלע is predicated of a person only once in the OT, namely Jacob, who "limped" when he was touched on the thigh (Gen. 32:32). Is the exilic community called "(the remnant) of Jacob" (2:12; 5:6f.) by way of allusion to this patriarchal tradition? Yet here in 4:6f. Jacob's name is not mentioned. Moreover, the word צלע occurs elsewhere only in a postexilic, secondary addition in Zeph. 3:19b. This saying bears more similarity to Mic. 4:6aβ than to Mic. 2:12a. There the image of the flock is also absent. Instead of "gathering" (אסף) the lame, Zeph. 3:19 speaks of "saving" (ישע *hiph.*) them. Nevertheless, it is most probable that Mic. 2:12; 4:6f.; and Zeph. 3:19 represent three variations of a single tradition dependent upon Ezekiel 34 and that they briefly summarize the message of that chapter (cf. B. Renaud, 187f.). In Ezekiel 34, the "gathering" (קבץ, v. 13) of the "scattered" (הנדחת, v. 4) is verbosely described; moreover, it is presented in the style of a first person Yahweh speech. There we also find the imagery of the "flock" (צאן, v. 2ff.) and with it the third person feminine singular, upon which our text was dependent. To be sure, the word צלה ("to limp," "to be lame") is not found there, but the cause of the suffering is apparently lameness or sickness (v. 4). Other exilic or postexilic texts speak of "gathering" (קבץ *piel*) of the "scattered" (נדח *niphal*), such as Jer. 23:3; Isa. 56:8; Deut. 30:3–5; Neh. 1:9. The relative clause in v. 6b expressly relates the promise to the disaster of the exile that Yahweh had brought on (cf. רעע *hiph.* in Jer. 25:6; Jos. 24:20; Exod. 5:22).

According to v. 7a, the purpose in gathering the scattered people is so that they become "a powerful nation." After the exile, the promise to Abraham (Gen. 12:2; 17:5; 18:18) is to be fulfilled anew (cf. Isa. 54:1ff.; Jer. 23:3; Deut. 30:5). Here שים ל means "to transform," as in 1:6; Gen. 21:13; Exod. 14:21; Isa. 42:15. Isaiah 60:22 reads like a commentary on v. 7aβ: "The least one shall become a thousand, and the smallest one a mighty nation" (on עצום, "mighty," "numerous," see above, p. 122 on 4:3). Here the word שארית stands parallel to the expectation of a "mighty nation"; the context ("the lame will become a remnant, . . . a mighty nation") removes every negative overtone from the word שארית, which refers to the new, lasting descendants (cf. Gen. 45:7 and H. Wildberger, *THAT* 2:847), the people who survive, with whom God will begin anew. Here, the "remnant" is not only the recipient of the promise (Isa. 37:32; 46:3; Jer. 23:3); rather, the word has clearly become a title that ascribes salvation to Israel (on this, cf. Isa. 54:1). With this promise, which the exilic community (see above) found in manifold variations, the redactor first of all expressly incorporates Israel into the promise to the nations (vv. 1–3); Israel, the גוי עצום, is placed side by side with the גוים עצומים. The saying, however, makes no reference to Zion.

[4:7b] The redactor supplements this promise with v. 7b (see above, p. 115). With the mention of "Mount Zion," the redactor makes a connection with 4:1ff.; with the word עליהם, he refers back to vv. 6–7a. Indicative of the redactor's hand is the shift from the third person feminine singular (vv. 6a–7 indicating the afflicted exiles) to the third person plural (עליהם), and also the transition from Yahweh's first person speech to speaking about Yahweh in the third person. The henceforth everlasting royal dominion of Yahweh on Mount Zion is announced. Whereas Yahweh's kingship was often praised at the time of Deutero-Isaiah and afterward (Isa. 41:21; 43:15; 44:6; Zeph. 3:15; Zech. 14:9; Isa. 33:22), the combination of the divine kingship motif with Jerusalem-Zion (Isa. 52:7; Obad. 21; Isa. 24:23), including the statement that it will also endure "forever," is mentioned elsewhere only in Ps. 146:10. This Psalm text also praises Yahweh as king because he saves and liberates the prisoners and the oppressed (146:7–9). The liturgical character of these verses well befits the celebration of the temple's dedication. Since the promise in vv. 6–7a is fulfilled in the return of the exiles, v. 7b says "from now on"; Yahweh's dominion and protection will be "everlasting," extending also over all other kings. The phrase מעתה ועד עולם is often used as a concluding liturgical formula (e.g., Ps. 115:18; 121:8; 131:3; cf. Isa. 9:6; 59:21).

[4:8] But what will issue forth from the throne of the Davidic ruler? In 4:8 the redactor attempts to answer on the basis of the promise which lay before him in 5:1 (see above, p. 116). In analogy to 5:1 (ואתה) he addresses Jerusalem-Zion (instead of Bethlehem). That "daughter of Zion" and "daughter of Jerusalem" do not refer to a daughter-city (suburb), such as Saul's Gibeah (thus H. Cazelles), nor to Migdal-Eder (RSV = tower of Eder) mentioned in Gen. 35:21, is indicated, aside from its common usage, by the verse's connection with the David traditions (B. Renaud [1977] 191–194; further, see below, pp. 143f. on 5:1). But what is meant by "tower of the flock" (מגדל־עדר) and by "hill" (עפל)? Let us begin with the second word. עפל denotes a certain formation of terrain: a "bulge" ("bump"), a "hill" (2 Kings 5:24). The word is used in a special sense for that "filling" (מלוא) built by Solomon in the breach south of the temple and palace areas of Jerusalem and north of the old city of David (on the southeastern hill) (1 Kings 9:15, 24; 11:27b; cf. M. Noth, *Könige* 1, BK 9/1, 219f.; H. Donner, *BRL²*, 160). Nehemiah 3:25–27 refers to a "great tower" (הַמִּגְדָּל הַגָּדוֹל) in the area of the wall of Ophel and of the royal palace; Isa. 32:14 knows of a hill (עפל) that stands next to a "watchtower" (בַּחַן) (H. Wildberger, *Jesaja*, BK 10/3, 1266, considers Isa. 32:9–14 to date from the postexilic period). Thus, in the postexilic time when v. 8 was composed, there might have been a tower standing among the ruins of the palace and hill area which once served the purpose of defense (G. Sauer, *BHHW* 2:1352) and is now called "tower of the flock." Could flocks have grazed there, decades after Jerusalem's destruction (cf. 3:12)? Or, in the light of 4:6f. (cf. 2:12), did the author use the imagery of a flock to picture the community returned from exile (see above, p. 124)? 2 Chron. 26:10 speaks of towers constructed to protect and watch over the flocks.

From the newly rebuilt temple, the speaker looks in a southerly direction upon the old palace and hill (Ophel) area. He declares to the community that in the new era of Yahweh's dominion (v. 7b), also this part of the city will not be left destitute: "To you shall come and enter the former dominion." This can only refer to the Davidic rule, whose return from Bethlehem the author found mentioned in 5:1. There the Davidic king is called מוֹשֵׁל (ruler) and not "king" (as Yahweh is called in v. 7b). Correspondingly, the verse speaks first of ממשלה, and only then (in a secondary addition?) of ממלכת, referring to the Jerusalem kingship. Thus the redactor has the expectation that, after the time of extensive disaster, of Jerusalem's destruction, and of the exile, then the new Jerusalem, overtowering and important, will also be accompanied by a restoration of earthly, royal rule in Jerusalem.

Purpose and Thrust

The redactor, according to what we have seen, was strictly guided by the question: After the experience of judgment Micah had prophesied concerning Zion-Jerusalem, what will become of the city in the future? For answers to this question, he drew upon prophetic traditions then current in exilic and postexilic times. The origins of these traditions are above all to be located in the hopes for salvation connected with the names of Jeremiah and Ezekiel, including the later and latest levels of tradition in the book of Isaiah. We may distinguish between three answers; they concern: (1) the future significance of the temple mount for the nations of the world (vv. 1–5); (2) Yahweh's sovereignty over the community returned from exile (vv. 6f.); and (3) the reestablishment of Davidic rule in Jerusalem (v. 8).

The redactor begins with a most comprehensive promise. The city that had to experience a total destruction according to 3:12 will become the center of a completely restored world of the nations. The explanation of what propels these nations toward Jerusalem is unique. They are neither to serve Israel (Isa. 60:3ff.) nor to bring treasures to the temple (Hag. 2:7–9) nor to participate in prayers and sacrifices of worship (Isa. 56:4–7; Zech. 14:16ff.). Rather, the grand theme of the nations' pilgrimage to the towering mount of Yahweh (vv. 1f.) is combined with the saving gift of consummate peace. This peace comes to the nations by means of Yahweh's word. The oracle of Yahweh, settling quarrels and upholding justice, paves the way to peace among nations (vv. 2f.). It will not be necessary for Yahweh to destroy their weapons (Ps. 46:10[9]); rather, the nations themselves, on the basis of their insight, will transform their weapons into instruments of peace (v. 3b; cf. the reversal in Joel 4:10[3:10]). For, as an alternative to learning how to make weapons (v. 3bβ), they will seek after Yahweh's instructions (v. 2a). Nothing is said about Israel's missionary work or the servant of Yahweh (cf. Isa. 42:1–4; 49:6). Israel is not even mentioned by name (see below, p. 161f., on 5:9–12).

In the passage transmitted in vv. 1–3 and also in the secondary addition in v. 4 (see above, p. 122), the accent lies on the saving word of God which brings peace to all. But the redactional placement of the passage in clear antithesis to 3:12 shifts the accent to the place where peace will be established, to the "mountain (of the house) of Yahweh" (vv. 1a, 2a). The same Zion that had to experience divine judgment will in the new era become the highest of all mountains and the center of salvation for the world of the nations. Zion, the place of salvation, will become the antithesis of Babel and its titanic self-security and self-praise, which made it impossible for people to understand one another (Gen. 11:1–9; Jer. 51:44).

The redactor knows that the choice between Zion and Babel is still a live possibility (v. 5). Thus the community that has experienced Yahweh's promise must even now walk persistently in the way that leads to the ultimate goal of peace that also includes all nations. The Christian community, gathered from the nations of the world, is in no less need of such resolve. For them, the Jerusalem-Zion theme has become, for the sake of the crucifixion and resurrection of Jesus Christ, the center of the world and the highest mountain peak. With their eyes on Christ, the Christian community lays hold of the promise that inaugurates for it—and also for the present history of the world—the future that brings peace.

The end of vv. 6–7 indicates that Mount Zion is the place of Yahweh's new and lasting kingly rule (v. 7b). The redactor takes up an oracle of Yahweh that applied to the exilic community in its misery (vv. 6–7a). The defeated people could not by their own strength alone escape their distress; the banished could not by themselves come together again; the sick in exile could not find their way home and recover. It is expressly recalled that Yahweh as judge was responsible for the doom (v. 6b). But now the same Yahweh makes good his promise: he brings them home, he gathers and strengthens them. The "remnant" will not be a lamentable vestige of an entire nation that has been broken; rather, saved by Yahweh, they become the pledge of a new, mighty people (v. 7a). Thus the returning community becomes a further model for the rule operative within God's kingdom: the small are made great, the weak are made strong (1 Sam. 16:1ff.; 1 Cor. 1:26ff.; Matt. 13:31–33; see below, pp. 143f. on Mic. 5:1). The end suffered by Israel was not the end of Yahweh's dominion.

The redactor places a new accent again upon the fact that the catastrophic end of Jerusalem (3:12) does not mean the end of Yahweh's authority. Rather, with the return of the exiles, Yahweh institutes his royal dominion anew and forever upon Mount Zion (v. 7b). Only for the sake of the promised royal dominion of Jesus (cf. Luke 1:32f. with Mic. 4:7) can this word of assurance to the liberated exilic community also strengthen the patience and hope of the community of faith drawn from the nations of the world.

The goal of the strengthened remnant is indicated in the two prophecies about the coming worldwide significance of the Jerusalem temple and about Yahweh's royal residence on Mount Zion. The redactor supplements these prophecies by appending a third promise in v. 8: the devastated area around the palace will see the return of the old Davidic rule. It is as though nothing can be lacking: alongside the expectation of a grand renewal of things, especially what the first prophecy says about the temple, the future must also include the previous glory of the earthly kingship. The redactor, according to all indications (see above, pp. 115f.), finds in the texts available to him—especially 5:1 among others—the grounds for his confidence: the promise of the messianic ruler from an old clan in Bethlehem suggests to him the restoration of the royal residence in Jerusalem.

The redactor's arrangement and reworking of these three sayings is indicative of an enormous theological struggle with the question of the new Jerusalem. Having researched the prophetic traditions belonging to the exilic period, the redactor now gives expression to his certainty that the divine promises will extend from the collapse of the nation to the postexilic times and beyond, wide open for the new acts of God.

Micah 4:9—5:5 [6]

Zion's Birthpangs

Literature

A. Bruno, *Micha und der Herrscher aus der Vorzeit* (1923). J. A. Fitzmyer, "*lᵉ* as a Preposition and a Particle in Micah 5:1 [5:2]," *CBQ* 18 (1956) 10–13. C. Westermann, "Micha 5,1–3," in *Herr, tue meine Lippen auf* 5, G. Eichholz (ed.) (1961²) 54–59. A. S. Kapelrud, "Eschatology in the Book of Micah," *VT* 11 (1961) 392–405. W. Harrelson, "Non-royal Motifs in the Royal Eschatology," *Israel's Prophetic Heritage: Essays in Honor of James Muilenburg* (1962) 147–165 (155–159). H. Gottlieb, "Den taerskende kuie Mi 4,11–13," *DTT* 16 (1963) 167–171. L. Gorgulho, "A Profecia sôbre Belem-Efratá em Miq 5,1–5," *RCT* 3 (1963) 20–38. S. J. Schwantes, "A Note on Micah 5:1 (Hebrew 4:14)," *AUSS* 1 (1963) 107. S. Herrmann, *Die prophetischen Heilserwartungen im Alten Testament*, BWANT 85 (1965) 146–153. G. Wanke, *Die Zionstheologie der Korachiten*, BZAW 97 (1966). H. Cazelles, "Histoire et Géographie en Mi IV 6–13," *Fourth World Congress Jewish Studies* 1 (1967) 87–89. Th. Lescow, "Das Geburtsmotiv in den messianischen Weissagungen bei Jesaja und Micha," *ZAW* 79 (1967) 172–207. H. P. Müller, "1. Weihnachtstag—Micha 5,1–4a.5b," *GPM* 22 (1967/1968) 35–41. J. T. Willis, *Mimmᵉkā lī yēṣēʾ* in Micah V 1," *JQR* 58 (1967/1968). Idem, "Micah IV 14—V 5—A Unit," *VT* 18 (1968) 529–547. K. J. Cathcart, "Notes on Micah 5,4–5," *Biblica* 49 (1968) 511–514. H. M. Lutz, *Jahwe, Jerusalem und die Völker*, WMANT 27 (1968) 91–97. W. H. Schmidt, "Die Ohnmacht des Messias," *KuD* 15 (1969) 18–34. J. T. Willis, "The Structure of Micah 3–5," *ZAW* 81 (1969) 191–214. H. P. Müller, *Ursprünge und Strukturen alttestamentlicher Eschatologie*, BZAW 109 (1969) 86–101. A. S. van der Woude, "Micah in Dispute with the Pseudo-Prophets," *VT* 19 (1969) 244–260 (248–256). J. Heer, "Der Bethlehemspruch Micheas und die Geburt Jesu (Micha 5,1–3)," *BiKi* 25 (1970) 106–109. P. Bordreuil, "Michée 4,10–13 et ses parallèles ougaritiques," *Sem* 21 (1971) 21–28. J. Coppens, "Le cadre littéraire de Michée V 1–5," *Near Eastern Studies in Honor of William Foxwell Albright*, ed. Hans Goedicke (1971) 57–62. K. Seybold, *Das davidische Königtum im Zeugnis der Propheten*, FRLANT 107 (1972) 106–115. H. S. Pelser, "Some Remarks Regarding the Contrast in Micah 5:1 and 2," *OTWSA* (1973) 35–44. J. Homerski, "Panujacy z Betlejem (interpretacja perykopy Mich 5,1–5)," *RTK* 22 (1976) 5–16. S. Vergone, "Micah 4,14," *BetM* 66 (1976) 392–401. O. Loretz, "Fehlanzeige von Ugaritismen in Micha 5,1–3," *UF* 9 (1977) 358–360. B. Renaud, *La Formation du Livre de Michée*, EtB (1977) 432f., provides further bibliography. K. J. Cathcart, "Micah 5,4–5 and Semitic Incantations," *Biblica* 59 (1978) 38–48. D. J. Bryant, "Micah 4:14—5:14., An Exegesis," *RestQ* 21 (1978) 210–230. O. Loretz, "Die Psalmen II,"

AOAT 207 (1979) 453–455. K. Adloff, "1. Christtag—Micha 5,1–4a," *GPM* 35 (1980) 42–52.

Text

4:9 Now!
>Why do you cry[a] so loudly?[b]
>Is the king not with you?
>>Has your counselor[c] disappeared,
>>>so that anguish grips you[d] like a woman in labor?

10 Writhe[a] and come forth,[b]
>>daughter of Zion—like a woman in labor!
>For now you must depart from the city,
>>you must dwell in an open field.
>To Babel you will go,
>>there you will be delivered,
>>>there Yahweh[c] will redeem you from the hand of your enemies.

11 But now!
>>There assemble themselves against you
>>>many nations.
>They say,
>"Let[a] her be polluted[b] and let[a] us feast
>>our eyes[c] on Zion."

12 But they do not know
>>the intention[a] of Yahweh;
>nor do they understand his plan,
>>that he ha gathered them like sheaves on the threshing floor.[b]

13 Arise and thresh,[a] daughter of Zion!
>>For "I will make your horn[b,c] into iron,
>>>your hooves[c] into bronze,"
>so that you can trample many peoples,
>>and can devote[d] their gain to Yahweh
>>>and their strength[e] to the Lord of the whole earth.

14[5:1] Now!
>Gash yourself,[a] daughter of the troops![b]
>>One[c] has laid seige to us.
>With the staff they strike on the cheek
>>the judge[d] of Israel.

5:1[2] But you, Bethlehem[a] Ephrathah,
>>you little one[b] '   '[c] among the thousands of Judah,
>"from you shall come forth one who is mine,[d]
>>to be ruler in Israel,"
>whose origins[e] lie in antiquity,
>>in ancient days.

2[3]   [Therefore he[a] will give them up until the time
>>>when[b] she who is in labor has given birth
>>>and the remnant[c] of his brothers will
>>>return to the children of Israel.]

3[4] He will stand and[a] shepherd in the majesty of Yahweh,
>>in the sovereignty of the name of Yahweh, his God.
>>[And[b] they will dwell[c] (undisturbed).]
>Indeed, now he[d] will become great
>>to the ends of the earth.

4[5]   And he[a] will achieve peace[b]
   [—Assyria, when it comes into our land
      and when it treads upon our fortresses,[c]
   then we[d] will have set up against it seven shepherds
      and eight princes[e] of men.
5[6]   They will shepherd[a] (the land)[b] of Assyria with the sword
      and the land of Nimrod 'with unsheathed dagger.'[c]—]
   and will deliver from Assyria,
      when[e] it comes into our land
      and when[e] it treads on our territory.

9a Gk (ἔγνως κακά) read תֵּדְעִי רָע, exchanging ר for ד, and understood רע to derive from רעע instead of from רוע: "Why do you know (love) evil?" Similarly a' (Syr) incorrectly read ἐκάκωσας ("you have done evil").

9b רֵעַ functions as the internal or absolute object *(figura etymologica)* of the verb, strengthening it; cf. Ges-K §117p; BrSynt §93d.

9c Gk (ἡ βουλή σου) presupposes עֵצָה with suffix as 4:12 instead of יוֹעֵץ; cf. also Isa. 9:5; Prov. 11:14. Is Gk thinking of the council of advisors? a' (ο συμβουλος σου), Vg *(consiliarius tuus)* support MT.

9d 4QpMi reads כִּי ה[חז]יקךה, i.e., the verb has a second person masculine singular suffix instead of a feminine suffix (MT) and thus is influenced by 4:8 (עדיך), whereas MT in v. 9 otherwise contains only feminine suffixes. MT may contain the original reading; cf. Renaud [1977] 196 with M. Collin, *VT* 21 [1971] 286.

10a Gk (ὤδινε καὶ ἀνδρίζου) apparently renders חולי with two verbs; the first has the sense of birthpangs (חיל *qal,* as MT: "writhe!"; cf. Isa. 23:4; 26:17; 45:10; 54:1), the second, a cry of encouragement: "be brave!" (cf. הָיֵל).

10b Gk (καὶ ἔγγιζε) may have read וְגַעִי, derived from נגע ("to touch"); but גְּעִי might also be the imperative of געה, "to low, bray" (of a cow, 1 Sam. 6:12; Job 6:5). The same meaning is found in גְחִי, the imperative of גיח (used for the "bursting forth" of a turbulent river in Job 38:8; 40:23). The context of the word here suggests rather an unusual imperative of גחה, which describes the "coming forth" of a child at birth in Ps. 22:10; Vg *(dole et satage)* apparently also thinks of labor and painful birth; see below, pp. 139f.

10c Gk (κύριος ὁ θεός σου) presupposes יהוה אֱלֹהֶיךְ; the expansion characterizes Yahweh as the coming savior God.

11a On the jussive used in an optative clause, cf. BrSynt §43.

11b Gk (ἐπιχαρούμεθα) presumably thinks of a malicious gloating. The Hebrew text followed by Gk is unknown.

11c The subject in the dual form is construed as a collective, with the preceding verb in the singular (Ges-K §145n; Joüon, *Gr* §150d). Gk (ἐπόψονται) has a plural verb; Vg *(aspiciat . . . oculus noster),* Syr, Targ, have a singular subject and predicate, thus providing a formal congruence.

12a Gk (τὸν λογισμὸν κυρίου) has the singular, in parallel to βουλή (עֵדָה), instead of the plural in MT, which according to content is to be correctly understood as an abstract plural; cf. BrSynt §19b and Seybold, *ThWAT* 3:251.

12b גֹּרֶן with an unaccented ה-*directionis.*

13a Instead of an expected וּ-verb, דוֹשִׁי, MT has דוֹשִׁי; perhaps the variation in sound next to קוּמִי is intended to effect a heightening; cf. Joüon, *Gr* §80k.

13b MT, Vg *(cornu tuum)* and Targ speak of "horn" in the singular, a sign of strength, as occurs frequently (1 Sam. 2:10; Jer. 48:25; Pss. 75:11[10]; 132:17; Lam. 2:3); Gk (τὰ κέρατά σου), Syr shift to the plural (cf. 1 Kings 22:11).

13c Targ interprets "your horn" as "the people in you" (עמא דביך), and "your hoofs" as "their remnant" (שארהון).

13d This is either an archaic form, with a י at the end for the second person feminine singular *hiph.* perfect (cf. Ges-K §44h), or an incorrect return to the first person of the twice-occurring אשים in v. 13aα. But with the word standing after

והדיקות and before ליהוה, the latter possibility is less likely. Targ (ותגמרין) presupposes והחרמתי (Sperber, IVB, 346, 355).

13e Gk (τὴν ἰσχὺν αὐτῶν) and Vg *(fortitudinem)* interpret this to mean military strength (see below, pp. 141f.).

14a In view of the context, the more usual I גדר *hithpolel* ("to gash oneself") is to be preferred to weakly attested II גדר ("to band together" KBL³). Gk (ἐμφραχ-θήσεται θυγάτηρ ἐμφραγμῷ) read forms of גדר for the verb and the noun ("the daughter is surrounded by a wall"; see note 14b), misreading, as is frequent, ר instead of ד (on a previous misreading, see note 4:9a).

14b בת־גדוד appears to have been formed in parallel to בת־ציון (cf. vv. 10, 13). In earlier times, גדוד usually had a pejorative sense ("band of robbers," Hos. 6:9; 7:1; Gen. 49:19; Jer. 18:22; thus also Vg, *filia latronis*). On grounds of its later occurrence, I. Willi-Plein, 88, and B. Renaud (1977), 198, prefer a neutral meaning ("troops," in 2 Chron. 25:9, 10, 13; 26:11).

14c The singular form is supported by Gk (ἔταξεν) and is to be preferred as *lectio difficilior*. Vg *(posuerunt;* likewise Syr) already presupposes a plural (שָׂמוּ), in parallel to the following יכו.

14d As at the beginning of the sentence, Gk (τὰς φυλὰς) apparently reads שֵׁבֶט for the second time, which could have been caused by the alliteration in the ancient text of the words שבט־שפט; here, however, Gk now gives the word the (second) meaning, "tribe," instead of "staff." Vg *(iudicis)* and the meaning of the sentence ("strike on the cheek") support MT.

5:1a In contrast to most names of towns, בית־לחם, like other place-names preceded by בית, is regarded as masculine (אתה—צעיר); cf. בית־אל in Amos 5:5; בֵּית חוֹרֹן in Jos. 16:5; cf. Joüon, *Gr* §134g. Following Gk (οἶκος τοῦ Εφραθα), since J. Wellhausen בית אפרתה is often taken as the original text and בית־לחם is considered a gloss. But בית אפרתה is otherwise unattested (B. Renaud [1977] 220f.), and Syr, Vg, and Targ support MT, as does the three-stress prosody. Gk can be explained as dittography or as emphasizing the personification of the town addressed here.

1b To take the ה from אפרתה and connect it with צעיר (see *BHS*) is not sufficiently supported by the superlatives in Gk (ὀλιγοστός) and Matt. 2:6 (ἐλαχίστη) (Gk: Εφραθα!). Both Gk and Matt. 2:6 understand צעיר as a predicate, whereas in MT the word functions as an appositive, without the predicate's occurring until v. 1aβ. A comparative sense for צעיר (without the article) also results from the parallel with the (remaining phrase) "thousands of Judah."

1c Here להיות has been incorrectly inserted from v. 1aγ (Hitzig; Rudolph); it can be explained as scribal haplography from צעיר to יצא (O. Loretz, 1977). Deleting the word results in two three-stress bicola in v. 1a; the twofold occurrence of להיות in quick succession is unlikely. Gk (τοῦ εἶναι) already presupposes MT. Matt. 2:6 (οὐδαμῶς ἐλαχίστη εἶ) also points to a text similar to MT and might have read לֹא הָיִיתָ (Th. H. Robinson). Vg *(parvulus es in milibus Judah),* instead, supports MT.

1d It is difficult to account for לי in connection with the question regarding the subject of יצא. Unlikely are the surmises that the word לי is a remnant of יֵלֶךְ (A. Bruno; *BHS*) or of מֶלֶךְ (E. Sellin), or an abbreviation of יהוה (J. Lippl). Gk (μοι) and Vg *(mihi)* support MT. It is probable that the word is an element from the tradition, since the saying recalls the messianic David tradition (cf. יצא in Isa. 11:1; 2 Sam. 7:12). Then, in spite of the word יהוה in the what follows (v. 3; cf. v. 2a), לי should be construed with Yahweh, perhaps as a single-member nominal clause functioning as the subject ("he who belongs to me"), whereas to understand לי as *dativus ethicus* would be problematic.

1e The plural (for "origin"), according to BrSynt §19b, serves "to give the expression a heightened sense of feeling."

2a Targ (יתמסרון, "they will be surrendered") smooths out the difficulty posed by the subject in the third person singular (MT יתנם), which cannot be the messiah of v. 1. However, Gk (δώσει) and Vg *(dabit)* confirm MT.

2b On the relative clause without אשר, cf. Ges-K §130d.

131

2c Gk (οἱ ἐπίλοιποι) and Vg *(reliquiae)* correctly understand יתר as a collective in light of the plural verb form (ישׁובֻן).

3a Gk inserts καὶ ὄψεται ("and will see"). Was this at first a misreading of ורעה as וראה?

3b Gk (ὑπάρξουσι) reads ישׁבו without a copula; rather, it connects the verb with v. 3aβ, making it into one sentence that begins with בגאין, a word Gk presumes to have a copula prefixed to it (καὶ ἐν τῇ δόξῃ . . .): "and in the majesty of the name of the Lord, their God, they live." In so doing, the masculine suffix attached to אלהים (MT, "his God") must be read by Gk as a plural (τοῦ θεοῦ αὐτῶν—"their God") to fit the plural subject (ישׁבו—ὑπάξουσι). This grammatical alteration speaks against Gk and in favor of MT, as does the resultant destruction of the *parallelismus membrorum* in v. 3aα//β.

3c Instead of יֵשֵׁבוּ the word יָשׁוּבוּ ("and they shall return") is frequently read; thus Syr, Vg, Targ, MT^MSSR (on this see D. Barthélemy, VTSuppl 10 [1963] 172). This may be explained as a mistaken reading influenced by v. 2b (ישׁובֻן), while the sense of the context supports MT (see below, pp. 146f.).

3d A majority of Gk^MSS translate with the plural (μεγαλυνθήσονται), incorrectly making the word congruent with וישׁבו instead of with ועמד ורעה.

4a Vg *(et erit iste pax)* is closer to the usual sense of the words than Gk (καὶ ἔσται αὕτη εἰρήνη, "and this one will be peace"), or than Targ (ויהי מבכין שׁלמא לנא, "and from now on there will be peace for us"); cf. Eph. 2:14. Otherwise worthy of note is the interpretation of זה שׁלום as a genitive construction like שׂר־שׁלום (Isa. 9:5[6]), corresponding to זה סיני (Judg. 5:5; Ps. 68:9[8]; cf. J. M. Allegro, *VT* 5 [1955] 311; K. J. Cathcart [1968]; W. Rudolph; B. Renaud [1977] 228: "He will be the Lord of peace").

4b Targ (יהי לנא) adds לנו ("for us").

4c Gk (ἐπὶ τὴν χώραν ἡμῶν) appears to have read בְּאַדְמָתֵנוּ ("in our land"). Support for this reading might be found in the parallels בארצנו in v. 4ba[1] and בגבולנו in v. 5bγ. But Gk is more easily clarified as secondary than MT (cf. also K. J. Cathkart [1978] 40f. and Jer. 9:20 MT and Gk).

4d The suggestion to read וְהֵקִים (A. Weiser; *BHS*) presupposes that the subject is the messianic shepherd (vv. 1, 3, 4a), but this reading receives no support in the textual tradition.

4e Gk (δήγματα, "bites") reads נֹשְׁכֵי instead of נסיכי. E. Sellin (388) accepted this variant reading ("biters of men"); however, the other ancient versions support MT.

5a The word's derivation from I רעה is preferable to II רעע ("to shatter," thus KBL); it is supported by Gk, Vg and also by the preceding sentence in v. 4b (רעים).

5b In its position parallel to ארץ, נמרד the word ארץ is more likely a secondary addition than original, especially since it overloads the rhythm and is not presupposed by Gk.

5c בִּפְתָחֶהָ and its meaning (cf. Ps. 55:22) are made more probable by α' (ἐν σειρομασταις αυτης), ε' (εν παραξιφισιν), Vg *(in lanceis eius);* MT ("with their gates"), thus also σ', θ', does not fit with the parallel בחרב; however, because פתח occurs frequently, a misreading of the seldom-occurring פְּתִיחָה is easily conceivable.

5d The word is elucidated in Targ (וישׁיזבינגא, "he will deliver us") by the addition of the first person plural suffix, but this should not lead to a change of MT (והצילנו; thus *BHS*). It is easier to account for the suffix as a later addition than to suppose that MT was later abbreviated. The pronominal object often can be omitted; cf. Joüon, *Gr* §146i. The singular subject is supported by all ancient translations.

5e Targ (ולא יתיל . . . ולא ידרוך) presupposes ולא יבוא . . . ולא ידרך: "that he *not* come into our land and that he *not* tread upon our territory."

Form

A new type of collection of prophetic sayings begins in 4:9 in which each saying is introduced by the word עתה(ו) ("and now," vv. 9, 11, 14). The preceding collection in 4:1–8, begun by והיה (4:1; cf. 4:6, "on that day"), points to the distant future ("then," "when the times change"; see above, p. 119. On the ["fixed"] expression והיה = "and/but then," cf. KBL³, 233, no. 2b). This same introductory formula (והיה) occurs in 5:6, 7, 9, the sayings which follow our present collection of prophecies. Thus these "now-sayings" are encircled by "then-sayings." Because of a further והיה in 5:4a (see below, p. 147), we must at the outset ask where the "now-sayings" come to an end. This requires an investigation into the unusual structure of these sayings.

[4:9–10] The first saying in 4:9f. indicates that the "now" is related to an acute situation of distress. Words are addressed immediately (second person feminine singular) to those who are suffering. The questions (vv. 9a,ba) and imperatives (v. 10a) point to a lively disputation style. Connected with the imperatives is a vocative which informs the reader that the "daughter of Zion" is the addressee. The vocative is followed by a כי-clause which initially provides further, explicit directives for the present distress, "now." Then the saying changes to the form of a promise of deliverance (v. 10b). At first Yahweh is the subject (in the third person) of this assurance of salvation. The direct address style continues until the end of the saying. As a whole the passage has an unusual form for an assurance of deliverance; it derives from a discussion concerning the people's present distress. The saying provides a new interpretation of the word "now." The rhythm is that of elevated prose, with an irregular alternation between two-stress and three-stress cola, which only seldom exhibit *parallelismus membrorum*. The latter occurs, for example, at points of climax, as in the double question about the dangerous situation referred to in v. 9ba (two-stress bicolon), or in the assurance of deliverance at the conclusion containing the double occurrence of שם.

[4:11–13] The structure of the second saying, despite considerable changes of theme, is remarkably like the first. Here, too, the "now" is immediately connected with an acute situation of distress. Here, too, those experiencing the trouble are addressed in the second person feminine singular. Here, too, the direct address style continues throughout the passage. The disputation is enlivened by words quoted from a third party; in v. 11b the voice of the enemy is introduced in a quotation; and, without any explicit introduction, the voice of Yahweh (in both sentences formulated in first person speech in v. 13aα²) blends in with the prophet's words. Although the transition from doom to salvation is prepared for in v. 12 by a statement which offers reflection on the matter, nevertheless an explicit announcement of salvation is not made until after a twofold imperative with the vocative ("daughter of Zion," as in v. 10a) in a כי-clause. Here the "daughter of Zion" herself becomes the agent of Yahweh's punishment of his enemies, but she is empowered and authorized to do this only by the word and deed of Yahweh (v. 13). The statements of reflection in v. 12 make explicit what was in essence recognizable already in vv. 9f.: in both sayings a new meaning of the word "now" results from the disclosure of Yahweh's plans. Here, too, we have a promise of deliverance which grows out of the discussion of present distress. The rhythm becomes somewhat more pronounced especially at the end, compared with the preceding saying: v. 13 contains two clear three-stress tricola with *parallelismus membrorum*.

More problematic is the relationship of the structure of the third "now-saying" to the preceding two sayings. To be sure, 4:14 also relates the "now" to a situation of distress, and here, too, we find the direct address style formulated in the second person feminine singular of the imperative form. However, it is not the "daughter of Zion" who is addressed in the vocative. The meaning of בת־גדוד is yet to be explained (see below, p. 143); in essentials, the parallels of v. 14 with vv. 9 and 13, as well as with the description of distress in the verses following v. 14, suggest that here, too, the phrase refers to inhabitants of Jerusalem or to certain groups belonging to Jerusalem. The description of distress changes stylistically. For the first time, the first person plural is used (v. 14aβ). Those who had been the addressees become the speaker, and the prophet himself is included.

Should v. 14 be considered a fragment of a saying (B. Renaud [1977] 214) because the following verses in 5:1ff. develop differently than the previous "now-sayings"? Or, should we not rather see v. 14 as the necessary introduction to 5:1ff. (thus J. de Waard, *RHPhR* [1979] 513)? The partial structural similarity of v. 14 to v. 9 and v. 11 raises the question whether the following verses in 5:1ff., despite all the variations, are not in fact so similar to the preceding verses that 5:1ff. appear indispensable after the description of distress in 4:14, and thus 4:14 would appear to be the necessary transition to the following promise of deliverance.

[5:1] In any case, after the discussion of distress there follows in 5:1 an assurance of salvation. There is a similarity of structure with 4:9f. and vv. 11–13, to the extent that 5:1 announces the arrival of a new "ruler in Israel" after the humiliation of the "judge of Israel" in v. 14.[1]

The prophecy is formulated in direct address style; now, however, the addressee is the Judean town of Bethlehem. Could this be the reason that previously in v. 14, Jerusalem ceased to be the addressee and, with the prophet, the city joins those who speak the lamentation (first person plural in v. 14aβ)? The promise addressed to Bethlehem is spoken by Yahweh. As in 4:13aα², no formula for introducing quotations prefaces the Yahweh speech. The liveliness of the discussion is to be seen here in the transition from the direct address in second person feminine singular in 4:14aα to direct address to Bethlehem (5:1aα, in the second person masculine singular). This liveliness is also apparent in the change in the prophet's voice: as the first person plural in v. 14aβ indicates, the prophet here speaks in the first person plural, thus including himself among those

---

1. Just as the chapter divisions of the Middle Ages separate Mic. 5:1ff. from the description of distress in 4:14, they also separate Isa. 9:1ff. and 11:1ff. from the immediately preceding passages that originally belonged to them in Isa. 8:23 and 10:33f. (?); cf. K. Koch, *Die Profeten* I, *Assyrische Zeit* [1978], 145ff.).

previously addressed by him. But then in 5:1, with the messenger style, the prophet's voice changes to the first person singular of the Yahweh speech.

The promise of deliverance cannot conclude with 5:1, for the preceding two sayings certainly exhibit a movement from Jerusalem's distress to her deliverance. (This was perceived especially by the consistent later interpretation of 5:1 found in 4:8; see above, pp. 115f.). The difficulty lies in the various places where vv. 2–5 have been perceptibly reworked.

[5:2–5] The first of the secondary additions is found in 5:2, for the subject of the sentence cannot be the "ruler" from v. 1, whose birth according to v. 2a is still to be expected. The subject must therefore be Yahweh. Nor is the third person plural suffix in the word יתנם to be explained from v. 1. Thus the connection to v. 1 made by לכן is not initially intelligible (see below, p. 145). The word יולדה quite unexpectedly recurs, taken from 4:9. The statements concerning the ruler in v. 1 are not directly continued until v. 3; the transition from Yahweh's first person speech (v. 1) to speaking about Yahweh in the third person (v. 3) corresponds to the same transition in 4:13a–b, if originally there was not a promise to "daughter of Zion" concerning the "ruler" from Bethlehem that was displaced by v. 2—something the later interpretation of 5:1 in 4:8 could have helped facilitate.

A second later addition is found in the first word of v. 3b. The plural form וישבו interrupts the flow of the sentence concerning the "ruler" (third person singular in v. 3a and b). If we ask to whom this secondary word of hope speaks, it is probable that the third person plural relates to the return of the "brothers" and "children of Israel" in v. 2b. Thus the secondary addition at the beginning of v. 3b may be attributed to the same redaction responsible for v. 2. It has been taken from the first word in 4:4 (B. Renaud). The original text in 5:3 is continued in v. 4a, beginning with the word זה, which points to the preceding context (on והיה, see below, p. 147).

A third, more extensive interpolation can be seen in 5:4b–5a (similarly E. Sellin; A. Deissler; A. George). Here the agent, presented in the first person plural (v. 4bβ), deploys a large number of armed rulers against "Assyria." The tension between a human agency announced here (vv. 4b–5a) and the action of Yahweh and his shepherd is too great for vv. 4b–5a to have come from the same author as vv. 1, 3, 4a. On the other hand, the older-appearing text is concluded in v. 5b, where, after the plural verb forms in vv. 4b–5a, the subject appears again in the third person singular, as in vv. 1, 3, 4a; the speaker is presented in the first person plural, which recalls the first person plural in 4:14. It is precisely this sentence in v. 5b which is later interpreted anew by vv. 4b–5a, as is indicated by the extensive use of its wording at the beginning of the secondary addition in v. 4ba.

If these literary critical conclusions are correct, then after the description of distress (4:14) and the proclamation of a new ruler (5:1), the passage contains the promise of a worldwide reign of peace (vv. 3–4a), concluding with the particular consequences, for Jerusalem as well (first person plural in 5:5b as in 4:14!), of the ruler's acts of deliverance from the hostile world powers (v. 5b). Thus also the third "now-saying" leads to a declaration of deliverance (והציל) from the enemy, as did the preceding first (in v. 10bβ תנצלי) and second (in v. 13) sayings. Whereas in the first saying Yahweh himself carries out the deliverance, in the second the "daughter of Zion" is empowered to conquer the nations, and in the third it is the ruler from Bethlehem.

The prosody in the third saying—corresponding to an intensification internal to the three sayings—is more strongly pronounced. Three-stress bicola predominate; at points of climax they are replaced by two-stress bicola. After 4:14—to be read as elevated prose, since it lacks *parallelismus membrorum*—5:1 begins with two three-stress bicola (v. 1a; cf. note 5:1c) and concludes with a two-stress bicolon (v. 1b), a passage "highly poetic in feeling" (G. von Rad, *Old Testament Theology* 2:170). After the three-stress bicolon in v. 3a, v. 3b can also be read (without the first word; see above, p. 135 and note the *maqqeph!)* together with v. 4a (syncopic accents!) as a three-stress bicolon. The saying concludes in v. 5b with a two-stress tricolon.

Setting

The three "now-sayings" in 4:9—5:5 in their essential content, on the one hand, exhibit a similar structure: as promises of deliverance, they discuss a present time of distress, give a new interpretation to the word "now," pledge deliverance, and thus present an unusual form for a prophecy of consolation. This similarity in structure indicates that they share a common situation from which the sayings originated. On the other hand, the themes of the three sayings are so different that they should be interpreted as a literary rather than as a rhetorical unit. J. L. Mays (105) traces the thrice-occurring introductory עתה(ו) to the hand of the redactor. Whereas arguments for a literary reworking of the sayings in 4:9–14 are not compelling, the evidence suggests redactional work within 5:2–5. But apparently the redactor's work has to do not only with the third saying: he reworks the promise in the third saying with an eye toward the content of the first two sayings. The interpretative commentary in v. 2 makes reference to the time (עת) in which the woman in labor will bring forth. Here the redactor picks up words concerning the time of distress (עתה) with its cries of a woman in labor (4:9f.). With the statement about the armed rulers who march against Assyria (5:4b–5a), he alludes to the conquest of the enemy by the "daughter of Zion" in 4:13. This supplement to the "now-sayings" apparently intends to address the problem of postponed fulfillment of their promises and to help the troubled people at the time of their "surrender" (v. 2a).

A postexilic origin for the redactional level in 5:2, 3bα (first word only), 4b–5a is supported first of all by the content of 5:2 (see below and Isa. 66:7–9), but also by the style. The style indicates not only that there was a reworking of material within the preexisting context of 4:9—5:5b; it especially shows that the preexisting text Isa. 7:14 (לְבֵן יִתֵּן . . . וְיֹלָדְה) was brought into the remarkable beginning in 5:2a (J. Wellhausen 145f.; O. Loretz [1977] 359). Furthermore, the word וישבו in v. 3bα, taken from 4:4a, presupposes the existence of this late text (see above, p. 135; on 5:4b–5a, see below, pp. 147f.). The redaction that arranged and supplemented the sayings in 4:9—5:5 inserted this entire complex into its collection of "then-sayings." Indeed, the complex was placed precisely (after 4:8) where the redaction's own statement in 4:8 was in need of evidence, which was provided by the climax of the "now-sayings" in 5:1 (see above, p. 119).

To which period do the original sayings contained in 4:9—5:5 belong? Our structural analysis of the three sayings indicated that the answer is to be sought in all three sayings that begin their discussion of distress with "now." The references to such distress given in 4:9f., 11, 14 are best understood around the time of the conquest of Jerusalem by the Babylonians in 587. Particularly the differences in content in the sayings support this supposition like no other. Micah 4:9f. recalls the situation immediately after the capture of the city. Now the inhabitants must "depart from the city" after the temple, along with the dwellings, had burned down (v. 10b; cf. 2 Kings 25:9–11). Outside "in the open field" (בשׂדה, cf. Jer. 40:[1], 7, 13; [41:8]) they formed encampments where the treks "to Babylon" were organized (2 Kings 25:7, 11–13, 28). Micah 4:11 is appropriate to the situation during and immediately after the siege. By then the people had experienced under Nebuchadnezzar II that "many nations gathered themselves against" Jerusalem (v. 11a; cf. 2 Kings 25:1–4). What is said about the composition of Nebuchadnezzar's military forces during his earlier campaign (598), as reported in 2 Kings 24:2, may similarly apply to 587, namely, that along with "Chaldeans were also Syrians, Moabites, and Ammonites." On the particular hostility of the Edomites around 587, see Obad. 11–14. The Edomites went about speaking words of mockery and derision (v. 11b) as Obad. 12; Lam. 1:7; Ezek. 35:14f.; Ps. 137:7 attest from the time of the large-scale attack on Jerusalem.

Micah 4:14 recalls a particular occurrence in the last phase of the siege. First, the term for "siege" (מצור) is used here, a term current in the Babylonian era (cf. 2 Kings 25:2; Jer. 52:5; Ezek. 4:3, 7, 8; 5:2). Then the verse goes on to speak of a particular humiliation of the "judge of Israel," probably a reference to the king (see below, p. 143). Conceivably the best commentary on this is given by the account concerning the fate of Zedekiah in 2 Kings 25:4–7. Moreover, that the people's hope turned toward Bethlehem (5:1) is at no other time so easily conceivable as immediately after the total destruction of Jerusalem and the expulsion of the Davidic kings from their royal residence. Hence, the descriptions of distress in the three sayings points to the same date, the time around 587.

This date finds a welcome confirmation in the diction of the sayings. The question, "Is the king not in your midst?" (4:9) corresponds to Jer. 8:19. That Zion is "gripped with anguish like a woman in labor" is said elsewhere precisely in these words only in Jer. 6:24 and 50:43; cf. 22:23; 30:6; 49:24; also 4:31; 13:21. The parallel placement of "intention" (מחשבות)—"plan" (עצה) of Yahweh (4:12a) is attested elsewhere only in Jer. 49:20 (cf. v. 30) and 50:45. On the imagery of sheaves on the threshing floor used for the nations (4:12b), cf. Jer. 9:21; 51:33. Thus the author is most likely to be found among the circle of Jeremiah's disciples (cf. B. Renaud [1977] 205–216). Furthermore, words addressed to the "daughter of Zion" (4:10, 13) occur in Jer. 4:31; 6:2, 23; and in texts belonging immediately after the destruction of Jerusalem (Lam. 1:6; 2:1, 4, 8, 10, 13, 19); cf. the Deuteronomistic addition in Mic. 1:13b and see above, pp. 50, 52 and Th. Lescow, *ZAW* 84 (1972) 69. On the postexilic origin of the designations of time in 5:1b, see below, p. 145.

The arguments for dating these texts in the postexilic time, or even in Micah's time, are appreciably weaker. In response to the claim that 4:14 is reminiscent of Micah's love for wordplays and for assonance (1:10–16; see above, pp. 59ff.), as W. Beyerlin (p. 17ff.) argues, it could be suggested instead that the author of 4:14 had a thorough knowledge of the Micah traditions in chaps. 1–3. Moreover, the structure of his sayings is indicative of a completely different intention. Thus A. S. van der Woude is of the opinion that even the sayings in our passage continue Micah's disputation with his opponents, and that 4:(1–)9, 11–13 and 5:4–5 stem from the pseudo- (salvation-) prophets (cf. A. S. van der Woude [1969] 249ff.; [1976] 125ff.; similarly W. Rudolph). However, there is as little indication here of an alternation of voices speaking at the same time as there is in 2:12f. and in 4:1ff. Rather, it is characteristic of these sayings of comfort, as demonstrated above, to point the way out of distress toward deliverance. This brings us to the question about the "setting in life" of the three prophecies of salvation, each of which begins with a marked reference to the present distress. During the disastrous time of 587, the sayings pick up the extremely threatening announcement of judgment uttered by Micah in 3:12. "Now" the hour of its fulfillment has come. In response to it, the generation experiencing great crisis must find an affirmative answer. Now, in the hour of judgment, it must come to the belief that Yahweh, the king, is in its midst, as had been so casually expressed in times of plenty (cf. 4:9 with 3:11). Yahweh would, indeed, save it from the disaster and lead it anew to salvation. This prophet of comfort, who belongs among Jeremiah's disciples, in the most difficult of times, therefore builds the bridge of hope that would lead from Micah's proclamation of judgment to God's new, saving deeds.

Such prophecies of consolation were conceivably spoken and transmitted (at first individually) in liturgies of lamentation which were used after 587 on anniversaries of the destruction of the city and the burning of the temple (Zech. 7:3, 5; 8:19). One can see from Obadiah's sayings that in these liturgies of mourning, along with prayers of lamentation, new interpretations of older prophecies also took their place (cf. H. W. Wolff, "Obadja—Ein Kultprophet als Interpret," *EvTh* 37 [1977] 273–284; idem, *Obadiah and Jonah* 19ff. and Th. Lescow, *ZAW* 84 [1972] 66–69). This collection of three sayings of consolation is not only rooted in various situations of distress during the time around 587; it also speaks of salvation from this distress in quite different ways. That these sayings are a compilation of prophecies drawn from the Jerusalem lamentation ceremonies accounts for such differences. This makes the variations in content more understandable than the supposition of a disputation between true and false prophets; in that case one would expect, according to 2:6–11 and 3:5-7, 11, appropriate formulas to introduce two different speakers.

In light of these considerations, it should not be surprising that these sayings were literarily attached immediately to chaps. 1–3 by the redactor. Only with the postexilic redaction were the sayings in 4:1–8 inserted before the "now- sayings," which at the same time were reedited and brought into the grand conception of eschatological proclamation found in chaps. 4–5.

Commentary

[4:9] That the first saying (vv. 9f.) begins with "now" becomes intelligible if the speaker himself experienced in his own present time the fulfillment of Micah's judgment against Jerusalem (3:12). The word "now" is picked up anew and elucidated in v. 10ba (כִּי-עַתָּה). Only there does the prophet mention details relating to military actions in the summer and fall of 587 (v. 10b). In v. 9 he initially speaks about the private reactions of Jerusalem's inhabitants. He inquires into the basis for the public "outcry"; he responds to it with rhetorical questions. Similar to Judg. 7:21, here רוע *hiph.* means a desperate, lamenting cry for help; it is the outcry of terrified people who have been hopelessly overpowered by the enemy's hostilities against a starving city after a year and a half of siege (2 Kings 25:1, 3f., 8). The imperfect (תָּרִיעִי) has the sense of present duration (Joüon, *Gr* §113d). The question about the king's presence probably does not relate in an ironic sense to Zedekiah's flight from the city (according to 2 Kings 25:4f.; cf. J. L. Mays 105). It is more conceivable that the question refers to Yahweh. This is suggested by the similar double question in Jer. 8:19, "Is not Yahweh in Zion? Is there no king in her?" That Yahweh as king (מֶלֶךְ) at the same time is called יוֹעֵץ ("counselor") not only corresponds to the frequently attested view of Yahweh as planner and counselor (Isa. 5:19; 19:17; Jer. 28:29; 32:19; etc.); it is also particularly suggested in this context by the immediately following saying in v. 12a. Finally, the double question that asks about Yahweh's presence becomes intelligible when we note that here the prophet refers back to 3:11b and is making a commentary on it. In 3:11b Micah quotes words that express the self-security of his audience: "Is not Yahweh in our midst?" Now a later disciple of Micah, during the Babylonian era, asks the desperate inhabitants of the conquered city what they now think concerning Yahweh's presence. Their fervent cry of anguish is likened to the anxious cry (חזק *hiph.*) of a writhing (חִיל) person who is suddenly seized and overcome by labor pains. This expression once again takes up language from Jeremiah: according to Jer. 6:24, as a result of a report about a conquering enemy (vv. 22f.), the "daughter of Zion" (v. 23) is "taken hold of" by "pain as of a woman in travail" (v. 24; cf. also Jer. 4:31; 13:21; 22:23; 30:6; Isa. 26:17f.; 66:7f.); labor pains grip Israel's enemies in Jer. 49:24; 50:43; Isa. 13:8; (21:3); Ps. 48:7[6]). But the birthpangs represent not only extraordinary pain and despair. חִיל begins with the first pains and ends with (liberating) birth (יֶלֶד; cf. Isa. 26:17f.; 66:7f.; cf. Baumann, *ThWAT* 2:899f.). Thus the metaphor is appropriate for illustrating the change from distress to liberation.

[4:10] Correspondingly, the "now" of the present, despairing conditions finds a new interpretation: the woman who writhes in pain is indeed one who gives birth. Apparently the daughter of Zion here, unlike 4:8 (see below, p. 125), is not a personification of the city, but one of the inhabitants of Jerusalem (cf. also 4:13). The double imperative ("writhe and come forth!"), like the words of a midwife, challenges the daughter of

Zion to put forth the final efforts of birth. חיל (חולי) leads further to the "breaking forth" (וגחי from גיח) or "going forth" (גחה, see note 10b) of the child from the womb (Ps. 22:10). In v. 10b the prophet explains the event without any imagery (כי־עתה). The present distress is comprised of three actions: exodus from the city (which has become uninhabitable; cf. 2 Kings 25:9–11); camping "in the open field" (outside the breached walls, until they are transported into exile; on בשדה, cf. Jer. 6:25; 14:18; 40:7, 13); arrival in Babylon (בוא is used for going into exile in 2 Kings 24:16; 25:7; cf. Jer. 34:3). However, these painful experiences will be followed in the end by liberation. Only "there" in Babylon, only "there"—the emphasis is made by repetition in the last two sentences—ensues the deliverance (נצל niph.) from all oppression. Not until the end of the saying is Yahweh named as the liberator: he redeems his property (גאל) from the dominion of the overwhelming enemies of Jerusalem: cf. גאל מכף with גאל מיד in Jer. 31:11. Thus not only is Micah's prophecy of judgment fulfilled; even beyond that, an entirely new life in freedom with Yahweh is announced. The accent at the end of the saying is upon the redeeming will of Yahweh, which is mightier than all the affliction from the present enemy.

[4:11–13] Even more clearly than the first saying, the second enters into a discussion with the conquerors. Here the themes of "the nations assault on the city of God" (v. 11) and of "Yahweh's war against the nations" (vv. 12b–13) are combined with each other in a singular manner (v. 12a). Whereas in vv. 9f. the "now" was reinterpreted with the image of birth-pangs, in vv. 11–13 it is done within sight of the assembled nations.

[4:11] Here ועתה does not have the oft-occurring sense of drawing a conclusion; rather, beginning a new saying, the word points in a strictly temporal way to the present situation, as עתה in vv. 9 and 14 (cf. H. A. Brongers, *VT* 15 [1965] 289–299). For a second time, the conclusion of the Micah traditions, with its announcement of punishment against Zion (3:12), is connected with the events that transpired in the meantime. As in 4:9f. the "daughter of Zion" is addressed (cf. עליך in v. 11 with בת־ציון in vv. 10 and 13; as in the first saying, she is not mentioned until the imperatives, which make a transition to the second part of the saying). The motif of the "nations assault against the city of God" (cf. Ps. 48:5[6]) is presented in a form which corresponds to a genuine report of observed historical events. "Many nations" did in fact "assemble" themselves and storm Jerusalem in 588/587 (cf. 2 Kings 24:2 with 25:1–4 and see above, p. 137). Unlike Joel 4[3]:2; Zech. 14:2; Zeph. 3:8, the saying does not immediately report that "Yahweh" assembled them. Initially, with a perfect verb followed by a participle, v. 11 only presents events which can be seen and heard, i.e., it presents facts capable of being substantiated. By quoting the words of the conquerors, the prophet demonstrates that the nations undertake war against Jerusalem on their own authority. Their will and desire is to "pollute" the city of God. חנף probably means a concrete "besoiling," which defiles the city with the blood of war (cf. Num. 35:33; Ps. 106:38 and Seybold, *ThWAT* 3:42; differently p. 44: "to do something improper"?), an action that burns down Yahweh's temple (2 Kings 25:9). That the enemy gloatingly "looks down upon" Jerusalem when the city is conquered in 587 is repeatedly attested (Obad. 12a; Lam. 1:7; Ezek. 35:12, 14f.; Ps. 137:7; on חזה ב, cf. also Ps. 118:7, ראה ב). The prophet can remember that the enemy opened his mouth in derision over the destroyed city (cf. Obad. 12a). Verse 11 therefore especially presents a report of actual events occurring after July, 587.

[4:12] But with v. 12 (as in vv. 9f.) the distress of the situation is placed in a new light. Behind the nations' willful intent to destroy Zion stands something concerning which they "do not know," into which "they have no insight," but something which will now be revealed to the over-powered "daughter of Zion," the inhabitants of Jerusalem. The deliberate intentions of the nations are merely a link in the chain of Yahweh's grand design. Already in Isa. 14:24–27 we find a military threat to Jerusalem in a certain historical situation that is drawn into a universal plan of Yahweh (cf. H. M. Lutz, 155ff. and Isa. 28:29). This passage speaks repeatedly of the עצה of Yahweh. However, only in the Jeremianic tradition do we find the abstract plural מחשבות יהוה parallel with עצת יהוה to designate the comprehensive plan of Yahweh (see note 12a) that stands opposed to the foreign nations (Jer. 49:20; 50:45; see Seybold, *ThWAT,* 3:255). מחשבות means a calculated intention and, together with עצה, a comprehensive plan. In that the prophet knows Yahweh's comprehensive plan, the present distress is placed in a new light.

The prophet begins the reinterpretation of the "now" with a simile: "He (Yahweh) has gathered them (the nations) like sheaves on the threshing floor." עמיר denotes the bundle of harvested and gathered sheaves of grain brought for threshing "to the threshing floor" (see note 12b); the sheaves are thus taken to their irrevocable end (cf. Jer. 9:21). This imagery, drawn from the harvest, is used to portray Yahweh's plan of judgment (cf. Joel 4[3]:13; Zech. 12:6). The apparent self-willed "gathering" of the nations in fact originates in the will of Yahweh. It is not they who have assembled themselves together; Yahweh has (cf. Isa. 8:9f.; 17:12–14; also Joel 4[3]:2; Zeph. 3:8; Zech. 14:2).

[4:13] Verse 13 describes how gathering for assault against Jerusalem prepares for Yahweh's war against the assembled nations. At first the simile of harvest in v. 12b is developed further. The "daughter of Zion," i.e. the inhabitants of Jerusalem previously under attack (cf. 4:10), are summoned to "thresh." The imagery presupposes that the bundles of grain are loosened and spread out on the threshing floor. Now the kernels can be trampled and crushed. As the subsequent mention of "bronze hooves" indicates, the notion here is one of cattle being driven over the threshing floor to crush the grain (Deut. 25:4; Hos. 10:11; cf. Dalman, *AuS,* 3:112–114). "Threshing" thus becomes an image of total destruction (Hab. 3:12; Isa. 41:15). The double imperative, addressed to the daughter of Zion, is like the "summons to battle" called out by a prophet in Yahweh's war (cf. R. Bach, WMANT 9 (1962), 66ff.; 71; 75; H. M. Lutz, 93f.). The prophet gives the motivation for his summons by means of two promises spoken by Yahweh in v. 13aα², which are introduced by כי. Besides v. 11, where the nations' consciousness of their superiority is elucidated by quotations, the prophet now equips the daughter of Zion with confidence of victory through God's words of assurance that he will provide them with superior strength. The "horn" is a general mark of strength—as is first of all characteristic of the wild ox (Num. 23:22)—and is provided by Yahweh to the king (1 Sam. 2:10; Ps. 132:17) and his people (Deut. 33:17) so they can overpower the enemy. The prophet Zedekiah, according to 2 Kings 22:11, used "iron horns" to symbolize Israel's military strength against Syria. In v. 13 Yahweh assures the daughter of Zion of her superior strength over the nations. Only with the second word of assurance is there a return to the imagery of the threshing floor. The sheaves of grain are just as thoroughly trampled under the tread of "bronze hooves" as by "iron threshing sledges" (Amos 1:3). After the quotation of Yahweh's word of assurance, the simile gives way to an interpretative clause in v. 13aβ. The consequence of the "threshing" done under Yahweh's authority is that the "daughter of Zion" will "trample" the multitude of nations: דקק‎ qal can of course be used for crushing grain (Isa. 28:28; cf. 41:15), but in the hiph. it especially denotes complete destruction (2 Kings 23:6, 15: "crush to dust"), even of the nations (2 Sam. 22:43). Whereas the nations are Yahweh's instrument against Israel elsewhere in prophetic texts, here the daughter of Zion is summoned as Yahweh's instrument against the nations of the world. There is further evidence of this motif from the time immediately after 587 in Obad. 18; Ezek. 25:14 (cf. also Isa. 11:13f.; Zech. 12:6 and Wolff, *Obadiah and Jonah* 66). It is clear that the war to be waged by the daughter of Zion is Yahweh's war. This is indicated by the stipulation to devote the spoil to Yahweh (see note 4:13d). The spoils of war are not retained by Israel, but must be devoted to Yahweh (cf. 2 Sam. 8:11; 1 Kings 7:51; 15:15; Lev. 27:28; and G. von Rad, *Der Heilige Krieg im alten Israel* 13f.). This, too, emphasizes the defensive character of the eschatological Yahweh war, especially since according to v. 11 the war is an immediate response to the nations' attack (cf. H. M. Lutz, 184). The word בצע‎ means (unjust) profit; חיל‎ refers rather to the means of military strength (cf. Eising, *ThWAT* 2:904ff.). Everything is at the disposal of Yahweh, "the Lord of the whole earth." The title here refers not only to Yahweh's sovereign disposition over the land promised to Israel (Isa. 3:11, 13), but also to his authoritative command and direction of all the powers within history (Zech. 4:10, 14; 6:5), and of all spheres of nature (Ps. 97:5) in the earth (cf. Isa. 54:5). It is for the comfort of the city conquered by the powerful nations that Yahweh, whose sanctuary is destroyed, will demonstrate through his chastised people that he is the absolute, universal Lord of all nations. He empowers the daughter of Zion anew so that she is able to rule over the sovereign powers of the nations. Here, too, in the novel content of this saying, the relationship of conqueror to conquered is reversed by Yahweh's intervention.

[4:14] For a third time the word "now" connects Micah's prophecy of destruction (3:12) with the events of 587. Support for this interpretation, in addition to the parallels in 4:10 and 11, is found especially in the mention of the conditions of siege and of the humiliation of the "judge of Israel." But unlike the previous two sayings, the imperative stands at the very beginning of the saying. A ritual of lamentation is commanded: "Scratch the skin until it bleeds" (see note 14a; Deut. 14:1; 1 Kings 18:28; Jer. 47:5); the ritual action of mourning for the destruction of Jerusalem is repeatedly mentioned in circles close to Jeremiah (Jer. 41:5; 16:6). As in the preceding two sayings, here words are addressed to a second person feminine singular; however, she is no longer called "daughter of Zion" (as in vv. 10 and 13), but "daughter of the troops" (see note 14b). To whom can this refer? While the following verses speak of the siege and then of the blow against the "judge of Israel," one could think of Zedekiah who, according to 2 Kings 25:4, attempted to break out of the city escorted by a detachment of troops. However, the king and the group with him were caught near Jericho; his sons were killed, and he was blinded, put in chains, and taken to Babylon. Is the "daughter of Zion" now characterized as the "daughter" (i.e., as a member) of the detachment that unsuccessfully tried to escape? Certainty in interpretation cannot be attained, especially since the alliteration probably influenced the choice of words. Undoubtedly, however, "daughter of the troops" means the inhabitants who found themselves within the walls under siege, among whom the speaker counted himself (עלינו). מצור is used elsewhere, particularly for the siege of Jerusalem: 2 Kings 24:10; 25:2; Ezek. 4:3, 7; 5:2 (cf. Jer. 10:17).

In this context, the "judge of Israel" can only mean the king; again, as with the summons תתגדדי בת־גדוד, here the alliteration שפט—שבט might have contributed to the choice of words. One should not conclude that the passage goes back to Micah himself merely because it is reminiscent of the alliteration in 1:10–16 (thus most recently, Jörg Jeremias, *ZAW* 83 [1971] 354). On the other hand, it is possible that this disciple of the prophet was familiar not only with his message but also with the linguistic forms of the old Micah traditions. One can also see a reference to the king in the phrase "judge of Israel," because (1) מלך not infrequently stands parallel with שפט (Ps. 2:10; 2 Kings 15:5; Isa. 16:5; (2) certain kinds of judicial decisions were made by the king (2 Sam. 15:2, 6; cf. G. Ch. Macholz, "Die Stellung des Königs in der israelitischen Gerichtsverfassung," *ZAW* 84 [1972] 157–182); (3) שפט as a verb plainly can have the meaning of "to rule" (1 Kings 3:9).

To "strike the judge of Israel on the cheek" is an insulting, humiliating act (1 Kings 22:24; Ps. 3:8; Job 16:10; Lam. 3:30; Isa. 50:6). To strike with the "staff" intensifies the shame. He himself who wields the royal staff is now abused and humbled by a foreign staff. Concerning Zedekiah, it is reported that the king of Babylon brought him to his headquarters in Riblah and had his eyes put out (Jer. 52:9–11). Such an insulting act further disgraces him and at the same time removes his authority. This is characteristic of the present hour: an imprisoned people, a dishonored king.

[5:1] But for the people of Zion and for all of Israel, something new can be expected with regard to its king. And something is also new with regard to the addressees of the promise. The assurance of deliverance, which expects the appearance of a new ruler, looks toward and directly addresses "Bethlehem-Ephrathah." Thus the words speak to David's hometown rather than to his royal residence. David's father, Jesse, is introduced in 1 Sam. 17:12 as an Ephrathite from Bethlehem (1 Sam. 16:18; 17:58; cf. 1 Sam. 16:1; 2 Sam. 20:1). Ephrathah means the clan; Bethlehem refers to its place of residence (cf. Ruth 1:2). It avoids confusion to append the name Ephrathah to Bethlehem because there is also a Bethlehem in Galilee in the region occupied by the tribe of Zebulun (Josh. 19:15). The connection of the words "Bethlehem-Judah" serves to make the same distinction in 1 Sam. 17:12. While the name Bethlehem means "house of bread," Ephrathah means "field of fruit" (KBL³). The prophet's glance turns away from Jerusalem to the country village situated 9 km to the south. What is presupposed here is that the former Davidic dynasty of Jerusalem has come to an end (4:14; cf. Jer. 22:30). It would appear that the viewpoint of Isa. 11:1 is picked up and developed further: the tree has fallen, but a new shoot springs from its stump (Jesse, David's father). Although the prophetic expectation looks toward the Judean country village, the passage need not be ascribed to Micah, who comes from the provinces of Judah; rather, the passage fits the situation after 587. However, this indirect revision of the Nathan promise (2 Sam. 7:16) does not expressly speak about a different line from the house of Jesse. In principle what is emphasized here is that this ruling line arises from the now-defunct Davidic dynasty: Bethlehem is "small among the thousands of Judah." Originally, a "thousand" was a unit levied by a clan for the tribal army (1 Sam. 8:12; Amos 5:3); it came to denote the clan unit itself (Judg. 6:15; 1 Sam. 10:19, 21) and its territory within the tribal domain, which can be identical with a city (Amos 5:3; Mic. 5:1). Among the tribes of Judah, Bethlehem represents a relatively small "thousand." צָעִיר ("small") means "few in number," "(militarily) insignificant"; the word is synonymous with "despised" in Ps. 119:141. The Gideon (Judg. 6:15) and Saul (1 Sam. 9:21) traditions also contain narratives about Yahweh's election of a deliverer from an insignificant clan; according to 1 Sam. 16:11–13, the elected David is the "smallest" (i.e., "youngest") within the family circle. According to Isa. 60:22 "the least shall become a thousand (אֶלֶף) and the smallest (הַצָּעִיר) a mighty nation" (גּוֹי עָצוּם). This thought is quite similar to that contained in Mic. 4:6–7a (see above, p. 124). Here in v. 1 an insignificant town, from which nothing great is expected, is the place of origin for the new ruler. Yahweh takes up anew his messianic work at an inglorious town among provincial people. Because Yahweh acts in this manner, Bethlehem paradoxically is "by no means the least" (Matt. 2:6; see note 5:1c).

An emphatic word of assurance is given to the little town: "*from you* will come forth. . . ." יָצָא can of course also mean "to be born," as in Job 1:21, or "to descend from" (Gen. 17:6; 35:11); but mostly it has the more comprehensive sense of "to proceed from," especially in the context of messianic expectations (2 Sam. 7:12; Isa. 11:1; Jer. 30:21). Hence, in v. 1 the word is not so much connected with giving birth, but rather with providing the details of the ruler's appearance, "for me . . . to become ruler in Israel." The word לִי (cf. also note 5:1d) emphasizes that he is entirely subordinate to the will of Yahweh: Yahweh clearly states that the coming ruler has his origins in Yahweh's election (1 Sam. 16:1), and that his very nature is defined by an enduring relationship with Yahweh (cf. Jer. 30:21). לִהְיוֹת accentuates Yahweh's intention. With this word the prophet takes up a further element from the Nathan promise (cf. 2 Sam. 7:8, just as previously יָצָא recalls 2 Sam. 7:12 and לִי, 1 Sam. 16:1). While the elected person in 2 Sam. 7:8 is called נָגִיד ("leader"), here (as in Jer. 30:21) he is called מוֹשֵׁל ("ruler"). In both instances the title of מֶלֶךְ is avoided. Is this reserved for Yahweh alone (cf. 4:7b and on 5:3 see below, p. 146)? In any case, what distinguishes the coming ruler from the representatives of the dynasty who have been cut off is that in his government, nothing other than Yahweh's sovereignty is executed. He reigns "over Israel." This is more than Jerusalem and Judah (1:9). Israel's salvation history will begin anew. Even if this history is not to be a direct continuation of the history of Jerusalem's royal line, nevertheless there is a correspondence to its "ancient origins." The abstract plural מוצאת (see above, note 5:1e) refers to the "origin" and picks up the root יצא "to proceed from" in v. 1aβ; the twice-occurring מן ("from antiquity, from ancient days"), taken again from the preceding ממך, makes prominent the identify of the ancient origins (similarly with Jesse in Isa. 11:1) in Bethlehem. Finally, the reference to the original starting-point emphasizes that it is the selfsame God who makes such promises, and that he is faithful to his original promises despite all human infidelity and historical changes. The expressions מקדם "from of old" and ימי עולם "since ancient days" occur in connection with David's time in Neh. 12:46 and Amos 9:11, and elsewhere only in exilic and postexilic texts (cf. Mic. 7:14; Isa. 45:21; 46:10; 63:9, 11; Mal. 3:4; etc.).

[5:2] The later addition in v. 2 (see above, p. 134) addresses those who in spiritual despair have waited in vain for the appearance of the ruler from Bethlehem (v. 1). The difficulty in understanding the connecting particle "therefore" is best explained if we see in v. 2 an allusion to Isa. 7:14 (see above, p. 136); there the text also has to do with (after לכן יתן) a woman who will conceive; with a time of waiting (vv. 15f.); and finally, in a wider context, with the return of a remnant (cf. Mic. 5:2b with Isa. 7:3). While in Isaiah it speaks of *giving* a sign, in v. 2, in a midrashlike use of the term נתן, it speaks of "giving up" (here נתן is an elliptical expression in the sense of נתן ביד אויבים, "to surrender into the hand of the enemy"; cf. 2 Sam. 5:19; 1 Kings 22:6). Those "given up" are people who suffer the consequences of the events of 587 (4:9f., 11, 14). Yahweh, whose plan goes back to ancient days (5:1b), also determines the end of the times of oppression. They will end when the woman in labor gives birth. Here the commentator draws together the statements about the woman in labor in 4:9f. with those about the new ruler in 5:1 and Isa. 7:14. As long as the woman in labor experiences birthpangs and cries out, the time of distress continues on. When she has finished giving birth (perf. ילדה), then the liberation and the time of salvation arrive (cf. Isa. 66:6–9; on birth as the end of the crisis, cf. Th. Lescow, *ZAW* 79 [1967] 204). Hence, the secondary addition in v. 2 teaches that times of trial are not to be met without hope.

One of the events which belongs to the ending of Judah's time of distress is the return of the "remnant of his brothers" from exile. Following 4:14—5:1, the suffix in אחיו should first of all be connected with the exiled princes of the royal house. However, to "his brothers" also belong, according to Deuteronomistic thought, all the others who survived the *golah* (Deut. 17:15, 20), especially in that they are to be united with the "children of Israel," that is, the people who remained in the land and formed the nucleus of the messianic community (v. 1aβ). The time of the new ruler from Bethlehem therefore coincides with the return of the rest of those in exile. This is the message of the secondary addition in v. 2, since it is written with an eye toward not only v. 3 but also v. 1. For the realm of the new ruler extends to "the ends of the earth" (v. 3b).

[5:3] Verse 3 is the original continuation of v. 1. After the statement about origins (v. 1), it initially proclaims the accession to the throne of the ruler from Bethlehem (וְעָמַד). The administration of his rule is described as the work of a shepherd (וְרָעָה). As a just shepherd, the ruler accomplishes three functions: he will lead his people, protect them, and provide for them. That a ruler is given the title of "shepherd" is a common practice in the ancient Orient (cf. W. Zimmerli, *Ezekiel* 2:218ff.). In the Old Testament the title is already applied to Israel's judges: Yahweh commissions them to "shepherd" his people Israel (2 Sam. 7:7). The same is said concerning David, whom Yahweh took from following after the flock in the meadow (2 Sam. 5:2; cf. 7:8). Jeremiah 23:1–4 is the first text to speak of Israel's future ruler as the good shepherd of Israel whom Yahweh— himself referred to as shepherd in the preceding verse—will appoint. The future Davidic king is proclaimed by Ezekiel (34:23; 37:24) to be the one shepherd; here too, it is said that Yahweh will appoint him, after Ezekiel speaks of Yahweh's own shepherding of the flock (34:11ff.). Verse 3 belongs to the same line of thought voiced in this Ezekiel passage, which is to be dated after 587 (W. Zimmerli, *Ezekiel* 2:218ff.). This verse emphasizes that the shepherding of the new ruler will be accomplished by the authorization of Yahweh. Here the word עֹז refers to Yahweh's "majesty" (A. S. van der Woude, *THAT* 2:254f.) and is synonymous with גָּאוֹן ("sovereignty"); likewise, שֵׁם יהוה is synonymous with Yahweh himself, with the nuance that the "name" of Yahweh recalls the God whom Israel proclaims and praises (Pss. 29:2; 96:8). By leading, protecting, and caring for Israel, the promised one from Bethlehem executes Yahweh's majesty; by subordinating himself to Yahweh's sovereign power, he acts as the shepherd of his people. That Yahweh is expressly named "his God" emphasizes again the shepherd's special and complete personal relationship with God (see above, p. 144 on לִי in v. 1).

The following sentence, connected by כִּי, is not in the proper sense a motivation clause; rather, it takes the promise further (on emphatic כִּי, KBL³ 448) by emphasizing, with a new reference to "now," that the present is already contained in the promise. The ruler will achieve greatness like unto the significance and meaning of the former great kings, as was already promised to David (2 Sam. 7:9); indeed, he will truly become a world ruler. His office as shepherd will embrace all lands and political powers "to the ends of the earth." The phrase "ends of the earth" is mostly found in eschatological (Isa. 45:22, 52:10; Pss. 22:28[27]; 98:3) and particularly in messianic texts (1 Sam. 2:10; Zech. 9:10; Pss. 2:8; 72:8) that belong especially to the exilic and postexilic eras.

At the beginning of v. 3b, the redactor has inserted the catchword וְיָשְׁבוּ, taken from 4:4a, which points back to the universal freedom proclaimed in 4:1–4. This is easily understandable, since the guarantor of this freedom now becomes the ruler from Israel by Yahweh's authority. He will remain undaunted by danger and oppression from every willful intrusion. Here the word יָשַׁב has the comprehensive, pregnant meaning of living in lasting peaceful contentment. At the same time, וְיָשְׁבוּ continues the redaction's later addition in 5:2b, thus especially including the remnant among those who return from exile.

[5:4a] The word זֶה refers back to the ruler in vv. 1 and 3. To be sure, critics recently have attempted to understand זֶה שָׁלוֹם as a genitive construction like זֶה סִינַי (Judg. 5:5) and שַׂר־שָׁלוֹם (Isa. 9:5) (see note 5:4a). But the evidence for this is weak, especially in passages that belong to the time of our text. Because of the reference זֶה makes back to vv. 1 and 3, וְהָיָה does not function as a connecting formula ("and then"), as in 4:1; 5:6, 7, 9; rather, it has the pregnant meaning "to become real," "to become effective," "to effect." Because he will save Israel from its overpowering enemies, the ruler from Bethlehem will bring about genuine שָׁלוֹם.

[5:5b] This is indicated by v. 5b. Not until v. 5b do we find the continuation of v. 4a, which offers an interpretation of "this one" (v. 4a; cf. the third person singular). The catchword for "deliverance" (in 4:10bα נצל *niph.* pass.) is now taken up in the active form (נצל *hiph.*): "he will deliver." The comprehensive promise now aims at the concrete situation of distress brought about by the attack of the powerful nations. As in the description of distress in 4:14aβ, so now the prophet's words once again include himself among the afflicted community: "Assyria, when it comes into *our* land . . . *our* territory." That the foreign conqueror is named "Assyria" is not unusual, even in the Babylonian or Persian periods (cf. Lam. 5:6; Ezra 6:22; Zech. 10:10f.; Mic. 7:12; Nah. 3:18 [see Jörg Jeremias, WMANT 35, 1970, 51]; Isa. 10:12, 24; 19:23; 27:13 [see H. Wildberger, *Jesaja 1–12,* BK 10/1, 402f.; 408; 419; BK 10/2, 743f.]). For after the military advances of Tiglath-Pileser III during the third quarter of the eighth century, Israel experienced threat from the great power to the north under the unforgettable name of "Assyria." Thus even after the collapse of the Neo-Assyrian empire, "Assyria" became the code-name for the succeeding empires that marched down from the north. If vv. 4a and 5b form the conclusion to the promises of deliverance in 4:9—5:1, 3, and if these verses originated in the time around 587, then in v. 5b the community in the Babylonian era makes a confession of its faith in response to the proclamation that the coming ruler from Bethlehem will save them from the power of the nations.

[5:4b–5a] The passage in vv. 4b–5a has been inserted between vv. 4a and 5b; this becomes intelligible if vv. 4b–5a were a secondary addition initially written on the margin of the manuscript. It takes up almost word for word the sentence about "Assyrian" attack in v. 5b. Here the code-meaning of Assyria is substantiated by the synonym "land of Nimrod" in v. 5a. For the word *Nimrod,* with reference to Mesopotamia, represents the archetypal image of a thoroughgoing rule by oppression (cf. Gen. 10:8–12). What is new in this later insertion is that (a) the first person plural of those under attack, mentioned in 4:14 and 5:5b, now becomes the subject that speaks about providing its own help against the enemy; (b) they will summon up numerous "shepherds" (seven or eight), in contrast to the one shepherd from Bethlehem (vv. 1, 3; cf. Ezek. 34:23; 37:24); (c) these shepherds are expressly called "princes of men," whereas the ruler from Bethlehem will "shepherd" by the power of Yahweh; (d) in their function as shepherds, they fight against their powerful enemy exclusively with "sword and dagger." This secondary addition contains no details which would enable us to date it reliably. The content of the text stands at a considerable distance from its older context. Was this addition intended to supplement the statements about the intervening conditions prior to the Messiah's birth mentioned in v. 2, perhaps depending on 4:13, which speak of the empowering of the daughter of Zion to thresh? Nevertheless, the final deliverance of Israel will be accomplished by the one who is promised (v. 5b, third person singular).

Purpose and Thrust

We have identified these three prophecies of consolation (4:9f., 11–13, and 4:14—5:1, 3, 4a, 5b), unique in their form-critical characteristics, as "assurances of deliverance" *(Rettungszusprüche)* (see above, pp. 133ff.). These prophetic sayings presuppose that a reading of the book of Micah, up to 3:12, immediately preceded them. They attest that the destruction of Jerusalem proclaimed there, including all of its accompanying terrors, is taking place "now," for all eyes to see (4:9, 11, 14). This event makes it necessary to consider and reflect upon the misfortunes of Jerusalem and all its inhabitants. Such misfortune is presupposed by these promises.

What these prophecies have in common is that in each case they describe, at the outset, the present, concrete situation of distress, but then clearly point the way to deliverance from oppression. At the same time, the present situation is given a new interpretation: the oppressive times are portrayed as necessary; indeed, the present sufferings become, under the new prophetic word, the preparation for liberation. The enemies' assault upon Jerusalem leads to the defeat of them all. In light of the prophetic promises, all present relationships are altered. The community that accepts the judgment proclaimed by Micah perceives itself to be on the way to surmounting its distress. Hence the people who have been beaten down are picked up and placed into a new reality by the promises of consolation and deliverance.

The details of the suffering and its alleviation are presented differently in each of these sayings. The first saying (4:9f.) speaks about the deportees, those who must depart from the city (see above, p. 137). As certainly as the woman in labor will successfully give birth only after she has suffered birthpangs (see also p. 145 on 5:2), just as certainly those expelled from Jerusalem will be saved from the violence of their enemies by Yahweh only after they make their way to Babylon. Israel arrives at the path to freedom only by experiencing the yes to the previously ordained punishment (cf. 1:16; 2:3f.; 3:12).

The second prophetic saying (4:11–13) sees the troops of foreign nations gathered to besiege, conquer, and occupy Zion (see above, p. 137). But this gathering together leads to their own destruction. As heads of grain are bundled into sheaves and brought to the threshing floor to be threshed, so the assembled conquerors will be threshed. The daughter of Zion herself, i.e., the inhabitants of the previously besieged city, will triumph over the nations, not by her own strength, but by the empowerment of her God; not for her own praise and profit, but for the glory of God, the "Lord of the whole earth" (v. 13). Of an active, positive turning of the nations to Yahweh, as attested in Hag. 2:7ff.; Isa. 60:7ff.; Mic. 4:1–

3 (on which see above, pp. 120f.), this exilic prophet as yet has nothing to say. Here the emphasis lies only on the notion that the threat to Zion by the nations presents a necessary but passing phase in the grand plan of Yahweh (v. 12a).

The third prophetic saying (4:14—5:1, 3, 4a, 5b) concerns the humiliation of the people under siege and of their king (see above, pp. 142f.). The no spoken to Jerusalem is superseded by the yes to Bethlehem. The promise of the new ruler from the small clan (צעיר, v. 1aα) declares that his dominion will extend to the whole world (יגדל, v. 3b). The shamefully treated "judge of Israel" (4:14b) is replaced by one whom Yahweh authorizes (v. 3a). As one who in his own person is the embodiment of peace, he defends against all the military maneuvers of the powerful nations. The people of God, attacked by foreign kings and disappointed by their political chiefs, can expect one who rules by God's authority. When Ephesians 2:14 (Αὐτὸς γάρ ἐστιν ἡ εἰρήνη ἡμῶν) alludes to Isa. 9:5f. [4f.] as well as to Mic. 5:4a [5a], the extension of the dominion from Bethlehem "to the ends of the earth" (v. 3b) is developed in such a way that in Jesus Christ even the hostility between the Jews and the nations is transformed into peace.

Thus these three promises of consolation provide encouragement by dealing with the actual terrors of the present situation, each in its own way: redemption by Yahweh (v. 10bβ); by Yahweh's plan (v. 12a); deliverance by the Messiah (vv. 4a, 5b). After Micah's message of judgment has been fulfilled, the voice of the prophets direct Israel toward these illuminating goals. These prophecies cast new light on the present.

The three eschatological sayings (see above, p. 119) concerning the new Jerusalem, now contained in 4:1–8, have been inserted into their present literary context between 3:12 and 4:9. They further develop the message of the three prophecies of consolation in 4:9—5:5 addressed to Zion, who now experiences birthpangs. Micah 4:6f. guides the exultant deportees back from Babylon (4:9f.), under the kingship of Yahweh, who reigns on Mount Zion. In 4:1–4 we see the warlike nations, gathered on Zion (4:11–13), transformed into a community of peace-loving persons (cf. also 5:3 and see above, p. 146); for now, however, this is only expressed as a hope (4:5). Finally, 4:8 awaits the appearance of the ruler from Bethlehem (5:1) as the new king who marches into Jerusalem (see above, p. 125). The joining of 4:8 to 5:1 possibly effected the present literary connection of the exilic prophecies of consolation with the postexilic promises.

In its own times of crisis, the church, together with Israel, will have to search these prophetic words for the kind of encouragement and direction they can impart to her.

The Remnant of Jacob
and the Nations

Literature

Th. H. Gaster, "Notes on the Minor Prophets. 2. Micah V 13," *JThS* 38 (1937) 163–164. W. Zimmerli, "Die Eigenart der prophetischen Rede des Ezechiel," *ZAW* 66 (1954) 1–26 (13–19); reprinted in ThB 19 (1963) 148–177 (162–169). A. S. Kapelrud, "Eschatology in the Book of Micah," *VT* 11 (1961) 392–405. J. T. Willis, "The Structure of Micah 3–5," *ZAW* 81 (1969) 191–214. Idem, "The Authenticity and Meaning of Micah 5:9–14," *ZAW* 81 (1969) 353–368. Jörg Jeremias, "Die Deutung der Gerichtsworte Michas in der Exilszeit," *ZAW* 83 (1971) 330–354 (343–346). J. P. van Zijl, "A Possible Explanation of Micah 5:13 in Light of Comparative Semitic Languages," *OTWSA* (1973) 73–76. G. E. Mendenhall, "The 'Vengeance' of Yahweh," in *The Tenth Generation* (1973) 69–104. W. Dietrich, "Rache. Erwägungen zu einem alttestamentlichen Thema," *EvTh* 36 (1976) 450–472. D. J. Bryant, "Micah 4:14–5:14. An Exegesis," *RestQ* 21 (1978) 210–230.

Text

5:6[7] And then the remnant of Jacob[a] will be
       in the midst of many peoples
    like dew from[b] Yahweh,
      like showers upon the plants,
    (inasmuch as) it hopes not in man,
      nor stays for any human.

  7[8] And then the remnant of Jacob will be [among the nations][a]
       in the midst of many peoples,
    like a lion among the beasts of the forest,
      like a young lion among the flocks of sheep,
    (inasmuch as) it, whenever it comes and tramples,
      then[b] it rends and none can save.

  8[9]   Raise[a] your hand against your foes,
        so that all your enemies will be cut off.

  9[10] And then, on that day, utterance of Yahweh,
     then I will cut off[a] your[b] steeds from your midst,
      and your chariots I will destroy.

10[11] Then I will cut off the cities[a] of your land,
    and I will demolish all of your fortresses.
11[12] Then I will cut off the means of sorcery[a] from your hand,[b]
    so that soothsayers no longer practice among you.
12[13] Then I will cut off your[a] carved images
    and the stone monuments[b] from your midst,
  so that you no more fall down
    before the inferior[c] work of your hands.
13[14]   Then I will root out your[a] 'enemies'[b] from your midst,
    and your 'foes'[c] I will destroy.
14[15]   And I will execute in wrath and anger
    vengeance[a] on the nations
    who have not heard.

6a Gk (ἐν τοῖς ἔθνεσιν), like MT, Syr, Targ, Vg in v. 7aa¹, presupposes בגוים also here. Thus Gk expressly interprets "remnant of Jacob" in terms of the diaspora. The shorter text in MT, supported also by the regular prosody of the three stress bicola is probably original in v. 6 as well as in v. 7.

6b Gk (πίπτουσα = "falling") seeks to explain the preposition מאת, although the reading does not presuppose a text different from MT.

7a See note 6a.

7b Where does the apodosis begin after the conditional clause? The same kind of verb forms (perfect) permit it to begin with ורמם, with וטרף, or even with ואין (thus according to the accents in MT). In such cases the speaking-pause decides. In the prosody of the three-stress bicolon, it is to be recognized before וטרף; cf. Joüon, *Gr* §176b and B. Renaud [1977] 255.

8a MT (jussive) intends to be understood as a petition. However, many Mss and the ancient versions (Gk, ὑψωθήσεται; Vg, *exaltabitur*), read תרום (imperfect, "you will raise up") and thus understand the sentence to be an expression of confidence that continues, and gives the motivation for, the promises in vv. 6–7. When an analysis of the context offers no compelling counter-arguments, one should keep to the (unusual) reading in MT.

9a Jerome softens the repetitiveness of the same verb form והכרתי here and in vv. 10, 11, 12 because he "strives to give variation in expression" (Jerome: *auferam —perdam—auferam—et perire faciam*); cf. B. Kedar-Kopfstein, "Die Wiedergabe des hebräischen Kausativs in der Vulgata," *ZAW* 85 (1973) 196–219 (209).

9b Targ considers the "peoples" (עממיא) to be the objects of Yahweh's wrath.

10a Here also Targ interprets the sentence in terms of the peoples: "the cities of the peoples (עממיא) from your land"; cf. note 9b.

11a Gk (τὰ φάρμακά σου = בְּשָׁפֶיךָ, "your sorcery") is to be understood as a misreading due to the frequent second person singular suffixes in this context; Vg *(maleficia)* and Targ support MT.

11b Gk (ἐκ τῶν χειρῶν σου) interprets the singular in MT (=Vg, *de manu tua*) as a collective.

12a Here, too, Targ interprets the idols as belonging to the peoples (צלמי עממיא); cf. note 9b, 10a.

12b Syr reads מִזְבְּחוֹתֶיךָ ("your altars"), but MT is supported by Gk (τὰς στήλας σου), Targ (רקמתהון), Vg *(statuas tuas)*.

12c Gk (τοῖς ἔργοις), Targ (לעובדי), Vg *(opera)* presuppose the plural לְמַעֲשֵׂי; thus in view of several statements in the singular within the immediate context, they interpret the singular form in MT as a collective.

13a Targ (שתלי עממיא) again relates the sentence to the peoples (as in vv. 9b, 10a, 12a).

13b On considerations that support understanding אשריך as a misreading of an original אֹיְבֶיךָ, see below, pp. 159f.

13c Although Gk (τὰς πόλεις σου), Vg *(civitates tuas)* support MT, nevertheless "cities" forms an unusual parallel to "Asherim" (cf. on the other hand the parallels in vv. 9aβ-12a); furthermore, the word "cities" already occurs in v. 10a. If one wished to see in v. 13 a summary of religious and political means of defense (I. Willi-Plein, 97), the parallel, "cities"—"Asherim," would hardly be representative of this. Therefore, critics have attempted various conjectures to replace עָרֶיךָ, such as עֲצַבֶּיךָ ("your images [of idols]," W. Nowack; *BHS*), or בְּעָלֶיךָ (*BHK*; R. Vuilleumier), as possible parallels to "Asherim"; cf. B. Renaud (1977) 262f. The more recent attempt to explain MT in terms of the Ugaritic word *'r,* which refers to a cultic object (Th. H. Gaster, et al.), seems uncertain, especially in that ערים would then be assigned two completely different meanings within the same context (cf. v. 10a with v. 13b). The only conjecture supported by the text's history is צָרֶיךָ ("your enemies"; Targ, בעלי דבבך; M. Buber: "your oppressors"). While this conjecture offers no more of a thematic parallel to the Asherim than does MT, it can nevertheless be understood as a transition to v. 14, thereby picking up צריך in v. 8. It also supports the surmise that אשריך is a misreading of an original אֹיְבֶיךָ (see above, note 13b and below, pp. 159f.). Text critical decisions should not be separated from the problems of the literary levels within the passage (see below, pp. 159f.).

14a On נקם as object of the verb עשה, cf. Judg. 11:36; Ezek. 25:17; Ps. 149:7 (עשה נקמה); a different view is represented by I. Willi-Plein, 97 (who does not take these texts into consideration).

Form

The three "now-sayings" in 4:9—5:5 (see above, pp. 133ff.) are followed by three "then-sayings" (והיה in 5:6, 7, 9) that point to the future. With these "then-sayings," the redactor continues the theme of hope that is rooted in the "now- sayings." In 5:6ff. this hope is primarily concerned with Israel's future relationship to the nations, while the sayings in 4:1–8 especially are shaped by the question about Jerusalem's future (see above, pp. 114ff.). As in 4:1–8, so also in 5:6ff. we must distinguish between a redactional level and an older nucleus of sayings that is taken up here. With the introductory formula in 5:9aα ("And then, on that day, utterance of Yahweh"), the redactor's hand most clearly recalls 4:6aα[1] (but also cf. והיה in 4:1).

Within the older, traditional material, two complexes are distinguished by the unusual similarity of their internal structure. The first complex (vv. 6f.) contains two promises, each with the same form, to the "remnant of Jacob." In both verses, each of which consists of three three-stress bicola, the parallelism is precisely carried out: the first bicolon proclaims *that* the "remnant of Jacob" will be significant among the nations; the second bicolon, each colon containing a double simile, tells by *whom* this takes place; the third bicolon, in which a relative clause continues the simile, explains *what* the similes intend to say. The genre employed here, an unconditional prophetic promise, expresses the content of the promise exclusively by means of a parable. In view of the extreme differences between the two similes, the pairing of the two sayings raises the question whether the structure is to be understood in an antithetic or a synthetic sense (see below, p. 157).

The second complex, set off by its stereotyped formulation, is found in vv. 9aβ–12. Each of the four Yahweh oracles is introduced in the same way by the expression "and I will cut off"; each is structured in synonymous parallelism. Utilizing the form of the preexilic "excommunication sayings" (vv. 9aβ, b, 10, 11, 12a), the oracles climax in a declaration of the goal (v. 12b). Analysis of the form's history indicates that the excommunication formula והכרתי can be traced back through Ezek. 14:8f. to the Holiness Code (Lev. 17:10; 20:3, 5, 6). The formula also occurs in the passive (Lev. 7:20f., 27; 19:8; 20:18; cf. W. Zimmerli, *ZAW* 66 [1954] 1–16, and idem, *Ezekiel* 1:303–305). Here we find a type of sacral-legal maxim used in connection with persons who, having committed serious crimes, are excommunicated from the worshiping community lest their fellowship with Yahweh be endangered. Yahweh himself, by "cutting off" (כרת *hiph.*) the designated persons "from the midst" of the people (מקרב, as in Lev. 17:4, 10; 18:29; 20:3, 5, 6, 18, so also in Mic. 5:9aβ, 12aβ), guarantees the life of the community (G. von Rad, *Old Testament Theology* 1:264f.). The present composition is distinguished from the above-mentioned excommunication sayings by three modifications: (1) not persons but things are handed over to destruction (cf. in addition Lev. 26:30; Zech. 9:10; Nah. 1:14); (2) the excommunication sayings are formulated in the style of direct address ("you," second person singular), without any closer identification (according to the form and the content of the saying, Israel is the only conceivable addressee); (3) the series of four excommunication sayings is united by the conclusion in v. 12b, which indicates that the purpose is to destroy the false worship of those addressed here. To this extent, this series of destructive threats (without any accusation!) proves in the end to be a special form of the promise, which gives assurance that the purification of the community will liberate it.

Just as v. 8 gives little indication of being an original part of the promises (vv. 6f.), so vv. 13–14 hardly belonged originally to the assurance of God's acts of purification (vv. 9–12), which reaches an intelligible conclusion in v. 12b. The secondary additions from the redactor's hand are unified by the theme of the nations as the enemy of Yahweh (on v. 13, see note 13c and below, pp. 159f.). In view of the yet unfulfilled promise in v. 7, v. 8 adds a petition addressed to Yahweh concerning this unfulfilled promise; at the same time, the wording of v. 8, with כרת *niph.*, makes a transition to vv. 9–12 (והכרתי), whose second person singular ("you") is reinterpreted to mean Yahweh's enemies (thus Targ; see above, note 13a). If the proposed conjectures pertaining to v. 13 are on the mark, then this verse expressly promises that Yahweh answers the petition in v. 8; indeed, v. 13 would then be a supplement to vv. 9–12 and in conformity with its style. A concluding, prosaic declaration of wrath characterizes Yahweh's enemies as "the nations who have not heard" (on גוים in v. 14, cf. also the second addition of בגוים in v. 7 and in v. 6 Gk; see note 6a).

Setting

Such considerations pose the question of the literary setting of these redactional additions. A connection between the concluding reference to the "nations who have not heard" with the summons to hear addressed to the nations in 1:2 can hardly be overlooked (Th. Lescow, 58; J. L. Mays, 125). The universalistic, certainly postexilic work of redaction (see above, p. 51 and Introduction §5) has framed chaps. 1–5 with 1:2 and 5:14. In particular this level of redaction has taken the sayings collected in chaps. 4–5 and joined them to the collection of the ancient Micah prophecies in chaps. 1–3.

It is probable that the later additions such as 4:5, 5:8, and v. 13 [conj.] belong to the universalistic redaction of the Persian era (see below, pp. 160f.). These additions, given the forms of the confession (4:5), the petition (5:8), and the Yahweh oracle against foreign nations (5:13 [conj.], 14), point to a connection with the lamentation ceremonies from the exilic and postexilic eras (see below, p. 138). Among circles of cultic prophets, who were responsible for such ceremonies, we can well imagine the setting in which the collection of such disparate material was made; moreover, this could be the setting for the above-noted structuring of the material by the redactor and also for the growth of the different levels of tradition (first the "now-sayings," then groups of eschatological "then-sayings").

The final process of redaction took up preexisting texts (vv. 6f. and vv. 9aβ–12) which provide us with only a few clues for determining their precise date. We can merely assert, with a high degree of probability, that both passages do not stem from the preexilic era, to say nothing of their belonging among Micah's original prophecies. The introductory formula in v. 9aα that links vv. 6f. to vv. 9aβ–12 recalls 4:6aα[1], where the same formula also begins a saying from the time after the beginning of the exile in 587 (see below, p. 118).

The double saying in 5:6f. may be more intelligible if we date it in the Persian rather than in the Babylonian era. For in the texts that can be dated with certainty, "the remnant" (שארית) is not used as a firmly fixed term until 520 (Hag. 1:12, 14; 2:2; Zech. 8:6, 11, 12). The ("now")-sayings, presumably from exilic times (see above, pp. 136f.), on the other hand, address themselves to the "daughter of Zion" (4:10, 13, 14; cf. 4:8). The theme in 5:6f. intensifies the promise from 4:7a, which states that the "lame" will become a "mighty nation."

As 5:6f. corresponds to the saying in 4:6f., so 5:9–12 corresponds, to a certain extent, to the universal promise in 4:1–4. For according to the original meaning of this "excommunication saying," Yahweh destroys from Israel's midst all man-made military appurtenances and heathen religious practices which would offer security; in this way Yahweh frees Israel, like the nations in 4:1–3, to seek after his instruction alone (5:12b), and to reject all that has to do with war. Whereas 4:1–4 says nothing about Israel, 5:9–12 indicates that by Yahweh's acts of purification, Israel will also be expressly equipped for the kingdom of world peace (on 4:5, see above, p. 123). This is the purpose of "being cut off" that is announced here. Perhaps the passage is to be dated in the exilic era (Jörg Jeremias). In this case, it would interpret the destructive blows of the Babylonian conquest as Yahweh's purifying act, at least at its beginning. This act separates Israel from "the works of your hands" (v. 12b). The (Deuteronomistic?) teachers have formed their inventory of these works by freely adapting Isa. 2:6–8 and Hos. 14:4. The passage (5:9–12) is not far removed from the later additions and revisions of the Micah's original prophecies, which, in 1:13b, characterize the chariots of Lachish as the chief work of "Israel's rebellion" and which, in 1:5, 7a; 2:10 MT, denounce cultic "uncleanness" (see above, pp. 61f., 84). In light of the passage's kinship to the statements in Hag. 2:22 and Zech. 9:10, an earlier postexilic date should not be excluded from consideration. In this case, the passage would then be comparable to 4:1–4 also in terms of the date (see above, p. 118).

Commentary

[5:6–7] The pair of sayings in vv. 6f. addresses words of promise to the "remnant of Jacob." The word שארית already occurred in 2:12 and 4:7 as a fixed key-term (see above, p. 123). Here and in those texts, the word "remnant" has lost any negative tone suggestive of a lamentable group of survivors who serve merely as a rear guard against complete destruction (Jer. 8:3). Now they are the saved remnant, the people of God, who will be founders of a new family. They are people gathered from the diaspora of the exile by the power of Yahweh's promises (Jer. 23:3; Isa. 46:3), summoned to make a new beginning in Jerusalem (Hag. 1:12, 14; 2:2; Zech. 8:6, 11, 12). Is it especially significant that here, but in no other instance, the remnant is referred to as the "remnant of *Jacob*"? Micah himself has treated Jacob and Israel as synonyms, using both terms to designate the people of Judah as his addressees (3:8; cf. 3:1, 9; 1:14f.). His opponents, apparently regarding themselves as the "house of Jacob" (2:7), appealed to the special blessing given to the patriarch (Gen. 27:27–29; 32:27–30), which he handed on further (Gen. 49:8–12). The Deuteronomist calls the inhabitants of the Northern kingdom "Jacob," and the Judeans "Israel." In the promise in 2:12, which is similar to 5:6f., the "remnant of Israel" and "all of Jacob" are synonymous; in 4:2 the temple is called "house of the God of Jacob"; in the promise directed to the exiles in 4:6f., those who were scattered are twice called "the lame" (flock; see above, p. 123), who will become "the remnant," although the name of Jacob is not used. Only the very infrequent word "to limp" (צלע; see above, p. 123) might allude to Jacob (Gen. 32:32). Haggai and Zechariah simply refer to "remnant of th(es)e people (texts noted above); Zephaniah speaks of the "remnant of the house of Judah" (2:7), "remnant of my people" (2:9), or "remnant of Israel" (3:13), as in Mic. 2:12. When we review this linguistic usage, it might be that the unique phrase "remnant of Jacob" is a quite intentional allusion to the patriarchs as the recipients of the promised blessings. It is uncertain whether the individual sayings, with their own particular statements, intend to make a connection with the various offers of blessing to Jacob (cf. N. Renaud [1977] 260f.). This might be a correct supposition, since Isaac's blessing of Jacob speaks of "dew from heaven" and also of Jacob's relation to the nations (Gen. 27:28f.), and since in Jacob's blessing, Judah (also in relation to the nations) is compared with a lion (Gen. 49:9f.). However, upon closer scrutiny no connection is evident.

[5:6] This is true particularly of the first saying (v. 6). The "remnant of Jacob in the midst of many nations" is compared with the dew. But here the dew of heaven means neither the gift of fertility for Jacob's field, nor is Jacob himself to become a blessing for the nation (cf. Gen. 27:28f.). "In the midst of the peoples"—thus the situation of the remnant of Jacob is straightforwardly described. Gk's interpolation (see note 6a) means to emphasize that this refers not only to the remnant of the community in Jerusalem and Judah, but includes the entire diaspora as well. The shorter text in MT, in accordance with its present context, might even presuppose the return of the "remnant of the brothers" (5:2). Here, as in 4:2f., 13 (see above, p. 120). עמים רבים refers to the profusion, to the totality, of the nations; the phrase is not intended to be understood in an exclusive (many, but not all), but in an inclusive sense: "in the midst of the multitude of peoples" exists the remnant of Jacob. The intention of the verse is to speak about this existence of the remnant in the pagan world (בקרב); it is not, therefore, about a certain significance of the remnant *for* the nations (as, for example, in Zech. 8:13). This is over-looked by numerous misinterpretations. The remnant of Jacob is com-pared to "dew" and "showers." Both make things very wet, but without doing damage (as in some cases of downpour). What is the meaning of the simile of dew and rain? Only in certain exceptions would it mean some-thing negative: according to Hos. 6:4; 13:3, dew stands for that which is erratic, impermanent, quickly disappearing (after sunrise); occasionally it refers to what is life-giving (Hos. 14:6; Ps. 133:3). But most often it means the gift of fertility (dew: Gen. 27:28; Deut. 33:28; Zech. 8:12; showers: Pss. 65:11 [10]; 72:6). None of these meanings applies to our passage. For immediately upon the introduction of the simile in v. 6aβ, the *tertium comparationis* is referred to: like dew, the remnant of Jacob comes "from Yahweh"; and the relative clause in v. 6b immediately emphasizes this twice, *via negationis,* for dew and showers upon the plants: they hope for nothing from mankind, nor expect anything from the children of men. (Here both verbs, קוה *piel* as well as יחל *piel* and *hiph.,* are used in the majority of instances in the OT in connection with Yahweh; see H. W. Wolff, *The Anthropology of the Old Testament* 149f.). Thus, "dew" has a different meaning here than in the evidence cited above. As in 2 Sam. 17:12 dew is plainly a surprising, mysterious thing that is not properly to be expected from humans. The rhetorical ques-tions in Job 38:28 correspond even more precisely to the meaning of our passage: "Has the rain a father, or who has begotten the drops of the dew?" Dew and rain are something special in that they are outside the realm of what humans can perceive; for the ancient Israelites, what causes dew is simply not explainable. Precisely in the same way, the future existence of a "remnant of Jacob" in the historical realm is also a wonder that can only be understood as coming "from Yahweh." It is the work of God alone; it is not an event that humans can account for. This does not exclude, but rather includes, the simile's allusion to the promise of fertility and increase (cf. Ps. 110:3[?]). The first saying therefore clearly asks not about the significance of the "remnant of Jacob" for the nations, but about the wondrous origin of its future existence in the midst of the nations. The survivors may for all time hope in Yahweh's work.

Verse 7 continues this certainty, in that now the simile of the lion enlarges upon the consequences for the future international significance of the "remnant of Jacob." In contrast to v. 6, now we find a reflection upon the place of the "remnant" in the outside world. This is already indicated at the beginning of the simile in v. 7aβ,γ: "like a lion among the beasts of the forest, like a young lion among the flocks of sheep." (Here too the interpolation בגוים in v. 7aα MT, and the preposition כ in v. 7aβ,γ, become intelligible as interpretative glosses; see above, note 6a.) Corre-spondingly, the relative clause in v. 7b further explains the imagery with its statement that the lion is incomparable and invincible. What the adult lion among the beasts (בבהמות יער) is capable of, even the young lion can do among the goats and the sheep (בעדרי־צאן). The comparison of Israel with the lion refers back to ancient tradition: Gen. 49:9; Num. 23:24. Wherever the lion imagery occurs, it points to superior courage and invincible strength (Isa. 5:29; Hos. 5:14; Pss. 7:3 [2]; 17:11ff.). As it is often said about Yahweh (Deut. 32:39; Hos. 5:14; Ps. 50:22; Job 10:7; cf. Isa. 43:13) and, e.g., in other instances about the historical Assyrian empire (Isa. 5:29), here, too, it is said of the "remnant of Jacob" as the eschatological people of God: they may be attacked by all, but none will overcome them.

[5:6–7] Thus the two similes in v. 6 and v. 7 do not stand in antithesis to each other, as though the remnant of Jacob were, in one instance, a blessing for the nations and, in another, a curse (A. Weiser; Th. H. Robinson; cf. Th. Lescow, 78, in reference to Prov. 19:12); or, as though quietists first speak, and then militant activists (W. Rudolph); first pacifists and then militarists (R. E. Wolfe, *IB*); or, following Gen. 12:3a, first Israel's friends are addressed, and then its enemies (Th. H. Robinson). Rather, the parallelism between the two sayings is to be understood as synthetic. Verse 6 states what will become of the remnant of Jacob "by the power of Yahweh": a wondrous deed of God, which cannot be humanly accounted for (cf. 4:6–7a). Verse 7 states what the remnant of Jacob will become in the midst of the other nations: superior and invincible in relation to all other powers (cf. 4:13). According to 5:5b the Messiah will save (והציל) Israel from Assyria; according to v. 7b no one will be able to save the nations from the remnant of Jacob (ואין מציל).

[5:8] If v. 8 is read as a promise (see note 8a), then its words of assurance merely interpret the imagery in v. 7b and hold out for the "remnant of Jacob" the prospect that it will successfully attack the enemy. But it is more probable, following the reading in MT, that the verse is a petition addressed to Yahweh (see note 8a). In light of the diction found in prayers in the Old Testament, to "raise your hand" more likely refers to Yahweh (Ps. 89:14; Isa. 26:11; cf. also Exod. 17:11; Pss. 57:6, 12; 108:6; 112:9 and Ackroyd, *ThWAT* 3, 443). As in the corresponding secondary additions in v. 13 [conj.] and v. 14, the nations are to be viewed as *Yahweh's* enemies. More significantly, as a later addition to vv. 6f., v. 8 is better understood as originating from a time when Israel was under attack; the remnant of Jacob, until such a time, by no means considered itself dominant over the nations, as v. 7 promises. The expectation that the enemies "will be cut off" (כרת *niph.*) makes a transition to the proclamation that Yahweh himself will cut them off (כרת *hiph.*, vv. 9–12). Apparently like v. 8, Targum Jonathan (see notes 9b, 10a, 12a) and even vv. 13 [conj.], 14 have understood the excommunication sayings in vv. 9–12 to be addressed to the nations.

[5:9] Originally, however, this saying was addressed to Israel. This is already made clear by a form critical analysis of the origin of the excommunication formula, which recalls the practice of purging the community of those whose misdeeds endanger its life (see above, p. 152). Everything that defiled Israel and therefore threatened its life before Yahweh had to be removed "from its midst" like an infectious bacillus. The first to be mentioned are Israel's "horses" and "chariots." Since the time of Isaiah, the people's trust had been drawn away from Yahweh and placed in military instruments as a means for waging war (Isa. 2:7; 30:15–17; 31:1–3; Hos. 10:13; Deut. 17:16). The Deuteronomistic interpreter of Micah's sayings had also made reference to this (1:13b). Horses and chariots are rendered harmless only by destroying them. (They are placed under the excommunication formula also in Zech. 9:10a.) In the announcement of Yahweh's punishment, the threat "I will destroy" (אבד *hiph.*) is placed next to the typical keyword in the formula: "I will cut off" (והכרתי).

[5:10] After the means for military attack have been mentioned in v. 9, v. 10 turns to fortifications that provide for defense. "Cities" and "fortresses," because of their elevation and their protective walls, are "inaccessible" (בצר) settlements. As a rule the fortresses are called עָרֵי הַמִּבְצָר (Num. 32:17, 36; Josh. 10:20; 19:35; 2 Kings 3:19; 10:2; 17:9; 18:8; Jer. 4:5; 5:17; 6:27; 8:14; 34:7; etc.). The people who work in the fields withdraw into the "cities" when the enemy approaches (Jer. 1:15; 4:16; 5:6; etc.); the fortified cities were especially equipped for military purposes by the addition of buttressed walls and watchtowers. In part they served as cities for storage of supplies, and for chariots and horsemen (1 Kings 9:19; 10:26; 2 Chron. 11:5; see above, pp. 61f., on Lachish). By taking its protection into its own hands, Israel has become separated from its true creator and protector (cf. Hos. 8:14; 10:14; and Wolff, *Hosea* 146). Now we find alongside the excommunication formula the technical military term הרס, which is characteristically used for the tearing down of city walls (cf. Lam. 2:2; Jer. 45:4; Ezek. 13:14). If Yahweh's destructive work is aimed at all military armaments (Ps. 46:10–12 [9–11]), then Israel itself is placed in the same situation to which God's instruction leads the nations: according to 4:2f., they destroy their own weapons.

[5:11] Following the removal of those things which provide military security (vv. 9f.), vv. 11–12a turn to the question of Israel's religious self-security. The word כשפים includes all the means for the practice of sorcery used by the professional magicians (cf. Nah. 3:4: בַּעֲלַת כְּשָׁפִים, the soothsayer as "mistress of the means of sorcery"). This refers to objects that can be cast "from the hand," such as arrows, oracular lots, liver (Ezek. 21:26), staves (Hos. 4:12), peeled rods, and mandrakes (Gen. 30:14f., 37ff.). The destruction of such implements of sorcery means the end of the sorcerers. It is remarkable that here, too, it is not persons who are threatened (as in Lev. 20:6; see above, p. 152). The transition from the perfect consecutive in v. 11a to the result clause in the imperfect, with inversion of the subject (v. 11b), merely indicates that, due to the destruction of the tools of divination, the sorcerers will no longer be found in Israel. Here as well, persons are not directly threatened, as in the older excommunication pronouncements (see above, p. 152).

[5:12] Finally, the idols and sacred pillars will be removed from Israel's midst. The word מקרבך, characteristic of the ancient excommunication pronouncements, appears once again (see above, pp. 157f. on v. 9aβ). It was forbidden to worship carved images (פסילים, Exod. 20:4; Deut. 7:25) and stone monuments (מצבות, Lev. 26:1; Deut. 7:5), which were often artistically shaped (Hos. 10:1). Yahweh himself will liberate his people from substituting for him images which they can control.

Cultic objects, together with attempts to achieve military security, are called "work of your hands." Military weapons and sorcery, along with idol worship, stand on the same level with false self-trust and insulting mistrust of the God of Israel. Hosea (14:4[3]) and Isaiah (2:6–8) had already characterized both as the "work of the hands" of men. Since the sixth century this catchphrase was commonly used to demystify all the overrated means for achieving self-defense, whether military or religious (Jer. 1:16; 10:3; 25:6; Deut. 4:28; 27:15; 31:29; 2 Kings 19:18; 22:17; cf. Pss. 115:4; 135:15; etc.). When in this passage Yahweh liberates his people from praying to the work of their own hands in an attempt to secure their own lives, he creates the presupposition for reestablishing their original relationship of trust. Perhaps standing in the background is the experience of helplessness in every sphere of life that seized Israel in the sixth century. Thus Israel saw itself placed anew before the truth of the prophetic word of judgment, but also before the word of promise. Here the words promising action that will purify Israel are only an indirect reminiscence of the accusations of the older prophets. The main thrust of these verses is to point Israel away from misleading attempts to save itself and to direct it toward a new community of peace. Ultimately, even the nations are to join this community (4:1–4).

[5:13–14] First, however, the nations must also face divine judgment. This is described by the later addition to the passage in vv. 13f. Verse 13 still exhibits a loose connection with the elevated style of vv. 9–12, but the parallel verbs in v. 13 already leave behind the excommunication formula in vv. 9–12; in v. 14 the style becomes entirely prose. The present form of v. 13 in MT at first makes it questionable whether this verse originally belonged with v. 14, or whether it represents a separate addition to vv. 9–12. The latter view is generally held.

[5:13] The problem is why the "Asherim" and the "cities" (according to Targ, "the foes"; see note 13c) stand parallel. The intelligibility of this, or even its necessity, is difficult to recognize. Therefore I propose what at first may appear to be a bold conjecture: might not אשריך be viewed as a misreading of an original אֹיְבֶיךָ? Let us examine the following observations which support this proposal. (1) This reading provides צָרֶיךָ (following Targ; see note 13c) with a meaningful parallel that corresponds to the parallel צריך־איביך in v. 8. (2) In no other instance in the Old Testament does the word נתש have אשרים for an object; instead, in every case it is a term for the deportation of nation, groups of people (Ps. 9:7[6]; 1 Kings 14:15; Amos 9:15; cf. H. J. Kraus, *Psalms 1–59,* 190), or even of foreign nations (Jer. 12:14, 15, 17; 18:7). It also refers to deportation when it is used metaphorically as an antonym for נטע ("to plant," Jer. 1:10; 24:6; 31:28; 42:10; 45:4; cf. Ezek. 19:12), having its original meaning of "to root out." It should be particularly noted that in the Jeremianic-Deuteronomistic writings, in a broader context than that found here (v. 14b!), נתש is used in connection with the "nations who do not hear" (Jer. 12:17;

18:7–10); and that Yahweh "in wrath and anger," roots them out also in Deut. 29:27 as here in v. 14a (cf. P. Diepold, *Israels Land,* BWANT 95 [1972] 205f.). (3) The destruction of אשרים is pictured in other passages with a variety of verbs, such as "to cut off" (כרת, Exod. 34:13), "to burn" (שרף, Deut. 12:3), "to break in pieces" (שבר *piel,* 2 Chron. 34:4), "to hew down" (גדע *piel,* Deut. 7:5); "to remove" (סור *hiph.,* 2 Chron. 17:6); but the verb נתש, except in Mic. 5:13, is not found in connection with the Asherim. (4) After the words פסיליך and מצבותיך (v. 12a), אשריך could easily have been read instead of אֹיְבֶיךָ. The frequency of the three-stress colon פסילים—מצבות—אשרים (Deut. 7:5; 12:3) makes this clear enough, but the recurrence of the duple series מצבות—אשרים (Deut. 16:12f.; 1 Kings 14:23; 2 Kings 17:10; 18:4; 2 Chron. 31:1) makes it even more intelligible, especially since in the Old Hebrew script the two different letters י and ש, as well as כ and ר, are graphically similar to each other.

If this conjecture is correct, v. 13 would provide, on the one hand, an appropriate supplement to vv. 9–12; on the other, it would make a clear connection between v. 8 and v. 14. Verse 13 thus promises what was requested in v. 8: the destruction of your enemies "from your midst." The catchword מקרבך is taken from the excommunication formula (vv. 9aβ, 12aβ). Thereby Israel's military and religious idolatry is characterized in this later addition as a kind of foothold for its foes, and the entire promise of a purifying judgment for Israel is turned into a threat to all the foes in her midst (cf. Targ and notes 9b, 10a, 12a).

[5:14] Verse 14 provides a complete exposition of the redaction's key ideas. The verse exhibits a kinship with those conceptions of the Deuteronomistic school which reflect upon Israel's relation to the nations. Such conceptions in the Deuteronomistic preaching call on Israel to make a choice, and they also include the possibility for the foreign nations to turn and repent (cf. W. Thiel, *Die deuteronomistische Redaktion von Jeremia 1–25,* WMANT 41 [1973] 162–168; 215f.; see above, pp. 159f., no. 2). With the summons to hear in 1:2, the redactor had included all inhabitants of the earth in his appeal for Israel's obedience. The nations even now are to pay attention to Micah's proclamation of Yahweh's judgment upon Israel and Judah, that they might understand the true basis for the course of history. This is similar to the didactic discourse the Deuteronomist holds with the nations in Deut. 29:21–27. The expression stating that Yahweh acts באף ובחמה ("with wrath and anger") has its origin in such didactic discourses (Deut. 29:22, 27; cf. further Jer. 21:5; 32:37 = Deuteronomistic redaction). In Deut. 29 Yahweh's burning fury is an indication that Israel's breach of covenant and its unfaithfulness ignite a passionate response from its God. This the nations must come to recognize. In Mic. 5:14 Yahweh also confronts the nations' unchecked lust for power. He turns his "vengeance" (נקם) against them in defense of an Israel that has become impotent. In the Old Testament such godly "vengeance" is, to a large extent, viewed positively as a just correspondence to the nations' arbitrary acts of injustice (Deut. 32:35, 41, 43; Isa. 34:8; 59:17; 63:4, 6; cf. G. E. Mendenhall; W. Dietrich).

The motivation for Yahweh's intervention is precisely stated in the concluding relative clause: his vengeance is directed toward "those who have not heard." The reference back to 1:2 is clear (see above, pp.

14f., 51, 153f.). Micah 1:2 contains the word עמים, while 5:14 has גוים; this is understandable in that the two words are used synonymously in chaps. 4 and 5 (cf. 4:1–3, 11–13; 5:7 MT). This does not speak against the supposition that both verses originated from the same redactor. That "not hearing" the voice of Yahweh is a fundamental sin accords well with the theology of the Jeremian-Deuteronomistic sermons which summon Israel to choose (Jer. 12:17 and 18:10; cf. Deut. 29:23ff. and W. Thiel, WMANT 41, 290–295). When the nations hear, the concrete result should be their "learning the ways of Yahweh's people" (cf. Jer. 12:16). The final redactor of the book of Micah has in mind not only the prophecies of Micah in chaps. 1–3 and their fulfillment, but beyond this, the sayings collected in chaps. 4 and 5 which apply directly to the nations. In this way, the prophecies in 1:2 and 5:14 recapitulate the words of Micah and the postexilic prophecies in chaps. 1–5 (cf. Th. Lescow, 58; J. L. Mays, 125).

Purpose and Thrust

The first part (4:1–8) of chaps. 4 and 5 focuses on the question, What will happen to Zion after the catastrophe that is threatened in 3:12? Then the "now-sayings" in 4:9—5:5 are concerned with the "daughter of Zion," from the time of the fulfillment of the prophecy of judgment in 3:12 until the time of deliverance. But in the concluding sayings (5:6–14) the significant question for the redactor becomes, What is to be the future of the nations as the enemy of Yahweh and of Israel (5:8, 13 [conj.], 14)?

To answer this question, 5:6f. presents two sayings that belong together, each containing similes. As originally independent sayings, they represent two aspects of the future existence of the "remnant of Jacob in the midst of the nations." To everyone's surprise, this future is a purely wondrous act of God (v. 6); this wonder will be demonstrated by the absolute superiority and stability of the remnant among all the nations of the world (v. 7). The people of God can expect their future to be a sudden act of new creation. No longer will they face the threat of disaster; instead, they will more likely pose a threat to the previous strength of the pagan world. The followers of Jesus can also believe this (cf. Matt. 16:18).

The series of excommunication sayings in vv. 9–12 emphasizes that Israel's continued existence lies by no means in the power of its own hand. Although these verses contain no accusation against Israel, they presuppose that Israel—with its offensive and defensive military weapons; with its sorcery and idols—offers its worship to, and places its hope in, its own human capabilities (the "work of its hands," v. 12b), which in truth can be offered to Yahweh alone. Since, according to this present word of promise, Yahweh alone destroys all these instruments of anxiety and self-security, he liberates his people for new trust in him. Perhaps in the fulfillment of Micah's judgment speech (3:12) in the year 587, this prophetic voice already perceived the beginning of such liberating actions and thus interpreted the divine punishment as an act of purification.

Both units, vv. 6f. and vv. 9–12, taken by themselves, are genuine promises made to an Israel which had previously been threatened and subjugated. But the redactor perceived here, above all, a threat directed to the enemies of Yahweh and Israel. After v. 7 this is certainly under-

161

standable. In a period when, for the longest time, the remnant of Jacob was by no means "like a lion" among the nations, the petition in v. 8 for Yahweh's intervention against Israel's foes becomes necessary. At the same time, the petition corrects an interpretation of v. 7 which conveys the impression that the remnant of Jacob, with its own means of gaining power, might be able to come out against its foes. That Yahweh alone can defend them is then explained by the redactor in v. 13 [conj.] and v. 14 with unambiguous dependence upon vv. 9–12.

The nations, for their part, stand before a choice. Either they hear Yahweh's voice and advance with the people of God toward peace (4:1–4:5b), or they refuse (4:5a; 5:14b) and become liable to the wrath of Yahweh (5:14a).

Walk Attentively
with Your God

Literature

F. C. Burkitt, "Micah 6 and 7: A Northern Prophecy," *JBL* 45 (1926) 159–161. A. S. Osborn, "The Nature of True Religion Micah 6:1–8," *BiblRev* 17 (1932) 232–239. H. Gunkel; J. Begrich, *Einleitung in die Psalmen* (1933) 408f. J. Begrich, *Die priesterliche Tora,* BZAW 66 (1936) 63–88; reprinted in *Gesammelte Studien,* ThB 21 (1964) 232–260. J. H. Hertz, "Micah 6:8," *ET* 46 (1934/1935) 188. D. W. Thomas, "The Root *sn'* in Hebrew and the Meaning of *qdrnyt* in Malachi 3:14," *JJS* 1 (1949) 182–188. Idem, "The Root צנע in Hebrew," *Actes du XXIᵉ Congrès international des Orientalistes* (Paris 1949) 115–116. G. W. Anderson, "A Study of Mic. 6:1–8," *SJTh* 4 (1951) 191–197. Ph. Hyatt, "On the Meaning of Micah 6:8," *AThR* 34 (1952) 232–239. R. Hentschke, *Die Stellung der vorexilischen Schriftpropheten zum Kultus,* BZAW 75 (1957) 104–107. A. Deissler, "Micha 6,1–8. Der Rechtsstreit Jahwes mit Israel um das rechte Bundesverhältnis," *TThZ* 68 (1959) 229–234. H. J. Stoebe, "Und demütig sein vor deinem Gott," *WuD* 6 (1959) 180–194. W. Beyerlin, *Die Kulttraditionen Israels in der Verkündigung des Propheten Micha,* FRLANT 72 (1959) 69–74. K. Koch, "Tempeleinlassliturgien und Dekaloge," *Studien zur Theologie der alttestamentlichen Überlieferungen. Festschrift Gerhard von Rad* (1961) 45–60 (54–56). E. R. Achtemeier, "How to Stay Alive (Exercising Love in Terms of Micah 6:8)," *Theology in Life* 6 (1963) 275–282. P. Watson, "Formcriticism and an Exegesis of Micah 6:1–8," *RestQ* 7 (1963) 62–72. Th. Lescow, *Micha 6,6–8. Studien zu Sprache, Form und Auslegung,* AzTh 1/25 (1966). J. T. Willis, Review of Th. Lescow, *Micha 6,6–8. Studien zu Sprache, Form und Auslegung,* in *VT* 18 (1968) 273–278. H. J. Boecker, *Redeformen des Rechtslebens im Alten Testament,* WMANT 14 (²1970) 101–105. Th. Lescow, "Die dreistufige Tora," *ZAW* 82 (1970) 362–379 (378f.). R. Zerfass, "Es ist dir gesagt, Mensch, was du tun sollst (Mi 6,8)," *BiKi* 25 (1970) 109–110. A. S. van der Woude, "Deutero-Micha, ein Prophet aus Nord-Israel?" *NedThT* 25 (1971) 365–378. Th. Lescow, "Redaktionsgeschichtliche Analyse von Micha 6–7," *ZAW* 84 (1972) 182–212 (182–193). G. Warmuth, *Das Mahnwort,* BBE 1 (1976) 58–60. J. Vermeylen, *Du prophète Isaïe à l'apocalyptique* (1977/1978) 595–598.

Text

6:1   Hear now [a]what Yahweh says!
      Stand, accuse[b] the mountains,
        so that the hills hear your voice!

2 Hear, O mountains,[a] Yahweh's lawsuit,
    'give ear,'[b] foundations of the earth!
  For Yahweh holds a lawsuit with his people,
    he contends with Israel.
3 My people, what wrong have I done to you?
    How have I required too much of you?[a]
    Testify against me!
4 I have surely brought you out of the land of Egypt,
    from the house of slavery I redeemed you.
  I sent before you
    Moses, Aaron, and Miriam.[a]
5 My people, remember now
    what Balak plotted,[a]
      [b]the king of Moab,[b]
    and what Balaam answered him,
      [b]the son of Beor![b]
  'Recall the passage'[b]
    from Shittim[c] to Gilgal,
      that (you) may know know (the proof of) Yahweh's saving
acts![d]

6 With what shall I come before Yahweh,
    bow before God on high?[a]
  Shall I come before him with burnt offerings,
    with calves a year old?
7 Would Yahweh[a] be pleased with thousands of rams,
    with streams of oil by the ten thousands?[b]
  Shall I give up my firstborn for my rebellion,
    my own child[c] for my sinful life?[d]

8 It has been told[a] you, O man, what is good
    and what Yahweh requires of you:
  Simply practice justice, love kindness,
    and walk[b] attentively[c] with your God.

1a Gk[W] (λόγον κυρίου· κύριος εἶπεν) and Gk[A] (λόγον κυρίου ἃ ὁ κύριος εἶπεν) appear
to presuppose an additional דבר יהוה or הדבר (Ms). But they more likely offer two
translation variants, one free, the other literal (W. Rudolph). For only Mur 88,
Syr, and Vg *(audite quae Dominus loquitur),* Targ (שמעו כען יתד יוי אמר) support MT.
1b Gk (κρίθητι πρὸς τὰ ὄρη) and Vg *(contende iudicio adversum montes)* do not
justify reading אל- instead of את- (E. Sellin; I. Willi-Plein).
2a Gk (λαοί), as in 1:2, reads "peoples" (עַמִּים).
2b Since Wellhausen it is usually assumed that this word is a misreading of an
original וְהַאֲזִינוּ ("listen!"), in accordance with the many parallels to שמעו (cf. Hos.
5:1; Isa. 1:2, 10; Deut. 32:1; etc.). With והאתנים standing next to מסדי ארץ, the
syntax of MT is unintelligible. The article attached to the word והאתנים is also
troublesome, because the parallelism of הרים and ארץ, here and often in similar
texts (Isa. 1:2; Mic. 1:2; Deut. 32:22), contains no article in a personification. MT
probably arose from an earlier gloss on the text which explained "foundations of
the earth" as "the objects." The scribe's eye may then have jumped over וְהַאֲזִינוּ,

omitting it from the text. Targ (עקריא "roots"), Gk (αἱ φάραγγες "chasms"), Syr ('wmk' "depths"), α' (τα στερεα "foundations"), σ' (τα παλαια "old things"), θ' (τα αρχαια "ancient things"), Vg *(fortia fundamenta terrae* "strong") confirm the difficulty of the reading in MT.

3a Literally: "tired out," "overworked." Gk translates the second question twice: "How have I made it difficult to for you? How have I pained you? (ἢ τί ἐλύπησά σε ἢ τί παρηνώχλά σοι;).

4a E. Sellin, A. Weiser, J. L. Mays, etc., take the first word from v. 5 and include it with v. 4, reading עמי; this results in a three-stress bicolon in v. 4b that corresponds to the same rhythm in vv. 3 and 4a, and an את־ before "Aaron and Miriam" is no longer wanting. But this proposed reading has no support in the history of the text. Nor is עמי, which stands parallel to the beginning of v. 3, so easily omitted. The sign of the accusative need not in every case be repeated.

5a Gk (κατὰ σοῦ) and Syr elucidate the verse by adding "against you."

5b–b It has been suggested that the two phrases in apposition to Balak and Balaam be deleted, especially in order to restore the rhythm to a three-stress bicolon (E. Sellin). Further, it has been supposed that בן־בעור is a misreading of בעברך (A. Weiser: "when you passed over"; R. Vuilleumier: "lors de ton passage"); or of בּ(י) עבור (A. Deissler: "remember the passing over"). This is as difficult to imagine as are the consequences of such a reconstruction, namely, that only after these corruptions crept in, the phrase "the king of Moab" was inserted into the text. Since in fact no further clause at the beginning of v. 5 functions as the object of the verb זכר־נא (v. 5a), nor does the text contain an imperative verb parallel to זכר, it is conceivable that there was haplography of בּ(י) בעור (assuming a defectively written בין and metathesis of ע/ב). Unanimously attested in the transmitted texts, the prepositions (השפים־)מן and (הגלגל־)עד require a word that denotes "to cross." In this respect, the suggestion that בּ(י) עבור be inserted ought to be carefully considered.

5c Gk (ἀπὸ τῶν σχοίνων) perhaps had the Reed Sea in mind.

5d On the plural, cf. D. Michel, *Grundlegung einer hebräischen Syntax* 1 (1977) 66. This phrase (צדקות יהוה) within the Yahweh speech is a fixed expression (cf. Judg. 5:11; 1 Sam. 12:7; Ps. 103:6); it is unlikely that צדקותי was the original reading (J. Lindblom) and that at a later point the suffix י was understood as an abbreviation of the Tetragrammaton.

6a Gk (θεοῦ μου ὑψίστου) read לאלהי. Gk usually translates עליון with the word ὕψιστος, especially in the Psalter (91:1, 9; 92:2; etc.), but sometimes this Greek word also translates מרום (Pss. 71:19; 92:2).

7a The word יהוה should not be deleted merely for the sake of the verse's rhythm (thus A. George, R. Vuilleumier, I. Willi-Plein), especially since it carries an important secondary accent, as in v. 6 and v. 8 (Th. Lescow [1966] 48), and since, in addition, the determination of each of the three stresses in vv. 6aα, 7aβ, 7bβ is not certain.

7b The correct translation χειμάρρων ("waterfalls") in Gk^V has been misread as χιμαρων ("goats"), a corruption internal to the Greek text.

7c Literally: "the fruit of my body."

7d Literally: "the sins of my person"; on the meaning of נֶפֶשׁ see H. W. Wolff, *Anthropology of the Old Testament* 1973), 21f., 23ff.; here נפש with suffix functions as an emphatic personal pronoun; see below, p. 178. On the translation, see Th. Lescow (1966) 54.

8a Since the third person masculine singular *hiph.* is probably correctly understood by Gk (ἀνηγγέλη) as an indefinite subject (Br*Synt* §36d; cf. Joüon, *Gr* §155d and σ' [ειπε σοι]; θ' [ερρεθη]), it is unnecessary to vocalize the verb as a passive (הֻגַּד, J. Wellhausen). Vg *(indicabo),* Syr, Arabic incorrectly continue the first person speech of vv. 6, 7b.

8b Essentially, "to live"; see below, p. 181.

8c The absolute infinitive of צנע *hiph.* functions as an adverb modifying the following infinitive construct לכת; cf. Ges-K §113,2; Br*Synt* §99b. On the meaning of the word, see below, pp. 181f.

Form

The transmission complex that begins in 6:1f. reaches its conclusion as a rhetorical unit, at the latest, with v. 8. For in v. 9 we find an unusual but unambiguous new beginning that introduces a new addressee (v. 9aα), with a new summons to hear (v. 9b), and a different theme (vv. 10ff.).

Yet it must be questioned at the outset whether 6:1–8 presents an original unit. How do the various introductory sentences in v. 1a, b and v. 2a, b relate to the divine speech in vv. 3–5? And how are we to understand the connection of this divine speech to the human questions in vv. 6–7 with their answer in v. 8?

Among the introductory sentences, v. 2b is certainly the beginning of the speech in vv. 3–5. For v. 2b announces Yahweh's legal dispute (ריב, see below, pp. 173f.) with "his people," which in the subsequent verses is precisely followed by the first person speech of Yahweh (vv. 3–5; on v. 5bβ, see note 5d) with words addressed to "my people" (v. 3a, 5a) and with the challenge to respond (v. 3b).

But v. 2a is not to be separated from the announcement of the lawsuit in v. 2b. This is already indicated by the conjunction כי at the beginning of v. 2b. Prior to this in v. 2a, before the actual beginning of the legal dispute, the mountains and the foundations of the earth are summoned to serve as the law court, similar to other examples of legal procedure in prophet texts (Isa. 1:2; Jer. 2:12; 25:31; cf. Deut. 32:1). Both sentences speak of the ריב (ל) יהוה; in the first (v. 2a), a cosmic law court is summoned, while in the second (v. 2b) the legal opponents are presented and the proceeding is introduced. Thus at least vv. 2a, 2b, and 3–5 represent a unified whole. Form critically, the passage is to be regarded as an inauguration of a judicial procedure; it already presupposes the peoples' accusation against Yahweh, or their rejection of him (cf. v. 3 and Jer. 2:5f.).

Verse 1 is clearly set off from vv. 2–5. To be sure, v. 1 also speaks of ריב. However, while the word in v. 2a and 2b means the judicial dispute as a whole (cf. ריב עם in v. 2bα and יכח *hithpael* that is synonymously parallel in v. 2bβ; cf. also Hos. 4:1; 12:3 and see below, p. 174), in v. 1 ריב has the more specialized meaning "to accuse" (ריב את/ב; Jer. 2:9; 25:31; cf. Hos. 2:4; Gen. 31:36 and Wolff, *Hosea,* 33, 66f.), for the accused "mountains" and "hills" are to "hear" (v. 1bβ) the voice of the plaintiff. Thus in v. 1 it is neither "Israel" nor Yahweh's "people" who are named as the legal opponents, as in v. 2b; rather, it is "the mountains" and "the hills." Accordingly, in v. 1b they do not have the same function as "the mountains" and the "foundations of the earth" in v. 2a, which act as the law court or the witnesses. And, whereas Yahweh conducts the legal proceeding in v. 2, an unidentifiable human figure, commissioned by Yahweh, is summoned to act as plaintiff in v. 1. To whom does Yahweh speak? Is it an unnamed prophet? In this case, "the mountains" and "the hills" could be interpreted as representing Israel, as is found occasionally in Ezekiel (6:3; 36:4,6; A. S. van der Woude, 202). Or is

Israel summoned to be Yahweh's witness against the foreign nations (A. Weiser)? In this instance, "mountains" and "hills" would be ciphers for the nations (and their cultic places; cf. W. Zimmerli, *Ezekiel* 1 [Hermeneia] 185f.; *Ezekiel* 2:238) that are being indicted by Yahweh (see below, pp. 172f.). In either case, not only the stylistic and thematic differences would become intelligible, but especially the redactional character of 6:1 as a transition from 1:2—5:14 to the last two chapters of the book (concerning this, see below, p. 169, "Setting").

According to its form, 6:1 should be interpreted as a redactional transition. The decisive support for this is found in the observation that the redactor borrows his terminology almost exclusively from the immediate context; at the same time, however, the words are given a different meaning or are negated. On שמעו, cf. 5:14; 6:2, and 1:2; on ריב and on ההרים, cf. 6:2; parallel to ההרים stands הגבעות in v. 1b and (האתנים) מסדי ארץ in v. 2a; concerning the transition from plural שמעו in v. 1a (cf. also 5:14b and 1:2!) to the imperative singular of the plaintiff who is summoned in v. 1b (קום ריב), cf. the corresponding collective singulars in 6:2ff. (. . . עמו ישראל). We must therefore interpret 6:1 as the redactor's composition for the purpose of connecting the preceding chapters with what follows.

It follows that 6:2–5 was provided to the redaction by the tradition. How are these verses related to vv. 6–8? We have noted that v. 2a contains the summons to the law court, that v. 2b is the presentation of the opponents in the legal procedure, and that vv. 3–5 contain Yahweh's lawsuit speech (see above, p. 166). This speech is to be more precisely defined as a speech of self-defense (*Selbstverteidigungsrede;* cf. Jer. 26:12–15; 1 Sam. 12:3–5; and H. J. Boecker 94ff.) by Yahweh; it responds to a previous but unquoted indictment brought by the people, or to some corresponding act of rejection (cf. especially Jer. 2:4–13!). Two elements are contained in this speech of self-defense: (1) a categorical declaration of innocence in the form of a question containing the challenge to give proof to the contrary (v. 3); (2) concrete evidence of Yahweh's fundamental saving acts, with the challenge to acknowledge Yahweh's will to bring salvation (vv. 4f.). The twice-occurring address, "my people," in v. 3a and v. 5a structures the speech into two strophes. Yahweh is justified and exonerated before the people in the first strophe by the exodus from Egypt (vv. 3–4); in the second strophe, by the Balaam tradition with reference to the crossing of the Jordan (v. 5).

At first glance, it appears that the text in vv. 6–8 does not fit with the speech of self-defense presented in the context of a legal proceeding. Verses 6–8 are reminiscent of speech forms belonging to priestly instruction. To the four questions about what constitutes acceptable sacrifices (vv. 6–7), an answer is given (v. 8) that simply leaves these questions aside and points to what Yahweh expects concerning the whole range of human conduct. Similar dialogues that offer instruction regarding cultic matters are found in the temple entrance-liturgies (Pss. 15:1 and vv. 2–5; 24:3 and v. 4; Isa. 33:14b and v. 15; cf. K. Koch) and in questions about the effect of holy and impure things (Hag. 2:12–13; cf. J. Begrich). The form of the instructional dialogue *(Unterweisungsgespräch),* therefore, has its origin not in the legal procedure, as in vv. 2–5, but in the cult. Corresponding to this decisive difference, there is another difference, namely, that in vv. 2–5 the dialogue partners are Yahweh and "his people" (vv. 2b, 3, 5); in vv. 6–7, however, the dialogue partners are an individual (first person singular, vv. 6–7; אדם in v. 8) and his teacher (v. 8).

Nevertheless, there are important reasons for seeing in vv. 2–8 a self-contained, artistic composition in which various speech forms have been fused together. Thus the sequence of questions in vv. 6–7 (see below, pp. 177f.), each masterfully more intense than the last, only becomes intelligible at all when, in correspondence to the questions, the knowledge of God's dissatisfaction with his people underlies the implied accusation in vv. 2–5. On the other hand, Yahweh's lawsuit speech in vv. 3–5 would be a fragment if it merely presented his self-defense, and would be left not only without an explication of the accusations, but also without any answer from the audience that was challenged to answer in v. 3b. If the temple entrance-liturgies known to us (Pss. 15:1; 24:3) are compared with this passage, here we find absolutely nothing said about the conditions for entrance to the sanctuary. Verses 6–7 inquire about the means for reconciliation with the God who has been previously accused (cf. v. 3); the concern is for encountering Yahweh himself as the (previously attested) "God on high." The question במה ("with what?"), verbosely developed in vv. 6–7 and presumably to be distinguished from the briefer מי ("who?") questions of the temple entrance-liturgies, alludes to the twofold מה ("what?") that commences Yahweh's speech in v. 3a. Then follows in v. 3b the challenge for an answer. The ceremonious counter-questions at first give absurd responses (vv. 6f.); then a prophetic answer, correcting the absurdity, instructs the audience in v. 8. Thus the text exhibits an effective tension from v. 3 to the correct answer in v. 8 (cf. I. Willi-Plein, 98f.).

The passage contained in 6:2–8 as a whole presents us with an artistically composed didactic sermon (for a comparison with Deuteronomistic paraeneses, see below, pp. 170f.), which employs rhetorical forms of various origins. With its (imaginary) dialogue presented as a disputation speech, the passage conveys a sense of great urgency. Whether it was originally a literary composition (cf. N. Lohfink, *Das Hauptgebot* [1963] 134ff.), or rather at first presented orally, must remain an open question. Nevertheless, the variety of form and color utilized in the composition suggests rather that the writer was educated by prophets and priests from within the Deuteronomistic school (see below, pp. 171f.). In that case, the present form of the questions in vv. 6f. was hardly shaped in a genuine dialogue; rather, they are imaginary questions that belong within the context of the speech. As the questions themselves grow in intensity, they almost reach the point of parody, exaggerating reality to the point of the grotesque for the normal participants in the Israelite cultic observances.

As regards the rhythm of the passage, the four prosodic units in vv. 6f. clearly consist of synonymous bicola which generally should be read as three-stress bicola. Three-stress bicola also predominate in the preceding lawsuit speech in vv. 2–4a; on the other hand, the prosody in the transmitted text of vv. 4b–5 becomes uncertain (on the text-critical problems, see notes 4a and 5b–b). In the redactional transition in v. 1, after the opening in v. 1a, v. 1b appropriates the catchwords and also the form of the three-stress bicolon from v. 2a; the transition in v. 1 is thus similar to the mixed style of the redactional verses in 5:13f. (see above, p. 153). The concluding exhortation in v. 8, with its graceful, four-stress bicolon (vv. 8a, ba^1 + 8ba^2, β) clearly is rhythmically set off from the bicola of the Torah-questions in vv. 6f.

The elevated style of the passage is indicated by occasional alliterations. Of particular note is the transition from v. 3aβ to v. 4aα, where the reference to Yahweh's "bringing out" of Egypt *(häᵉᵃlitîka),* an answer exonerating Yahweh, is made to sound similar to the charge that Yahweh has "overburdened" Israel *(häl'ētîkā).* Indeed, it has been rightly pointed out that the climax of the didactic passage is possessed of phonetic refinement (Th. Lescow [1966] 49f.). In the concluding prosodic unit containing the series of Torah-questions, the *i* sound is heard seven times in v. 7b, five of which are the first person singular suffix, in which a human speaker challenges himself with questions formulated in the first person style. The first two syllables of the answer in v. 8 again pick up the *i* sound *(higgîd),* but in the proclamation of the will of God the *i* sound is immediately replaced by the multiple recurrence of the clear, soothing and sustaining *a* sound.

Setting

The attempt to understand v. 1 as a redactional transition should not overlook the fact that the "summons to hear," expressed by the form-element שִׁמְעוּ־נָא, already occurs in 3:1, 9. Whereas the summons in those verses directly addresses leading circles in Jerusalem, here it introduces words which Yahweh speaks to his people as a whole. Since 6:1 immediately follows not chap. 3 but chap. 5, we must also pay attention to the final redaction found in 1:2 and 5:14 (see above, p. 153), which in 1:2 summons the nations of the world to hear, and in 5:14 threatens them for not hearing. Consequently, it can be assumed that with the transitional verse in 6:1, the redaction intends that the collection of sayings in chaps. 6–7 be subsequently understood as a kind of model of prophetic accusations which also apply to the nations. Remarkably, Gk translated הרים in 6:2 with λαοί (or did it read עַמִּים?), which is certainly incorrect, but in 6:1ba, in light of 5:14b, it could certainly be intelligible. As in Ezek. 6:3; 36:4, 6, where "mountains" and "hills" represent Israel, so here these words might stand for the nations of the world (perhaps also in reference to the sense of the context in 4:1a; cf. J. L. Mays, 33), which, according to 4:1a, are summoned to the mountain of Yahweh; here, however, they are at first included in the accusation against Israel. Redactional work of this kind would not be possible until postexilic times (see above, p. 51 on 1:2 and pp. 153f. on 5:14).

In addition to 1:3—5:12, another group of sayings was available to the redaction from the tradition, of which 6:2–8 was the first. The attempts to establish the setting and date of 6:2–8 differ greatly, since the text offers no concrete references. Today few commentators (in addition to W. Rudolph) think that Micah was the author. The language, the manner of conception, and the themes depart considerably from Micah's sayings in chaps. 1–3. The detailed reference to Israel's traditions in this passage is completely foreign to Micah. Whereas Micah makes concrete accusations and proclamations of disaster, here instead we find fundamental instructions; whereas Micah precisely addresses his words to certain leading circles on behalf of his fellow countrymen, here Yahweh's people as such are his conversation partners. It is of great significance that the meaning of עַמִּי in 1:9; 2:8f.; 3:3, 5 (Micah's fellow countrymen[!]; see above, pp. 59 and 82) is different from עַמִּי in 6:3, 5 (the people of God!). Other attempts to find the author in the eighth century in the Northern Kingdom (A. S. van der Woude); in Judah at the time of Manasseh in the seventh century (already H. Ewald, 1867); or as late as the fifth or fourth centuries (K. Marti, Ph. Hyatt, Th. Lescow), find supporting data mostly in isolated observations. More recent investigations endeavor to compare the diction, themes, and intention of the passage as a whole with parallel Old Testament texts in order to ascertain the author's historical context (I. Willi-Plein, J. L. Mays, B. Renaud, J. Vermeylen).

As a didactic piece, it clearly presupposes characteristics of Deuteronomistic paraenesis and of the extended discourses found in the Deuteronomistic history. Indeed, the retrospect of Yahweh's deeds in the form of a speech of self-defense within the framework of a lawsuit speech (vv. 2–5) recalls the speech of Samuel in 1 Sam. 12:6ff. (merely cf. ענה ב in 1 Sam. 12:3 with Mic. 6:3b). Further, the expression צדקות יהוה for salvation history in 1 Sam. 12:7 occurs in Mic. 6:5; on the sending (שלח) of "Moses and Aaron" to bring up (עלה *hiph.*) the people "from the land of Egypt" in 1 Sam. 12:6, 8, cf. Mic. 6:4a, b; on the mention of the "king of Moab" in 1 Sam. 12:9, cf. Mic. 6:5. Similarly, Joshua's speech in Josh. 24:5 refers to the sending of Moses and Aaron at the exodus from Egypt; it mentions, additionally, the king of Moab, named "Balak" and also "Balaam, the son of Beor" in Josh. 24:9; cf. Mic. 6:5a. Moreover, this part of Joshua's speech, like Mic. 6:3–5, is presented in the form of a Yahweh speech. In the following verses from the Deuteronomist in Josh. 24:17, after the expression "brought up from the land of Egypt," there occurs the typical Deuteronomic- Deuteronomistic apposition, "out of the house of bondage" (cf. מבית עבדים in Mic. 6:4a with Deut. 5:6; 6:12; 7:8; 8:14; 13:6, 11; Exod. 13:3; 20:2; Judg. 6:8). With this apposition the term פדה ("to ransom") repeatedly occurs; it is a typical Deuteronomic-Deuteronomistic interpretative word for the exodus from Egypt (as in Mic. 6:4aβ, so in Deut. 7:8; 13:6; beyond this, without this apposition, in Deut. 9:26; 15:15; 21:8; 24:18; Ps. 78:42; etc.). The reference to the towns of "Shittim" and "Gilgal" for the crossing from Transjordan into the region west of the Jordan corresponds to the report in Josh. 3–5 (cf. 3:1; 4:19) edited by the Deuteronomists. Hence all the significant data in Mic. 6:3–5 in essence belong exclusively to specific Deuteronomic-Deuteronomistic traditions.

This is equally true of the rhetorical intention with which this data is given expression. Its formulation corresponds to Deuteronomistic paraenesis which, as here in Mic. 6:5, makes stereotyped exhortations with the words זכר and ידע: "Remember so that you may know" (Deut. 7:9, 18; 8:2; 9:6f.; etc.). The object of the remembrance and knowledge is always the great saving acts of Yahweh; the goal of the remembrance and knowledge, however, as in vv. (6–)8, is new obedience, new love, and walking in the way of Yahweh (Deut. 5:12–15; 6:20–25; 8:6; 11:22; etc.). Among the rich variations of Deuteronomic didactic sermons, Deut. 10:12–22 is noticeably similar to Mic. 6:2–8. The structure of the beginning of the sermon in Deut. 10:12: "(Israel,) what (does) Yahweh (your God) (require) of you? Only that (you fear Yahweh, your God . . .)" (מה יהוה . . . ממך כי אם) corresponds precisely to the climax in Mic. 6:8. Also according to the summary in Deut. 10:13, the concern is simply with what is "good" (טוב ל) (for the audience). The will of God is declared with the same words, or certainly with similar words, as in Mic. 6:8b: "Do justice" (עשה משפט, v. 18), "demonstrate love" (אהב, vv. 18f.) and "follow in the ways of God" (לכת בכל דרכיו, v. 12). As in our passage (vv. 4–5), this new conduct has its motivation not in a particular revelation of the law but in the remembrance of Yahweh's mighty deeds (Deut. 10:17ff., 21), which, as acts of God's love, give birth to human acts of love (vv. 15, 18f.); nor is there lacking a reference to Egypt (v. 19). It is repeatedly emphasized, as at the end of 6:8, that Yahweh is "your God" (vv. 12, 14, 22).

The juxtaposition of critique of the cult (indirect in Mic. 6:6f.) with the requirement of obedience (v. 8) is one of the particular characteristics of Deuteronomistic interpretation of the prophets (cf. Amos 5:25 and Wolff, *Joel and Amos* 112f.; 264f.; on Jer. 6:19f.; 7:21ff., cf. W. Thiel, *Die deuteronomistische Redaktion von Jeremia 26–45*, WMANT 52 [1981] 111, etc.). Evidence of this is seen in the creative use of langauge in v. 8b, where new formulations of the will of God are couched in dense summaries (see below, p. 180): "Once again [we find] the Deuteronomistic school's rich shading of langauge (L. Perlitt, WP KG 66 [1977] 119).

Accordingly, this didactic passage must be located within the broader circle of Deuteronomic and Deuteronomistic sermonic activity, although a more precise date between the end of the seventh century and the fifth century cannot be demonstrated. (On a preexilic origin, cf. B. Renaud [1977] 326 and I. Willi-Plein 100). The speech certainly also intends to proclaim the fundamental, saving deeds of Yahweh as valid and meaningful for later ages, without limit. Thus it addresses its audience not only as a community of Israelites (vv. 2–5), but as individual "persons" (v. 8). Whereas most classic prophetic texts are very precisely aimed at a given audience, this didactic speech from the Deuteronomic-Deuteronomistic school is intended to be "timeless."

Observations concerning details in the text speak in favor of a relatively late date within the assigned span of time. Miriam is mentioned alongside of Moses and Aaron; this series of names occurs neither in Deuteronomic-Deuteronomistic texts, nor in prophetic texts, but only in 1 Chron. 5:29; Num. 12:1, 4, 10f. and 26:59. The author reviews the historical reminiscences of the Pentateuch as a whole and apparently also those in the book of Joshua in its final form (on Shittim and Gilgal, cf. Josh. 3:1; 4:19). Among the variations of vocabulary in the related passage Deut. 10:12–22, perhaps the most significant is that "Israel" is addressed, whereas in the comparable passage in Mic. 6:8, it is "man." This should not be surprising, however, since אדם is used in Deut. 5:24; 8:3. Moreover, the address to "my people" in Mic. 6:3, 5 should be compared with Pss. 50:7; 78:1; 81:9[8] (12[11], 14[13]). This points to a certain connection of style and function with parts of Psalms 50 and 81 (cf. Ps. 50:4, 8ff., 14ff.; 81:11ff.[10ff.], 14[13]), psalms which are also to be seen in connection with Deuteronomistic circles and, more precisely, with Levitic cultic activity. These psalms are probably to be dated in the postexilic period (cf. Jörg Jeremias, *Kultprophetie und Gerichtsverkündigung in der späten Königszeit Israels,* WMANT 35 [1970] 126f.; H. J. Kraus, *Psalms 1–59,* 490, *Psalms 60–150,* 149). Indeed, the prehistory of the didactic sermon in Micah 6 may go back to the early Deuteronomic period, but presumably it did not receive its present form until the postexilic period.

Admittedly, it remains difficult to date more precisely within the broader confines of the exile a text that embraces hundreds of years of Israel's history; and it is equally difficult to determine more exactly the function of its speaker. The artistic composition of this text, with its sharply contrasting colors and its stirring succession of rhetorical forms, places us in the presence of a priest who utters exhortations intimately connected with Israel's history, and who at the same time is a teacher educated in prophetic circles. The less we know about his person and his time, the more precisely we must apply his "timeless" words.

Commentary

[6:1] Verse 1 stems from the work of the final redactor (see above, p. 167), who again issues a new summons to hear (as in 1:2). Whom does he address in v. 1a? Since neither the mountains, hills, foundations of the earth, nor even Israel is introduced until vv. 1b–2, the redactor first of all intends to address his readers. Only the redactional connection with 5:14 suggests more precisely that the nations are spoken to here (see above, p. 169). With v. 1 the redactor once again briefly refers back to 1:2 with an eye toward the last section of the book, which had been recently joined to the previous chapters. The summons to hear is emphasized by the particle נא- (as in 3:1, 9), since according to 5:14 there had previously been a refusal to hear. In spite of and because of the nations' refusal to hear, Yahweh speaks further. With the inversion of the subject in a relative clause, the participle אֹמֵר—in an unusual expression that probably betrays the written character of the verse—emphasizes the incessant nature of Yahweh's speaking (on the durative, cf. Meyer³, §§101,7b; 104,2b). The new appeal to hear is meaningful only because Yahweh (in spite of his wrath, 5:14!) does not cease in his efforts to open the ears of the nations.

What Yahweh says is communicated first in v. 1b. To whom is the new, imperative—now in the singular—addressed? It cannot be the plural, ecumenical readership of v. 1a. The word קוּם often occurs in proclamations charging someone to rise up and go to a distant place (Num. 22:20; 1 Kings 17:9; Jon. 1:2; 3:2); but the witness or the plaintiff can also be commanded to stand before the law court (Deut. 19:15f.). Here both of these two aspects are reflected, since the verse refers to stepping forward to make an accusation (רִיב) and to the "mountains" and "hills" as the audience. Since no specific prophet is mentioned, but the redactor without exception works with the words of the context (even though he reinterprets them), the plaintiff summoned here can presumably only be Israel (cf. H. J. Boecker, 102; J. L. Mays, 128, 131, and see above, pp. 166f.).

But the accused party, as remarkable as it may first appear, is the "mountains" and the "hills." הרים differentiates the elevated, individual mountains and mountain ranges from the smaller rises (גבעות); however, here the words are used synonymously, as is often the case. They occur in parallel 31 times in the Old Testament (cf. 4:1 and A. Schwarzenbach, *Die geographische Terminologie im Hebräischen des Alten Testaments* [1954]). It is unlikely that "mountains" and "hills" in v. 1b, as well as "mountains" and "foundations of the earth" in v. 2a, represent the law court. In this case, v. 1b would be a poor doublette of v. 2; and the preposition את- would have to mean "in the presence of," "before," or something similar (cf. Th. H. Robinson, W, Rudolph, J. L. Mays), a meaning which, in context with ריב, is not demonstrable (but cf. ריב את- in Jer. 2:9; Judg. 8:1; Neh. 5:7; 13:11, 17). If, however, the mountains and hills do not represent the law court (corresponding to v. 2b), but instead are the accused party, what would the redactor of (5:14—)6:1 have meant? To me it appears most likely that he found in the mountains and hills a cipher for the nations (see above, p. 169). Already according to 1:2, the redactor recognized in the melting of the mountains the fate of the pagan nations (1:4; see above, p. 46; cf. Ps. 97:5). In Nah. 1:5 "mountains" and "hills" clearly stand parallel to "earth and all that dwells in it," against which comes the wrath of Yahweh (cf. Isa. 34:1f.). That the redactor places before us a difficult metaphor that needs to be deciphered is most easily understood in relation to his dependence on the context. It should be emphasized that this interpretation remains uncertain. If our supposition is correct, then Israel is challenged in v. 1b to take part in Yahweh's lawsuit as the plaintiff against the nations, as is similarly presupposed in 4:13; 5:7.

[6:2] The original beginning of the text in v. 2 (and reinterpreted in v. 1b) opens with a solemn introduction to the legal procedure. By means of a two-part summons to hear (see note 2b) the law court is constituted, and at the same time dependable witnesses to the proceedings are appointed. "Mountains" and "foundations of the earth" are called upon as though they were personal dignitaries (the omission of the article preceding the word הרים [v. 2a] is noticeable in comparison with ההרים in the more recent text in v. 1b; see note 2b). More frequently it is "heaven and earth" that are summoned; this we find, for example, in the execration texts of Arslan Tash (*KAI* no. 27,13) from the seventh century. In the international treaty of *Sefire* (*KAI* no. 222 A 11f.) from the eighth century, heaven and earth as well as the "bottom [of the sea?] and the springs," are summoned, among others, as guarantors of the treaty. (Cf. further, H. Wildberger, *Jesaja 1–12,* BK 10/1, 9f.). In the Old Testament, comparable texts about the summoning of heaven and earth as witnesses are to be found, in addition to Isa. 1:2, especially in Deuteronomistic passages (Deut. 4:26; 30:19; 31:28; 32:1). In v. 2 the "mountains" and the "foundations of the earth" have the same function. Together, as the topmost and bottommost boundary, both expressions point to the entire earthly cosmos. The mountains, moreover, represent height and power (see above, p. 56); the rocky "foundations of the earth" (cf. the laying bare of the "foundations" of the buildings in Samaria in 1:6b) stand for what is imperturbable and constant, and of lasting stability (cf. Mosis, *ThWAT* 3:673f.). The interpolation והאתנים emphasizes such permanency (cf. Deut. 21:4; Jer. 5:15; Amos 5:24; Ps. 74:15). The earthly cosmos, which outlasts human nations, is called to be witness to Yahweh's dialogue with his people. Indeed, this lawsuit belongs to a public that is global in breadth.

Unlike v. 1b, here ריב means Yahweh's indictment against his people. The following context in vv. 4f. further indicates that the entire legal procedure is meant. The synonymously parallel יכח, a *hithpael* form occurring only here, also emphasizes the dialogical character of the dispute. We will see that the reproaches against Israel remarkably recede. That the party in Yahweh's lawsuit is called "my people" already at the outset suggests that the proceedings are not to be a dispute between enemies but a disagreement among allies. The verse recalls the language of Deuteronomy (7:6; 14:2; 26:18; Exod. 19:5; cf. Hos. 2:25b), both with its understanding of the people as Yahweh's own possession, and, at the same time, with the introduction to a legal proceeding reminiscent of Hosea (4:1; 12:3). To be Yahweh's people—that is Israel's identity in the midst of the cosmic witnesses.

[6:3] There is no accusation following the summons of the law court (as in Hos. 4:1; 12:3; cf. Jer. 25:31), to say nothing of a sentence of judgment; rather, we find Yahweh's speech of self-defense, whose words are animated more strongly by the keynote of love and courtship than by the desire for self-affirmation. The address to "my people!" which is repeated in v. 5, already indicates that Yahweh's own commitment to Israel remains valid as the unconditional basis for the lawsuit. The subject of the legal proceeding is not Israel's guilt, but Yahweh's deeds and demands. Hence, with a double question, Yahweh calls himself into question: "What have I done to you?" In the course of usual legal proceedings, this is the question asked by a person who sees himself charged with some wrong (1 Sam. 17:29; 26:18; 29:8); it is identical with the question, "What is my guilt?" (thus 1 Sam. 20:1). It stands in antithesis to the question asked by one who makes the accusation: "What have you done?" (cf. Judg. 8:1 with 8:2!). With the question asked by the person who considers himself accused ("What have I done?") there begins the "speech of appeasement" (H. J. Boecker, 103). The Yahweh speech, which presupposes the indictment from the people, does not state from which direction the indictment is made.

This might become somewhat clearer in the second question. The verb לאה *hiph.* has Yahweh as its subject elsewhere only in Job 16:7; there Job laments that Yahweh has "worn him out" with troubles. The root לאה expresses overload, annoyance, exhaustion (cf. Isa. 1:14; Jer. 12:5; see note 3a). The noun derived from it (תְּלָאָה) denotes the hardship which Israel experienced in Egypt and in later periods of affliction (Exod. 18:8; Num. 20:14; Lam. 3:5; Neh. 9:32). The question in our passage, "How have I required too much of [overburdened, troubled] you?" in this context fits only at a time that is not characterized by significant political troubles between Israel and foreign nations, yet a period in which Israel was dissatisfied with Yahweh. This applies somewhat to the time of Josiah (cf. Jer. 2:5–9), but even better to the early Persian era, when such a question could allude to the heavy demands of the cult. The wearisomeness of sacrificial worship is referred to by the word לאה is Isa. 16:12; Mal. 1:13 (with reference to Yahweh in Isa. 1:14). If that is also the case here, then the questions about pleasing sacrifices in vv. 6f. and the answer in v. 8 in tension with v. 3 become intelligible ("In what way have I expected too much of you?").

In that case, it is theologically significant how Yahweh takes upon himself the burden of guilt and is prepared to let himself be accused. He expressly challenges his people to offer the grounds for their indictment of him. ב ענה, a fixed expression belonging to the law court, introduces a person's reply within the legal proceeding (Num. 35:30; 1 Sam. 12:3f.; 2 Sam. 1:16; Isa. 3:9; Job 9:14; cf. F. Horst, *Hiob* BK 16/1, 148). Yahweh expects, therefore, that the people will present reasons for their apparent dissatisfaction with their God by declaring what are his unjust deeds or his troublesome requirements. A teacher who expresses the will of God in this manner is intent on a new arrangement between Yahweh and his people; he is certain that God will not abandon his covenant.

[6:4] Instead of the people's response called for in v. 3b, Yahweh continues with his speech of self-justification (v. 4)—after a period of embarrassed silence on the part of the audience (thus W. Rudolph)(?). Since no reasons for the complaint are forthcoming, an emphatic כי cites the reasons which "on the contrary" must lead to praise of Yahweh and to a recognition of his saving deeds (v. 5bβ) (after an expected negative answer following the questions in v. 3a, the particle כי is similar to the English "indeed," or "on the contrary," KBL³ 448). Even the first word, with its clear assonances, replies to the indirect reproaches in v. 3aβ: *häl'ētîkā? – hä'ᵃlitîkā!* This must have sounded to Israel something like: "I am said to have *over*burdened you? I have rather *un*burdened you!"; or "I am said to have pressed *down* upon you? I have rather led you *up!*" עלה *hiph.* ("to bring up") instead of יצא *hiph.* ("to bring out") is used by the Deuteronomic-Deuteronomistic literature for the Exodus event when it appears alongside the gift of the land (Deut. 20:1; Josh. 24:17; Judg. 6:8, 13; 1 Sam. 12:6; cf. Wolff, *Joel and Amos* 169f.). The objection voiced against the secret reproaches of the people is strengthened in v. 4 by characterizing the land of Egypt as "house of bondage" and the Exodus as "ransom" (פדה; on the appropriation of Deuteronomic-Deuteronomistic language, see above, p. 170). פדה denotes first of all the redemption of a person or an animal by the payment of its equal value: Exod. 13:13; 34:20; Lev. 27:27. But Yahweh has accomplished the redemption of Israel out of the house of bondage in Egypt by his own initiative alone. Thus Israel's original confession concerning the fundamental redemptive deeds of its God is impressed anew upon the people in the name of Yahweh as the first and permanently valid reason for its knowledge of God. Joined to this is the recollection of the commissioning of the first leaders of the people. It is most unusual that together with Moses and Aaron (Josh. 24:5; 1 Sam. 12:6, 8; Pss. 77:21; 105:26) Miriam is also mentioned (see above, p. 171). We are unable to tell what different functions were attributed here to these three figures—they were even thought to be brother and sister according to 1 Chron. 5:29. Nevertheless, the reference is probably to their task as leaders, as we know from the Pentateuchal traditions; לפניך ("before you") recalls not only the ancient historical data, but also the tradition that provides orientation for the present. Moses, Aaron, and Miriam, who were once sent as Israel's leaders, even down to the present time prepare the way for Yahweh's mission. According to the Targum the "three prophets" are "Moses, who teaches the tradition and the law; Aaron, who brings reconciliation to the people; Miriam, who instructs the women" (תלתה נביי משה לאלפא מסרת ודינין אהרן לכפרא על עמא ומרים לאוראה לנשיא).

[6:5] The repetition of the vocative "my people!" (cf. v. 3a), together with the summons to "remembrance" in v. 5, indicates once more that Yahweh's speech of self-defense aims at conciliation (H. J. Boecker 103, 108, 119). זכר ("to remember") does not understand historical events as belonging to the past; rather, they provide orientation for the present (thus especially in Deuteronomy; see above, p. 170). Recalling the Pentateuchal traditions preserved in Numbers 22–24, there is further mention of Yahweh's acts of unburdening and liberating Israel. The brief reference presupposes knowledge of the Balaam traditions. The audience must have known the content of what Balak "planned" (the word יעץ does not occur in Num. 22–24), namely, that Israel was to be cursed by Balaam (cf. Num. 22:6, 11, 17; 23:7; 24:10). They also must have known what Balaam *answered;* refusing to curse Israel, he blessed them according to Yahweh's direction (ענה in Num. 22:18; 23:12, 26; cf. 22:13; 24:13).

Immediately after the reference to Balaam, *Shittim* is named, a place also mentioned in the Pentateuch in Num. 25:1 immediately after the Balaam narrative. In our text, however, Shittim is mentioned as the place of departure for crossing the Jordan on the way to *Gilgal.* Accordingly, this basic outline of salvation history combines the Balak-Balaam narrative with the entrance into promised land in a manner similar to the combination of the commissioning of Moses, Aaron, and Miriam with the Exodus from Egypt. Yahweh's saving deeds are accompanied by his witnesses. That the history of the entrance into the land begins with the departure from Shittim, the last encampment before crossing the Jordan (Josh. 2:1; 3:1), is in agreement with the traditions in Josh. 2–5. The place is to be located at the modern *Tell el-hammâm,* about 10 km east of the ford of the Jordan that leads to Jericho (cf. K. Elliger, *BHHW* 3: 1812). The first stop on the other side of the Jordan is Gilgal (concerning its location in the neighborhood of Jericho, cf. K. Elliger, *BHHW* 1: 572f.). These details are in agreement with Josh. 4:19b. Gilgal became, therefore, the place of remembrance and celebration for Israel, since there, finally, "the reproach of Egypt was rolled away" from her (Josh. 5:9f.; cf. 4:19ff.). Thus in the Deuteronomistic presentation, as in our text, the themes of the Exodus and the gift of the land are joined together. It is probable that the beginning of the original text in Mic. 6:5ba contained the most important key word for the crossing of the Jordan—עבר, found in Josh. 3:1, 11, 14, 16f.; 4:1, 5, 7, 10–13, 22f.; 5:1 (see note 5b–b).

The function of the remembrance of the Exodus and of the entrance into the land is to show that the reproaches against Yahweh, as the questions in v. 3 presuppose, are untenable. This is precisely what is meant by the goal of the remembering in v. 5bβ: "that you may know the saving deeds of Yahweh." Thus the ultimate direction of the act of remembering and also its present significance become completely clear (cf. also Josh. 4:24a, b and W. Schottroff, *THAT* 1:510, 517). The tenor of

Deuteronomistic-Levitical paraenesis is perceptible (see above, p. 170). The person who remembers Yahweh's redemptive and guiding actions comes to a contemporary knowledge of Yahweh and is able to correct the misdeeds in his life. The phrase צדקות יהוה expresses, on the one hand, the concept of Yahweh's righteousness; but it indicates, on the other, that such righteousness is the result of his deeds of salvation from disaster (cf. Judg. 5:11; 1 Sam. 12:7; Ps. 103:6; Dan. 9:16 and F. Crüsemann, "Jahwes Gerechtigkeit [ṣᵉdāqā/ṣäddäq] im Alten Testament," *EvTh* 36 [1976] 427–450 [436f.]). צדקות יהוה therefore has become the particular expression in the Old Testament for, and at the same time an interpretation of, Yahweh's "saving history." At the same time, the phrase expresses Israel's liberation by Yahweh's acts and his continuing acts of righteousness. Thus with Yahweh's speech of self-defense, our preacher has achieved his first goal.

[6:6] Having been brought to a thorough understanding, the listener's answer—after the challenge in v. 3b—is overdue. The prophet as teacher leaves behind the form of the lawsuit speech and introduces in v. 6 first of all a series of counter-questions that heighten the tension in the passage. He loosely appropriates the form used by an individual who seeks priestly instruction (see above, p. 167). The questions are supposed to touch upon the right response of an individual in the Yahwistic cult; to this extent, they refer back to the questions concerning Yahweh's excessive demands in v. 3bβ; but at the same time the questions completely misunderstand Yahweh's own witness to his saving deeds. To be sure, the questions presuppose quiet and humble agreement with Yahweh's justification of himself. But they do not perceive that the reproach concerning Yahweh's excessive demands has long since been abrogated by the remembrance of Yahweh's liberating acts (see above, pp. 175ff. on vv. 4–5).

First, the basic question is formulated (v. 6a); then it is developed in three further questions containing proposals, each increasing in intensity (vv. 6b–7). "With what shall I come before Yahweh?"—thus the general question is put. Still present in it is the dread of the legal encounter arising from the questions asked in the legal proceeding. In a similar way, Jacob once was in dread of again meeting Esau (Gen. 32:8ff.); as a result, he attempted to assuage Esau with gifts (vv. 14ff.). In our verse the question concerns the appropriate sacrificial offering for atonement (cf. 2 Sam. 21:3; בַּמָּה אֲכַפֵּר). It is formulated in an unconventional manner. קדם *piel* denotes a meeting between persons (Deut. 23:5[4]; Isa. 21:14) as well as a coming into Yahweh's presence (elsewhere only in Ps. 95:2). כפף occurs in the *niphal* only here. In Isa. 58:5 the *qal* form of כפף is used ironically to describe the figure of a fasting person who *bows* his head over like a reed; in Ps. 57:7[6], the word appears to belong to the language of the hunt; in Pss. 145:14; 146:8 it describes persons who are suffering in a nonspiritual sense as *bowed down*. The writer of our text appears to be unacquainted with the technical language of the cult. With the word כפף *niphal* he describes a person in an attitude of deep humility who, self-abased at prayer, *bows down* his whole body before the "God of the heights" (in the form of an inverted כ; כף = the cupped hand; cf. Th. Lescow [1966] 22). Moreover, "God on high" is a most unusual expression in the liturgical language of Israel, although מרום is not seldom used for heaven as the throne and dwelling place of God (Isa. 33:5; 57:15; Ps. 93:4; etc.). God is also said to come from the "heights" to save (Pss. 7:8[7]; 18:17[16]; 68:19[18]; 102:20[19]; 144:7; Job 16:19) or to punish (Jer. 25:30; Lam. 1:13). This is a powerful expression of the reason for humility before the majesty of God.

The question of with what one should come before God receives its first concrete answer in v. 6b. עולות, whole offerings, are burnt offerings meant to be completely consumed and to rise as smoke toward heaven. This general question, whose meaning and efficacy are apparently not entirely self-evident to the speaker, is immediately followed by a refinement. "Calves one year old," because of their tenderness, are a favored delicacy; in connection with burnt offerings, the expression occurs elsewhere only in Lev. 9:3. According to Lev. 22:27, calves are acceptable as sacrificial animals from their eighth day on (as are lambs and kids). Apparently v. 6b presents a first heightening in the quality of the offering. What is of course naturally presupposed here is a consciousness of guilt (cf. v. 7b) and a desire for atonement (cf. Num. 15:22–26; Judg. 20:26; 21:2–4; Job 1:5).

[6:7] Verse 7a continues with the more precise question (using the official technical expression of the priests) concerning what would be "pleasing to Yahweh." רצה refers to the act of (pleasingly) accepting the sacrifice according to regulations for approval and reckoning in the cult; this is expressed by the priest in the name of Yahweh, on the basis of his special knowledge of such matters. When the priest accepts the sacrifice, God at the same time accepts the person offering the sacrifice (cf. Lev. 1:4; 7:18; 19:7; 22:23, 25, 27; Jer. 14:10, 12; Ezek. 20:40f.; Hos. 8:13; Amos 5:22; Ps. 51:18[19], and Wolff, *Joel and Amos* 263). Now there follows an immense increase in the quantity of the offering (after an increase in quality suggested in v. 6b). That an individual would offer a thousand rams is a somewhat unusual act of this kind, for otherwise only kings such as Solomon are reported to have done so, and only on unique occasions (1 Kings 3:4; cf. 8:63; 1 Chron. 29:21; 2 Chron. 29:32). The escalation of the proposed sacrifices continues not only in numbers, from a thousand to ten thousand (cf. 1 Sam. 18:7; Ps. 91:7; Dan. 7:10) but also in the offer of oil, which departs from all units of measurement that are customary in the cult; now (as nowhere else) the verse speaks of "streams of oil." Usually the word נחל means a full stream or river (Ezek. 47:5; Amos 5:24; Ps. 104:10; etc.). For the cereal offering (later offered daily) oil was necessary for the preparation of cereal and baked goods (Exod. 29:40; Lev. 2:1, 15; 7:12) and also for preparation of oil used for anointing (Exod. 30:24). In such cases, the amount of oil used is always one-fourth, one-half, or one *hin* (about 1.5 to 5.5 liters; cf. Num. 28:5; 15:9; Exod. 30:24). "Ten thousand streams of oil" is an absolutely excessive amount of oil to be sacrificed by an individual. At the least, this raises the issue here whether the teacher who formulates the question in this way intends to make a caricature of what is becoming more and more nonsensical, especially the great size of sacrificial offerings.

In the last question (v. 7b), the teacher exaggerates in the extreme by pushing his examples of boundless sacrifices toward what is plainly frivolous. He portrays the sheer despair of the intention to give oneself fully to acts of propitiation; going beyond all legal possibilities provided by the Yahwistic cult, he offers to *sacrifice his firstborn.* In doing so, it is as though he reverts to the time preceding the story of Abraham's sacrifice (Gen. 22:2ff., 12ff.; cf. Exod. 22:28; 13:2 with Exod. 13:15; 34:20; Lev. 18:21; 20:2–5; Deut. 12:31; 18:10) and gives himself to the practices of the sex cults (2 Kings 3:27; 16:3; 21:6 and K. Elliger, *ZAW* 67 [1955] 17; idem, *Leviticus,* HAT 1/14 [1966] 241; cf. also Hos. 4:13f.; 5:7 and Wolff, *Hosea* 14f.; 85ff.; 101; the first child fathered in the sacred grove was sacrificed to the fertility god). According to 2 Kings 23:10 child sacrifice was made to the abominable god Moloch in the valley of Hinnom. Jeremiah (7:31; 19:5; 32:35) and Ezekiel (16:20f.; 20:26, 31) waged a vigorous polemic against this. Whoever thinks that he is able to heal dissension with God himself can only approach such extreme and long-since abolished sacrifices with questions. But at the same time, this is a confession that one cannot make amends for excessive rebellion against God, for the mistakes of one's own life (see above, p. 56 note 7b on פשע and חטאת). The teacher who formulated the questions in vv. 6f. has masterfully presented ad absurdum the possibility of cultic sacrifices and indirectly indicates to the individual that Yahweh does not make these kinds of demands upon his people.

[6:8] What Yahweh desires of people is communicated to them. The answer to all the questions in vv. 6f. may be well known. In any case, the preacher declares now in the perfect tense that it has (long ago) been "mediated" (on הגיד, see above, p. 105 and C. Westermann, *THAT* 2:31–37). "Communicating" the will of God in v. 8 corresponds to "declaring" Israel's sin in 3:8. The exegetes would like to know what kind of "communicators" the preacher is referring to. Is it perhaps priests who, as in Psalms 15 and 24, in allowing entrance to the temple, respond to the pilgrims' questions in a manner similar to, but not the same as, those in vv. 6f.? And are their answers, though somewhat removed, similar to v. 8 (cf. Pss. 15:2+3–5; 24:4 and K. Koch, *Probleme biblischer Theologie: Festschrift Gerhard von Rad* [1971] 239, note 8)? Or does our preacher have in mind certain prophets whose key themes can be recognized in the answer given in v. 8, such as Micah (3:1, 8, 9), Hosea (6:6; 12:7) and Amos (5:7, 24; 6:12) (Th. H. Robinson)? Or does he think of Moses, who has "declared" the covenant and the decalogue (Deut. 4:13; 5:5; E. Sellin; A. Weiser)? If the mediator of God's will remains unnamed here, it is particularly because, for the preacher, the content of the verse is more important than the speaker. Moreover, if he belonged to a larger circle of Deuteronomistic preachers (see above, pp. 170f.), he would have knowledge of more than figures who could be easily named. For example, corresponding to the sketch in vv. 4f., he knows the saving history from Moses to Balaam, from Egypt to the giving of the land; but he also knows the classical prophets, whose prophecies his school transmitted and interpreted, from Amos and Hosea to Micah and Jeremiah. The language of the beginning of the verse—"it has been told you"—expressly recalls Deut. 4:13; 5:5.

The singular address form is in accordance with the genre of priestly Torah used here (cf. אדם in the context of the laws regulating sacrifices in Lev. 1:2; 13:2; Num. 19:14; etc.). But according to Deut. 5:24; 8:3, אדם also denotes the person who hears the proclamation of the divine will; indeed, "man" is the one, standing in danger, who can exist before the "God on high" (cf. Mic. 6:6) only in an attitude of humility (cf. אדם in Isa. 2:9, 11, 17, 22). As an individual member of the people of God, אדם is reminded, in the light of the absence of direction from the sacrificial system, "of what is good." Here the preacher does not refer to a particular revelation of the law but rather to the good of the entire saving history according to vv. 4f. As in Deuteronomy, the remembrance of the redemption out of Egypt, the "house of bondage," as well as of all the saving deeds of God, serves the righteous obedience of the command-ments (cf. Deut. 5:15; 6:21; 15:15; 16:12; 10:12–22). It has to do with the good that brings well-being to people (cf. Deut. 10:13), not with what is oppressive, burdensome, tiring (v. 3a), not the "yoke" of the law (vv. 6f.). It has to do with that which redeems, not with that which enslaves (v. 4a); it has to do with the blessing that resists the desire to curse (v. 5a). To do "what is good" allows no room for the reproach that God's requirements are excessive.

What Yahweh "requires" (דרש) of human beings is therefore nothing other than what he has done for them. He does not require that a person ask the question "With what?" (במה v. 6a) in connection with offering sacrifices; in principle, God only asks the question "Who?" (מי Pss. 15:1; 24:3). "It's you, not something, God wants" (J. L. Mays, 136). מה . . . כי אם ("what except" = "nothing other," KBL³ 449) emphasizes here as in Deut. 10:12 the exclusive character of what follows, in contrast to the offering of sacrifices in their ever-increasing variety and number (vv. 6f.). In the exclusive *summa* presented in v. 8, three elements are to be noted: (1) three infinitive clauses express the new actions that God expects. (2) Well-known key words are employed ("it has been told you"). (3) At the same time, unique phrases that have a new ring disclose what Yahweh "requires" of human beings.

The first thing that is "good," expressed unpretentiously and con-cisely, is "to practice justice." The term משפט takes up a key theme in Micah's preaching (3:8; cf. 3:1, 9, and see above, pp. 104, 109). It means the orders of justice that are maintained and reinstituted by peaceful actions, by just court decisions and by conciliation within the community. Everyone in Israel is "to know" justice, especially every official (3:1b; cf. 2 Sam. 8:15); it is particularly these who "detest" justice (3:9). Besides "knowing justice," "*deeds* of justice" are expected, in correspondence to Yahweh's deeds (cf. Gen. 18:25; 1 Kings 8:45, 59; cf. Mic. 7:9). In the Old Testament, עשׂות משפט is more often predicated of persons than of God (cf. G. Liedke, *THAT* 2:1004). In Deut. 10:12ff., a passage closely related to our text, the phrase is taken up in v. 18 and given concrete expression: "He executes justice for the fatherless and the widows." To support persons who have no other legal counsel, or to reconcile those who have otherwise become alienated, or to heal broken communities—that is the good deed which deserves to be called justice. Justice should also be established between disputing parties (Jer. 7:5; Ezek. 18:8). Prov. 21:15 calls such execution of justice (עשׂות משפט) "a joy to the righteous, but a dismay to evildoers."

While the first requirement merely takes up a frequently occurring expression, the second phrase has a new ring to it. The genitive construction אהבת חסד occurs only here in the entire Old Testament. (In Qumran the phrase occurs in 1QS V,4; VIII,2, apparently with the context taken from Mic. 6:8; additionally, in II,24; V,25; X,26). To be sure, חסד occurs not seldom next to משפט (Jer. 9:23; Hos. 2:21; 6:5 [conj.]; 12:7; Zech. 7:9; Ps. 101:1). Even in these instances, something new is suggested by this familiar word. One could say that חסד has the goal of establishing justice; but it also gives the presupposition for this, namely, the constancy and closeness within the community. Of course, the secular usage of חסד never refers to the people as a whole, but always to a closer relationship between persons, such as man and wife, father and son, hosts and guests, relatives and friends (thus Zobel, *ThWAT* 3:58). A significant example is provided by Ruth 3:10; there Boaz says to Ruth, "You have made this last kindness [חסד toward Boaz] greater than the first [loving-kindness toward the mother-in-law]." The word's intimate quality, which has also given it a beloved place in lyric poetry (Zobel, 50), is strongly heightened by the connection with the infinitive construct אהבת, which functions as the *nomen regens* (cf. Bauer-Leander, 43g). Similar to those statements in which חסד and אהבה stand parallel, e.g., in Jer. 2:2; 31:3, this unique construct chain underscores the heartfelt love that belongs to the Old Testament's sense of community. The phrase characterizes the personal experience of loving affection, and also its object, the community, by a sense of kindness, an element necessary to life. Again the related text in Deut. 10:12ff. offers a concrete example: on the basis of Yahweh's love for the sojourner (vv. 15, 18b), Israel is encouraged to practice kindness toward the sojourner by providing loving gifts of food and clothing for them (v. 19). The "practice of justice" (עשות משפט) apparently has not achieved its goal if it has not accomplished the "love of kindness" (חסד אהבת).

Only the third infinitive construction explains the relationship between human conduct and God's deeds; it again sounds a new, unique note and indicates already with its comprehensiveness the accent that rests on this final statement. Not until these final words are the first two statements placed in the proper light. Last but not least, Yahweh requires that human beings "live attentively with your God." The final word, אלהיך, recalls the gift-giving God who leads forward, who in his love and sense of community, and with his deeds of justice, is devoted to human beings. "Your God"—that remains the final, life-giving word that echoes in one's hearing. "With" his God a person may "walk" and find the path that leads to what is good. In following upon this path, justice and love become new realities. Therefore such "walking" (לכת) expected by God is characterized by the unusual adverbial modifier, הצנע (see note 8c). Here we find an example of the liveliness, the empathy, and the ever-fresh linguistic capacity with which the Deuteronomistic preachers make clear to their audience how "walking with God" is rightly done. In Deut. 10:12, the most important comparable text (see above, p. 170), the expression first of all explains what "fear of Yahweh" means; then it elucidates the "love" for God with the better-known Deuteronomic formula "with all your heart and soul" (with conscious devotion of the will and genuine desire; cf. H. W. Wolff, *Anthropology of the Old Testament* 53; on this topic, cf. further Hos. 12:7bβ[6bβ] and Ps. 101:1–2). What does the new adverbial modifier הצנע bring to the phrase "to walk with your God"? The root צנע occurs within the Old Testament canon elsewhere only in Prov. 11:2 as an adjective (צְנוּעַ plural): "When pride comes, then disgrace; but with the צְנוּעִים is wisdom." The word thus stands in opposition to זָדוֹן = "pride," "arrogance." Consequently, in the light of the Vg *(humilitas)*, the translation "humble" might at first recommend itself. However, three observations make this explanation in Prov. 11:2, as in Mic. 6:8, appear inadequate: (1) it does not entirely fit with the resulting "wisdom" (see below on Sirach); (2) the *hiph.* form as such in Mic. 6:8 leads one to expect a more active characteristic for "walking with your God"; (3) Gk also points in this direction when it translates ἕτοιμον εἶναι τοῦ πορεύεσθαι μετὰ κυρίου θεοῦ σου, indicating that it thinks of "readiness." Only with the fourfold occurrence of the root in Sirach do we find any further help: Sir. 16:25; 32:3 (both instances are צנע *hiph.*, as in Mic. 6:8) and 34:22; 42:8 (צנוע) (on what follows, cf. Ph. Hyatt and H. J. Stoebe). Sirach 16:25 says, "I will impart my spirit by weight (בְּמִשְׁקָל), and declare my knowledge בְּהַצְנֵעַ." The saying is related to Yahweh's works (of creation); it characterizes an intellectual endeavor (as does Prov. 11:2). בהצנע stands parallel to במשקל, which means a "well-considered" speech (see its antonym, "arrogance," in Prov. 11:2). Accordingly, Gk translates בהצנע appropriately with ἐν ἀκριβείᾳ. Here the meaning of הצנע is given as "prudent," "circumspect," "shrewd." Sirach 42:8 supports this meaning, where the synonym זָהִיר = "discrete" occurs. The remaining texts in Sirach also confirm this conclusion (cf. Hyatt and Stoebe). In Qumran, the word possesses a meaning that is no different, although in the translations of it the rendering "humble" (in light of the traditional translation in Mic. 6:8) has incorrectly slipped in. This can be most clearly recognized as a mistake in 1QS IV,3–5, for there "humility" is expressed by the proper word עֲנָוָה, which stands next to הצנע לכת; this expression is given the meaning "prudent dealings"; cf. also 1QS V,4 and VIII,2, where, moreover, it is not "walking with God" but human interactions that are meant. On the other hand, the Deuteronomistic preacher in Mic. 6:8, as in Deut. 10:12–22, has in mind the right discipleship of the person who gives attention to Yahweh's history with his people and his prophets. For him it is good to walk "prudently," "attentively," "alertly" (thus one can now translate הצנע) with the God to whom history witnesses. But this does not mean that Yahweh makes a third requirement, something religious, that would be different from doing justice and acts of loving-kindness. Here, rather, each of these actions aids the other to achieve the entirety of life's goodness which God prepares and requires: execute justice, accomplish deeds of personal kindness, and be attentive to godliness.

Purpose and Thrust

No other saying in the book of the prophet Micah is cited so often or has become so influential as 6:8. Within the framework of the verse's prehistory and its later interpretation, we must note the intention of the verse within its own particular context in 6:2–8. Placed in the book of Micah, this passage gives to the book a completely different tone. Not one word of indictment is detectable here, to say nothing of a sentence of judgment passed on the entire nation or on certain groups (as in chaps. 1–3). Nor is there to be found any proclamation of future, or even eschatological, salvation in connection with the history of foreign nations (as in chaps. 4–5). While a solemn legal proceeding is undertaken (v. 2), the content of the passage calls Israel to remember the forgotten elements of saving history (vv. 3–5). Then increasingly demanding sacrificial require-ments are brought into the discussion (vv. 6f.); but at the conclusion of the passage, there is merely a brief, urgent reference to common, goodly conduct of human affairs that accords with the will of Israel's God as it is known from the tradition. What is silently presupposed is the possibility of repentance and amendment of life (otherwise than in chaps. 1–3). However, instead of compelling Israel to act, it merely calls for an impressive remembering (vv. 5, 8a). A didactic sermon-in-outline, the passage leads the reader from the present reality of Yahweh's great deeds of salvation, through a discussion of inappropriate cultic responses, and then on to clear statements of "what is good" for human beings. The emotion within the text is sustained throughout, from Yahweh's wooing address to "his people" (v. 2; "my people!" vv. 3a, 5a), to the trust-evoking reference to God in words that counsel them to "walk attentively with your God" (v. 8). The terms עַמִּי and אֱלֹהֶיךָ, words that provide the foundation for the passage, attest to the unbroken covenant relationship on God's part, although it is in need of renewal on Israel's part. The passage lends support to the believing community as it stands between the monumental catastrophes of history and the dawning of the new world.

The preacher's schooling in Deuteronomic-Deuteronomistic thought is unmistakable in all of this (see above, p. 170). In the literary context into which it has now been inserted, the concluding verse (v. 8), surely not by chance, takes up the commission "to practice justice" (see above, p. 180); however, now it is not intended to provide evidence for a prophetic accusation. Rather, it introduces a terse summary of Deuteron-omic-Deuteronomistic exhortations (on Deut. 10:12–22 cf. above, pp. 170f.). Just as Deuteronomy often exhibits a connection with Hosea (Wolff, *Hosea* xxi), so our preacher appropriates form-elements of the lawsuit speech in Hosea (4:1; 12:3); however, he employs them not to indict or condemn the people but to make room for Israel's indirect accusation against Yahweh. Yahweh takes it upon himself to testify in his own defense (see above, pp. 174f.). He speaks as one who is under attack, opposed, compromised (v. 3). The God of Israel is "not a prisoner of His own exalted status" (K. Barth, *Church Dogmatics* 4/2, trans. G. W. Bromiley [Edinburgh: T & T Clark, 1958] 42), but with humility calls himself into question. In refusing to bring an accusation against his people, and in placing himself into question, the way is being paved for the divine condescension of the redeemer. Whoever would serve him with sacrificial gifts as the "God on high" (v. 6a), misunderstands the history of his will to save.

Only by remembering God's saving deeds and his saving will does one become aware of God's goodness which brings blessings to him and to his neighbor. Thus the classic words of v. 8 are intended to be seen in the light of vv. 2–7. Verse 8 is at once an admonition to, and a description of, those whose lives have been redeemed. It presents the key words of faith that set life on the right path. The verse welds together what readily alienates secular from religious persons, bringing together civil righteousness and private humanitarianism. "Practice justice" (see above, p. 180)—that is the common, essential task of life that restrains cheating, covetousness, deception, and everything else that hinders or destroys life in community. Within the human community this zeal for "objective" justice, with its goal of creating a new community, should not be separated from the "subjective" desire to overcome the disruptions of life in community and "to love kindness" (see above, pp. 180f.). In his hymn for Pentecost, Paul Gerhardt called the "spirit of love," which is the "spirit of the Father and the Son," the "friend of kindness." The God of Israel has shown to people what kind of life-giving help it is when his justice and our love go hand in hand. His divine condescension in Israel, and above all in Jesus Christ, makes it easy for us "to walk attentively" with him who is called "your God" (see above, pp. 181f.). In his ways we find united the desire for justice and the zeal for love.

The didactic passage in Mic. 6:8b, with its three-part structure, is one of the greatest attempts to formulate, briefly and to the point, the *summa* of what is good. In Hosea we find a similar attempt (12:7[6]):

> You shall return to your God,
>> preserve love and justice,
>> and continually wait upon your God.

In the middle clause חסד and משפט stand side by side, while in Micah (v. 8b) these two words form the first and the second clauses. In the third clause, Hosea, wanting to evoke trust (and developing further the first clause), also speaks of "your God"; yet he prefaces these words with the phrase "continually waiting upon." In Hosea, this expectant waiting for God's deeds and directions makes possible the new, living community of loving care and justice, whereas in the Micah text, the thought is of the God who leads the way for his people with his deeds of salvation. In the New Testament the double commandment about love (Mark 12:28–31) provides a briefer summary. Conceptually, Paul stands closer to Micah in Rom. 13:8–10, in that he portrays love as "the fulfillment of the law," which is in accordance with the "mercies of God" (Rom. 12:1f.; cf. E. Käsemann, HNT 8a [1973] 344f.). Paul's words in vv. 11–14, which continue vv. 8–10, recall Hosea's phrase, "wait continually" (Hos. 12:7bβ [6bβ]). On the New Testament's understanding of Mic. 6:8b, it is useful to compare Galatians 5.

The theological summary found in Mic. 6:8 gives us insight into what is absolutely indispensable; and it offers clear directions on how we are to live in the interim period of history. These words are as simple as they are inspiring.

Micah 6:9-16

The Deceived Deceiver

Literature

F. C. Burkitt, "Micah 6 and 7: A Northern Prophecy," *JBL* 45 (1926) 159–161. A. Ehrman, "A Note on שׁי in Mic. 6:14," *JNES* 18 (1959) 156. R. Tournay, "Quelques Relectures Bibliques Antisamaritaines," *RB* 71 (1964) 504–536 (Michée VI,9–16: 514–524). Jörg Jeremias, "Die Deutung der Gerichtsworte Michas in der Exilszeit," *ZAW* 83 (1971) 330–354. I. Willi-Plein, *Vorformen der Schriftexegese innerhalb des Alten Testaments,* BZAW 123 (1971) 100–104. Th. Lescow, "Redaktionsgeschichtliche Analyse von Micha 6–7," *ZAW* 84 (1972) 182–212 (193–196). A. Ehrman, "A Note on Micah VI 14," *VT* 23 (1973) 103–105. O. Loretz, "Hebräisch *tjrwš* und *jrš* in Mi 6,15 und Hi 20,15," *UF* 9 (1977) 353–354. G. W. Ramsey, "Speech-Forms in Hebrew Law and Prophetic Oracles," *JBL* 96 (1977) 45–58.

Text

9 Yahweh's[a] voice calls to the city:
　　　　[It is prudent to fear your name.][b]
　　　Listen,[c] O tribe[d] and [e]'assembly of the [v. 10] city'![e]
　　'Can I forget'[a] the 'unjust liquid measure'[b]
　　　　　　[riches of injustice][c]
　　and [d]the cursed, diminished dry measure?[d]
11 Can I 'pronounce'[a] justice when the scale is unjust,
　　　when the bag contains deceptive (weight-)stones?
12 Because[a] her wealthy are full of violence
　　　and her inhabitants speak lies,
　　　　　[their tongue is deceitful[b] in their mouth,][c]
13 so I have surely 'begun'[a] to destroy you,
　　　to make you desolate because of your sins.
14 You will eat, but not be satisfied.
　　　　[Your physical pain (remains) in you.][a]
　　　You will put away,[b] but not save.
　　　　[And what you save I will give up to the sword.][c]
15 You will sow, but not reap.
　　　You will tread olives, but not anoint yourself with oil,
　　　　you will (tread) must, but not drink wine.

185

16   ['You have'ᵃ kept the precepts of Omri
and every deed of the house of Ahab;
you live according to their counsels,
so that I will give you up to destruction
and 'your'ᵇ inhabitants to a hissing;
the scorn of 'the peoples'ᶜ you shall bear.]ᵈ

9a Targ (נבייא דיוי) interprets by adding "the prophet of Yahweh's" voice.
9b R. Tournay translates: "Then your name will see success." But the word order
(object-verb-subject) presupposed by this seems forced. The ancient versions
without exception derive the word from יָרֵא ("to fear," "to honor") rather than
from ראה (MT, "to see," "to experience"); e.g., Vg: "et salus erit timentibus (יִרְאֵי)
nomen tuum." Gk (καὶ σώσει φοβουμένους τὸ ὄνομα αὐτοῦ) read each word differently (וְהוֹשִׁיעַ יְרְאֵי שְׁמוֹ [?] see *BHS*) from MT. Most likely the clause speaks of
Yahweh's name; and יראה should be vocalized as the infinitive of ירא (= יִרְאָה); cf.
Ps. 86:11b. The sentence interrupts the content of v. 9aα and 9b. It should be
taken as an interpolation. On the meaning of תושיה, cf. Prov. 3:21, and see below
for commentary on the verse.
9c Gk (ἄκουε) presupposes a singular form (שְׁמַע) because it considers only "tribe"
as the vocative connected with the verb.
9d Also Gk (φυλή) and Vg *(tribus)* translate "tribe" instead of "staff"; otherwise
Sellin, who supposes that here the "rod" is the instrument of God's punishment.
9e–10e MT ("and who has determined it; yet"), as a completion of the vocative, is
hardly intelligible. Since J. Wellhausen it is usually assumed that MT arose from
a misreading of וּמוֹעֵד הָעִיר, especially in that also Gk (πόλιν) read עִיר instead of עוֹד.
In other respects, Gk (καὶ τίς κοσμήσει πόλιν;) appears to presuppose וּמִי יַעֲדֶה עִיר
("and who adorns the city?"). Accordingly, I. Willi-Plein (101) proposes the
reading וּמִי יְעַד הָעִיר ("Hear this, tribal peoples, and whoever gathers in the city").
But מ is hardly a relative particle, and it would be unusual for יעד *niph.* to have a
subject in the singular (B. Renaud [1977] 328).
10a MT asks (without recognizable sense) about "fire" (אֵשׁ = אִשׁ in 2 Sam. 14:19;
Prov. 18:24), as also Gk (μὴ πῦρ), Syr and Vg *(adhuc ignis).* Targ (דאית) apparently
understood אֵשׁ = יֵשׁ. The parallel sentence in v. 11 leads one to expect a verbal
form. J. Wellhausen's proposed reading, הַאֶשֶּׁה (נשה, "to forget"), is to be preferred
to B. Duhm's suggestion to read הַאֶשָּׂא (נשא, "to bear").
10b Instead of "unjust house" (MT, בֵּית), it is quite likely that בַּת (liquid measure
for wine, oil, and other liquids) should be read in parallel to איפה (v. 10b) (B.
Duhm). The misreading of בַּת as בֵּית (as well as the interpolation of אצרות רשע)
brought with it the incorrect vocalization of the original רֶשַׁע as רָשָׁע ("house of the
guilty one").
10c The misreading בֵּית (see note 10b) may have led to the rhythmically superfluous interpretative phrase "treasures of injustice," especially since the combination of the two word "treasure house" is frequent (KBL³ 23). Both the repetition
of רשע as well as the extended length of v. 10a, compared with the three-stress
colon in v. 10b, suggest that אצרות רשע is an interpolation. I. Willi-Plein (100),
loosely following Gk, proposes a different but much too complicated solution.
10d–d Literally: "the scant ("lean") ephah that is accursed"; cf. Vg *(mensura
minor);* Gk (ὕβρεως) read זָדוֹן ("audacity") instead of רָזוֹן ("leanness").
11a MT ("to be pure") is not likely to have been spoken by Yahweh. Vg *(iusti-
ficabo)* and the sense of the context require the *piel* vocalization הַאֲזַכֶּה.
12a As a rule אשר is understood as a relative particle. Gk (ἐξ ὧν) and Vg *(in quibus)*
connect v. 12 to v. 11; but then the third person singular feminine suffixes in v. 12
(עשיריה—וישביה) would have no antecedent. Th. Lescow (195) thinks that the
relative particle that precedes עשיריה is secondary, due to dittography, especially
since without the particle the three-stress bicolon in the context is restored. The

third person singular feminine suffixes reach back for their antecedent beyond vv. 10–11 to "the city" in vv. 9–10aα (in addition to הָעִיר in 9a, see also note 9e–10e); to rearrange v. 12 after vv. 9–10aα (first word) is unnecessary (otherwise, K. Marti; A. Weiser; R. Vuilleumier). Heretofore, too little attention has been directed to the connection of v. 12a with v. 13, which is even closer than v. 12a is to v. 9. Even Syr understands אֲשֶׁר as a causal connection ("because"; see KBL³ 95, IIc). אֲשֶׁר in v. 12a introduces the motivation clause for the result clause begun by -וְגַם אֲנִי in v. 13a. Thus here a relationship of correspondence is established between guilt (v. 12a) and punishment (13). It should be noted that the same syntactic and stylistic device is used as in Jer. 13:25b–26; Ezek. 16:43 (further, cf. Ezek. 20:24f.; 5:11; 8:17f.; 9:10; Mal. 2:9), whereby אֲשֶׁר is given the same meaning as יַעַן; cf. Jer. 13:25b–26 (אֲשֶׁר) with Ezek. 16:43 (יַעַן אֲשֶׁר) and Ezek. 20:24 (יַעַן).

12b Gk (ὑψώθη) incorrectly derived רמיה from רום ("to exalt").

12c That v. 12b is a later interpolation (as v. 9aβ) is suggested by (1) the transition from the third person singular feminine suffixes to the third person plural masculine suffixes in v. 12b, as well as by (2) the superfluousness of a further three-stress colon.

13a MT (חלה *hiph.* "I have made ill") cannot be followed by the infinitive "to smite you." Gk (ἄρξομαι), α' (ἠρξάμην), Vg *(coepi)* fittingly read הַחִלּוֹתִי חלל *hiph.*). Perhaps the incorrect reading in MT was influenced by Isa. 1:5.

14a The meaning of יֵשַׁח has not yet been explained (KBL³ "filth"; W. Rudolph, "hunger"; A. Ehrman [1973] "dysentery"). Owing to metathesis of ח/שׂ, Gk (σκοτάσει) misread יֶחְשַׁךְ (*qal,* "it will become dark"), or even יַחְשִׁךְ (*hiph.,* "he darkens"; cf. Jer. 13:16; Ps. 105:28, thus A. Deissler). Since v. 14aβ departs from the stereotyped form of the main clauses within this context, which have a double verb (direct address) and the word וְלֹא in the futility curses (see below, p. 189) (cf. vv. 14aα, 14bα, 15a, 15b), v. 14aβ (as v. 14bβ, see note 14c) is to be taken as an interpolation. Since v. 14aβ, like v. 14bβ after it, is intended to explicate the immediately preceding sentence, the translation "hunger" is not improbable (cf. W. Rudolph, 116f.). However, the textual tradition suggests instead some kind of stomach illness (Syr *'brt',* "dysentery"; Targ ויהי לך למרע במעך) has a similar understanding: "you will become weak in your stomach"; cf. also Rashi (see A. Ehrman 1973). J. Wellhausen proposes: "Your fodder will give you a stomachache."

14b סוג *hiph.* (used for displacement of a landmark, Hos. 5:10; Deut. 19:14; Prov. 22:28; etc.) appears to have been similarly understood by Gk (καὶ ἐκνεύσει). Also worthy of consideration is וְתַשֵּׂג (נשׂג *hiph.*), "you will become rich"; cf. Lev. 25:47; also note 2:6c and Jörg Jeremias 341, note 44.

14c This sentence also departs from the recurrent form of the futility curses (see note 14a); by picking up the word תפלט, yet changing from the *hiph.* of the context to the more usual *piel,* it gives the impression of being a commentary on v. 14bα (cf. B. Duhm, 53).

16a Instead of the unusual verb form in MT (שׁמר *hithpael,* "and he will watch himself"), which interrupts the direct address style (second person) and which is to be considered a scribal error, since J. Wellhausen וַתִּשְׁמֹר has been read, following Gk^Mss, θ' (ἐφύλαξας), Vg *(et custodisti),* it is to be assumed that there is metathesis of ר/שׁ in the unvocalized consonantal text.

16b Instead of a third person singular feminine suffix ("her inhabitants"), a second person suffix would be expected after אֹתֵךְ. B. Duhm proposed וְיֹשְׁבַיִךְ. Does MT derive from וישביה in v. 12? In that case, it would refer to "the city" (vv. 9a, 10aα [conj.]), whereas the direct address forms of the second person singular and plural refer to the inhabitants (as in vv. 13–15) or to the "tribe" (v. 9b).

16c Given the sense of the context, MT ("my people") is less probable than Gk (λαῶν), which presupposes עַמִּים. On the phrase נשׂא חרפת עמים, cf. Ezek. 36:15.

16d On the secondary character of v. 16, see below, pp. 189f., 197f.

Form

The passage 6:2–8, incorporating the forms of the lawsuit speech and the didactic sermon, is addressed to the people of God and to the individuals in their midst. Following this text, v. 9 commences a different rhetorical unit concerning "the city," which in its entirety is formulated in the style of a first person Yahweh speech. Not until 7:1 is this replaced by a human voice, speaking in the first person, and by a different theme. Such an abrupt caesura before 6:9 and after 6:16 is not to be found within 6:9–16, even though the rhetorical forms within the passage are diverse. But it would not do justice to the clear linkages of these forms if the passage were said to be merely a "connecting of fragments one after the other" (thus T. H. Robinson, 147f.).

On the whole, the text according to its structure is a self-contained prophetic judgment speech which in several places has been reworked by the insertion of secondary material. The original basic text exhibits two main parts, the accusation (vv. 10–12) and the announcement of punishment (vv. 13–15), which are clearly distinct from each other. Verses 9b–10aα (conjecture concerning the first word) begins the prophecy with a summons to hear. In v. 9aα an introduction (merely literary?) prefixed to the passage presents Yahweh as the one who calls and "the city" as the party he addresses. Between this introduction and the summons to hear we find a prayer—a parenthesis, as it were, in the present form of the transmitted text (see note 9b)—in v. 9aβ which reminds the reader of the aforementioned name of God (v. 9aα), and which is intended to provide the motivation for "hearing" (v. 9b).

The accusation in vv. 10aα (second word)–12a, which is the first main section of the judgment speech, contains two parts that can be distinguished on the basis of style. Verses 10–11 speak of the concrete transgressions arising from a deceitful attitude that infests commercial dealings. These transgressions are expressed in the form of rhetorical questions intended to establish the impossibility that such deeds can go unpunished by Yahweh. Thus even the unique style of the questions that present the accusation suggests the necessity of Yahweh's punishment. The second part of the accusation in v. 12a, which expands and summarizes the catalogue of guilt, places oppression and lying in a direct syntactic relationship to the corresponding reactions of Yahweh (in v. 13), if indeed אשר in v. 12a introduces a motivation clause for the announcement of Yahweh's intervention in v. 13a (. . . וגם־אני), precisely as in Jer. 13:25b (cf. Ezek. 16:43 and see note 12a). Thus in an impressive way both parts of the indictment already make a connection with and point toward the announcement of judgment.

The second main section also exhibits two parts that are form-critically differentiated. First, the expression וגם־אני (as in Jer. 13:26 and in the Ezekiel texts mentioned in note 12a) in v. 13 announces in the style of a first person Yahweh speech that Yahweh's retributive action is already beginning; with the reference back to "your sins" (v. 13b), the announcement itself again brackets together guilt and punishment in a relationship of correspondence. In the second part of the announcement of judgment, the prophet, continuing the direct address style (second

person singular masculine of v. 13), elucidates the consequences of Yahweh's punishing blows by means of five futility curses (A. S. van der
Woude [1976] 231f. calls them "sayings of inefficacy"; cf. "futility curses"
in D. R. Hillers, *Treaty-Curses and the Old Testament Prophets,* Biblica et
Orientalia 16 [Rome 1964]), which render fruitless significant human
actions that are supposed to promote life. The fivefold ולא ("but not")
effects the total frustration of an action. In each instance an important
life-sustaining action is mentioned (direct address, second person singular), but then its expected result is immediately negated with a curse-
like ולא. This form of the curse already occurs in Amos 5:11; Hos. 4:10;
Lev. 26:26b; Deut. 28:30, 39–41, as well as in the ancient Near East, e.g.,
in the treaties of the Sefire texts (*KAI* 222 A 22–24; cf. Wolff, *Amos and
Joel* 247, and A. S. van der Woude [1976] 231f.).

The five stereotyped futility curses, characterized especially by ולא,
contain clearly recognizable secondary additions similar to the interpolations within the introduction (v. 9aβ) and the accusation (v. 12b). The
later addition in v. 14aβ is presumably intended to declare that the
famine will increase in intensity (see note 14a). Again borrowing the first
person style of the Yahweh speech from v. 13, the interpolation in v.
14bβ (see note 14c) vividly shows that any attempt "to save" will be
frustrated by Yahweh's intervention with military weapons in war.
Finally, the interpolator extensively broadens the historical horizon by
appending v. 16 (again appropriating the first person style of the Yahweh
speech in v. 16ba). Here the correspondence of guilt and punishment is
viewed in light of the history of the Northern Kingdom under Omri and
Ahab. From a form-critical perspective, the secondary character of the
verse is especially evident in that the issue of guilt (after the announcement of punishment already made in vv. 13–15) is treated once again and
in a manner entirely different from vv. 10–12. This later reference to guilt
appropriates individual catchwords from the older text which the redactor had before him; cf. יושביה in v. 16b with v. 12a; לשמה in v. 16b with
השמם in v. 13b. As noted above concerning the interpolation in v. 14bβ,
here too it appears that v. 16 is an interpretation that derives from a
different situation (see below, "Setting"). On the whole, therefore, we
have in 6:9–16 a judgment speech, editorially reworked at several points,
which makes use of various form elements in the individual parts of the
passage.

The change of persons in the pronouns and verbs corresponds to
the lack of unity in style. While the third person singular feminine suffixes
in v. 12a are to be construed with "the city" (v. 9) as their antecedent, in
the interpolation in v. 12b the third person plural suffixes refer to the
city's inhabitants. The announcement of punishment in v. 13 shifts to the
second person singular masculine, which addresses (in a collective sense)
the "tribe" (and 'the assembly', see note 9e–10e) as the inhabitants who
are guilty and who are the objects of judgment. This form of address
(second person singular masculine) continues through vv. 14–15. Uncertainty does not arise again until the later addition in v. 16. There in the
transmitted text the second person singular masculine and plural, as well
as the third person singular masculine and third person singular feminine, which refer back to the addressees of the passage, change irregu-

larly—a further indication of the verse's secondary character. On conjectural emendations, cf. notes 16a and 16b.

In the synonymously parallel prosodic units of the original passage, the rhythmical structure is mostly cola of three or four stresses.

Setting

This complex of sayings concerns the "city" (v. 9aα). Its name is not given. This in itself would suggest that the city is most likely Jerusalem. At least since Jeremiah and Ezekiel, none but Jerusalem is so conspicuously called העיר (cf. Jer. 6:6; 8:16; 17:24f.; Ezek. 4:3; 5:2; 7:15; Lam. 1:19; 2:12, 15, etc.). Moreover, it should be taken into consideration that the later Samaria is never compared with the precepts of Omri and Ahab, kings of the Northern Kingdom (6:16; A. S. van der Woude [222f.] considers the unnamed city to be Samaria), although Jerusalem apparently is, according to the Deuteronomistic history (2 Kings 21:3, 13; cf. 2 Kings 8:27; on further reminiscences of the Deuteronomistic history in the passage, see below, pp. 197f.). Furthermore, the expression נתן לחרב (v. 14bβ; cf. Jer. 15:9) and especially נתן לשמה ולשרקה (v. 16ba; cf. Jer. 19:8; 25:9, 18!; 29:18; on v. 16bβ, cf. Ezek. 36:15) belong to the closely related Jeremiah tradition. These linguistic connections, on the whole, are hardly to be dated before, and are more likely after, the middle of the sixth century (cf. Jörg Jeremias, 342f.; B. Renaud, 338ff.). Nor are these connections in 6:9–16 to be separated from Jerusalem.

To be sure, 6:16 (as v. 14aβ,bβ; see above, p. 189) belongs to a later redaction of this complex of sayings. The interpolations in v. 9aβ and v. 12b, which recall the language of wisdom, are at least as late, if not even postexilic. To what time, therefore, should we date this text (vv. 9aα,b–12a, 13–14aα,ba, 15), to which later interpretations have been added?

Given the structure and theme of this judgment speech, critics have tried to argue that the passage comes from Micah (recently, W. Rudolph). But the ancient prophecies of Micah in chaps. 1–3 are more tightly knit; nor do they exhibit a comparable multiplicity of forms which have been dovetailed together, as in 6:9ff. The linking of accusation and corresponding announcement of punishment in vv. 12f. by the peculiar syntactic form אשר ... וגם־אני points to the time of Jeremiah and Ezekiel (see above, note 12a), i.e., to the Babylonian era, around the beginning of the exile. Consonant with this period is the initial content of Yahweh's threat in v. 13a: "Thus also have I 'begun' to smite you." The sentence can be understood as a reference to the Babylonian danger around 600. We may surely assume that the passage in all its parts, including the futility curses (vv. 14f.) joined to the preceding verses, as well as the rhetorical questions that present the accusation (vv. 10f.), appropriates older material. But this, finally, is hardly reason to consider Micah its author, for remaining is the difficulty of how to account for the literary differences between 6:9–16 and the other original prophecies of Micah (cf. J. L. Mays, 14f.). Hence, the formation of the complex of sayings in 6:9–16 is best understood if we date it toward the end of the sixth century. Purely in terms of its date, the passage is not far removed from 6:2–8 (see above, p. 171). Nevertheless, in 6:9ff. we meet threat instead of admonition, judgment instead of hope.

Commentary

[6:9] The Yahweh speech in v. 9aα is introduced by an unusual form; instead of the messenger formula "Thus said Yahweh," as in 2:3 (cf. 3:5 MT), we find the phrase "voice of Yahweh." קול is not to be understood as an interjection ("Hear!"), which occurs frequently in Isa. 40:3, 6 (thus J. L. Mays; cf. KBL), although even there such an interpretation is without compelling arguments (cf. K. Elliger, *Exodus,* BK 11, ad loc.). Nor is there any indication here of a theophany description, in which case the threatening voice would be the thunder of a cloudburst (cf. Amos 1:2; Isa. 30:30f.; Ps. 29:3–5, 7–9). Rather, because of the following "summons to hear" (v. 9b), the expression refers to the proclaiming voice of Yahweh which calls for a decision to obey, as we find in more than a dozen instances in Deuteronomy (4:36; 5:25–28; 8:20; 13:19; 15:5; 18:16; 26:14; 27:10; 28:1, 2, 15, 45, 62); for Yahweh's voice determines whether there is blessing or curse, life or death. Nevertheless, in no other instance in the Old Testament is קול יהוה connected with the predicate קרא(י). Thus the initial phrase in v. 9 provides a unique introduction to a prophetic saying. The phrase can be understood to make a literary connection with 6:2–8, especially since that text also appropriates Deuteronomistic language (see above, p. 170). The redactor formulated יקרא (Yahweh's voice "proclaims") as a presupposition for inserting the שמעו-passage ("Hear!"; cf. שמע את-/בקול יהוה in the above mentioned texts of Deuteronomy) which he appropriates, making the addressee ("the city") correspond to the beginning of the original rhetorical unit in vv. 9b–10a (first word in Gk; see notes 9e–10e). Moreover, the third person singular feminine suffixes in v. 12a and v. 16bα have their antecedent in "the city." The initial sentence, announcing the "voice of Yahweh which calls," is an appropriate beginning insofar as the "I" of Yahweh speaks in the accusation (vv. 10–11), also in the announcement of punishment (v. 13), and even in the redactional additions in v. 14bβ and v. 16bα.

A prayer addressed to Yahweh (שמך) in v. 9aβ (on its vocalization and translation, see note 9b) was added later to the redactor's introduction. It contains wisdom language, as the occurrence of תושיה indicates in Prov. 2:7; 3:21; 8:14; Job 6:13; Isa. 28:29. Although the word's etymology is uncertain (cf. H. Wildberger, *Jesaja 1–12,* 10/3, note "b" on Isa. 28:29), nevertheless its usage as a synonym for עצה in Prov. 8:14 and Isa. 28:29, and its occurrence in Job 6:13, make clear that its meaning lies between "prudence," "shrewdness," and "success." The word summarizes what Ps. 111:10a develops under the theme of "fear of Yahweh." The word "prudent" in this compound noun clause is the predicate of the subject (sentence) "to 'fear' your name." The expression picks up the wording of the petition in Ps. 86:11b: "Unite my heart to fear thy name" (cf. also Mal. 3:20[4:2]; Ps. 61:6; 102:16; 112:1). The content of the prayer inserted here is related to the speaking of Yahweh's voice (v. 9aα) and to the summons to hear his voice (v. 9b). When the following verses present the voice of the divine judge, the interpolator confesses before God his insight that respectful obedience (ירא) toward the proclamation of the "name" is true intelligence, the opposite of foolishness, shortsightedness, and failure.

The "summons to hear" (v. 9b) commences the judgment speech available to the redactor from the tradition. The vocatives connected with the summons are unusual in the prophetic material. The word מטה occurs mostly in the Priestly document for "tribe" (cf. also Josh. 7:1; 1 Kings 8:1). Does this refer to the tribe of Judah and thus to Judeans who came from the provincial settlements to "the city" of Jerusalem to engage in trade (cf. Jer. 7:2b)? If the conjecture offered in 9e–10e is correct, the "assembly of the city" is to be distinguished from the "tribe" in that the former refers to the gathering of permanent residents in "the city," i.e., the Jerusalemites. In this case, these words of address would correspond to the expression, frequent in Jeremiah, "men of Judah and inhabitants of Jerusalem," which almost always (except for 36:31) occurs in this word-order (Jer. 4:3f.; 11:2, 9; 17:25; 18:11; 32:32; 35:13; according to W. Thiel, WMANT 41 [1973] 142, among others, the words are a Deuteronomistic formula). The unusual character of the expressions designating the addressees may have to do with the accusation in vv. 10–12, which is concerned with commerce and trade. The rarity of these designations presumably contributed to an early misreading of the text. That "city and tribe" were likely mentioned next to "assembly and city" accounts for the various interchanges of feminine and masculine, singular and plural pronouns.

[6:10] Beginning with the second word in v. 10, the legal indictment is initiated by two double questions which, as rhetorical questions, allow the intended audience to confirm indirectly their own culpability. The first question (v. 10) is concerned with false measures used in trade, the second (v. 11) with scales and weights. The most important cubic measures for liquid and dry goods are mentioned first. *Bath* is used for water, wine, and oil (1 Kings 7:26, 38; Isa. 5:10; Ezek. 45:14; 2 Chron. 2:9); *ephah,* for grains of all kinds, groats, and meal (Lev. 5:11; Judg. 6:19; 1 Sam. 17:17; Ruth 2:17). According to Ezek. 45:11, bath and ephah are of equal capacity. It is hardly possible to determine their precise volume, which varied in ancient Israel according to location and time. During the Neo-Assyrian and Neo-Babylonian eras, bath and ephah were about 30–32 liters (cf. G. Schmitt, *BRL*² 205; concerning factors that remain uncertain, see R. de Vaux, *Ancient Israel: Its Life and Institutions* [1961] 199–206; further, Barrois, *Manuel* 2:250; *IDB* 4:834f.; W. Zimmerli, *Ezekiel* 2 [Hermeneia] 476f.; on the archeological data, see P. Welten, 50–54). While there was of course no international office of weights and measures, we may assume that a city such as Jerusalem and its dependent provincial settlements would have had binding units of measure. When the Old Testament occasionally speaks of אֶבֶן הַמֶּלֶךְ, the "king's (weight)-stones" (2 Sam. 14:26), and more often of שֶׁקֶל הַקֹּדֶשׁ, the "weights of the sanctuary" (Exod. 30:13, etc.), such expressions refer to the measures of the royal court and of the priesthood in the temple which served as valid norms.

This prophetic text is concerned with intentional departures from such norms. It condemns the falsification of liquid measure as בת רשע (see note 10b). The expression is formulated in antithesis to בַּת צֶדֶק, the "accurate bath" (cf. Ps. 45:8[7]; and Ezek. 45:10). The statement about the "inaccurate bath," corresponding to the official language concerning just measurements, receives a drastic heightening in its parallel concerning the dry measure, which is called "the emaciated, accursed ephah." The unfalsified ephah is called אֵפָה צֶדֶק (Ezek. 45:10; Lev. 19:36). Here the expression "ephah of emaciation" for a falsified ephah is unique; רזון is otherwise used in connection with the human body (Ps. 106:15); in Isa. 10:16 רזון ("leanness") stands in contrast to "stoutness." With this word the prophet portrays the unlawful "reduction" of the ephah (Amos 8:5); he thus presupposes "two kinds of ephahs" (as in Deut. 25:14; Prov. 20:10), a "small" and a "large" one (Deut. 25:14), whereas there ought to be only a "full and just measure" (Deut. 25:15; אֵיפָה שְׁלֵמָה וָצֶדֶק). The "emaciated ephah" deceives the buyer with a small amount of goods. It is therefore an "execrable," an "accursed" ephah. זעם is a rather seldom-used word for curse. It is used for human "malediction" (Prov. 24:24) as well as for the "curse" of God (Num. 23:7f.; Mal. 1:4). Here the word is to be understood as a "terrifying threat" (W. Schottroff, *Der altisraelitische Fluchspruch,* WMANT 30 [1969] 28). It occurs in appropriate contexts in older prophecies (Amos 8:5b, 7), teachings of the wise (Prov. 20:10), and in legal maxims (Deut. 25:16; cf. Lev. 19:36b).

The presumable interpolation (see note 10c) calls the profit from the falsified measure אצרות רשע, "unjustly gathered supplies," something that is also denounced by Amos (3:10). In addition, the interpolation mentions "the house of the guilty one" (by changing the vocalization of "unjust bath"; see note 10b); there the deceptive merchants store their supplies. Moreover, such a house stands under the curse of Yahweh (Prov. 3:33; 14:11).

The statements about false measures provoke questions from Yahweh: "Can I forget . . .?" Here the word נשה (see note 10a) stands in antithesis to זכר, the legal term for "to remember," " "to call to remembrance," "to declare," "to speak" (before the court). Yahweh's righteousness forbids "forgetfulness"; it requires that one "remembers." In the face of a similar transgression (Amos 8:5!), Amos 8:4–7 speaks of Yahweh's oath "never to forget" (שכח, v. 7b) such deeds. In the language of the prophets, "not to forget," "to remember guilt," "to punish transgression," are synonymous expressions (cf. especially Hos. 8:13; 9:9 [also 7:2] and Wolff, *Hosea* 145). The accusations formulated as questions demand the agreement of the audience and call upon them to have an understanding of righteousness.

[6:11] Similarly, v. 11 contains questions concerning the use of balances and weights. The dual form מאזנים refers to both pans of the scale required by the stationary scale as well as by the hand-held scale (cf. H. Weippert, *BRL*² 355). The scale-pans from Old Testament times that have been found have a diameter of only ca. 10 cm. They were used especially for weighing money (not yet in coin; Jer. 32:10) and also for certain wares that were sold only in small amounts (such as spices; Exod. 30:24). (Amounts of grain, meal, wine, and oil were determined by cubic measure.) Items were weighed by means of standardized weights, for which stones (אֲבָנִים) were used (numerous in Judah); most of them were round, with a flat side on which the size of the measure was inscribed (H. Weippert, *BRL*² 93f.). They were kept in a (leather) bag (כיס, Deut. 25:13; Prov. 16:11).

In the ancient Near East, scales and stone weights were the most common means of deception in the trading of wares. The Code of Hammurabi already prescribed: "If a merchant lent grain or money at interest and when he lent (it) at interest he paid out the money by the small weight and the grain by the small measure, but when he got (it) back he got the money by the [large] weight (and) the grain by the large measure, [that merchant shall forfeit] whatever he lent" (*ANET* 169:94). In the extensive hymn to Shamash it says: "He who handles the scales in falsehood, He who deliberately changes the stone weights (and) lowers [their weight], will make himself lie for the profit and then lose [his bag of weights]. He who handles the scales in truth, much . . . As much as possible . . . He who handles the measure . . ." (*ANET* 388:51–56; also A. Falkenstein and W. von Soden, *Sumerische und akkadische Hymnen und Gebete* [1953] 244). In the Egyptian *Book of the Dead* (Saying 125, lines 16f.), we find these words in a negative confession of sin: "I have not added anything to the weight of the balance. I have not diminished anything in the plummet of the scales" (*Near Eastern Religious Texts Relating to the Old Testament,* ed. W. Beyerlin [1978] 66). Also, in the Old Testament false weights and scales are the most frequently mentioned as instruments of the merchant's deception; references are found in the prophets (Amos 8:5; Hos. 12:8; Ezek. 45:10), in proverbial wisdom (Prov. 11:1; 16:11; 20:10), and in legal statutes (Lev. 19:36; Deut. 25:13, 15).

In our text the "just scale" (מֹאזְנֵי צֶדֶק Ezek. 45:10; Lev. 19:36; cf. Job 31:6), which belongs to Yahweh's just ordinances (מֹאזְנֵי מִשְׁפָּט, Prov. 16:11), has become מֹאזְנֵי רֶשַׁע, "unjust scale." To alter the scale so that it was no longer true, one used heavier scale-bowls or bent the crossbeam (see Amos 8:5 and Wolff, *Joel and Amos* 327). Such actions turn it into a מֹאזְנֵי מִרְמָה (Prov. 11:1), "deceptive scale." Our text calls the stone weights אַבְנֵי מרמה. This means not only that the weights depart from the norm of the אַבְנֵי צֶדֶק (Lev. 19:36); they are also used with the intent of giving the seller an unfair advantage (on מרמה [רמה], see M. A. Klopfenstein, *Die Lüge nach dem Alten Testament* [1964] 310ff.). In this case the deception arises from the fact that the merchant uses "two kinds of stones" (Prov. 20:10), namely, "a large and a small stone" (Deut. 25:13), not only a "just, full [i.e., intact] stone" (אֶבֶן שְׁלֵמָה וָצֶדֶק, Deut. 25:15; cf. Prov. 11:11). The smaller stone, which the merchant uses for his own advantage deceptively to weigh the money for making a purchase, could have lost its normal weight through damage or many years of usage. The "bag" conceals the false as well as the authentic stones. Thus the deceptive stones as well as the bent scales and the falsified cubic measures enable one to obtain more goods for less money. Yahweh again asks, "Shall I pronounce just?" (see note 11a). Shall I declare not guilty such acts of deception, secret cunning, and covert fraud? The preposition ‍ב introduces the instrument of deception, "in whose presence," "in the face of which," Yahweh utters his judgment.

[6:12] After the preparation made by the questions in vv. 10f., the Yahweh speech takes a new turn in v. 12, summarizing and then proceeding further. The "rich people" are expressly said to be inhabitants of the city (the suffixes of the third person singular feminine in v. 12aα,β are to be construed with עיר in vv. 9f.; see note 12a). They have not only pocketed profits, exploiting the poor by sordid methods; their superior position enables them to act with violence. This accusation recalls Mic. 2:1f., 8–10; 3:2f., 10. The word חמס means the aggressive attack upon life and limb of one's neighbor; it means naked force, which can take all forms of oppression and violation of one's legal rights, including the arbitrary and brutal shedding of blood (Amos 3:9f.; Jer. 22:3; Ezek. 45:9; Isa. 59:7; see Wolff, *Joel and Amos* 193f.). To say that the rich "are full" (מלא) of violence means that they are completely controlled by it (cf. pp. 104f. on Mic. 3:8). Justice and righteousness, love and mercy, are unable to dwell in them. Thus in this context עשיר refers to the rich who are unscrupulous, as in 2 Sam. 12:1–4; Prov. 18:23; 22:7.

Almost essential to their acts of violence is the speaking of lies, which they must conceal (חמס and שקר occur together, e.g., in Ps. 27:12; further, cf. Zeph. 1:9; Isa. 53:9). False statements are found not only in every type of aggressive speech and arbitrary insult; they are made especially in bearing false witness before the court (Pss. 27:12; 101:7; 1 Kings 21:10ff.). Moreover, שקר denotes all actions and deeds connected with swindling and cheating in everyday life, especially in commercial dealings (vv. 10f.), with and without words (cf. M. A. Klopfenstein, *Die Lüge* 155–158).

The gloss in v. 12b (see note 12c), using familiar vocabulary (cf. Pss. 120:2f., 52:4), lends emphasis to the accusation against deceptive speech in v. 12aβ. The gloss refers not only to individual false statements; it also indicates that in the mouth of those accused here, nothing is to be found but a lying tongue, thus preventing one true word from passing between their lips.

[6:13] The word אשר in v. 12a is already an indication that the verse functions as the motivation clause for v. 13 (see note 12a); at the same time, the declaration of punishment in v. 13 twice refers back to the preceding accusation. In the first instance, the initial phrase וגם־אני emphasizes the strict correspondence between Yahweh's intervention and human wickedness; in the second, the phrase על־חמאתך summarizes the previously mentioned sins as the reason for Yahweh's punitive actions. The phrase וגם־אני, which introduces Yahweh's deeds of judgment, indicates that they correspond to human transgression. Used to connect two sentences together, this phrase is familiar from Ezekiel where, following the phrase, Yahweh's punishment is expressly and repeatedly emphasized with the assertion, "I will requite their deeds upon their heads" (i.e., I will cause them to encounter their own conduct; Ezek. 9:10; 16:43; cf. further the similarly structured sayings mentioned in note 12a). Thus in our passage also, Yahweh's announced deeds of punishment are to be understood in connection with the city's culpable deeds. This is indicated by the following futility curses (v. 14f.), which develop Yahweh's acts of "smiting" and "destruction" (v. 13). When v. 13a initially speaks of the "beginning" (see note 13a) of Yahweh's .blows, this suggests harvest failure as well as political and military disaster. The meaning of שמם *hiph.*, in light of Lev. 26:31f.; Jer. 10:25; 49:20; Ezek. 30:12, 14; Ps. 79:7, is more likely the desolation and destruction resulting from military actions, in which connection the personal object (found only in Ezek.

20:26, in addition to Mic. 6:13) here suggests human involvement in the "devastation" and "shocking horror."

The form of address in the second person singular masculine (in contrast to the third person singular feminine in v. 12a!) can be explained without difficulty. First, in prophetic judgment speeches, it is not unusual to find a shift to direct address at the beginning of the announcement, after the accusation in the third person (merely cf. Mic. 2:3; 3:6, 12; Amos 4:2f.). Second, this has been influenced by the direct address form of the immediately following fertility curses, in view of which v. 13 was apparently formulated. This also accounts for the singular, since the curses are addressed primarily to individuals (cf. Deut. 28:29–31, 38–40). (On the form of the original text and its expansion, see above, pp. 188f.)

[6:14] The series of presumably five original curses begins with the declaration of famine; it occurs frequently in familiar series of curses and related forms of a similar type (cf. Hos. 4:10; Amos 4:8; Isa. 9:19; Hag. 1:6; Lev. 26:16). The amount of food is not enough to satisfy hunger. An elementary requirement for human survival is endangered. Famine can be caused by a bad harvest (Hag. 1:6), locust plague (Deut. 28:38), as well as by attack of an enemy (Lev. 26:25f.). In this context (v. 13a!) the connection with vv. 10–12 is of interest. Yahweh's intervention corresponds to the dishonest trading and violent oppression which endangers the neighbor (on v. 14aβ, see note 14a). The next curse refers even more clearly to deceptive business dealings, if indeed סוג hiph. connotes a secret "putting away" that corresponds to the nocturnal "removal" of the "boundary (stone)" (cf. Hos. 5:10; Deut. 19:14; 27:17; Prov. 22:28; 23:10). No "sharp practices" will result in success ("deliverance").

Like v. 14aβ, v. 14bβ does not fit the pattern; at the same time, v. 14bβ introduces a new theme. The glossarist shifts from the individual sphere of city and provincial commerce (vv. 9–12) to the arena of military actions that plunder and are immediately life-threatening ("sword"); here the phraseology is reminiscent of Jer. 15:9b; 21:7; Ezek. 6:12, suggesting that v. 14bβ belongs to the time around 587.

[6:15] With three further futility curses, v. 15 clearly addresses itself to agrarian themes. The threat that the sower will not reap the harvest is a frequent theme in comparable series of curses (Deut. 28:30, 38; cf. Hos. 8:7; Hag. 1:6; Job 31:8). In the context of this passage, the prophet, standing at the marketplace in Jerusalem (see above, p. 192 on vv. 9f.), now turns his gaze more upon the traders who come from the provinces, or upon farmers who live in Jerusalem, whereas v. 14 also included the city's buyers and traders. Besides sowing and harvest, the verse also speaks of preparing oil and wine. The phrase דרך זית is a general description of processing olives, although "to tread" (דרך) is not to be taken literally for olives—as it is for grapes (Amos 9:13). The olives (containing pits) as a rule were crushed in a mortar; then the pulp, placed in a folded cloth, was pressed out by wringing the cloth (see D. Kellermann, BRL² 238–240). Most probably, תירוש is not to be understood as a noun ("grape juice," "must," or "new wine"), but as a verb, II ירש (imperfect, second person singular masculine // דרך) = "to tread." Preparation of oil and wine becomes meaningless, since those addressed here will not be able to anoint themselves with oil, nor will they enjoy the wine. To be deprived of enjoying one's wine after the hard work of preparing it is, given all the variations, a fixed part of the futility curse (cf. Deut. 28:30b, 39; Amos 5:11b; Zeph. 1:13bβ).

Whereas in Amos (5:11) and Hosea (4:10) we find only a simple doubling of the futility curses, Deuteronomy (28:30, 31, 38–41) contains a longer series which as such has a parallel only in Mic. 6:14f.; in both instances there is also a tendency toward varying the strict form by means of expansions (see above, p. 189). The series of curses in vv. 14ff. means to indicate that, when the presupposition for honest and upright personal dealings no longer exists (vv. 10–12), the futility of all vital, human activities becomes a concrete example of Yahweh's punishing blow (v. 13). In Deut. 28 the curses fall upon all who "do not obey the voice of Yahweh" (cf. Deut. 28:15 with Mic. 6:9aα,b).

[6:16] We already noted that when the introduction (v. 9aα) was literarily attached to the older, original saying, the latter was presumably incorporated into Deuteronomistic tradition; now in v. 16 the presence of Deuteronomistic language is even clearer. The shift of the style of address from second person singular to second person plural—familiar from the strata in the book of Deuteronomy—also occurs here (singular: v. 16aα,bα; plural: v. 16aβ,bβ) and might also point to two literary phases in the verse. In both we find a new formulation of guilt (v. 16a) as well as a new kind of announcement of punishment (v. 16b).

"Omri" and "the house of Ahab" are named as prominent representatives of the Northern Kingdom of Israel. The Assyrians named the Israelite state after Omri, founder of the royal residence at Samaria (886–874; cf. 1 Kings 16:23–28), calling it *Bît-Ḫumrî* (*ANET* 280; *TGI²* 51; by Shalmaneser III in the year 841) not only during the time of Jehu, who overthrew the Omri dynasty. Even almost one and a half centuries after Omri's death, the annals of Tiglath-Pileser III call the Northern Kingdom of Israel "House of Omri" (*ANET* 283f.; *TGI²* 57f.; cf. *RLA* 2:43). In the Old Testament, except in our passage, Omri is named later only once more within the Deuteronomistic history (according to 1 Kings 16:23–28), which speaks of him as the grandfather of Athaliah (2 Kings 8:26; 2 Chron. 22:2). Nevertheless, it is not surprising that Omri's name as the founder of Samaria, and on account of his notorious wickedness (1 Kings 16:25), appears in our text. His son Ahab (875–853) is repeatedly mentioned in the Deuteronomistic history: in 2 Kings 21:3 the idol worship of the Jerusalem king Manasseh is compared with that of Ahab (cf. already 2 Kings 8:26f.). And in 2 Kings 21:13, the disaster that befell Samaria because of the guilt of the house of Ahab, is, correspondingly, proclaimed against Jerusalem. In our passage the accusation and the threat directed against "the city" exhibit precisely the same line of thought found in the Deuteronomistic history. The expression שׁמר חקות, "to keep the statutes," is also Deuteronomistic; it is used particularly in connection with human, specifically pagan, customs: cf. Deut. 4:40; 1 Kings 2:3; 9:6; 11:11, 34, 38; 2 Kings 17:13; 23:3 with 2 Kings 17:8, 19, 34 and 1 Kings 3:3. On the parallel מעשׂה//חקות, cf. Jer. 10:3 (post-Deuteronomistic); on הלך במעצות, cf. Jer. 7:24; Ps. 81:13. Concrete transgressions are not mentioned. Perhaps the house of Ahab is named particularly in reminiscence of the Naboth story, where a connection is made between lie and violence (cf. 1 Kings 21:8ff. with Mic. 6:12a). Otherwise, the verse could be a succinct statement of what the Deuteronomistic history emphasizes: the wickedness of Omri, like that of Ahab, is worse than that of all his predecessors in the eyes of Yahweh (1 Kings 16:25, 30).

Since the inhabitants of Jerusalem followed in the same path, they will meet the same end—their own destruction (2 Kings 21:10–15). Micah himself had already viewed Jerusalem in the light of Samaria's destruction (see above, pp. 47f. on 1:6–9). The word למען can introduce the result ("so that") as well as the intention (here it is ironic, as in Hos. 8:4). Moreover, the wording used to express Yahweh's acts of punishment borrows catchwords from the Deuteronomistic school. On לשמה in v. 16b, cf., on the one hand, v. 13b (see above, p. 189); on the other, 2 Kings 22:19 (". . . this place and its inhabitants . . . will become a desolation and a curse"). The connection of לשמה with the verb נתן occurs only in four other instances (Jer. 25:18; 29:18; 2 Chron. 29:8; 30:7; elsewhere, usually with היה; or, we find the expression שום לשמה), always in connection with Jerusalem. In the first three of these instances, as also in v. 16, לשרקה comes after the word לשמה, and in Jer. 29:18, even the word וּלְחֶרְפָּה also occurs (cf. with v. 16bβ). Once again, the proximity to Deuteronomistic language is confirmed (on the Jeremiah passages, cf. W. Thiel, WMANT 52 [1981] 17f., 113).

While the word שמה in this context announces the objective destruction that strikes the whole (cf. the singular object אתך), the word שרקה drones in the ears of "its inhabitants" as individuals (plural), like that hissing and whistling that is experienced in the horror of desolation during the defense against the powers of destruction; שרקה occurs only with or in parallel to שמה (Jer. 19:8; 25:9, 18; 29:18; 51:37; 2 Chron. 29:8). Moreover, the city's inhabitants will be exposed to the scorn and the reproach (חרפה, as in Jer. 29:18) of the "peoples" (see note 16c). Thus the literary addition in v. 16 places the injustices that are internal to the city not only into the framework of Israel's history, but also into the wider horizon of the misfortunes of world politics.

Purpose and Thrust

After 6:8, vv. 9ff. at first appear to be a concrete and detailed exposition of that verse. Utilizing contrasting images, vv. 10–12 illustrate what those who are called to practice justice and love in attentive obedience to Yahweh are by all means to avoid doing. Moreover, these verses do not mince words concerning the merchants' deceitful practices and their fraudulent use of weights and balances. The prophet offers his commentary by posing questions that provoke them to admit their own inexcusable deeds. Thus the prophet's words are instructive for preachers on how to leave aside the trite and commonplace. He challenges each reader to scrutinize his business dealings in the light of God's claims.

The punishment Yahweh declares to the swindlers is presented as corresponding to their deception of and brutality toward other people (v. 12f.: ". . . but I too . . ."; see above, p. 195). Those who engage in deception will themselves be deceived. People who have no respect for their brothers and sisters will not be respected. What they sow they will not reap (vv. 14–15). Just as cheating one's neighbor, in false hope, does not finally lead to the desired goal of increased wealth, so the God of Israel will demonstrate that the misuse of economic power truly leads to one's own ruin. The futility curses cause inconsiderate persons to see that the punishment for their guilt fits the crime.

The interpretation added later to the passage, as is clearly evident in vv. 14bβ, 16, goes beyond this. It indicates that everyday mistreatment of the neighbor must be seen in the light of its political and historical dimensions. As a consequence of "the city's" internal dishonesty and violence, it must experience historical catastrophe in the midst of the nations. The initial words in v. 9aα, together with the introductory summons to hear in v. 9b, propound a comprehensive, all-embracing insight: this complex of prophetic sayings, using examples of deceitful and malicious dealings, including the proclamation of destruction, teaches what Deut. 28:15 formulates in this way: "If you will not obey the voice of Yahweh your God, . . . then all these curses shall come upon you. . . ." As the later expansions of the text in Deuteronomy 28 as well as in Mic. 6:14–16 indicate, these illustrations in the text suggest how they can be further applied to other concrete actions and their corresponding curses.

Chaos Now!

Bibliography

B. Reicke, "Liturgical Traditions in Micah 7," *HTR* 60 (1967) 349–368. A. S. van der Woude, "Deutero-Micha: Ein Prophet aus Nord-Israel?" *NedThT* 25 (1971) 365–378. Th. Lescow, "Redaktionsgeschichtliche Analyse von Micha 6–7," *ZAW* 84 (1972) 201–210. J. T. Willis, "A Reapplied Prophetic Hope Oracle," VTSuppl 26 (1974) 64–76.

Text

1 [a]Woe is me!
For me it is like[b] the gathering[c] of fruit,
   like[b] the gleaning of the vintage:
Not one grape to eat!
   (Not)[d] one early fig, which[e] I longed for!
2 Disappeared from the land is the pious man,
   and not one upright person remains among the people.
All of them lie[a] in ambush (to shed) blood.
   One brother hunts[b] the other to death.[c]
3 'Their hands are skillful at doing evil.'[a]
The official makes demands,
   the judge . . . for payment.[b]
The great man—he makes judgments according to his greed.
   And they twist[c] it.
4 The best among them[a] is like a brier,
   the 'most upright (like) a thorn hedge.'[b]
      The day[c] of your watchmen [your punishment][d] has arrived.
         Now their chaos[e] has come.
5 Believe not the neighbor!
   Trust[a] not the friend!
From her who lies in your bosom,
   guard the doors[b] of your mouth!
6 For the son considers the father to be foolish.
   The daughter rebels against her mother,
the daughter-in-law against her mother-in-law.
   A man's enemies are the people of his own house.

7 But I will watch for Yahweh;
I will wait upon the God of my salvation.
My God will answer me.

1a Targ (אמר נביא) explains that the prophet speaks in what follows.
1b Nouns introduced by the comparative particle כ are usually descriptions expressing a state or condition, which are to be translated into English with prepositions (Ges-K §118s,w); cf. Isa. 17:5; 24:13.
1c Plural construct of the noun אֹסֶף ("in-gathering," "harvest"); cf. Isa. 32:10, KBL³ 72b and Bauer-Leander §§19f. The plural form is chosen to make a parallel with עללת. Gk (ὡς συνάγων) reads the singular participle (כְּאֹסֵף), or the word with ־compaginis (cf. Bauer-Leander §65j). The parallel supports MT (plural noun). The words refer not to persons (harvesters) but to the action (harvesting). Vg *(sicut qui colligit in autumno racemos vindemiae)* reads כְּאֹסֵף as does Gk; however, overlooking כ, Vg understands עללת as the object of the verb (". . . grapes of the vintage") and קיץ as a reference to the season (in autumn). Nevertheless, it is clear also according to Isa. 17:5; 24:13, that as a particle of comparison in the original text in v. 1aα and 1aβ, כ refers not to persons but to an act.
1d An elliptical style is present here, which also omits repeating the negative.
1e Further, the asyndetic relative clause belongs to the harsh staccato style; see below, p. 203.
2a Gk (δικάζονται, "to conduct a lawsuit") overlooks the א in the word יארבו, reading יָרְבוּ.
2b Gk (ἐκθλίβουσιν) incorrectly reads יָצוּרוּ ("to oppress") by mistaking ר (MT) for ד.
2c Gk (ἐκθλιβῇ), α´, σ´ (ἀναθέματι), Targ (לגמירא), Vg *(ad mortem),* Syr all understand I חֵרֶם to mean an "act of destruction and death" (N. Lohfink, *ThWAT* 3:201; cf. Isa. 43:28; Zech. 14:11; Mal. 3:24). On account of the metaphors of "chase and hunting," L. C. Allen, N. Lohfink, 194, and B. Renaud, 346, understand the word to be II חֵרֶם "(with the) net." However, an *accusative instrumentalis* in connection with the word צוד is not otherwise attested. To delete the word on metrical grounds (frequently suggested) appears to be arbitrary in view of the unified witness of the translations. On the syntax, cf. Mal. 3:24.
3a MT ("Against evil [there are] hands to do good") is in this context less probable than the presumable literary antecedent available to Gk (ἐπὶ τὸ κακὸν τὰς χεῖρας αὐτῶν ἑτοιμάζουσιν): לְהָרַע כַּפֵּיהֶם הֵטִיבוּ. Does MT seek to improve the text by moralizing (על instead of ל)? Vg also presupposes כַּפֵּיהֶם instead of כַּפַּיִם *(malum manuum suarum dicunt bonum).*
3b Gk (καὶ ὁ κριτὴς εἰρηνικοὺς λόγους ἐλάλησε) offers a paraphrase by reading שָׁלוֹם instead of בַּשִּׁלּוּם. However, the context leads one to expect elliptical parallels of two stresses in v. 3aβ,γ, in which שֹׁאֵל accordingly would be construed as the predicate to הַשֹּׁפֵט, and at the same time (ב)שלום would function as the object to שֹׁאֵל.
3c On עבת = עות = עבט = "twist," "change," "distort"; cf. Wolff, *Joel and Amos,* note g on Joel 2:7; B. Renaud, 349f. Certainty in reconstructing and translating the text of v. 3 seems impossible, although the meaning of the statements may be ascertained in light of v. 2.
4a The suffix lends to the adjective the meaning of a superlative (Br*Synt* §60c).
4b MT ("more upright than a thorn hedge") does not fit with the preceding parallel sentence (but cf. Ges-K §133e: "worse than a thorn hedge"). According to the parallelism (v. 4aα//aβ), MT incorrectly divided the two words; more likely is the reading יְשָׁרָם מְסוּכָה. Given the elliptical staccato style here, it would appear improbable that a כ should be inserted (כחדק/כמסוכה). Vg *(et qui rectus quasi spina de sepe)* translates v. 4aβ as precisely parallel to v. 4aα.
4c E. Sellin, R. Vuilleumier, BHS, propose that הוֹי (following Gk, οὐαὶ οὐαί) be read instead of יום. But Gk definitely supports יום (ἐν ἡμέρᾳ σκοπιᾶς σου).

4d Without a copula the appended word (פְּקֻדָּתְךָ) appears to be a secondary gloss.
4e Gk (κλαυθμοί, "wailing") incorrectly derives the noun from בכה ("to weep"); see also Joel 1:18 Gk. The root, however, is בוך ("to wander about aimlessly"; cf. Exod. 14:3). On the word's meaning, see below, p. 107.
5a Mur 88 (וְאַל) and Gk (καὶ μή) connect the two cola in v. 5a with the copula. The asyndetic-elliptical style of the entire context supports MT; only in v. 2aβ and v. 3aβ, b does the copula ו otherwise occur.
5b The Hebraic dual expresses the notion that the (two) lips are the doors of language; cf. Wolff, *Anthropology of the Old Testament* (1973) 77.

Form

The entirely unusual cry of personal lamentation (see below, p. 204) marks the beginning of a new rhetorical unit. Changing from the excited, first person lament (v. 1) to accusations in the third person, including superlative formulations (vv. 2ff.), the unit unquestionably continues until v. 4a. Thereafter, three problems arise concerning the conclusion of the unit.

1. In v. 4bα there is an abrupt shift to direct address in the singular, followed again by a declarative statement (v. 4bβ) having to do with a plurality of persons (third plural). Nothing stands in the way of identifying this last third person plural with the plural in vv. 2–4a. But what is the significance of the transition to direct address in the singular? It can only be understood as a prayer (I. Willi-Plein). In the prayer it is established (perfect) that, with the situation described in the preceding verses, the "day" has finally arrived—the "day" proclaimed by Yahweh's "watchmen," i.e., the (earlier) prophets (see below, p. 207). An interpolation (see note 4d) explains that this is (the day of) "punishment"; the second person singular suffix attached to "punishment" points again to Yahweh as the subject of the punishment (see below, p. 207). The following reference to "now" (עתה) is a part of the later explication, its purpose being to clarify the word "today." Thus v. 4b contains an interpretation of vv. 1–4a that views the lamentable troubles as the fulfillment of prophetic threats (v. 4bα); but above all, v. 4bβ calls the results of this "chaos" (see below, p. 207). That we have a later addition in v. 4b, with its change from third to second person, may also be concluded from the fact that the sentence, begun with יום and continued with עתה, is similar to the later additions in 7:11–12. Moreover, the prose style indicates it is later; but above all, vv. 1–4a are continued by vv. 5f., verses which appear to be interrupted by v. 4b (cf. Jörg Jeremias, 351, and B. Renaud, 353).

2. But here the second problem is to be discussed: Do vv. 1–4a and vv. 5–6 belong together as an original unit? That the answer is in the affirmative is not self-evident, because following the accusations, v. 5 contains admonitions and warnings that are completely different. Yet these admonitions and warnings find their motivation in renewed lamentations (v. 6) that are thoroughly related to vv. 2–4a. Moreover, such a combination of admonitions and accusations on a quite similar theme has parallels in Jer. 9:1–5; 12:6, in which the similarity of expression is especially noticeable: "they all" are adulterers (Jer. 9:1[2]; cf. Mic. 7:2); they proceed from evil to evil" (Jer. 9:2[3]; cf. Mic. 7:3); "let everyone beware of his neighbor"; "let none trust" "his brother" (Jer. 9:3[4]; 12:6;

cf. Mic. 7:5). hence vv. 1–4a are closely connected with vv. 5–6 according to form critical as well as thematic considerations.

3. Finally, it disputed whether v. 7 belongs to vv. 1–6 (thus B. Duhm, A. Weiser, W. Rudolph, R. Vuilleumier, I. Willi-Plein, L. C. Allen, A. S. van der Woude, et al.), or is itself already a part of vv. 8ff. (thus J. Wellhausen, H. Gunkel, O. Eissfeldt, J. T. Willis, Th. Lescow, et al.). Unquestionably, v. 7 is no longer a part of the lamentation. Since reasons for both positions can be advanced, J. L. Mays (155f.) inclines toward a compromise that considers v. 7 to be a redactional seam between vv. 1–6 and vv. 8ff. Nevertheless, considering merely the syntax, it seems to me that the ı-*copulativum* in the first word of v. 7 connects it more closely to the preceding verses than v. 8 is connected with v. 7. This is all the more noticeable in that no such copula occurs in the preceding or subsequent context. Moreover, the three sentences with imperfect verbs point to hope in Yahweh and thus are oriented toward the future, whereas in vv. 8ff. the statements in the first person, with verbs in the perfect, emphasize the present preparation of defense against an enemy who is personally addressed there. Thus v. 7, with its self-summons (first person) to persistent watchfulness for Yahweh's answer, rounds off the preceding disclosure of destructive, public injustice that was begun by the first person lament in v. 1. The "I" that expresses bitter disappointment moves from weeping and lament, in spite of everything, to the "I" that trusts in his God. Elsewhere we find in Hab. 3:18 a similarly formulated sentence that, looking toward the future (... באלהי ישעי ואני ביהוה), unequivocally brings the passage to a conclusion after a series of laments (see below, p. 208).

The passage appears to have a certain rigidity of style. Following the prelude containing two stresses, we find together with three-stress cola an unusual number of two-stress cola (vv. 3aβ, b, 4a, 5b, 6aβ, 7b); these intensify the whiplike sharpness of the accusation, insofar as this is not rooted in a corrupt text (which must be taken into account in v. 3). Corresponding to this style we find the asyndesis of the relative clause in v. 1bβ and the extraordinarily frequent omission of the ı-*copulativum* in parallel cola: vv. 1a, 2b, 3a, 4a, 5a (see note 5a!), 6a, 6b, 7a, 7b. This makes for a harsh staccato style, which is also accompanied by ellipses such as the omission of a negative in v. 1bβ in parallel to אין in v. 1bα (cf. on the other hand v. 2a and Jer. 8:13!) or the omission of an object or predicate in v. 3aβ,γ (see note 3b).

Setting

This lamentation is connected with the preceding judgment speech in 6:9–16 only in that it laments conditions that are partially similar. In 6:9–16 such conditions are denounced as sin, especially deceit, cheating, and brutal acts of oppression. But here they are not presented as the basis for judgment; rather, they are the cause of suffering for which hope in Yahweh is the only answer.

Who is the speaker? According to Targ, it is a prophet (see note 1a; thus also E. Sellin, J. Lindblom, R. Vuilleumier, B. Renaud, et al.). This supposition is to be preferred to the suggestion that the community of Zion offers this lament (thus J. Wellhausen, J. M. P. Smith, J. L. Mays).

For a community such as a city, with its responsible heads and families, is precisely the entity over which the isolated speaker expresses his lamentation. The image of deep disappointment in v. 1 (see below, pp. 204f.), as well as the expressions of hope in v. 7, are better understood in the mouth of an offended individual, indeed, a lamenting prophet (cf. Jer. 8:23—9:5; 5:1; 12:1ff.). But v. 4b may belong to the final redaction of the book, which is also recognizable in 7:11f. (see Introduction §5).

Neither Micah nor a contemporary in the Northern Kingdom in the eighth century (A. S. van der Woude, 240f.: the time of Pekah, 740–730) can be considered the author of 7:1–4a+5–6. How different are Micah's words in 1:8 and 2:1 from the lament here! How differently Micah designates the responsible authorities (see below, p. 206 on v. 3)! Texts similar to 7:1–7 in language and theme are found chiefly in the early postexilic period, especially in Trito-Isaiah (Isa. 57:1–2; 59:4–8; cf. Jer. 9:1–5 [2–6]; 12:6; Mal. 3:24[4:6] might presuppose 7:6; see I. Willi-Plein; J. L. Mays). The life of the community of that time must have been characterized by demoralization and instability. The dissolution of the social and economic orders must have misled the most important officials to selfish, arbitrary acts. Moreover, relationships within families and with neighbors were deprived of all trustworthiness; each person greedily looked after his own survival. Only a few isolated individuals, saddened by the collapse of Yahweh's saving ordinances, could in their lamentations preserve something of Israel's prophetic tradition.

Commentary

[7:1] As to details, even the present form of this quite unusual introductory phrase expressing a cry of lamentation supports a postexilic date. The phrase אללי לי occurs elsewhere in the Old Testament only in Job 10:15. The root II אלל means "to lament" (KBL³ 55b). Job utters his "Woe is me!" out of the particular circumstance of his own guilt. It is an expression of complete helplessness. Spewing forth his lamentation, our prophet is threatened by a sea of injustice and encircled by a host of cunning, deceit, and malice. The cry אללי לי stands closer to the anxious cry אוי לי (Isa. 6:5) than to the cry of the death-lament, הוי (Mic. 2:1; see above, p. 77).

First, the prophet explains his situation by using a simile drawn from harvest time or, more precisely, from the experience of gleaning at the end of the harvest. He feels like one of the poorest among the people who, after the main harvest, is allowed to see whether something remains for him; but he is mournfully disappointed. When the Israelite farmers harvest grain and olives as well as grapes, they are commanded to leave in their fields a not-too-sparse gleaning for the needy and the foreigners (Lev. 19:9–10; 23:22; Deut. 24:19–22). Boaz serves as an example of this (according to Ruth 2:3, 7, 15f.). When only two or three olives are found in the topmost bough, or four or five in the extreme branches, it brings deep disappointment (Isa. 17:6; cf. H. Wildberger, *Jesaja 13–27,* BK 10/2, 647–649). That the hungry are disappointed at the gleanings is an image often used to picture extreme distress (Jer. 49:9; Isa. 24:13).

Our text speaks not of the grain or olive harvest, but of figs and grapes as desirable delicacies. While the word בציר denotes the main vintage, whose gleanings are referred to here (אללת, as in Judg. 8:2; Isa.

24:13), so קִיץ denotes the most important summer fruit, namely, the fig
(cf. 2 Sam. 16:1 and Wolff, *Joel and Amos* 319). בכורה means the early
fruit on the young shoots from the previous year that already ripens in
May-June (in contrast to the תְּאֵנָה, the fruit on the sprouts of the new year
that can be harvested in August-September). אשכול is a less frequent word
for grape (instead of עֵנָב), which appears to have been chosen here
because of its alliteration with לאכול. The juicy early fig, the first fruit to
ripen in early summer, was especially popular and desirable (cf. Isa.
28:4b and H. Wildberger, *Jesaja 28–39*, BK 10/3, 1049). The asyndetic
relative clause (see note 1e) modifying the word בכורה emphasizes strong
desire (אוה *piel*); the subject is נפש ("throat, the seat of hunger"), which in
Hebrew can be used as a synonym for mouth (Eccl. 6:7). With the first
person suffix, as here, the word can denote the first person, "I" (cf. also
Eccl. 7:28 and H. W. Wolff, *Anthropology of the Old Testament* 11ff.;
23ff.). In this declaration the accent lies in v. 1b upon the painful disappointment of a person who experiences great hunger. The gleanings of
the harvest are not merely sparse; rather, there is nothing to be found: "no
grape, no fig!" (see note 1d; cf. Jer. 8:13). Thus the speaker characterizes
himself as one whose experiences are unfulfilled, whose yearnings are
unmet, and whose bitter disappointment is complete.

[7:2] The scene portrayed in v. 1 by means of a simile is interpreted in v.
2. אין is picked up from v. 1bα, making a connection between v. 1 and v. 2
(אין is emphasized by its placement at the end of v. 2aβ); it is strengthened
by the word אבד in the parallel sentence (v. 2aα). If at the gleaning of the
harvested fields one seeks grape and early fig completely in vain, this
corresponds to the prophet's mood: he finds not one God-fearing person
in the land, nor an upright person among the people. אבד מן (v. 2aα)
essentially means "to be swept away" (from the earth). The result is that
"no honest person any longer exists among the people" (v. 2aβ). A quite
similar formulation is found in Isa. 57:1; 59:4; on this theme, cf. Jer. 5:1
and Eccl. 7:28f. The singular of חסיד and ישר (as of grape and fig in v. 1b)
emphasizes that not *one* is to be found. The חסיד is a person who practices
חֶסֶד, particularly one who lives in a conscious relationship of trust in
Yahweh (Pss. 12:2; 31:24; 85:9; etc.); it is seldom presupposed that, in
addition to this, the חסיד has close, friendly relations with his fellow
human beings. The word belongs almost exclusively to the language of
the prayers in the Psalms (28 out of a total of 32 occurrences); within the
prophetic corpus it occurs elsewhere only in Jer. 3:12 (in reference to
God) (cf. H. J. Stoebe, *THAT* 1:601, 618ff.). At the same time, the word
ישר is more related to justice between persons; it denotes the "honest,"
"upright," "upstanding," "conscientious" person who shuns all that is
crooked and who loves righteousness (Hos. 14:10; Mic. 2:7b; cf. 3:9); not
infrequently, ישר occurs as a synonym for צַדִּיק (Pss. 32:11; 33:1; 64:11;
etc.). According to Eccl. 7:28f., only one person in a thousand remains
"upright" (ישר), just as God created him; all the rest "seek out all kinds of
intrigue." Our passage is not far removed from Ecclesiastes' discovery of
the corruption of all human beings (cf. A. Lauha, *Kohelet,* BK 19, 143).
Verse two emphasizes in what follows that enmity among people knows
no exceptions. "They all" seek after the "shedding of blood" (on דמים, see
above p. 106 on 3:10); indeed, they do so in a cunning manner. The word

ארב indicates that their violence is not accomplished in the open; rather, they lie in ambush (cf. Judg. 9:34; Ps. 10:8f.). Such malicious conduct brings everyone into conflict with everyone else: each person treats his brother like a wild animal that is hunted (צוד, Gen. 27:3; often used to denote the hunting of wild game) "to its death." To translate the word חרם "with the net" is neither warranted by the syntax nor supported semantically by the ancient versions (see note 2c). Nor is the concept of the "ban" expressed here (N. Lohfink, ThWAT 3: 201); the idea is merely that of reciprocal destruction (otherwise, 4:13bα; see above p. 142).

[7:3] The prophet therefore laments over the malice and hostility existing within all levels of the people; his lament is not limited to certain circles of leaders, as in Mic. 2:1–11 and 3:1–12. Trustworthiness, honesty, helpfulness, and security have given way to a criminal attitude among the entire breadth of the people. Skill is exhibited only in doing evil. In this sense, the sentence in v. 3aα quite probably presents a summary statement (on textual criticism, see note 3a); it is to be interpreted in light of Jer. 4:22b: "They are skilled in doing evil, but how to do good they know not."

From all the people, however, three particularly responsible groups of leaders are set apart: "the official," "the judge," and "the great man." None of these three groups was named by Micah; he addressed only the following administrative officials: קָצִין "leader," 3:1, 9; כֹּהֵן "priest," 3:11; נָבִיא "prophet," 3:5, 11; the "judge" (שֹׁפֵט) Micah calls רֹאשׁ "head," 3:11 (cf. 3:1, 9 and see above, pp. 97f.). In v. 3 the official who comes from the civilian as well as the military sphere is called שַׂר. If we have correctly understood this brief lament, the official is characterized by his "demands" (שָׁאַל "to ask," "to require"). Similarly, it says that the "judge" seeks after "payment" (שָׁלוֹם) (on the brevity of the expression, see note 3b). The basic meaning of שׁלם is "to make complete," "to reconstitute into a whole" (cf. W. Eisenbeis, Die Wurzel שׁלם im Alten Testament, BZAW 113 [1969] 350f.). In Exod. 21:36 שׁלם piel means "to make restitution." Otherwise שׁלוּם speaks only of the "retribution" of Yahweh (Deut. 32:35; Isa. 34:8; Hos. 9:7; Ps. 91:8). However, like the word שַׁלְמֹנִים (//שֹׁחַד "bribery") in Isa. 1:23, in v. 3 it means "payment," "compensation." The judge is not guided by justice, but by the "recompense" he expects. The "great man" refers to confidants of the king and to higher administrative officials, such as Abner, Saul's field marshal (2 Sam. 3:38; cf. 1 Sam. 14:50f.); to the guardians of the princes in Samaria (2 Kings 10:6); or to the writers of royal decrees (Jon. 3:7; see Wolff, Obadiah and Jonah 152). During the postexilic period perhaps these were special counselors who were commissioned by the Persian emperor to particular jobs in the satrapy (cf., e.g., Ezra 7:14). In our passage "the great man" is accused of allowing his word, decree, or decision to be dictated by his own willfulness. הוַּת נפשׁו recalls the simile in v. 1bβ (נפשׁי אותה). In contrast to the prophet's longing for fresh fruit, here we find a willfulness that only craves recompense (cf. Prov. 10:3; 11:6; on נפשׁ as the organ of desire, see above, p. 205). Thus total chaos spreads from the upper as well as from lower levels of society. The result is a perversion of all relationship (see note 3c).

[7:4a] This thought is emphasized once more. Even the "best" and the "most upright" are like a "thorn hedge" (on the superlatives, see notes 4a and b). Thus it is asserted again that among the masses there is no exception. Even among those of good repute, no one can in fact be found who is not engaged in bloody struggle. They all obstruct the way of their neighbor, with the result that it becomes impossible to achieve one's purposes ("to obstruct" is the function of a thorn hedge; cf. Prov. 15:19).

[7:4b] Perhaps the word "thorn hedge" (מסוכה) suggested the assonance מבוכה ("disorder") to the commentator who speaks in v. 4b; with this word the interpolated prayer reaches its climax (see above, p. 202). In the national confusion surrounding him the commentator sees the arrival of "the day of your watchmen." According to Hab. 2:1; Isa. 21:6; מצפה (like צֹפֶה in Hos. 9:8; Jer. 6:17; Ezek. 3:17; 33:2, 6, 7; Isa. 52:8) designates the function of a prophet. As a visionary, he assumes the office of watchman and sentinel in times of war. "Your watchmen" are thus Yahweh's prophets who have declared the very disaster which is "now" taking place (באה) with the dissolution of all institutions of justice, and with the threat to all of life. Like an apocalyptic visionary, the commentator looks back to the ancient prophetic word and sees that it has become fulfilled in his present day. An additional explanatory gloss (see note 4d) interprets the day of Yahweh's watchmen as the day of his "punishment." The second person suffix attached to this word is also to be syntactically construed with Yahweh; cf. Hos. 9:7; Isa. 10:3 and the large number of prophetic announcements of disaster in which Yahweh is the subject of the punishment (פקד): Amos 3:2, 14; Hos. 1:4; 4:9; 9:9; Jer. 5:9, 29; 6:15; 9:8, 24; 11:22; etc. From Yahweh's perspective, it is the day when the watchmen's word is fulfilled, the day of punishment; from a human perspective, it is מבוכה, the national "disorder" which is lamented in vv. 2–4a. The word seldom occurs; here it denotes chaos and confusion. The root בוך refers to perplexed, agitated disorder (Exod. 14:3), helpless dismay (Joel 1:18) and general shock and consternation (Esther 3:15). The noun מבוכה occurs elsewhere only in Isa. 22:5; there, as in v. 4b, it describes the effects of the day of Yahweh as וּמְבוּכָה יוֹם מְהוּמָה וּמְבוּסָה. With this phrase, an all-encompassing, disastrous chaos is elucidated in three ways: מְהוּמָה means national consternation and panic; מְבוּסָה means trampling, in the sense of brutal subjugation; finally, מְבוּכָה refers to the total confusion and chaotic dissolution of all orders of society. When our passage takes up this last word (מבוכה), one perceives the further shades of meaning suggested by the two preceding words in Isa. 22:5, which form an assonance with it. What Yahweh's prophets had foreseen, and what, e.g., the immediately preceding text (6:9–16) had spoken about, is taking place "now." The one who speaks in v. 4b expresses this sympathetically in prayer before Yahweh.

[7:5] This sketch of chaos continues in v. 5, first in the form of warnings. These warnings draw the consequences resulting from the deceit and falsehood which dominate all of life and even penetrate into the personal sphere of everyday life, destroying neighborliness and friendship, marriage and family. It should be noted that within v. 5 there is a heightening of the natural relationships of trust; it moves from one's neighbor and fellowman (רֵעַ), to trusted friend (אַלּוּף), and then to beloved wife. The greater the natural expectations of trust, the greater the caution against mistrust. No longer should one trust his colleague, whose path is crossed each day. אמן hiph. "to believe," when used for relationships between persons, has a predominantly negative sense (A. Jepsen, ThWAT 1:322ff.). Only the inexperienced put their confidence in others (Prov. 14:15). Above all, when people no longer trust in God, their words no longer truly express their convictions. Psalm 12:2f. contains the image of the person with a "double heart," the model of the ἀνὴρ δίψυχος (James 1:8), the divided soul. While his words are friendly, his heart is an abomination (Prov. 26:25; cf. Ps. 28:3; Jer. 12:6). As with neighbor and companion in times of great deception (Ps. 55:12[11]!), so one must beware of the close friend (the "confidant," אַלּוּף; cf. Ps. 55:13–15[12–14], 21f.[20f.]). As in the parallel containing the word אמן hiph., בטח warns against an attitude of false confidence (cf. also Ps. 41:7[6], 10[9], and A. Jepsen, ThWAT 1:612). Finally, even one's most intimate companion, the beloved wife, presents danger. "The wife of your bosom," is the person with whom the husband has tender, intimate relations (1 Kings 1:2; Deut. 13:7; 28:54) and begets children (Gen. 16:5). Although the husband has to mistrust the words of neighbor and friend, with his wife he must especially pay attention to the words he himself speaks; he must reckon with betrayal (cf. Ps. 41:7b[6b]). Hence, his lips must remain tightly sealed (see note 5b).

[7:6] The demand for thorough skepticism toward human relationships is given its motivation in v. 6: as the primary unit of all community life, the family is thrown into confusion. The son, instead of giving honor to his father (Exod. 20:12) and bringing him joy (Prov. 15:20), despises him like a blockhead (cf. Prov. 30:17); he treats him like a נָבָל (נבל piel), like one who withers away (נבל qal) because of his age (Prov. 23:22). Instead of honoring the mother (Lev. 19:3), the daughter rebels against her; קוּם ב means "to stand up against someone in a hostile manner." In the Old Testament, disgraceful treatment of elders is deserving of the death penalty (Exod. 21:15, 17; Lev. 20:9; Prov. 20:20). Within the unit of the extended family, the daughter-in-law is supposed to be subordinate to the mother-in-law. Belonging to the extended family are slaves born into the house, as well as foreign slaves bought with money. Both groups are attached to the head of the family as "men of his house" (cf. Gen. 17:23, 27; 39:11, 14). Those who are supposed to help him have become his opponents (cf. Isa. 3:5). Consequently, the family is disintegrated by disrespect and strife. When the nucleus of all community—certainly the first and last place where security is experienced—is undermined, then every refuge is turned into chaos. This is the end of all community.

[7:7] In this truly eschatological situation, the voice of the completely isolated prophet turns to Yahweh. There is no need to look for another alternative. צפה piel means the "watching" done by the individual at prayer who, as in the Psalter, waits for an answer (Ps. 5:4[3]). If the present distress is the fulfillment of what was seen earlier by the watchmen (v. 4b), then in his desperation all the prophet can do is to watch and wait for Yahweh's new deeds. For the moment, he peers only into the abyss. But whoever prayerfully performs the task of watchman (Hab. 2:1) waits in suspense; the word יחל *hiph.* also typically expresses the waiting for an answer in the Psalms of lament (Pss. 38:16[15]; 42:6[5], 12[11]; 43:5; on the hopeful waiting of a prophet, cf. Isa. 8:17). In the midst of nothingness, the prophet waits for Yahweh, "the God of my salvation," to come forth and make himself known. The phrase אלהי ישעי, a motif expressing confidence, occurs frequently in the petitions in individual laments (Pss. 25:5; 27:9; 62:8[7]; Hab. 3:18) and in community laments (Pss. 79:9; 85:5[4]; Lam. 4:17; 1 Chron. 16:35). Despite all human unfaithfulness and deception, God will make this new salvation a reality. The solitary prophet waits for an answer to his prayer with a confidence that resolutely faces the depression resulting from a disrupted community life. Hence v. 7, which has parallels to the psalms of lament, as noted above, is more intelligible as the conclusion to vv. 1–6 than as the prelude to vv. 8ff. (see above, p. 203).

Purpose and Thrust

When we consider the special character of vv. 1–7, we recognize that its uniqueness lies in its presentation of lament upon lament, down to the conclusion, but with absolutely no announcement of judgment. This is all the more remarkable because when concrete human guilt is indicted (vv. 2–4a, 5–6) throughout the prophetic texts, it is followed by the announcement of punishment (most recently 6:9–16; cf. 2:1–5; 3:1–4, 5–7, 9–12). (On the function of the warning in v. 5, see above, pp. 207f.) The reason such announcements are not to be found here is that the injustice proclaimed in the text is the judgment itself. The interpretative sentence added later in v. 4b (see above, p. 207) explains the national "confusion" (מבוכה) as the fulfillment of the sayings of (previous) prophetic watchmen. In that betrayal, desire for blood, greed, and duplicity reign, the guilty are already experiencing disaster.

The particular characteristics of the text are further exhibited in the emphasis upon the totality of the injustice. Not only officials, judges, the "great men" (v. 3), but "everyone" (v. 2) lies in wait to do evil to the other. Not merely the degenerate riffraff, but even those considered to be the best and most upright, tear open wounds and split the community by insurmountable obstacles (v. 4a). Not only has public life fallen into chaos; even among circles of friends and family, contempt, mistrust, and hostility reign (vv. 5f.). It is a haunted world in which each makes life hell for the other; and it is all-embracing.

Thus it is human beings who prepare the end for each other. This eschatological viewpoint connects our text with 4 Ezra (cf. 3:12ff.), which appropriates several of its main themes: "When you see that one brother delivers another to death, children rebel against parents, the wife leaves her own husband; when nation makes war against nation, then you will recognize that the end is near!" (U. B. Müller, *JSHRZ* V/2 [1976] 94).

Even the author of our passage is unable to imagine how history is to continue, either by Yahweh's deeds of judgment or by acts of purification. That he does not stand totally helpless is only because he looks to Yahweh anew and is certain that his name is a guarantee of salvation; he does not know, however, the how of Yahweh's answer or action. Concrete ideas concerning Yahweh's answer, such as those presented by the person at prayer in Psalm 12 (vv. 6–8[5–7]) in a similar situation (vv. 2–5, 9[1–4, 8]), escape him.

Moreover, from the very beginning (vv. 1f.!), his isolation is greater. Seeking (in vain) for one pious and upright person, the figures closest to him in the Old Testament are Jeremiah (5:1–5; 9:1–5; 12:1–6) and Trito-Isaiah (57:1–2; 59:4–8).

Thus in a limited way, he is one of the few forerunners of the person before whom all are sinners and who, suffering for all their sins, takes them upon himself and bears them away (Isa. 53:4–7; Rom. 3:23; 4:25). In the New Testament's testimony to Jesus Christ we meet the One who suffers alone, who seeks in vain for one just person; and we meet the God who becomes the Savior of a world filled with injustice.

Verse 6 (cf. also v. 2bβ), which attests to the collapse of family life, is taken up in two different contexts in the Jesus tradition within the Synoptic Gospels. Jesus alludes to it in his speech about the end of the world in Mark 13:12 (Luke 21:16; cf. Jesus' words of commission in Matt. 10:21). The verse indicates that the disciples, even within the closest family circles, are inescapably threatened; that this, too, belongs to the signs of the end (note the reference above to 4 Ezra); and that the disciples will experience salvation (Mark 13:13; Luke 21:18; cf. Matt. 10:22) in waiting and endurance (cf. Mic. 7:7aβ).

In Jesus' commission of the disciples in Matt. 10:34–36 (Luke 12:51–53), Mic. 7:6 is appropriated with more precision and detail. Here the quotation clarifies the logion of Jesus which states that he "comes not to bring peace . . . but a sword." It is unavoidable, and a sign of the eschaton, that to confess Jesus divides even families. Just as the picture of hostility among parents, children, and persons within the household sketched out in Mic. 7:6 is so carefully appropriated in this passage (an admonition that such is to be endured for Jesus' sake), so it is remarkable that the admonitions to be distrustful in Mic. 7:5 are not taken up in the New Testament (cf. on the other hand Matt. 15:3ff.; 19:1ff.; 5:27ff.). The provisional hostility within the family itself is supposed to intensify—according to the concluding verse of our passage—the watchfulness for the God of salvation and his answer.

This precipitous pessimism, in spite of every thing, drives our prophet not to despair but into the arms of God. Thus in our own confused and chaotic generation, he shines like a star in the heavens (Phil. 2:15).

The Response
of the Community

Literature

B. Stade, "Streiflichter auf die Entstehung der jetzigen Gestalt der alttestament-lichen Prophetenschriften," *ZAW* 23 (1903) 153–171 (164–171: 5. Micha 7:7–20 ein Psalm). H. Gunkel, "Der Micha-Schluss. Zur Einführung in die literatur-geschichtliche Arbeit am Alten Testament," *ZS* 2 (1924) 145–178. F. Praetorius, "Zum Micha-Schluss," *ZS* 3 (1924) 72f. Ph. Calderone, "The Rivers of *'Maṣor,'*" *Biblica* 42 (1961) 423–432. O. Eissfeldt, "Ein Psalm aus Nord-Israel. Micha 7:7–20," *ZDMG* 112 (1962) 259–268; idem, *Kleine Schriften* 4 (1968) 63–72. J. Dus, "Weiteres zum nordisraelitischen Psalm Micha 7:7–20," *ZDMG* 115 (1965) 14–22. B. Z. Luria, "Das übriggebliebene Land und der Rest Israels," *BetM* 12 (1966–1967) 18–28. B. Reicke, "Liturgical Traditions in Micah 7," *HThR* 60 (1967) 349–368. I. Willi-Plein, *Vorformen der Schriftexegese innerhalb des Alten Testaments*, BZAW 123 (1971) 106–109. A. S. van der Woude, "Deutero-Micha: ein Prophet aus Nord-Israel?" *NedThT* 25 (1971) 365–378. L. Grollenberg, "Micha 7: eine Buss-Liturgie?" *Schrift* (Dutch) 17 (1971) 188–191. Th. Lescow, "Redactionsgeschichtliche Analyse von Micha 6–7," *ZAW* 84 (1972) 196–209. J. T. Willis, "A Reapplied Prophetic Hope Oracle," VTSuppl 26 (1974) 64–76. B. Renaud, *La Formation du Livre de Michée*, EtB (1977) 357–382. R. P. Gordon, "Micah VII 19 and Akkadian *kabāsu*," *VT* 28 (1978) 355.

Text

7:8 Do not rejoice over me, O my enemy![a]
　　For[b] although I have fallen, I shall rise up.
　　Whenever[c] I sit in darkness,
　　　Yahweh is surely my light.
9 [a]I must bear Yahweh's wrath
　　　—for against him I have transgressed—
　　until he pleads my case
　　　and executes justice for me.
　　He will direct me to the light,
　　　I will see his salvation.
10 When[a] my enemy[b] sees (it),
　　　shame will cover her,
　　she, who now says to me,

> "'Where' is ' 'c your God?"
> My eyes will look down on her—
> dnow she lies there trampledd
> like mud in the streets.

11 [A day (will come)a for buildingb your walls,
    a day on whichc 'your borders'd will be extended,
12   a day on whicha they will comeb to 'you'c
    fromd Assyria 'to'e Egypt,
      from Egyptf to the Euphrates,
        g'from sea to sea, from mountain to mountain.']g
13   [Then the earth will become desolate because of her
      inhabitants,a asb the fruit of their deeds.]c
14 Shepherd your people with your rod,
    the flock of your possession,
who dwellsa isolated there in the scrub
    in the midst of an orchard.
May they find pasture inb Bashan and Gilead
    as in ancient times.
15 As in the days of your exodus out of [the land]a of Egypt
    'let us'b see wonders!
16 May the nations see (it) and be ashamed—
    despitea all their superiority.
May they lay their hand on their mouth,
    may their ears become deaf.
17 May they lick dust like aa serpent,
    like those that creep on the ground.
May they come quaking out of their strongholds,
    [bto Yahweh our Godb];
may they come trembling
    and in fear before you.

18 Whoa is a God like you,
    who takes away transgression,
who overlooks rebellion
    bof the remnant of his possession!b
He does not retain his wrath forever,c
    for he is one who loves gracious kindness.
19 He will againa have mercy on us,
    our transgressions he will trample under foot.
Youb will sink into the depths of the sea
    all 'our'c sins.
20 You will bestow faithfulness upon Jacob
    and upon Abraham gracious kindness,
which you swore to our fathers
    froma the days of old.

8a איבתי = אֹיֶבֶת (אֹיֵב fem.) + first person singular suffix; cf. Bauer-Leander, §77d. Targ (רומי) interprets the enemy as "Rome," also in v. 10.
8b According to Gk (ὅτι) and Vg *(quia),* only the immediately following word (נפלתי) is governed by כי, so that it possibly gives the reason for the enemy's (malicious) pleasure; however, the rhythm of synthetic parallelism permits the כי to commence the entire following sentence (v. 8bβ), with the tone on the last word (כי ... קמתי); consequently, the reason for not rejoicing is given.
8c Gk (διότι ἐὰν) considers the causal particle כי, which is construed with v. 8aα, at the same time to begin the following clause (imperfect; v. 8ba) as a conditional

sentence that precedes the nominal clause in v. 8bβ. With the כִּי (here with imperfect of duration, cf. Gen. 4:12; Job 37:4b), MT presumably intends merely to introduce a temporal clause (cf. Vg, *cum*).

9a Targ prefixes to the beginning of the verse אמרת ירושלם, thereby expressly interpreting the speaker of the text as the city of Jerusalem.

10a Cf. Joüon, *Gr* §167a, on the formation of conditional sentences by the simple juxtaposition of two sentences with וְ followed by the imperfect.

10b See note 8a.

10c B. Renaud (359) considers it probable that the original text read אַיֵּה אֱלֹהֶיךָ. In the mouth of Israel's opponents, this shorter question is in fact more likely without the additional naming of "Yahweh" (cf. Pss. 42:4, 11; 79:10; 115:2; Joel 2:17). The present text ("Where is he, Yahweh your God?") could have arisen from incorrectly reading the last two letters of אַיֵּה twice, then understanding them as an abbreviation of the Tetragrammaton. Consequently, the original אַיֵּה became אַיּוֹ, in order to avoid a twice repeated יי. Moreover, a two-stress colon fits the preceding context better than a three-stress colon.

10d–d Literally: "Now she becomes the trampled one."

11a The three phrases that begin with יום in vv. 11a,b, 12aα appear to be fragmentary interpretative additions which, as commentary on the passage, conform to the syntactic rules of neither poetry nor prose.

11b Gk (πλίνθου) reads לִבְנוֹת (= לִבְנִים?) = brick(?).

11c The article in the word ההוא is understandable in view of the frequently occurring phrase ביום ההוא, but here it is probably secondary; cf. v. 12a. As a copula, הוא introduces a more precise definition of "day" (I. Willi-Plein, 107). It takes the place of a relative particle.

11d Following Gk (σου) perhaps חֻקֵּךְ is to be read.

12a Mur 88 (ביום ההוא) brings the text into conformity with a frequently occurring formula. MT is unusual and is to be viewed as original; see note 11a and G. W. Nebe, *ZNW* 63 [1972] 288).

12b יבוא could have as its subject יום הוא ("that day comes to you"); however, the logical subject is instead to be recognized in v. 12aβ, understood as an indefinite subject ("one") (W. Rudolph), unless, following Gk (ἥξουσιν), the plural יָבֹאוּ is not to be read (I. Willi-Plein: metathesis ו/א).

12c In relation to v. 11 the feminine suffix is to be expected: וְעָדַיִךְ; the feminine suffix may refer to the city or to the "daughter" of Jerusalem, the masculine suffix to the inhabitants (cf. v. 14).

12d למני is an alternative form of מִן ("from . . . to"; see KBL³ 565a and 566b).

12e As frequently, MT misread ר instead of ד; וְעַד is probably original; cf. v. 12bα.

12f Gk (ἀπὸ Τύρου) read מָצוֹר ("from Tyre"); however, it is unlikely for מ to follow immediately after למני within an otherwise strictly parallel sentence, just as it is likely, as is conjectured, for the מ to be repeated in the following v. 12bβ (see below, note 12g–g).

12g–g MT ("sea for sea, mountain to mountain," thus O. Eissfeldt, 266ff./70f.) is interpreted or even corrected by Gk^{W,etc.}: και απο θαλασσης εως θαλασσης και απο ορους εως (του) ορους. Is there present in יום and in והר an unusual accusative of movement: "to the sea . . ., to the mountain . . ." (B. Renaud, 361)? If the phrase מִיָּם עַד־יָם וּמֵהַר עַד־הַר, gained by translating back into Hebrew what is suggested by Gk^{W} and Vg (*et ad mare de mari et ad montem de monte)*, is unnecessary, then perhaps the small change to מֵהַר instead of הָהָר is sufficient (J. Wellhausen).

13a Gk^{W,B} (σὺν τοῖς κατοικοῦσιν) presupposes עִם ("with its inhabitants"); but the remaining Gk^{Mss} (μετα των κατοικουντων) support MT (עַל). In light of Lev. 10:3; Deut. 11:4; Jer. 6:7, A. S. van der Woude (258) proposes that עַל be translated "before the eyes of" (= עַל־פְּנֵי).

13b Actually, "owing to" or "as a result of"; מִן can also indicate "the cause of" (cf. KBL³ 566a).

13c See below, p. 225.

213

14a Participle with ‫-‬*compaginis,* as in Deut. 33:16; Jer. 49:16; Obad. 3; see H. W. Wolff, *Obadiah and Jonah,* Obad. note 3c; also Joüon, *Gr* §93n. Only in Deut. 33:16 does this form refer to Yahweh's dwelling; in Jer. 49:16 and Obad. 3 the subject is Edom. With the plural form, the ancient translations of our passage also have in mind a human entity (the people of God). The plural forms in Gk (κατασκηνοῦντας), Vg *(habitantes),* Syr, Targ do not justify the reading ‫שֹׁכְנֵי‬ (BHS), since the antecedents ‫עַם‬ and ‫צֹאן‬ can be appropriately understood as collectives; thus Gk even translates ‫צֹאן‬ with πρόβατα.

14b Following Targ perhaps ‫בְּבָשָׁן‬ is to be read (Sperber, IV B 90).

15a Gk (ἐξ Αἰγύπτου) does not presuppose ‫מֵאֶרֶץ‬; the briefer expression ‫מִמִּצְרַיִם‬ fits with the *Qina* rhythm of the context (3 + 2).

15b MT ("I cause him to see") unexpectedly jumps from the petition addressed to Yahweh to a promise by Yahweh in which the object ("him") has no antecedent in this context. The proposal to read ‫הַרְאֵנוּ‬ (J. Wellhausen) fits the context. Although MT possibly arose from a scribal error (‫א‬ instead of ‫ה‬), it is even more likely a conscious change of the petition into a promise of salvation (see below, p. 227). Moreover, MT is a result of the more usual understanding that ‫צֵאתְךָ‬ in v. 15a refers to the people's exodus, not Yahweh's (Exod. 13:3; 23:15; Deut. 11:10; Ps. 114:1, etc.).

16a Here ‫מִן‬ actually means separation, removal "out of the way," and comes close to being a negation: "shame *instead* of might"; cf. Hos. 6:6; Prov. 8:10 and Ges-K §119w.

17a In comparisons, the designation of the class is indicated in Hebrew by the article; see BrSynt §21cβ.

17b–b ‫אֶל־יהוה אֱלֹהֵינוּ‬ is probably a later interpretation (K. Marti; J. M. P. Smith; R. Vuilleumier, et al.); in the context, Yahweh is addressed (vv. 14f. and 17bβ, 18); moreover, in vv. 14–17aα only bicola occur; here a third colon seems out of place. The purpose of the interpolation is to insure that in the word ‫מִמְּךָ‬ ("before you" in v. 17bβ) Yahweh is seen as the one who is addressed and not, incorrectly, Israel. All the ancient versions already presuppose MT. Gk, Vg, Syr connect ‫אֶל־יהוה‬ ‫אֱלֹהֵינוּ‬ with the following word, ‫יִפְחָדוּ‬, as does the accentuation in MT ("to Yahweh, our God, they come trembling"; cf. Hos. 3:5b and H. W. Wolff, *Hosea,* note 1:2b). To the place of departure (‫מִן‬, "out of their strongholds"), the nations' destination (‫אֶל‬) "to Yahweh" has been added later. It is less likely that, instead of ‫אֶל־יהוה אֱלֹהֵינוּ‬, the last three words of v. 17 are a secondary addition; and that in ‫מִמְּךָ‬ Israel is addressed (thus B. Renaud, 367f.). For there is absolutely no indication in the text that vv. 16f. are not the continuation of the prayer in vv. 14f. Rather, a clear connection of these verses is supported by the following observations: (1) there are petitions in v. 15b (conj.): "let us *see!*" and in v. 16a: "may the nations *see!*"; furthermore, (2) the alliteration ‫יִרְאוּ־יִירָאוּ‬, which connects v. 14 with v. 16; finally, (3) the *Qina* rhythm throughout 14–17, which is preserved when the phrase ‫אֶל־יהוה אֱלֹהֵינוּ‬ is bracketed.

18a Targ (‫לֵית‬) reads ‫אֵין‬ ("none") instead of ‫מִי‬.

18b–b K. Marti, J. M. P. Smith, et al., consider v. 18aβ to be an interpolation, which "as a secondary addition excludes the heathen from forgiveness" (A. Weiser, 288). However, the transition from the direct address form in v. 18aα to the third person cannot be used as evidence here because vv. 18b–19a also contain the third person; see below, pp. 216f. ("Form").

18c Gk (εἰς μαρτύριον) has incorrectly vocalized the word as ‫לָעֵד‬ ("as witness").

19a In light of the following verb, here ‫יָשׁוּב‬, in the same imperfect tense without a ‫ו‬, has an adverbial meaning: "again," "once more" (cf. Joüon, *Gr* §177b).

19b MT is to be retained, for the imperfect is secured by the context; the transition to the second person singular is supported by v. 20a,b. The reading ‫וְהִשְׁלִיךְ‬ (BHS) is not, therefore, based upon sufficient grounds, even if Gk, Syr, Vg, Targ continue the third person from the preceding sentences. See below, pp. 216f. ("Form").

19c MT ("their sins") may have arisen in order to rhyme with יָם (v. 19bα) (?); however, חַטֹּאאתֵנוּ is secured by Mss, Gk, Syr, Vg, and supported by the first person plural suffixes in vv. 19aα,β, 20b.

20a Gk (κατὰ τὰς ἡμέρας), probably influenced by vv. 14b, 15a, incorrectly reads כִּימֵי ("as in the days . . .").

Form

According to its form and content, 7:8–20 stands in contrast to almost all of the previous passages in the book of Micah. Not one word of prophetic complaint or accusation is to be found here, neither threat, nor instruction, nor promise. (Only the insertion in vv. 11–13 is an exception; see above, note 11a and below, pp. 223ff.) Rather, the style and the forms contained in the psalms are to be recognized; perceptible here is the voice of the community, which was often previously addressed. That the community speaks here is noticeable in various ways. In vv. 8–10, the community confesses, as a collective "I" (first person singular), its guilt and especially its trust in God's salvation. In vv. 14–17, as the people of God (עַמְּךָ v. 14a), the community presents its petition with its lamentation to its God. In vv. 18–20 the members of the community (first person plural in vv. 19a, b [see note 19c], 20b) extol in hymnic exaltation the incomparability of their God, whose readiness to forgive is the basis for their new trust. Each passage, therefore, presented either in the style of a confession (vv. 8–10, 18b–19a: Yahweh in the third person) or in the form of an address (vv. 14–17, 18a, 19b–20: Yahweh in the second person), is primarily concerned with the relationship of the community to its God. Consequently, the text contains liturgical forms: confession of trust, elements of laments within a petition, and hymns of praise (cf. H. Gunkel, Th. Lescow, et al.).

Although such liturgical passages are thus to be recognized here, nevertheless in the composition of the text we do not find the structural ordering of a realized liturgy with responses. This is the case even if one maintains that vv. 11f. and v. 13 each contain a prophetic promise uttered from within the cultic sphere. Such a promise would not precede the words of lament in vv. 14–17; rather, it would have to belong after it (cf. Ps. 85). On the other hand, in such an instance the confession of confidence in vv. 8–10 would have to follow vv. 11–13, not precede it. Moreover, we find neither catchword connections nor thematic correspondences that would be expected in liturgical responses (cf. Psalm 12). Although the hope for Israel's salvation is common to all four passages, the path to this goal is nevertheless described quite differently.

After this preliminary sketch of the four units, we must now analyze each one according to its own characteristics.

An "I" speaks throughout vv. 8–10. From the content it is clear that this is a collective expression for the community. It is addressed in v. 10a as feminine (אֱלֹהָיִךְ), as it is in the later addition in v. 11a (גְּדֵרָיִךְ). This probably refers to the "daughter of Zion" (see 1:13; 4:8, 10, 13). Targ (see note 9a) expressly adds that here the city of "Jerusalem speaks." Correspondingly, its "enemy" (feminine) is a political entity. It is addressed in v. 8a in a negative summons to rejoice. This form occurs not infrequently —also in a positive formulation; as a rule the enemy is also in the feminine, as we find here. The reason for this may be that in its positive formulation, the summons to rejoice occurs in fertility oracles (as a promise of salvation in the sphere of the fertility cult, as in Isa. 54:1; Hos. 9:1; cf. Lam. 4:21[bβ!]). In v. 8 apparently a different reason is predominant: the form occurs in oracles against foreign nations in which cities and countries generally are addressed as feminine (cf. Isa. 14:29; Lam. 4:21; differently in Obad. 12). The negated summons to rejoice can be a typical element in oracles against foreign nations, as is especially indicated by Lam. 4:21, which is a positive but ironically intended counterpart (cf. F. Crüsemann, *Studien zur Formgeschichte von Hymnus und Danklied,* WMANT 32 [1969] 60–65). What follows appears to be nothing other than the motivation for the prohibition to rejoice: the occasion for the previous joy of the enemy, Israel's fall, exists no more (vv. 8aβ,b 9); moreover, the victress herself will fall (v. 10). This extensive motivation transforms the oracle against foreign nations into a song of confidence in salvation. It begins with three-stress bicola (vv. 8–9aα), changes to two-stress bicola at the climax (vv. 9b–10a conj.), concluding with a prosodic unit with three cola (3 + 3 + 2 stresses).

In vv. 11f. we find initially a threefold יום (at the beginning of vv. 11a, b and 12a). Instead of a *nomen rectum,* at first יום is more closely modified by an entirely unusual construction of the infinitive with ל; then by expressions to which ההוא or הוא (as relative particles; see note 11c) form the transition. The third elucidation of the word יום (v. 12aα) is expanded by three synonymous phrases. This commentary on יום— extremely unusual from a syntactical point of view—apparently is intended to explain more precisely a certain day, presumably the point in time designated by the word עתה at the conclusion of the previous unit. Here we find the style of a gloss that in the surrounding context is comparable only with 7:4b (see above, p. 203).

Verse 13 is separate from vv. 11f. according to style and content. A later prose addition, it expands the prophecy in v. 10 into universal dimensions and at the same time takes away the glimmer of hope for the nations expressed in the future expectation in vv. 16f. (see below, pp. 227f. on 7:17 and cf. 5:14).

Verses 14–17 present a song of lament which merely alludes to the distress of the people of God (v. 14a); the passage proceeds immediately to the offering of petitions whose concern is first the people of God (v. 14b, 15) and then the nations (vv. 16f.). That both groups of petitions belong together is indicated by the continuation of the optative style in vv. 16f., which contain verbs in the same imperfect tense that began in v. 14b (further, see note 17b–b). The prayer appears to be self-contained also in that it exhibits throughout the rhythm typical of laments (3 + 2 stresses, *Qina* verse) (on v. 17aβ,b, see note 17b–b).

Like vv. 8–10 and 14–17, vv. 18–20 are also to be viewed as an originally self-contained unit. These verses develop the theme of forgiveness of sins in a completely different way than what is suggested in v. 9. Concerning the foreign nations, to which considerable room is devoted in the preceding lamenting petition, there is not one syllable in vv. 18–20. Critics have questioned the internal unity of the passage, since the statements about Yahweh in the third person (vv. 18aβ, b, 19a) occur between sentences which address Yahweh in the second person (vv. 18aα, 19b, 20). The former has been considered a secondary addition (cf. B. Stade;

K. Marti; W. Nowack). But the change from second to third person may not be sufficient reason for such a conclusion. For sentences formulated as direct address which first present a closer description of the addressee with participles often shift from participial expressions to clauses containing finite verbs in the third person (cf. 3:1ff., 9ff.); however, this can lead later to clauses that again are formulated in direct address (merely cf. 3:12 after 3:9b–11 with 7:19b, 20 after 7:18b, 19a). Thus here, forms of the hymn of petition (second person) and of the hymn of confession (third person) are closely united.

Of more significance is the transition from the statements with participle and perfect verbs in v. 18 to sentences with imperfect verbs in vv. 19–20. The former have a declarative meaning and are to this extent constitutive for the hymn; they sing about experiencing the mercy and love of Israel's God. The latter (vv. 19–20) are intended (on the basis of former!) to be understood in a future sense. After v. 18 they cannot have a optative sense, as in vv. 14b, 16f. Rather, vv. 19–20 are expressions of steadfast confidence and trust (as in v. 9b); they relate the deeds of Yahweh to the singers themselves (first person plural in vv. 19aα,β, 20b; on v. 19b see note 19c). The rhythm changes within this hymn of praise. Three bicola with two stresses in vv. 18a, 19a are interrupted by a three-stress bicolon in v. 18b; then there is a shift to three prosodic units with 3 + 2 stresses in vv. 19b–20.

The variety of form and structure of the three psalmlike passages in vv. 8–10; 14–17; 18–20, and the later additions in vv. 11f., 13 make it improbable that vv. 8–20 present the original unit of a self-contained liturgy. These passages were not combined until the work of the redactor (cf. J. L. Mays, 155f.; B. Renaud, 379ff.). Thus the unit is a literary compilation. Each of the three miniature psalms is itself an echo that responds to the reading of all or a part of the preceding passages in the book of Micah (cf. Isa. 12:1–3 and 12:4–6). This will have to be shown in detail. But when and where was such an echo from the community given to these prophetic sayings; when and where was such a collection of answers made?

Setting

Let us first inquire into the probable date of this collection of psalms and then into the setting-in-life both of the individual units and of their compilation.

Most of the passages in 4:1—7:7 show evidence that their origin is from the exilic or postexilic time. This already makes it improbable that the concluding psalm-collection and its individual units came into existence before the exile; indeed, without exception the latest literary stratum of the prophetic books is found at their very end. In general the Psalms seldom mention any details that provide a basis for determining their date. Concerning our passage, scholars think they find some indication of the date in the geographical references in v. 14 (Carmel, Bashan, and Gilead), where place-names point to the area of the Northern Kingdom, which was brought to its final collapse with the conquest of Samaria in 722. But the Northern Kingdom had already lost the areas mentioned here because of the Syro-Ephraimite war in 733 (2 Kings 15:29; see below, pp. 225f.). Thus on the basis of geographical references, it has been thought that the entire passage could be understood in terms of the time prior to 733 (e.g., O. Eissfeldt, A. S. van der Woude, J. T. Willis). In this regard O. Eissfeldt (262ff./65ff.) connected v. 14aβ,γ with the words that directly address Yahweh ("you who dwell alone in the forest/in the midst of Carmel"). Had there been such a Northern Israelite view of Yahweh's dwelling place on Carmel as a counterpart to the dwelling place of Yahweh on Mount Zion, then one would at least expect (בְּרֹאשׁ) ("on the peak") instead of בתוך כרמל ("in the midst of Carmel"); on this and other counter-arguments cf. the detailed critique of B. Renaud, 372ff., and see above, note 14a.

If we seek an answer to the problem of the date of this concluding passage by comparing its language and theme with related strata in the Old Testament, then the geographical references themselves in v. 14 already point in an entirely different direction. Gilead and Bashan are mentioned together elsewhere only in Deut. 3:10, 12f.; 4:43; Josh. 20:8; 2 Kings 10:33, passages that belong to the Deuteronomistic history; together with Carmel, they occur only in Jer. 50:19. All of these texts, at the earliest, stem from the exilic period. Jeremiah 50:19 is of particular significance. This text speaks of the time after the fall of the Babylonian Empire, i.e., the time when the exiles returned to their own land. According to v. 19, the future Israel will be restored to these fertile areas named in our text; located particularly in the region east of Jordan, they belonged to the former Northern Kingdom, but had not been under Israelite control for the past two hundred years. The petition in Mic. 7:14b corresponds to the promise in Jeremiah (50:19), especially in that there Bashan and Gilead, as in v. 14, are characterized as a (fertile) pastureland (רעה) for Yahweh's flock, the people of God.

That the concluding psalms could not have been composed before 587 is also indicated by their numerous reminiscences of Lamentations, a book which belongs to the exilic period. The clearest of these is found in the prohibition of the "enemy's" (malicious) joy ([Schaden-] Freude) in 7:8, which appears to be a freely composed imitation of Lam. 4:21 (cf. also Lam. 1:21 and see above, pp. 215f.); to be sure, here the omission of the name "Edom" might not be by chance. Edom's hostile position concerning the fall of Jerusalem in 587 is repeatedly emphasized in the early exilic period (as in Lam. 4:21 and especially in Obad. 11–14; see Wolff, *Obadiah and Jonah* 42f.). On the other hand, corresponding to the connection of v. 14 with Jer. 50:19, the author of Mic. 7:8 might instead be thinking of Babylonia as the enemy (cf. the context with Jer. 50:1ff.). Other reminiscences of Lamentations are also found: the arrogant scorn of the enemy (cf. vv. 8a, 10 with Lam. 1:21; 2:15–16); the lament over the darkness (cf. v. 8b with Lam. 5:17); the confession that disaster, as a plague from Yahweh, stems from guilt (cf. v. 9a with Lam. 1:5, 8f., 17f.; 5:16); the complaint about loneliness (cf. v. 14a with Lam. 1:1; 3:28); the expectation of the return of the ancient time of deliverance (cf. vv. 14b–15 with Lam. 5:21); and the hope in Yahweh's mercy and goodness (cf. vv. 9b and 18–20 with Lam. 3:31–33). These motifs in the book of Lamentations recur throughout the period of the exile and beyond, but in Mic. 7:8–20 they are used with a particular clarity and frequency.

The present shape of our text is rather to be dated during the postexilic era. This conclusion derives not only from our general considerations of this concluding piece (see above, p. 217), but even more from its special proximity to texts in Trito-Isaiah. Let me mention only the following motifs from Isa. 59:9–15 and 63:7—64:11[12]: the reference to "darkness" and "light" (cf. v. 8b with Isa. 59:9b); the confession of guilt (cf. v. 9a with Isa. 59:12a; 64:4b, 8[5b, 9]); "justice" and "righteousness" as saving gifts (cf. v. 9b with Isa. 59:9a, 11b, 14); the imagery of "shepherding" the flock (cf. v. 14 with Isa. 63:11) in connection with Yahweh's people ("your people," Isa. 63:14; 64:8[9]); the reference to the "days of old" (cf. v. 14 with Isa. 63:10, 11); the desire that the "peoples may tremble" (cf. vv. 16f. with Isa. 64:1[2]); the praise of Yahweh's "mercy" and "gracious kindness" (cf. vv. 18–20 with Isa. 63:7, 15b); Israel as Yahweh's "possession" (cf. v. 18 with Isa. 63:17); the expression "our fathers" (cf. v. 20 with Isa. 64:10[11]); and, finally, the mention of "Abraham" (cf. v. 20 with Isa. 63:16). It should be noted that in prophecy prior to Ezekiel (33:24), Abraham is never mentioned! Not until Deutero-Isaiah (41:8; 51:2; cf. also the post-Isaian passage, Isa. 29:22) does Abraham become theologically significant as the agent of blessing. The reference to Abraham in Isa. 63:16 is made as critically as in Ezek. 33:24. By contrast, it is unique in Mic. 7:20 that "Abraham," as well as "Jacob," have become the names of the present and future people of Israel (see below, p. 231).

These individual observations confirm the date of this group of psalms as the (late) exilic or (more probably) postexilic period; such was proposed by J. Wellhausen, B. Stade, and H. Gunkel, and subsequently given frequent scrutiny, up to J. L. Mays (155) and B. Renaud (376f.). If the gloss in v. 11 presupposes that the building of the wall under Nehemiah was not yet completed (see below, pp. 223f.), then the composition of these later additions in vv. 11f., 13, at the latest, would have to have been in the first half of the fifth century. The songs very probably arose from within the Jerusalem community (see above, p. 215 and note 9a). Presumably the individual units within the psalm at first functioned in connection with the lamentation ceremonies, celebrated at such times as are attested in Zech. 7:3, 5; 8:19, which recalled the fall of Jerusalem and the destruction of the sanctuary. In such a setting the reminiscences of words addressed to foreign nations (v. 8a; cf. v. 16f. and Wolff, *Obadiah and Jonah* 42ff.), and of the songs collected in the book of Lamentations, become intelligible (cf. H. J. Kraus, *Threni,* BK 20, 11f.). Here, confession of guilt, acceptance of punishment, petition for redemption and new leadership, as well as praise for the mercy and faithfulness of God, have their meaningful place. To such worship services belong, first, the reading of ancient prophecies which had announced disaster (cf. above, p. 52 on chaps. 1–3; also 6:9–16); second, contemporary and applicable prophetic sayings which cast a critical or comforting light on the present situation (see above, p. 138 on chaps. 4–5; also 6:2–8; 7:1–7); finally, the psalmlike answer of the worshiping community in response to the preceding proclamation. Those redactors who collected, supplemented, and handed on the most varied prophecies probably also pieced together these concluding psalms. Although this passage does not present a self-contained liturgy (see above, p. 215), at first its individual units, and perhaps later the passage as a whole, function within the liturgy as the community's response to the words of the prophets. To these redactors the commentaries which supplement the passage in vv. 11f. and 13 are also to be attributed.

Commentary

[7:8] The song of confidence in 7:8–10, which is a response to the harsh message contained in the book of Micah, completely presupposes the historical experience of catastrophe. Jerusalem understands itself to be confronted by the malicious joy of its enemies. Obadiah attests to the gloating of the Edomites at the subjugation of Jerusalem in the year 587: the enemy opens wide its mouth and delights in the disaster of the city and its inhabitants (Obad. 12f.). The book of Lamentations (1:7; 2:15f.) attests to the resounding laughter over the ruin of the city. According to Ps. 137:7 the destroyers incite people further with the cry, "Raze it! Raze it!" Triumphantly they call out, "They are laid desolate! They are given us to devour!" (Ezek. 35:12, 14). In such a manner the enemy expressed its "joy" over the fulfillment of Mic. 3:12 (cf. 4:11).

But now the Jerusalem community need not tolerate such words of scorn. The direct address to the "enemy" (fem.), characteristic of the style of an "expressive gesture," suggests that the community turns toward the enemy in a kind of symbolic action. Such expressive gestures occur elsewhere in the context of lamentation ceremonies of the postexilic community (cf. W. Zimmerli, *Ezekiel* 1: 182ff.; H. W. Wolff, *Obadiah and Jonah* 43f.). Thus confidence in Yahweh in the face of the enemy is first expressed by denying the enemy its malicious joy *(Schadenfreude)*. The opponents are called "my enemy" (on the feminine singular, see above, p. 215). To whom does this refer? Edom is not mentioned, as in Obadiah, Ezekiel 35, and Psalm 137. The community's gaze may be directed to its chief opponent, Babylon, including its army (see above, p. 137, and cf. גוים in v. 16). In the preceding liturgical reading, at first the "enemy" is an oppressor from among their own people (cf. 2:8); later, it is the multitude of the nations (4:11; cf. 5:5b, 8, 14).

What kind of rejoicing is the "enemy" to be denied? In the style of a confession, Jerusalem gives expression to its confidence with two words which comprehend its present and future history: "(Although) I have fallen, (nevertheless) I shall rise up." נפל refers to military defeat. Lam. 2:21 says, "In the dust of the streets lie the young and the old; my maidens and my young men have *fallen* by the sword" (cf. Lam. 1:7; Jer. 25:27; Amos 5:2; 8:14). Different from what Amos (5:2) expects, however, this fall will be followed by a rising up. Hence, the essence of the comforting message in 4:9f. and 4:11–13 from the preceding liturgical reading is confidently appropriated. It is not impossible, however, that this refers not only to political destruction and reconstitution, but—corresponding to the following confession—also to guilt and return to Yahweh, after the manner of Jer. 8:4; Prov. 24:16. (Cf. the Agraphon of Jesus, "As often as you fall, stand up, and you will be saved!" Cf. J. Karawidopulos, *ZNW* 62 [1971] 299f. and *TRE* 2:106.)

The second כי-clause (see notes 8b, c) expresses the same trust, despite a hopeless situation that will yet continue: they will "sit in darkness"; i.e., they will be exposed to complete helplessness. In darkness one can only "grope like the blind" and even stumble at noon (Isa. 59:9f.). He who lives in darkness is in principle like the dead (according to Lam.

3:6; Pss. 88:7[6]; 143:3; Job 10:21). In the reading of the ancient words of Micah, the worshiping community has heard that the false prophets will be handed over to darkness, no longer able to discern the word of God, and thus they will lose their existence as prophets (3:6; see above, pp. 103f.). At the same time the existence of Jerusalem (3:11f.) and of the people of God is at stake. Out of the midst of this threat upon of their very life, they are nevertheless able to confess, "Yahweh is my light." Here "light" not only has the general meaning of life and its possibilities for self-direction and action; even more, it refers to concrete salvation from the threat of death (Ps. 27:1; etc.), including death in war (Isa. 9:1[2]; Ps. 18:29f.[28f.]). Jerusalem will partake of this "light" of Yahweh's beaming presence, whereas the nations will be swallowed up by darkness (Isa. 60:1). According to Micah's ancient prophecy (2:1), the oppressors will execute their evil plans by the help of the morning light. However, Yahweh, as the creator of light and darkness, remains the sovereign Lord of salvation and doom; the people he has tested will ultimately be liberated (Isa. 45:7f.).

[7:9] In light of the prophetic word, the worshiping community soberly confesses that it has yet to bear the punitive wrath of its God. A word that occurs infrequently, זַעַף can be used to describe the raging of the stormy sea in Jon. 1:15. Otherwise the word is used in connection with Yahweh only in Isa. 30:30, where it emphasizes the tempestuous and fiery raging of his wrath (cf. H. Ringgren, *ThWAT* 2:627f.). With this word the community accepts the threats of judgment attested to in 1:6—6:16 as expressions of the wrath of Yahweh which has become a reality. The awakened anger of God corresponds to the passion of his love, by which he elected his people and provided them with his gifts. The daughter of Zion understands her history not as a struggle of nations against one another and against her but rather as God's dealings with her, which she willingly takes upon herself and bears (נשא). The enemy also must come to know this. Only by the acknowledgment of one's own guilt and transgression is it possible to accept the wrath of God. But in so doing the community accepts at the same time the accusations spoken by the voices of the prophets—accusations proclaimed to it through the centuries down to the present time (on חטא[ת], cf. 1:5, 13; 3:8; 6:7, 13).

The history of Yahweh with his community is founded upon confidence, because his wrath has a purpose: ". . . until he pleads my case and executes justice for me. . . ." The purpose of oppression and disaster is not to destroy the transgressor but to bring about his dedication to a new life (Isa. 57:15; Ezek. 33:11; 1 Cor. 11:32). As the "light" of his community, Yahweh liberates it not only from its enemies (v. 8), but even more from its own guilt (v. 9a). The word ריב denotes the lawsuit, indeed, the legal process in its various stages, as well as the disputation as such (see above, pp. 173f.). It indicates that the history of Israel, and in particular Israel's history with its enemies, is understood as a legal suit between Jerusalem and its God. In our passage the reconstituting of the lawsuit unambiguously means that the way is being paved for redemption. The judge, strange to say, acts as lawyer and defense attorney. This is summarized in Lam. 3:58 by the statement, "Thou hast taken up my lawsuit, thou hast redeemed my life." In this manner, v. 9 in our psalm of trust also recalls a previously read prophetic word, which has been presented as a lawsuit speech (cf. 6:2). Now the goal of the legal process is "to execute justice." We met the expression עשׂה משׁפּט in 6:8. According to Deut. 10:18, it is Yahweh who stands in a gracious relationship to orphans and widows (see above, p. 180); then Mic. 6:8 states that Yahweh expects his people to "execute justice." Now Yahweh is said to execute justice for the entire community. We can comprehend Yahweh's deeds only as help, the pronouncement of innocence, and redemption. The proximity of such language to Trito-Isaiah confirms this interpretation, where in Isa. 59:11 we find the parallel יְשׁוּעָה // מִשְׁפָּט. There, too, the context contains a confession of sin, as well as the imagery of light and darkness; in Isaiah 59 the mood is one of tense expectancy, here by contrast it is one of trust.

It is characteristic that the expression about "light" (v. 8b) is altered and taken up again in v. 9bβ. "He will lead me to the light," says the community, expressing its trust. יצא hiph., a traditional term for the Exodus (see above, p. 175)—especially when it is connected with the goal (לאור, "to the light he will lead me")—is an unambiguous witness to the fact that the reconstitution of the legal process, as well as of the "execution of justice," can only be understood as a saving deed. This is no less true for the last statement in the verse. The צדקה anticipated by the confessing community is *his* צדקה, Yahweh's deed. It is an event which the community will "see" (ראה ב; or, better), "experience," "encounter." The community experiences liberation and redemption. Borrowing the language of Deutero-Isaiah, צדקה occurs in synonymous parallelism with אור, with שׁלום, and ישׁע ("light," "salvation," and "liberation," Isa. 45:7f.); further, it stands parallel with תְּשׁוּעָה ("redemption," Isa. 46:13) and with יְשׁוּעָה ("help," Isa. 51:6). Moreover, one should consider such psalm texts as Pss. 5:9[8]; 31:2[1]; 40:11[10]; 71:2, 15, 24; 98:2, in which צדקה denotes the event of redemption from disaster (cf. Mic. 6:5 and see above, p. 177, and F. Crüsemann, "Jahwes Gerechtigkeit *(ṣᵉdāqā/ṣādāq)* im Alten Testament," *EvTh* 36 [1976] 427–450). In this way Yahweh's deeds of salvation make an end to the rejoicing of the enemy (cf. Ps. 35:24). Here Yahweh's saving "righteousness" is related to external disaster as well as to guilt (cf. v. 9a and v. 8b).

[7:10] To be sure, in v. 10 reference is again made to the enemy's oppression. The style of confession found in the words addressed to foreign nations (v. 8aα) is also characteristic of the conclusion of this psalm of confidence. Here, however, the "enemy" (fem.) is no longer addressed. She must now become a witness to Yahweh's redemption and justification of Jerusalem. Rejoicing (v. 8aα) now changes places with shame (v. 10aα,b; cf. Ezek. 35:14f.). Like Jerusalem, the enemy will "see" Yahweh's saving deed (cf. v. 10aα with v. 9bβ). Thus Yahweh's צדקה is again presented as an historical event which can be seen by the public eye. Zion's opponents must stand there ashamed. Disgrace "covers" the enemy, "cloaks her," so that nothing but her disgrace can be seen. In particular, the enemy herself is now exposed to scorn and derision to the extent that she had previously scorned Jerusalem with the taunting question, "Where is your God?" (see note 10c). In the Old Testament this question always occurs as a derisive reproach made by the heathen nations (thus Joel 2:17; Pss. 79:10; 115:2; cf. Ps. 42:4[3], 11[10]). Yahweh's redemptive deeds for Zion pose anew the question about God not only for Zion but for the nations as well. Thus the community's confidence, which has replaced the scorn of the enemy, is strengthened in a multiplicity of ways.

Again, there is a correspondence between the "seeing" of the "enemy" and the "seeing" of Zion in v. 10b. Now, however, what Zion sees is not Yahweh's saving deed, as in v. 9bβ, but the "enemy" and her misfortune. When the object of ראה is indicated by the preposition ב, here as in v. 9b, the emphasis is placed on the intensity of the experience of "seeing." What is seen becomes a feast for the eyes; the view is pleasing (cf. also 4:11, חזה ב). Zion's trust in Yahweh also has its basis in the present collapse of the victor, who to this point has had an attitude of superiority. The new situation ("now!") is pictured in a drastic manner: the enemy is trampled like dirt in the streets. One cannot be brought down any lower. היה למרמס means "to be trampled down" (referring to a field or vineyard, long cultivated and protected, which has been broken into by cattle or wild animals; Isa. 5:5; 7:25; Ezek. 34:18f.); "to be suppressed" (referring to the nations, who are assailed by an enemy; Isa. 10:6; 28:18; and here). The simile with טיט, "dirt," "slime," "mire" of the streets (cf. Zech. 9:3; 10:5; in 2 Sam. 22:43 = Ps. 18:43[42], עָפָר//טיט, "dust," "filth") again elucidates the depth of the humiliation. With this action, all fear and despondency in the presence of the "enemy" is removed. Trust in Yahweh and a serene estimate of one's opponent belong together.

[7:11] Like 7:4 (see above, p. 202), the following phrases (v. 11) appear to be notes by the commentator, although here the word יום occurs at the beginning of each of the three phrases. They are connected with that point in time anticipated in vv. 9b–10. In Obad. 11–14 יום is noticeably repeated (ten times in four verses) in order to describe one and the same prominent historical event. But what is missing here, in contrast to the passage in Obadiah, is syntactic clarity (see note 10a). The fundamental changes that are yet to be expected according to vv. 9b–10 are suggested here in catchword fashion. The community in Zion, the speaker in vv. 8–10, is now in v. 11 the addressee (second person singular feminine). However, vv. 11–14 are not something like an answer or rejoinder to vv. 8–10, the oracle against foreign nations which has been transformed into a psalm of confidence. Rather, vv. 8–10 is presupposed by vv. 11f., 13, which offer a supplementary commentary on this text.

The day of Yahweh's righteousness, a day of victory over the enemy, is initially interpreted for the community in Zion as a time in which the walls of their city will be rebuilt. Instead of the usual word for the city walls, חוֹמָה (cf. Neh. 1:3ff.; Ps. 51:20[18]; Isa. 60:10), here the word גָּדֵר is used. גָּדֵר (גדרה) frequently denotes a protective wall that encloses field and vineyard (1 Sam. 24:4[3]; Ps. 80:13[12]; etc.); however, it can also quite possibly be used (metaphorically) for the city walls (Jer. 49:3; Ps. 89:41[40]; Ezra 9:9; but cf. I. Willi-Plein, 107f., and F. M. Cross, "A Reconstruction of the Judean Restoration," *JBL* 94 [1975] 4–18; note 60 on p. 14). In any case, this meaning is not to be ruled out here, if the text is to be dated before the time of Nehemiah (445–433), and if the

author uses גדר in a metaphorical sense (cf. Pss. 80:13[12]; 89:41[40];
Ezra 9:9). The word's connection with the verb בנה is reminiscent of the
future hope expressed in Trito-Isaiah (Isa. 60:10). In that event, in v. 11a
the building of an actual enclosure is counted among the anticipated
saving deeds of Yahweh.

In v. 11b the second explication of the expected "day" is more
difficult. It will have to be understood in its context between v. 11a and v.
12. Then the word חק is best interpreted as "border," "barrier" (Isa. 5:14;
Jer. 5:22; and cf. note 11d). Accordingly, רחק indicates that such a border,
if not completely eliminated, will certainly be enlarged. Since we often
find the conceptions of Trito-Isaiah in this context, here, in addition to
the words about building of the walls in Isa. 60:10, רחק recalls the opening
of the gates in Isa. 60:11; it is even more reminiscent of Isa. 26:15b (וְרִחַקְתָּ)
and Zech. 2:8f. The expectation that the borders will be extended provides a further commentary on the certainty of liberation from the enemies as it is expressed in vv. 8–10.

[7:12] With v. 12 the interpretative commentary on "that day" reaches a
climax. The realization of "that day" is expressed by the phrase, "They
will come to 'you'" (see notes 12a, c). Although the subject of the sentence
in v. 12aα initially appears to be unclear, nevertheless the three adverbial
modifiers in v. 12aβ,bα,β, by giving the places of departure for those who
are to come, at the same time limit the possibilities of interpretation. One
can only ask: Does v. 12 refer to the entirety of the nations or to the
Israelites of the diaspora? One might understand this to mean people
from all over the world, on the basis of Mic. 4:1f. (= Isa. 2:2f.); Zech.
14:16; Isa. 60:3f., 10 (thus, e.g., O. Eissfeldt); however, in these passages,
the destination and goal of the journey to Zion is always mentioned as
well (see above, pp. 120f., 126). This is not the case here. Hence, the
ancient interpretation is more probable, preserved by Targ (דמן אתור
גלותא), which thinks the verse refers to the Golah, for whom the "coming
(home)" as such would of course mean everything. This interpretation is
confirmed by those texts which also speak of the return home of the exiles
from all over the world, texts which always refer particularly to Assyria
and Egypt as the lands of exile: Zech. 10:10 (8–12); Isa. 11:11(–16);
27:13. To be sure, Assyria and Egypt appear not infrequently side by side
already in preexilic prophecy (Hos. 7:11; 11:5; Jer. 2:18); Lam. 5:6 is
reminiscent of this. Here in v. 12 one would expect to find Babylon
instead of Assyria (as in Mic. 4:10; see above, p. 140); nevertheless, even
in the Babylonian and Persian era, Assyria continued to a large extent to
be the name for the empire to the north (see above, pp. 147f. on Mic. 5:4f.
and Zech. 10:10; Isa. 11:11; 27:13). Along with the (Assyrian) Babylonian
diaspora, the Egyptian diaspora can also be mentioned (Jer. 43:7). In v.
12, as in 2 Kings 19:24 (= Isa. 37:25); Isa. 19:6, Egypt is called מצור. This
word, to be compared with the Akkadian *muṣur,* would sound like I מָצוֹר
to the Hebrew and thus convey to the ear the meaning of "oppression"
(see above, p. 143, on 4:14) (otherwise, Ph. Calderone [1961]). It remains
uncertain whether the reading presupposed by Gk (צר, Tyre; see note 12f)
in v. 12bα is original, even though the rule of alternation in *parallelismus
membrorum* could support this reading; for נהר in v. 12bα, which denotes

the Euphrates, in substance repeats Assyria from v. 12aβ. (Cf. the descriptions of Israel's horizon and of the far reaches of the inhabited earth in Mic. 5:3[4] [see above, p. 146]; further, Gen. 15:18; Deut. 11:24; 1 Kings 5:1; Isa. 11:15; Zech. 9:10; Ps. 72:8.) The concluding sentence in v. 12bβ (see note 12 g–g) is intended to show that the promise is broad enough to include the last dispersed Israelites as well, wherever they might be scattered between the Mediterranean and the Persian Gulf, between Sinai and Lebanon. With this description of the area inhabited by the exiles, these verses of commentary ascribe to the coming time of salvation a condition which is missing from the other promises of return from exile in the book of Micah (2:12f.; 4:6f.; 5:2). With this interpretation of 7:8–10 in 7:11–12, the commentator suggests that, with the consummation of Yahweh's lawsuit with his people, the end is coming not only to the judgment upon Jerusalem and its (hitherto narrowly drawn) borders, but also to Israel's dispersion.

[7:13] The independent prose sentence in v. 13 expands the threat uttered against the "enemy" in vv. 8a, 10, and also anticipates the thoughts expressed in vv. 16f. It juxtaposes a destroyed earth with the Zion community that is protected, extended, and gathered from every part of the world (vv. 11f.). Jerusalem will become something like an oasis in the desert of the earth. A similar portrayal is found in Obad. 16f.; Joel 4:18–20; and Zech. 14:10ff. The "desolation" (שממה) of the earth, which breaks in "upon its inhabitants," is the "fruit," i.e., the yield, the result of "their deeds" (cf. 3:4). The sentence could be a brief summary of Isa. 24:1–6.

[7:14] A lament commences in v. 14; it mentions the distress only briefly by name (v. 14aβ), but it presents in detail a petition for Yahweh's people (v. 14f.) and for the nations of the world (vv. 16f.). The lament is different from the song of trust in vv. 8–10 in that it imploringly calls upon Yahweh, but without mentioning his name. The threefold pronoun ךָ (second singular masculine) is noticeable in the first line; it attests to an awareness of the close relationship: "*Your* people shepherd with *your* rod, the flock of *your* possession!" The petition "to shepherd" (רעה) immediately addresses Yahweh in terms of his office as royal shepherd (2:12; 4:6f.; cf. 5:3 and see above, p. 146). This corresponds with the people's calling itself the "flock of his possession." Yahweh as shepherd and people as flock are motifs of trust that appear frequently in the psalms of prayer (Pss. 80:2[1]; 74:1; 28:9); they also function as the motivation in the hymns (Pss. 95:7; 100:3). Here the prayer, recalling Mic. 2:12; 4:6f., appropriates exilic traditions of promise (see above, p. 86). צאן נחלתך emphasizes less the thought of inheritance than the permanence and inviolability of property; Yahweh has created, by the power of his free choice (Ps. 33:12), the flock as his possession, for which he considers himself responsible. In this, too, we find a motif of trust from the songs of prayer (Isa. 63:17; Joel 2:17). Of the three functions of the shepherd (leading, protecting, feeding; cf. Psalm 23), initially there is indirect mention of defending the flock against the enemy, and then of leading it. For the "rod" (v. 14aα), the shepherd's main tool, serves especially to protect the flock from dangerous attack; its function is also to lead the flock to the good pasture areas of Bashan and Gilead in v. 14b. (A distinction between "rod" as weapon of defense and "staff" as implement for leading does not ensue here as in Ps. 23:4; cf. H. J. Kraus, *Psalms 1–59*, 308.) The function of feeding, together with that of leading, stands behind the reference to the pasture as the destination in v. 14b.

But this does not become intelligible until the sketch of the distress presented in v. 14aβ. The problem consists in the loneliness and seclusion in the wilderness of the scrub. יער is the bush or thicket ruled by wild animals (5:7; cf. 3:12 conj.; on this subject, cf. Isa. 7:23–25). Here the word stands in clear antithesis to כרמל, the fruitful orchard. כרמל is therefore probably not the proper name for that mountain forest on the Mediterranean which, according to its location and significance, hardly corresponds to Bashan and Gilead; nor, in the present structure of the sentence, is Carmel syntactically coordinate with these two areas. "Orchards" were hardly accessible to Jerusalemites, who were largely poor peasants in an expanse of ruins (cf. 2 Kings 25:12). Perhaps the word יער is intentionally chosen to make a connection with Micah's best-known prophecy (3:12). When in this prayer it says that "the thicket" is situated "in the midst of the orchard," the words refer to the narrowly circumscribed territory which alone is accessible to the people as inhabitable land, and as a farming and grazing area. "The orchard" itself (cf. Isa. 29:17; 32:15) is located in the unreachable outlying territory. As is immediately indicated, the reference is to particularly fertile areas such as Bashan and Gilead (see below). The generations of exilic and postexilic times found themselves in a narrow area in and around Jerusalem, cooped up as it were in a wretched scrub. They were "cut off" (לבדד) from the large pasture areas. בַּד is that portion separated from the whole (H. J. Zobel, *ThWAT* 1:511–518). Such "solitude" is an important theme in the songs of lament (Ps. 102:7f.; Lam. 1:1, 3; cf. Ps. 4:9[8]). Hemmed in and cut off—that is the distress which is voiced in this prayer.

But the people uttering this prayer seek an extensive pasture land (v. 14b). The subject of ירעו is now the suffering flock. In this verse, רעה means "finding pasture," "grazing," "feeding on," whereas with the shepherd as subject (v. 14aα), it means "tending," "leading," "looking after." The chief purpose of "tending" is to provide the flock with sufficient grazing. The community, cooped up in a limited space, takes the "days of old" (כימי עולם) as the criterion for its expectations. The early days are considered to be a model for the future and a basis for hope (cf. v. 20b). The petition instructs the community to reclaim "Bashan and Gilead" as pasture land which had been allotted to Israel in early times (Num. 32:1, 26, 33). This is explicitly promised anew in Jer. 50:19 for the return from exile (see above, p. 218). Bashan is the name of a fertile pasture and wooded area situated eastward from the Sea of Tiberias, on either side of the Yarmuk River (Nah. 1:4; Zech. 11:2; Deut. 32:14; Amos 4:1; Ezek. 27:6; 39:18; cf. Wolff, *Joel and Amos* 205). Gilead is situated eastward from the middle of the Jordan on either side of the Jabbok River; according to Num. 32:1 Gilead is particularly suited for raising cattle; Zech. 10:10 mentions it as the (yearned for) region to which the exiles will return. Gilead and Bashan are therefore fertile Transjordan areas for which the community prays, perhaps not only because these areas would provide room for the returning exiles; they would also contribute to the food supply necessary for the inhabitants of Jerusalem (on food shortages in Jerusalem in early postexilic times, cf. Hag. 1:6). Israel, having lost its landed property because of its guilt (cf. 2:3–5, 10; 4:11–13; 5:5b[6b]), now in prayer asks for its return.

[7:15] The days of the distant past are the criterion of hope for a new allotment of the land. Verse 15a, by picking up כִּימֵי from v. 14b, more precisely defines the early time as the days of the exodus from Egypt. Here "your exodus" does not mean that of the people, as it usually does elsewhere (Exod. 13:3; 23:15; Deut. 11:10; Ps. 114:1); rather, it is the exodus of *Yahweh,* which, thematically, is not surprising in light of texts such as Exod. 13:21; 33:14; Judg. 4:14; 2 Sam. 5:24; Ps. 68:8[7]. For those uttering this prayer, everything depends upon Yahweh, to whom these words are addressed. In the period of the diaspora and of the progressive deterioration of Jerusalem, as also in earlier times, help comes only from what is totally unexpected; from what, according to human considerations, is unlikely; indeed, help can only come from the marvelous leading forth of Yahweh and from his redemptive actions. The word נִפְלָאוֹת ("wonders") embraces the incomprehensible deeds of Yahweh's power and help (Exod. 3:20; Judg. 6:13; Pss. 78:11; 98:1; 105:2; cf. Exod. 15:11). "'Let us' see them"—thus the community cries out (probably; see note 15b).

[7:16] The community immediately proceeds with its petition, asking that the nations, too, "may see" (v. 16; cf. רָאָה in vv. 9bβ, 10aα and 10bα). Now their words of supplication concern not only the deeds of Yahweh for his people, but also their effects upon the rest of the world. This train of thought is not seldom found in thematically related songs of praise and prayers (see Exod. 15:13 and vv. 14–16; cf. Pss. 98:2f.; 126:2). What Yahweh's people hope to see as the wonder of his redemption, the nations are to experience as the intervention of his power, which is greater than their own. This continuation of the prayer corresponds to those words which, after the fulfillment of Micah's prophecy against Jerusalem, expected divine judgment upon the nations (cf. Mic. 4:11–13; 5:8[9], 14[15]). Here follows a series of seven verbs which describe the convulsive effect upon the nations when they see Yahweh's saving deeds for Israel. Upon viewing this, the nations will first experience a feeling of *shame,* which is so much the greater because all of the nations' valor and might (on גְּבוּרָה, see above, p. 105) is powerless against Yahweh's unexpected deeds (cf. Isa. 45:15f., 24; Ps. 83:18[17]; also Mic. 7:10aα). Their shame leads to *speechlessness;* for the speaking of scornful words—such as the question, "Where is your God?" (see above, pp. 222f. on v. 10aγ)—their mouth will be closed (cf. Prov. 30:32; Job 40:4[?]; also Mic. 3:7, where after they become ashamed, the false prophets are silenced; see above, pp. 103f.). Why do their *ears* become deaf? Job 26:14 speaks of the "thunder" of Yahweh's deeds. The nations will cease to hear and to speak.

[7:17] As subjugated enemies (cf. Ps. 72:9; Isa. 49:23), they shall become like "serpents" and other "crawling animals"; they shall prostrate themselves flat upon the ground and "lick the dust" like that serpent in Gen.

3:14 upon whom the a curse has fallen. But what is the meaning of the wish that they will "come forth trembling" ממסגרתיהם? רגז has the sense of "quaking" (of the earth) or "trembling" (of humans) (KBL); with the preposition מן in *constructio praegnans,* an unexpressed verb of movement is presupposed (Ges-K §§119ee–gg). Accordingly, the phrase has the sense of "to come forth trembling in dread" (KBL), something like the word חרג ("come out trembling") in Ps. 18:46[45]. What is unclear, there as well as here, is the place of their coming forth. The root I סגר means "to shut," "to lock"; accordingly, מִסְגֶּרֶת is often understood as "prison," "dungeon" (KBL³, E. Sellin, A. S. van der Woude). However, in this context, an act of (external) liberation is hardly conceivable. It probably has to do with the fearful coming forth of nations from their last "hiding places," "fortresses," or "citadels" (A. Weiser, W. Rudolph, L. C. Allen, et al.), so that here an act of nonresistance and capitulation is described. They surrender themselves to Yahweh, as the interpolation אל־יהוה אלהינו (see note 17b–b) expressly emphasizes. The final two verbs underline once again the nations' quaking (on פחד, cf. Hos. 3:5) reverence before Yahweh, for which Yahweh's people have petitioned. ירא with מן corresponds to Deuteronomistic linguistic usage (cf. 1:29; 2:4; 7:18; 20:1; Josh. 10:8); here the phrase denotes the basis and origin of their awe: it is Yahweh. At the end of a series of verbs expressing excitement and motion, the phrase can have a particular meaning. וְיִרְאוּ ("may they fear") takes up not only the sound of the word יִרְאוּ ("may they see") from the beginning of the petition for the nations; it also denotes the results of that experience. Similarly, in the narrative about the sailors in Jon. 1:16, after their provocative, agitating experience, the same word is used: they stand before Yahweh in fear and obedience (cf. H. W. Wolff, *Obadiah and Jonah* 121). If such a turning to Yahweh by the nations is one purpose of this prayer, then its impulse may derive more from Mic. 4:1–3 (and 5:3[4]) than from 4:11–13. In any event, however, the prayer also indicates an awareness that the history of Israel and that of the nations, in the final analysis, are indissolubly connected with each other.

[7:18] The last passage is a two-part hymn which, on the basis of what is known about Yahweh (v. 18), further extols what may be confidently expected from him (v. 19f.; see above, p. 217). The rhetorical question, "Who is a God like you?" is a typical hymnic form used by Israel to praise the uniqueness of its God. Usually, as is found here, the question is formulated in the style of direct address (Exod. 15:11; Jer. 10:7; Ps. 89:9[8]; etc.). Similar questions also occur in Israel's environment (cf. H. Gunkel; J. Begrich, *Einleitung in die Psalmen* [1933]; C. J. Labuschagne, *The Incomparability of Yahweh in the Old Testament,* POS 5 [1966]; G. Johannes, "Unvergleichlichkeitsformulierungen im Alten Testament," Dissertation, University of Mainz [1968]; F. Crüsemann, *Studien zur Formgeschichte von Hymnus und Danklied in Israel,* WMANT 32 [1969] 177f.). It is not impossible that the redactor, in placing at the end of the book a hymn begun with such a rhetorical question, has the hymn respond to the liturgical reading of these prophecies; and that he has done so also because the hymn can and ought to be understood as an interpretation of the name "Micah" (see above, p. 35).

In what does Yahweh's uniqueness consist? Often his incomparable greatness, power and glory are praised (e.g., Ps. 89:7–9[6–8], as with many deities of foreign nations). At the same time, and to a greater degree, his marvelous (redemptive) deeds are extolled (Pss. 71:19; 77:14 [13]; 86:8; Exod. 15:11; cf. Exod. 9:14), especially on behalf of the poor and helpless (Pss. 35:10; 113:5–7); his faithfulness to his covenant and word (1 Kings 8:23; Isa. 44:7; 46:9f.); and his nearness to those who call on him (Deut. 4:7). However, here as nowhere else—especially not in the pagan world, as far as I can determine—the incomparability of Yahweh's forgiveness of sins is celebrated in song. In a highly solemn manner, in seven sentences, each with different expressions and with the three most important Old Testament words for sin, Yahweh's forgiveness is praised as unique among his inconceivable deeds.

The series of expressions begins with two participial clauses. נשא עון is the most frequent (figurative) expression for forgiveness in the Old Testament (cf. J. J. Stamm, *Erlösen und Vergeben im Alten Testament* [1940] 67). The expression is most intelligible when understood in terms of the ritual of the great day of atonement, when the scapegoat bears away (ונשא) "all the transgressions" (כָּל־עֲוֹנֹתָם) of Israel into the desert (thus Lev. 16:22; see R. Knierim, *Die Hauptbegriffe für Sünde im Alten Testament* [1965] 119). In Isa. 53:12 it says that the servant of Yahweh "takes away the sins of many." עון is the first of the three chief words for sin (occurring 231 times in the Old Testament); it is a noun formed on the root עוה ("diverge," "transgress"), which originally meant "divergence," "perversity," "transgression" (R. Knierim, 237ff.). The word's own particular meaning becomes diminished due to usage that intermingles it with the synonymous nouns for sin and guilt, even though its particular nuance should not go unnoticed (R. Knierim, 238f.).

The second participial clause denotes sin with the word פשע, the most severe of the three synonyms; occurring only 93 times in the Old Testament, it means "revolt," "apostasy," "rebellion" (see above, pp. 56, 105 on 1:5; 3:8). The act of forgiveness is called עבר על־, "to pass by," "to overlook," "to let go unnoticed"; with this meaning, the phrase also occurs in Prov. 19:11: "A man's insight makes him slow to anger, but the best thing about him is that he overlooks offense" (עֲבֹר עַל־פֶּשַׁע). עבר על־ (construed with sin) may be a shade stronger than עבר ל (construed with persons) in Amos 7:8; 8:2 ("to pass by benignly," "not to intervene with punishment"; see H. W. Wolff, *Joel und Amos* 301). The forgiving indulgence toward "rebellion" spoken of here is for the שארית. With the word שארית, the passage takes up the prophecy concerning the redemption of the "remnant," Israel, a word which is heard repeatedly in the prophecies of promise within the book of Micah (2:12; 4:7; 5:6–7[7–8]; see above, pp. 154f.). When the phrase שארית נחלתו occurs here (its only occurrence in the book of Micah), it emphasizes the particularly intimate connection of the "remnant" with its God; this is similarly expressed in 7:14 with the phrase "flock of his possession" (see above, p. 225). According to 2 Kings 21:14 (Deuteronomistic), where the phrase from Mic. 7:18aβ occurs once again, Yahweh says prior to the exile that the "remnant of my possession" will be given into the hand of the enemy. Such a "giving up" of the remnant means total destruction of its existence, life, and future, with nothing at all remaining. On the other hand, forgiveness as "overlooking rebellion," as "forbearance for the remnant of his possession," now means nothing less than a revocation of the entire prophecy of judgment; thus renewal of existence and of life means that there is a future. Those of Yahweh's possession who survive can expect forgiveness of the guilt which Micah formerly declared. פשע picks up one of the catchwords from Micah's accusations in 3:8 (cf. 1:5, 13b; 6:7). Hence, the second sentence recalls the prophet's exposure of guilt as well as the exilic and postexilic promises (Isa. 43:25; 44:22; etc.).

The third sentence states that forgiveness is the end of Yahweh's wrath. Yahweh "does not retain his wrath for ever." לעד (cf. above, p. 123 on 4:5) points to what is final. That Yahweh's wrath is not continuous but limited by time is extolled in the Psalms, such as in 30:6[5] and 103:9; this also belongs to the message of Trito-Isaiah, according to Isa. 57:16; but also cf. 54:7f. and Jer. 3:12. Similar to Isa. 54:8, here the following sentence in v. 18bβ tells what, in contrast to his wrath, Yahweh essentially (and permanently), indeed, ultimately (Isa. 54:8!) takes pleasure in: חסד. חסד means that gracious kindness of Yahweh which endures as an unconditional trustworthy bond (on the use of the word between persons, see above, p. 181). Yahweh has a relationship of love with such gracious kindness, as is especially characteristic of him (חפץ חסד הוא). This delight in kind and gracious relationships that is proper to Yahweh provides the foundation for his readiness to forgive; forgiveness, in contrast to wrath, possesses the quality of permanence. Thus it is for a theological purpose that the fourth sentence, a כי clause in v. 18bβ, provides the essential motivation for the three preceding sentences about forgiveness. Concluding the first part of the hymn in an impressive manner, the כי-clause points to that quality of Yahweh which determines and limits all of his deeds. Pss. 86:5; 130:4, 7f.; Neh. 9:17 also attest that חסד is the foundation of forgiveness.

[7:19] In v. 19 we find a transition to imperfect verb forms and a shift to sentences expressing confidence which, after the more traditional formulations in v. 18, present expressions that describe the acts of forgiveness in an original way. At the same time, the singers of the hymn now formulate their statements in relation to themselves (first person plural in v. 19aα,β, 20b; on v. 19b, see note 19c). That the passage speaks no longer of Yahweh's actions in general (as in v. 18), but of specific deeds yet to be expected, is first indicated by the adverbial (see note 19a) function of שוב (imperfect), which points to a renewal of Yahweh's "compassion." רחם *piel* means the loving affection of a mother for her children (cf. רֶחֶם = "womb" and Isa. 49:15); or of a father for his sons (Ps. 103:13); or of a powerful person for the weak (1 Kings 8:50; Isa. 13:18; Jer. 42:12). Thus it always points to the loving affection of a superior, who is able and willing to help one in need. Accordingly, here in the fifth sentence, רחם means the renewed affection of Yahweh for the persons themselves who are at prayer.

An absolutely unparalleled sixth sentence, which speaks of "treading down our transgressions," also presupposes that Yahweh's mighty sovereignty expresses itself in acts of forgiveness. כבש generally is construed with persons. It can have as its object slaves who have been subdued with force (Jer. 34:11, 16), or women who have been assaulted (Esther 7:8). Thus here Israel's sins are personified as hostile powers which are subdued and destroyed, as in a massacre by Yahweh. The meaning of the verb, "to tread," "to trample down," is attested by Akkadian *kabāsu* I ("to trample out fire"; but also "to extinguish guilt" *[ka-ba-su ša ḫīṭīšu]*; W. von Soden, *Akkadisches Handwörterbuch* I 415, G 5).

The personification of sin as the archenemy of the people of God is also found in the seventh sentence, likewise uniquely formulated, according to which Yahweh will "throw all of our offenses into the depths of the sea." Such a statement compares the act of forgiveness with Israel's liberation at the Exodus from the power of Egyptians. According to Exod. 15:4f., Pharaoh's chariots and warriors sunk "into the depths of the sea" "like a stone." The sentences of confidence contained in the second part of the hymn, reaching their high point in v. 19b and returning to direct address of Yahweh, exhibit still a further heightening, in comparison with the confession v. 18, in that alongside עָוֹן, a third word for sin, חַטָּאת, has been added (293 times, the most frequently occurring in the Old Testament; on its meaning, see above, pp. 56, 105). Moreover, both words are in the plural, with a first person plural suffix. Finally, v. 19b speaks of "*all* of our sins." Thus the second part of the hymn apparently intends to present in a comprehensive manner the profusion of transgressions for which Israel has been indicted by the prophetic word; then it places them under the power of Yahweh's love and forgiveness which destroys them.

[7:20] In the conclusion, the expression of confidence is directed toward the reliability of the *promise to the patriarchs*. The verse has to do with the oath Yahweh swore "to our fathers in the days of old," words which pick up a typical Deuteronomic-Deuteronomistic expression (cf. Deut. 1:8, 35; 4:31; 6:10, 18, 23; 7:8f., 12f.; further, Ps. 105:8–11). The content of all these proof-texts has to do with the gift of the land; Yahweh promises it in a unilateral commitment of himself. The petition in 7:14b already recalled the extent of the ancient land-allotment (see above, p. 226). Now in v. 20, in contrast to the divine oath of ancient times, the gift to be awaited is "trustworthy loyalty" (אֱמֶת), and, again, that "gracious kindness" (חֶסֶד) already extolled in v. 18bβ as the foundation of the forgiveness of all sins. Once again, אֱמֶת, together with חֶסֶד, as regards the future, is the ultimate motivation for trustingly anticipating the destruction of all guilt. With חֶסֶד and אֱמֶת comes a new, expanded gift of land to Jerusalem, although here such a hope is not expressly stated.

When "Abraham" (along with "Jacob") is named as the recipient of the promise made under oath, this—as with "Jacob" (see also 1:5; 2:12; 3:8; 5:6, 7)—does not mean the patriarch as person (as is the case in Isa. 51:2; 63:16); rather, it refers (unique in the Old Testament!) to the present generation and their offspring, who are called "the remnant of his possession" in v. 18aβ, and who in Isa. 41:8 are correctly named זֶרַע אַבְרָהָם ("offspring of Abraham"). Israel, understanding its future in light of Yahweh's sovereign forgiveness of all its transgression, calls itself "Abraham" (and "Jacob"). Israel attests to its certainly that, in spite of its own faithlessness, it can remain sure of the unconditional faithfulness and gracious kindness of Yahweh. Hence, Micah's message of judgment does not have the final say; instead—after all the suffering brought by this judgment—the message of salvation, proclaimed since Deutero-Isaiah (cf. Isa. 51:1–3), has the final word. Here that message is taken up and sung as a hymn.

Purpose and Thrust

The collection of liturgical pieces in 7:8–20 apparently has brief antecedents in the theophany hymn in 1:3f.; in the different types of confessional passages in 4:5 and 7:7, as well as in the prayer of 5:8 (in each instance see the commentary ad loc.). But taken as a whole, the extent and the content of this collection at the end of the book of Micah make it a novum. No prophecy of judgment is any longer to be heard, neither accusations nor announcements of punishment, such as fill the ancient collection of Micah's sayings in 1:6—3:12 and still find an echo in 6:9–16. Neither assurance of salvation nor eschatological promise is any longer to be perceived, such as accompanied the community through its times of crisis when the message of judgment was fulfilled, or during its period of new orientation, according to 4:1—5:14[15] (excluding the fragmented commentary in 7:11–13). Neither didactic admonition, as in 6:2–6, nor cry of despair, as in 7:1–6, is to be heard any longer; its conclusion (7:7), however, precisely intones in a solitary voice the community's psalms which now follow in 7:8–20.

These psalms allow one to hear how the believing community understands itself in its relation to prophetic proclamation. It is presupposed that the community has listened to the reading of the previously written sayings of Micah and of the succeeding exilic and postexilic prophetic voices (see above, pp. 219f.). In the three different songs we have recognized in detail how the community responds entirely in its own words.

The first hymn (vv. 8–10) indicates, on the one hand, how the exilic-postexilic community's worship services struggle to come to terms with the scorn of the enemy (see above, pp. 220f.); however, the community finds the solution only by acknowledging how its God further executes the "lawsuit" with his people. In so doing, the community not only appropriates the conceptions of the lawsuit, as it confronted them in the reading of 6:2ff.; at the same time, the community also affirms both main themes from Micah's message: (1) "I must bear Yahweh's wrath" (v. 9aα)—thereby embracing Micah's proclamation of judgment and, at the same time, the suffering under the scorn of the enemy as the deserved punishment from God. (2) "For against him I have transgressed" (v. 9aβ)—thereby accepting Micah's accusations and therefore confessing their sins as transgressions against Yahweh. This confession of guilt before Yahweh proves to a presupposition for patient trust. Its basis lies in the future ("until . . .," v. 9b) righteousness of Yahweh, which executes justice and brings liberation and redemption. The expectation of Yahweh's צדקה ("redemptive act"; see above, p. 222), translated by Gk with δικαιοσύνη, theologically considered, points in the direction of the Pauline conception of justification (cf. Rom. 3:21–26). When in addition to the law Paul appeals to the prophets as witnesses to his gospel, then Mic. 7:8–10 provides an especially clear example. However, as a messenger of Jesus, Paul goes a step further than our Old Testament text in that he also includes the nations—here still the enemies of Israel—within the fellowship of those justified and redeemed by God (Rom. 3:27–31). In the New Testament proclamation, the walls of enmity, against which Mic. 7:8aα, 10 still make an attack, have been torn down by Christ Jesus (Eph. 2:13–16). Looking back from Jesus and Paul to Mic. 7:8–10, however, the New Testament community as well has its confidence strengthened and nourished in the words of the psalm: "And when I sit in darkness, Yahweh is surely my light."

This gospel message brings light to a world that has grown hopeless. Whoever asks the self-satisfied question, "Where is your God?" can see (cf. ראה in vv. 9bβ, 10aα,bα) a victorious answer already now in the message of Christ Jesus and in the future consummation of God's "lawsuit." In addition, the fact that this psalm of trust, which commences with the "rising up" of those who are fallen (v. 8aβ), is passed down from generation to generation, means already a "leading to the light" (v. 9bβ) for those who can accept it.

(On vv. 11–13, see above, pp. 223ff.)

A different echo of the preceding proclamation in the book of Micah is presented to the reader in vv. 14–17. Here a radiant trust is not exactly perceptible. Nevertheless, those who are oppressed may also approach God through the words of the prophets. In supplication lies sufficient anticipation of the turning point. Initially, however, the shameful present situation—in spite of the promise of Yahweh's or his messiah's function as shepherd-king (2:12; 4:6f.; 5:3)—is that of "dwelling alone in the wilderness," cut off from the fertile pasture. יער in v. 14aβ is reminiscent of יער in 3:12bβ. Along with the temple mountain, all of desolate Jerusalem and its nearer environs has become an uninhabited, wretched scrub. Its remnant of a community is cut off from all productive regions of the land. On what should these supplicants base their hope? Only God's deeds at the Exodus from Egypt come to mind. These, too, were events which were hardly considered possible—"wonders." The exilic and postexilic community can also turn to the God of an earlier time. No less can the new people of God, in all its wretchedness and need, rise up in prayer to him who in Jesus Christ has shown himself to be the "Good Shepherd," who not only protects, cares for, and leads, but who also gives up his life for the sheep (John 10), and whom God, in his resurrection from the dead, has made to be the "Great Shepherd" (Heb. 13:20). Israel's supplication for its own future (vv. 14f.) is accompanied by the petition for the nations (vv. 16f.). To the extent that this prayer is a request for insight (v. 16a) and the fear of God, it remains grounded in the promise in 4:1–3 and is a prayer that remains necessary until the end of days. To the extent that Israel's supplication expresses its lovelessness (cf. also 4:13; 5:7), it stands in need of forgiveness, which is the concern of the following verses.

After all the harsh words contained in the book of Micah in 1:2—7:6, the concluding psalm (vv. 18–20) alone extols the forgiveness of all guilt. In an unsurpassable way, it expresses for Israel what in the New Testament concerning all the nations cannot be sung more beautifully. It has been confirmed in Jesus Christ that the uniqueness and incomparability of the God of Israel is to be discerned in his "taking away" of sin. After all the harsh prophecies of judgment with their motivations; after Micah himself has defined his prophetic office as the work of exposing rebellion and transgression (3:8), here our passage celebrates the sole possibility for survival, indeed, for new life: the "renewed mercy" of God. In addition to the words פֶּשַׁע and חַטָּאת ("rebellion" and "offense") used for sin in Mic. 3:8, here the third word in the Old Testament, עָוֹן ("transgression"), is used in the singular (v. 18) and plural (v. 19). Moreover, v. 19 expressly speaks of the "totality" (כָּל־) of the offenses. Thus in retrospect of the numerous accusations in the book of Micah, it is unmistakably emphasized that no misdeeds remain which would not be "sunk in the depths of the sea." In the commentary on individual verses, it was noted how graphic and diverse are the glorious descriptions of the act of forgiveness itself. Particularly in v. 19, forgiveness becomes an act of victorious struggle against sin as a personified archenemy. Thus after the seriousness of the prophetic words of judgment, forgiveness is and remains the sole basis of all hope and the only foundation for true freedom before God and among human beings. The hymn appropriates from the prophecy of the exilic and postexilic periods the new word of God which, after Micah and the other preexilic prophets, makes a new beginning possible. By citing the reference back to the promise to the patriarchs in v. 20, the final sentence of the Magnificat (Luke 1:55) makes a connection between the concluding verse in the book of Micah and the appearance of the Messiah, Jesus.

What the three concluding, quite different psalms have in *common* with each other can be summarized in three points: (1) They all presuppose that *judgment* upon sin has been proclaimed and fulfilled: in the confession, "Yahweh's wrath will I bear" (v. 9a); in the characterization of the situation of distress of those "who dwell alone in the scrub" (v. 14aβ); in the various and oft-repeated references to "all our sins" (v. 19). (2) They all await a great *turning point:* in which God will again take up his lawsuit on behalf of his people (v. 9b); in a great act of redemption modeled after the Exodus from Egypt (vv. 14f.); in the victory over guilt and sin (v. 19). (3) The certainty of the turning point is solely grounded in *Yahweh,* who alone can make a completely new beginning: in his consummation of the lawsuit for Israel's redemption (vv. 8f.); in the evidence of his office as shepherd (v. 14); in his mighty acts of forgiveness (vv. 18f.); and in fulfilling his promises to the patriarchs (v. 20).

The probable origin of these psalms is in the liturgical reading of prophetic texts (see above, pp. 219f.) within formal worship services. This would indicate how the prophetic traditions came to be used in the community. These psalms do not intend to sketch the chronology of salvation history. Rather, each generation is to acknowledge that its own place is between judgment and redemption (cf. B. S. Childs, *Introduction to the Old Testament as Scripture* [1979] 437f.). In each case, the acknowledgment of guilt can achieve concrete form only in light of the prophetic indictment. From the prophetic announcements of judgment, the listener discovers, in analogy to his own history, that paths of folly lead to disastrous ends. The petitions uttered out of deprivation and oppression help lead one to God's fundamental promises and deeds of salvation. But the hymn of praise which stands at the conclusion is concerned with God's forgiveness, which, in spite of everything, sets people free for a new beginning. After hearing the message of the prophets, it is forgiveness that is absolutely indispensable.

Thus we see in this present collection of Israel's responses to the prophetic word the evidence of a liturgical orientation between remembrance and expectation. The worshiping community and the individual reader, whatever the time and place, stand before the question whether, in the present moment, the appropriate response to the prophetic witness is confession, petition and supplication, or praise.

Hebrew Grammars Cited

Bauer-Leander	H. Bauer and P. Leander, *Historische Grammatik der hebräischen Sprache des Alten Testaments* I, Halle 1922.
BrSynt	C. Brockelmann, *Hebräische Syntax,* Neukirchen 1956.
Ges-K	[F. H. W.] *Gesenius' Hebrew Grammar as edited and enlarged by the late E. Kautszch,* second English edition revised in accordance with the 28th German ed. (1909) by A. E. Cowley, Oxford 1910, reissued 1946.
Joüon, *Gr*	P. Joüon, *Grammaire de l'Hébreu Biblique,* Rome 1947[2].
Meyer[3]	G. Beer, *Hebräische Grammatik,* 2nd ed. of R. Meyer I (1952; 1966[3]), II (1955).

Abbreviations

a'	Aquila
AAAbo.H	Acta Academiae Aboensis, Humaniora
AHw	W. von Soden, *Akkadisches Handwörterbuch* (1966f.)
AJSL	*American Journal of Semitic Languages and Literature*
ANET	J. Pritchard, ed., *Ancient Near Eastern Texts Relating to the Old Testament* (1955²)
ANEP	J. Pritchard, ed., *Ancient Near Eastern Pictures Relating to the Old Testament*
AOAT	*Alter Orient und Altes Testament*
AOB	*Altorientalische Bilder zum Alten Testament*
AOT²	*Altorientalische Texte zum Alten Testament*
Arab	Arabic
ATD	Das Alte Testament Deutsch
AThR	*Anglican Theological Review*
Aug.	*Augustinum.* Rome
AuS	G. Dalman, *Arbeit und Sitte in Palästina,* 6 vols. (1928–1942)
AUSS	*Andrews University Seminary Studies*
AzTh	Arbeiten zur Theologie
BA	*The Biblical Archeologist*
BASOR	*Bulletin of the American Schools of Oriental Research*
Barrois, *Manuel*	A. G. Barrois, *Manuel d'Archéologie Biblique* I (1939), II (1953)
BBB	Bonner Biblische Beiträge
BBE	*Beiträge zur Biblischen Exegese*
BetM	*Beth Miqra*
BEvTh	Beiträge zur Evangelischen Theologie
BHHW	*Biblisch-Historisches Handwörterbuch*
BHTh	Beiträge zur historischen Theologie
BHK	*Biblia Hebraica,* ed. R. Kittel
BHS	*Biblia Hebraica Stuttgartensia*
BiBe	*Biblische Beiträge*
Bibl	*Biblica*
BibOr	*Biblica et Orientalia*
BiblRev	*Bible Review*
BiKi	*Bibel und Kirche*
BJPES	*Bulletin of the Jewish Palestine Exploration Society*

Abbreviations

BK	Biblischer Kommentar Altes Testament
BL	*Bibel-Lexikon*
BRL²	K. Galling, *Biblisches Reallexikon,* HAT I, 1 (1977²)
BrSynt	C. Brockelmann, *Hebräische Syntax* (1956)
BWANT	Beiträge zur Wissenschaft vom Alten und Neuen Testament
BZ	*Biblische Zeitschrift*
BZAW	Beihefte zur *ZAW*
CAT	*Commentaire de l'Ancien Testament*
conj.	conjecture
CBQ	*Catholic Biblical Quarterly*
CRB	*Cahiers de la Revue Biblique*
DB	*Deutsche Bibel*
Diss	Dissertation
DissAb	Dissertation Abstracts
DJD	*Discoveries in the Judean Desert*
DTT	*Dansk Teologisk Tidsskrift*
EAT	J. A. Knudtzon, *Die El-Amarna-Tafeln,* Vorderasiatische Bibliothek 2 (1915)
Ehrlich	A. B. Ehrlich, *Randglossen zur hebräischen Bibel* V (1912)
EHS.T	Europäische Hochschulschriften. Reihe 23: Theologie
ET	*The Expository Times*
ÉtB	*Études Biblique*
EvQ	*Evangelical Quarterly*
EvTh	*Evangelische Theologie*
f.(ff.)	Designates page(s) or verse(s) immediately following page or verse cited
FRLANT	Forschungen zur Religion und Literatur des Alten und Neuen Testaments
Ges-B	W. Gesenius and F. Buhl, *Hebräisches und aramäisches Handwörterbuch zum AT* (1921ff.¹⁷)
Gk	The Septuagint
GPM	*Göttinger Predigtmeditationen*
HAT	Handbuch zum Alten Testament
HNT	Handbuch zum Neuen Testament
HS	F. Feldmann and H. Herkenne, eds., *Die Heilige Schrift des Alten Testament*
HThR	*Harvard Theological Review*
HTS	Hervormde Teologiese Studies
IB	*The Interpreter's Bible*
ICC	The International Critical Commentary of the Holy Scripture
IDB	*The Interpreter's Dictionary of the Bible*
IDBSuppl	*The Interpreter's Dictionary of the Bible, Supplementary Volume*
IEJ	*Israel Exploration Journal*
Interp	*Interpretation*
JBL	*Journal of Biblical Literature*
JJS	*Journal of Jewish Studies*
JNES	*Journal of Near Eastern Studies*
JQR	*Jewish Quarterly Review*
JSOT	*Journal for the Study of the Old Testament*
JThS	*Journal of Theological Studies*
KAI	*Kanaanäische und aramäische Inschriften*
KAT	Kommentar zum Alten Testament
KBL	L. Koehler and W. Baumgartner, *Lexicon in Veteris Testamenti Libros* (1953; 1967ff.³)
KD	K. Barth, *Die Kirchliche Dogmatik*

KlSchr	*Kleine Schriften*
KuD	*Kerygma und Dogma*
MT	The Masoretic text
NedThT	*Nederlands Theologisch Tijdschrift*
OrAnt	*Oriens Antiquus*
OrSuec	*Orientalia Suecana*
OTL	Old Testament Library
OTS	*Oudtestamentische Studien*
OTWSA	*Die Oud Testamentiese Werkgemeenskap in Suid-Afrika*
PalCl	*Palestra del Clero*
PJB	*Palästinajahrbuch*
POS	*Pretoria Oriental Studies*
Q	Qumran, preceded by an arabic numeral
RB	*Revue Biblique*
RCT	*Revista de Cultura Theologica*
RestQ	*Restoration Quarterly*
RGG³	*Religion in Geschichte und Gegenwart* (1957–65³)
RHPhR	*Revue d'Histoire et de Philosophie Religieuses*
RHR	*Revue de l'Histoire des Religions*
RLA	*Reallexikon der Assyriologie* (1932ff.)
RSEHA	*Revue Sémitique d'Épigraphie et d'Histoire Ancienne*
RTK	*Roczniki Teologiczno-Kanoniczne*
σ'	Symmachus' Greek version of the OT
SBT	*Studies in Biblical Theology*
SBJ	*Sainte Bible Traduit en Français sous la Direction de l'école Biblique de Jérusalem*
SEA	*Svensk Exegetisk Årsbok*
Sem.	*Semitica. Cahiers publiés par l'Institut d'Études Sémitiques de l'Université de Paris*
SJTh	*Scottish Journal of Theology*
Sperber	A. Sperber, *The Bible in Aramaic*
ST	*Studia Theologica*
Syh	Syrohexeplaris
Syr	The Syriac version (Peshitta)
θ'	Theodotion's Greek version of the OT
Tarb	*Tarbiz.* Jerusalem
Targ	Targum
TDNT	*Theological Dictionary of the New Testament,* ed. G. Kittel
TGI²	K. Galling, ed., *Textbuch zur Geschichte Israels* (1978²)
TGW	*Tydskrif vir geesteswetenshappe*
THAT	E. Jenni, ed., *Theologisches Handwörterbuch zum Alten Testament*
ThB	Theologische Bucherei
ThR	*Theologische Rundschau*
Theol	*Theology.* London
ThSt	Theologische Studien. Zurich
TThZ	*Trier Theologische Zeitschrift*
ThWAT	*Theologisches Wörterbuch zum Alten Testament*
ThWNT	*Theologisches Wörterbuch zum Neuen Testament*
TRE	*Theologisches Realenzyklopädie*
UF	*Ugarit-Forschungen*
UT	C. Gordon, *Ugaritic Textbook*
v.(vv.)	verse(s)
Vg	The Vulgate
VoxTh	*Vox Theologica*
VT	*Vetus Testamentum*

Abbreviations

VTSuppl	Vetus Testamentum Supplements
WA	M. Luther, *Werke.* Kritische Gesamtausgabe (Weimarer Ausgabe)
WMANT	Wissenschaftliche Monographien zum Alten und Neuen Testament
WdF	Wege der Forschung
WuD	*Wort und Dienst*
ZAW	*Zeitschrift für die Alttestamentliche Wissenschaft*
Ziegler	J. Ziegler, *Septuaginta vol. XIII: Duodecim prophetae* (1967²)
ZDMG	*Zeitschrift der Deutschen Morganländischen Gesellschaft*
ZNW	*Zeitschrift für die Neutestamentliche Wissenschaft*
ZDPV	*Zeitschrift des Deutschen Palästina-Vereins*
ZS	*Zeitschrift für Semitistik und verwandte Gebiete*

Index of Biblical References

(The numbers are those of the Hebrew Bible.)

Index of Biblical References

Index of Biblical References

Index of Biblical References

250

Index of Names and Subjects

Index of Hebrew Words

Index of Names and Subjects